Springer Series in Supply Chain Management

Volume 22

Supply Chain Management (SCM), long an integral part of Operations Management, focuses on all elements of creating a product or service, and delivering that product or service, at the optimal cost and within an optimal timeframe. It spans the movement and storage of raw materials, work-in-process inventory, and finished goods from point of origin to point of consumption. To facilitate physical flows in a time-efficient and cost-effective manner, the scope of SCM includes technology-enabled information flows and financial flows.

The Springer Series in Supply Chain Management, under the guidance of founding Series Editor Christopher S. Tang, covers research of either theoretical or empirical nature, in both authored and edited volumes from leading scholars and practitioners in the field – with a specific focus on topics within the scope of SCM.

This series has been accepted by Scopus.

Springer and the Series Editor welcome book ideas from authors. Potential authors who wish to submit a book proposal should contact Ms. Jialin Yan, Associate Editor, Springer (Germany), e-mail: jialin.yan@springernature.com

Christian Mandl

Procurement Analytics

Data-Driven Decision-Making in Procurement and Supply Management

Springer

Christian Mandl
Applied Economics
Deggendorf Institute of Technology
Deggendorf, Germany

ISSN 2365-6395 ISSN 2365-6409 (electronic)
Springer Series in Supply Chain Management
ISBN 978-3-031-43280-4 ISBN 978-3-031-43281-1 (eBook)
https://doi.org/10.1007/978-3-031-43281-1

This Springer imprint is published by the registered company Springer Nature Switzerland AG
The registered company address is: Gewerbestrasse 11, 6330 Cham, Switzerland

Paper in this product is recyclable.

Preface

Advanced analytics is disrupting procurement. This is the first textbook that explicitly focuses on the intersection between advanced analytics and procurement from a conceptual, technical, and implementation perspective. The book was developed in the context of my lectures at Technical University of Munich (TUM) and Deggendorf Institute of Technology (DIT) and is motivated by one core question: How to generate (economic) value and insights from data in order to make better procurement decisions? Besides students at business schools, this book addresses two further target groups: (i) Procurement professionals with or without specific knowledge in advanced analytics and (ii) data scientists with or without specific experience in procurement and supply management. The objective is to present use cases for advanced analytics in procurement and give a method-based overview (in the sense of a playbook) for leveraging data and optimization for purchasing decisions. Besides presenting concepts and applications, we particularly focus on implementation (e.g., using standard programming languages or optimization solvers). This should help procurement managers and data scientists to quickly evaluate the value generated from a data-driven solution—prior to installing expensive (commercial) software. The readers should get an idea how to apply advanced analytics for data-informed procurement optimization. The textbook therefore presents methodological approaches from the fields of operations research (OR) and machine learning (ML) in a procurement context. Procurement applications cover a wide range from spend analytics, supplier management, and inventory control to risk management. Rather than presenting existing commercial (and non-commercial) software solutions, the textbook aims at providing a general understanding for procurement managers on data-driven methods, their implementation, and the value in the field of procurement. The contribution of this textbook is the combination of rigorous state-of-the-art methodology from academic research and first-hand experience from various application-oriented consulting and implementation projects across different industries where industrial support tools were developed for various procurement problem settings. I want to thank Stefan Minner (TU Munich), who motivated me to start working on procurement analytics around 10 years ago and whose work inspired several sections of this textbook.

Deggendorf, Germany Dr. Christian Mandl
July 2023

Contents

Acronyms

AA	Advanced Analytics
AHP	Analytic Hierarchy Process
AI	Artificial Intelligence
AIaaS	Artificial Intelligence as a Service
ANN	Artificial Neural Network
ANP	Analytic Network Process
API	Application Programming Interface
APS	Advanced Planning and Scheduling
ARIMA	Autoregressive Integrated Moving Average
AUC	Area Under the ROC Curve
B2B	Business-to-Business
BAFO	Best and Final Offer
BATNA	Best Alternative to a Negotiated Agreement
BBC	Buy-Back Contract
CAD	Computer-Aided Design
CAP	Combinatorial Auction Problem
CapEx	Capital Expenditure
CART	Classification and Regression Tree
CBOT	Chicago Board of Trade
CME	Chicago Mercantile Exchange
COGS	Cost of Goods Sold
COMEX	Commodity Exchange
CPO	Chief Procurement Officer
CV	Coefficient of Variation
CVaR	Conditional Value-at-Risk
CZK	Czech Crown
DCE	Dalian Commodity Exchange
DDA	Data-Driven Approach
DEA	Data Envelopment Analysis
DiF	Delivery in Full
DiFoT	Delivery in Full on Time

DL	Deep Learning
DME	Dubai Mercantile Exchange
DoT	Delivery on Time
DPS	Dynamic Purchasing System
DSaaS	Data Science-as-a-Service
EDI	Electronic Data Interchange
EEX	European Energy Exchange
ELO	Expected Leftovers
ELS	Expected Lost Sales
EOI	Economic Order Interval
EOQ	Economic Order Quantity
ERP	Enterprise Resource Planning
ES	Expected Sales
ESG	Environmental, Social, and Governance
ESI	Early Supplier Involvement
EUR	Euro
FFA	Freight Forward Agreement
GBP	Great British Pound
GSCPI	Global Supply Chain Pressure Index
GSR	Gold-Silver Ratio
HDPE	High-Density Polyethylene
ICE	Intercontinental Exchange
IP	Inventory Position
IPV	Invoice Price Variance
JD	Jump Diffusion
JIT	Just-in-Time
JPY	Japanese Yen
kNN	k-Nearest Neighbor
KPI	Key Performance Indicator
LDPE	Low-Density Polyethylene
LLDPE	Linear Low-Density Polyethylene
LLM	Large Language Model
LME	London Metal Exchange
LP	Linear Program(ming)
LPP	Linear Performance Pricing
LPPM	Linear Price Performance Measurement
MAE	Mean Absolute Error
MAPE	Mean Absolute Percentage Error
MCDM	Multi-Criteria Decision-Making
MCX	Multi Commodity Exchange
MDA	Mean Directional Accuracy
MDP	Markov Decision Process
MGEX	Minneapolis Grain Exchange
MILP	Mixed-Integer Linear Program(ming)
ML	Machine Learning

MR	Mean Reversion
MRO	Maintenance, Repair, and Operations
MRP	Material Requirements Planning
MRS	Markov Regime Switching
MSE	Mean Squared Error
MT	Metric Ton
mUSD	Million US Dollar
NLP	Natural Language Processing
NLPP	Nonlinear Performance Pricing
NPV	Net Present Value
NYMEX	New York Mercantile Exchange
OCR	Optimal Character Recognition
OEM	Original Equipment Manufacturer
OLS	Ordinary Least Square
OR	Operations Research
ORM	Operating Resource Management
OTC	Over-the-Counter
OTIF	On Time In Full
P2P	Purchase-to-Pay
PaaS	Platform-as-a-Service
PAT	Principal-Agent-Theory
PCA	Principal Component Analysis
PLN	Polish Zloty
PMI	Purchase Manager Index
PO	Purchase Order
POA	Price of Anarchy
PP	Polypropylene
ppm	Parts per Million
QDC	Quantity Discount Contract
QFC	Quantity Flexibility Contract
RCFLP	Reliable Capacitated Facility Location Problem
REO	Reoptimization
RFI	Request-for-Information
RFID	Radio-Frequency Identification
RFQ	Request-for-Quotation
RFP	Request-for-Proposal
RFX	Request-for-X
ROC	Receiver Operating Characteristic
ROI	Return on Investment
RPA	Robotic Process Automation
RSC	Revenue-Sharing Contract
RW	Random Walk
S2C	Source-to-Contract
S2P	Source-to-Pay
SaaS	Software-as-a-Service

SAW	Simple Additive Weighting
SCM	Supplier Chain Management
SKU	Stock-Keeping Unit
SLA	Service-Level Agreement
sqm	Square Meter
SRC	Sales Rebate Contract
SRM	Supplier Relationship Management
SS	Safety Stock
SV	Semi-Variance
SVM	Support Vector Machine
TBS	Tailored Base Surge
TCA	Total Cost of Acquisition
TCO	Total Cost of Ownership
TIOLI	Take It or Leave It
TLC	Total Landed Cost
TOCOM	Tokyo Commodity Exchange
TOPSIS	Technique for Order Preference by Similarity to Ideal Solution
TS	Tracking Signal
USD	US Dollar
VaR	Value-at-Risk
VUCA	Volatility, Uncertainty, Complexity, Ambiguity
VMI	Vendor Managed Inventory
WACC	Weighted Average Cost of Capital
WDP	Winner Determination Problem
WLC	Weighted Linear Combination
WLP	Warehouse Location Problem
WPC	Wholesale Price Contract
WPM	Weighted Product Model
WSM	Weighted Sum Model
ZOPA	Zone of Possible Agreements

Chapter 1
Introduction

Abstract This chapter aims at pointing out the potential of data-driven procurement optimization and shows the current state of digitization in procurement and supply management. It gives a brief overview of latest technologies, innovations and trends in digital procurement along the source-to-pay (S2P) process such as artificial intelligence (AI), robotic process automation (RPA), chatbots, text mining or blockchain and highlights concrete procurement applications for advanced data analytics.

Keywords Procurement · Supply management · Source-to-pay · Artificial intelligence · Advanced analytics

1.1 The Status Quo of Procurement

For a long time, the objective of procurement as a major discipline in supply chain management was to provide the right quantity, at the right quality, in right timing, to the right location at the right price (*5R of procurement*). **Cost-centered procurement** was reasonable because purchase cost makes up a huge proportion of the total cost of a firm (e.g., 50–60% in mechanical engineering). This proportion steadily grew over the last decades due to companies' constantly growing outsourcing activities. Today, more than 80% of the value add of a car does not come from the car producer itself but from its suppliers (compared to around 55% in the 1980s). Therefore, a typical company from the automotive or mechanical engineering industry with a profit margin of 10% and a material cost share (i.e., purchase cost in % of revenue) of 50% can increase its profit margin by 5% through a 1% reduction in purchase cost and even by 25% through a 5% purchase cost reduction (procurement leverage effect). In retail industry with even higher material cost shares and lower profit margins, the leverage effect of purchase cost reduction is even more effective: For a company with 5% profit margin and 75% material cost share, a 1% reduction in purchase cost yields a 15% increase in profit margin, a 5% reduction even results in 75% profit growth. Therefore, procurement is a major profit lever, which explains the strong orientation of procurement toward

C. Mandl, *Procurement Analytics*, Springer Series in Supply Chain Management 22, https://doi.org/10.1007/978-3-031-43281-1_1

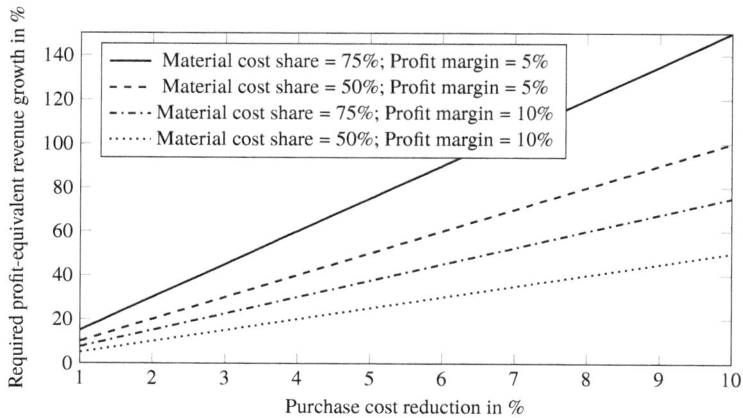

Fig. 1.1 The purchase cost leverage effect: Required revenue growth for profit implications equivalent to purchase cost reduction

cost reduction through demand bundling, optimized supplier selection, best-cost country sourcing, effective tendering processes, successful supplier negotiations and auction mechanisms.

Figure 1.1 illustrates the leverage effect of procurement compared to the sales function of a company. It shows that sales needs to increase revenue by a multiple in order to obtain the same profit effect as purchase cost reductions do. For instance, a company with a profit margin of 5% and a material cost share of 75%, which are typical numbers in retail industry, needs to more than double its revenue to generate the same profit as a 7% purchase cost reduction does. A company with a profit margin of 10% and a material cost share of 50%, which are typical numbers in automotive and mechanical engineering, need to increase its revenue by 25% in order to achieve the same profit effect as a 5% reduction in purchase cost does.

However, even though cost-cutting is still a major objective of any procurement organization, the area of responsibility of procurement extended significantly over the last years. Besides the traditional triangle of cost-time-quality, there are now further objectives such as (i) revenue generation and growth through innovation, (ii) sustainability and (iii) risk minimization or resilience.

Revenue Generation and Growth Today's procurement organizations are asked to contribute to product and process innovation through early supplier involvement (ESI) and intensified supplier relationship management (SRM) as it is already very common in the automotive and IT sector. ESI and SRM can ensure exclusive or prioritized supply, access to latest technologies and innovations and therefore generate a competitive advantage. According to an industry survey from McKinsey & Company, profound supplier collaboration can decrease cost by 5 to 10% and at the same time increase revenue by 7–10% (see [2]). Therefore, optimal supplier selection and collaboration are key for revenue maximization.

Sustainability Procurement is a major contributor to reach environmental, social and governance (ESG) goals with regard to decarbonization. Scope-3 emissions[1] from purchased goods and transportation along the value chain make up around 80–90% of total emissions. Therefore, procurement has an immense leverage effect through sustainability-optimized supply networks and optimized supplier selection decisions.

Risk Minimization Severe supply disruptions with lead time increases of more than 200% and price inflation for raw materials of more than 50% in the early 2020s have highlighted the importance of adequate risk management. *De-risking* of supply chains is an important goal of today's supply chain departments as a result of geopolitical instability and uncertainty driven by, e.g., the Russian invasion in Ukraine and the conflict in Taiwan. Procurement as the link between a company and its suppliers is responsible to assess risk and implement countermeasures such as hedging, dual sourcing or inventory optimization in order to increase supply resilience.

1.2 Digital Transformation of Procurement

The aforementioned procurement goals and challenges can only effectively and efficiently be addressed through the use of digital and data-driven approaches. Therefore, digitization is not only a buzzword but can be a real enabler in procurement even though only a small fraction of available data is currently used to address those goals. Nevertheless, companies recognize that digitization and data are a competitive advantage for procurement. According to PwC's *2022 Digital Procurement Survey* (see [3]) with 800+ participating procurement professionals across more than 60 countries, companies plan to invest on average 1.28 million Euro on short-term for digitization of their procurement processes. Many companies even define digitization of supply as a major strategic goal such as Volkswagen as stated in its 2021 annual report:

> "We are working systematically to implement a completely digitized supply chain. This is intended to help us to safeguard supply and leverage synergies throughout the Group in order to take a leading position in terms of cost and innovation. We are therefore creating a shared database and using innovative technologies to enable efficient, networked collaboration in real time—both within the Group and with our partners. The Purchasing division aims to standardize transactions with our suppliers in the future and automate them where possible. This will not only reduce transaction costs but will also accelerate business

[1] A firm's greenhouse gas (GHG) emissions are divided into scope-1, scope-2 and scope-3 emissions. Scope-1 emissions are those emissions resulting from own production facilities and the own vehicle fleet. Scope-2 emissions are resulting from purchased electricity, steam, heating or cooling, and scope-3 emissions come from any other players along the value chain such as direct and indirect suppliers, which includes all procurement activities related to raw materials and semi-finished products.

processes. Potential supply risks can be reported in an automated way in order to identify measures and alternatives faster together. The cornerstone for the future of Purchasing was laid in 2018 in the form of Group Purchasing's digitization strategy. This strategy aims not only to eliminate the weaknesses of Purchasing's IT system environment but also to increase the organization's effectiveness, efficiency and future viability. The initial systems, such as a bot project for automating supply chain business processes, were developed and integrated into the existing system environment."

In the course of digitization, both academia and industry increase the focus on data-driven business models and optimization in procurement. Companies started to routinely collect immense amounts of data including both internal data (e.g., spend cube data, inventory data) and external data (e.g., supplier data, market data) having access to various databases such as Bloomberg or Refinitiv. Furthermore, data quality improves steadily through real-time tracking (e.g., RFID technology). And there are significant advancements on methodologies from the fields of artificial intelligence and operations research that benefit from increasing computational power in order to solve procurement problems. Consequently, during the last decade, we saw many *ProcureTech* companies being founded (e.g., Coupa, Jaggaer, Ivalua, Scoutbee, Sievo, Lhotse, Simfoni or GEP) that strive to digitize procurement activities.

From an organizational point of view, procurement changed as well. Companies initialize new departments such as *Procurement Analytics*, *Procurement Intelligence* or *Digital Procurement* that focus on data-driven decision-making in procurement using latest technology from the fields of artificial intelligence (AI), machine learning (ML) and operations research (OR). And procurement offers the best possible environment and potential for data-driven optimization and decision-making, which is already recognized in industry. Roland Berger's CPO survey of 87 Fortune 500 companies shows that applied artificial intelligence is one of the top 3 priorities for 67% of the CPOs (see [4]). In the future, CPOs need to understand the potential of digital technology for enhancing procurement efficiency.

Furthermore, job profiles in procurement change as well. Procurement professionals increasingly need to build technological competencies in order to understand and quickly be able to apply data-driven methods to derive insights from procurement data and make better procurement decisions. This is already something we can observe in procurement job offers that increasingly ask for know-how in business intelligence tools such as `PowerBI` or `Tableau` or basic programming knowledge in `Python` or other languages. Future procurement professionals are more and more asked to develop tailored in-house solutions for planning tasks such as forecasting or algorithm-based decision-support tools in collaboration with data scientists.

1.3 Technologies and Trends in Digital Procurement

This book does not aim at deep-diving into all existing digital technologies related to the procurement function that are available at the market but rather wants to sensitize managers how to use data and analytics for specific procurement problem settings. However, we still want to give a brief overview on the current status of digital procurement technologies and trends that include applications in three main procurement areas, i.e.,

- *sourcing*, i.e., all processes related to procurement strategy, market screening, demand forecasting, supplier selection, negotiation, supplier relationship management (SRM) and contract management,
- *purchasing*, i.e., the actual buying process including item request, approval, purchase orders, item delivery and inspection,
- *accounts payable*, i.e., all processes related to invoice receipt, invoice verification, invoice processing and payment.

Most of the following technologies and trends in digital procurement/electronic procurement focus on the *source-to-pay (S2P)* process that is divided into the *source-to-contract (S2C)* process and the *purchase-to-pay (P2P)* process with the goal to automate labor-intensive or highly repetitive tasks such as contract management, purchase order approvals, invoicing, payment management and category management as much as possible (Fig. 1.2).

1.3.1 X-as-a-Service (XaaS)

The standard ERP and APS systems from well-established software providers such as SAP and Oracle are more and more extended by customized software for specific applications. Software-as-a-Service (SaaS), Platform-as-a-Service (PaaS), Data Science-as-a-Service (DSaaS) and Artificial Intelligence-as-a-Service (AIaaS) are pay-per-use models and become increasingly popular. They allow to access software as a service whenever needed without a complicated and time-consuming installation process. In the procurement context, many software products are

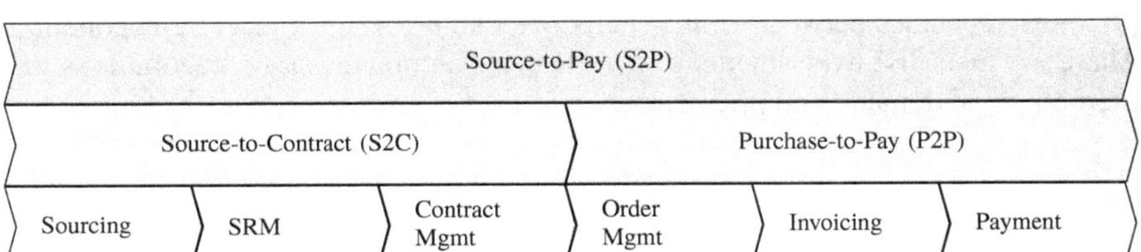

Fig. 1.2 The source-to-pay process

nowadays provided as SaaS or PaaS solutions (e.g., Coupa, SAP Ariba, GEP Smart or Sievo for spend management). They are used for efficient tender processes including request for information (RFI), request for quotation (RFQ) and e-auctions but also for should-cost modeling or performance pricing.

1.3.2 Platform Solutions

Platform solutions allow to efficiently match providers (i.e., suppliers) and consumers (i.e., buyers). In the procurement context, platform solutions are used twofold: (i) as digital or electronic marketplace (e.g., Amazon Business, Chembid) and (ii) as end-to-end (cloud) solution for electronic procurement (e.g., SAP Ariba, Coupa, Workday, Jaggaer, Ivalua). Electronic procurement marketplaces are particularly used for identifying new suppliers and are typically industry-specific (e.g., https://chemondis.com/ for chemicals, https://www.marketparts.com/ for automotive, https://foodtraderstore.com/ for the food industry, https://timocom.de/ for transportation services). These marketplaces increase market transparency (e.g., with regard to prices) and allow buyers to quickly and effortless connect with adequate suppliers. In public procurement (e.g., EU tender processes), dynamic purchasing systems (DPS) are common platforms that allow purchasers to quickly access a pool of pre-qualified suppliers that fulfill the specific requirements of the public sector.

1.3.3 Robotic Process Automation (RPA)

Robotic process automation (RPA) is an artificial intelligence-based approach to automate processes that are characterized by repetitive, manual, time-consuming or error-prone tasks. In the procurement context, RPA is used for the update of supplier data, automated ordering of standard material (e.g., office material), search for data from ERP systems, web crawling to identify new suppliers or the automation of reminder mechanisms in payment. RPA can also be used for similar parts analysis based on the scan of hundreds of computer-aided design (CAD) models in order to find similar parts than can be aggregated for price negotiations or to find price discrepancies between similar parts that can be used for price re-negotiation. There are also first experiments to use RPA for automated price negotiations and predictions of demand and price patterns.

1.3.4 (Chat)Bots

(Chat)bots are virtual artificial assistants that can interact with humans or other technical systems. Their actions are based on a knowledge database with answers and specific recognition patterns. In the procurement context, chatbots are used for guided buying, supplier support and as virtual negotiation agents, which potentially describes an interesting use case for automated price negotiations in the future. Given that companies such as a major German first-tier automotive supplier execute around 800 supplier negotiations per year, this can significantly reduce manual effort. Generative AI chatbots that are based on large language models (LLMs), such as OpenAI's ChatGPT and Google's Bard, are already in use in procurement to support the preparation of supplier negotiations by conducting deep market research, screening for potential new suppliers or evaluating incumbent suppliers based on a quick (financial) KPI assessment. It can also be leveraged for market reports on specific raw materials or summarizing the options to hedge procurement risk.

1.3.5 Natural Language Processing (NLP)

Natural language processing (NLP) translates human language to text (speech-to-text, speech recognition) or text to human language (text-to-speech, natural language understanding or natural language generation). The technology combines linguistics and statistics and is based on machine learning of text and speech. In the procurement context, this is, for instance, used for contract management or supplier management. In contract management, NLP can translate, analyze and interpret a large amount of contract documents with regard to (critical) information such as expiration dates, payment terms or opportunities for re-negotiations. In supplier management, NLP can automate communication with suppliers (e.g., supplier hotlines).

1.3.6 Text Mining

Text mining is the systematic semantic analysis of textual data via algorithms. It is able to go through a vast number of documents and to quickly identify relevant information. In the procurement context, text mining helps to quickly analyze contract documents and to identify potential supply risks. Today's supply chains are global, which makes it difficult for procurement professionals to keep track on local developments (e.g., political issues or weather events) in the sourcing regions. A systematic text mining approach with the use of a web crawler analyzing local news, social networks, weather databases or information systems of sea ports or customs authorities can signal early warnings on potential supply disruptions. Based on this information, procurement organizations can counteract.

1.3.7 Optimal Character Recognition (OCR)

Optical character recognition (OCR) is a technology that translates handwritten or printed text from images into a machine-readable format. In the procurement context, this is used to transfer invoices from suppliers and contracts of any format and layout to digitally encoded text. OCR can even be used via smartphone apps, which makes it a user-friendly application for purchasers.

1.3.8 Electronic Data Interchange (EDI)

Electronic data interchange (EDI) is a technology to transfer documents between companies in a standardized format. In the procurement context, EDI allows for electronic transmissions of purchase orders (PO), invoices and payment between the buyer and the supplier. This reduces manual effort in the purchase-to-pay process and reduces errors from system interface inconsistencies. EDI can be seen as the link between a supplier's and a buyer's ERP system(s).

1.3.9 Blockchain

Blockchains are virtual chains of data blocks that can continuously be extended by new data and information. They are characterized by decentralized storage, encryption, transparency and a consensus mechanism, i.e., all participants need to agree on any changes. This makes the technology tamperproof. In the procurement context, blockchain technology is considered as a technology with large potentials in the field of smart contracts and transparency enhancement along the supply chain. For instance, two companies agree on a unit price of 50 Euro. This price is documented in a smart contract based on blockchain technology. Therefore, the price can only be changed if both companies agree. Furthermore, both parties can add additional clauses such as extra payments for each day of delay. Delivery is tracked in real time and documented in the smart contract as well. One benefit over traditional contracts is that it cannot be manipulated and, furthermore, history is tracked in detail, i.e., every single change to the contract is documented. Another application is real-time tracking of the supply chain, including a calculation of the supply chain's carbon footprint or simply the secure data exchange between buyers and suppliers.

1.3.10 Digital Twins and Multi-Agent Systems

Digital twins are virtual mappings of real-world systems, processes or products that are modeled and improved with optimization or simulation techniques. In the procurement context, this can be the virtual replication of the buying process with decision-support tools (e.g., inventory control systems). The digital twin gives a data-driven recommendation when the buyer should buy which quantity. In physical reality, the buyer can subsequently use this information together with his own judgment for real-world decision-making. A second application is the digital mapping of the physical supply network in order to increase supply chain transparency and to quickly identify potential disruption risks such as bad weather conditions through the use of text mining in geographically selected newspapers and social media. A third application is virtual supplier audits via digital twins of the supplier's production facilities.

Multi-agent systems are systems with multiple agents that collectively solve a problem (distributed artificial intelligence). From a methodological perspective, this is referred to as multi-agent simulation. In the procurement context, this can be the simulation of customer or supplier behavior that affects the optimal purchase decision (e.g., timing and quantity). A benefit of digital twins and multi-agent systems is that different scenarios of the future can easily be analyzed with regard to decision implications. This is particularly useful for data-informed risk management decisions.

1.4 Data Analytics in Procurement

Rather than focusing on specific technologies for digital procurement, this textbook regards procurement more from a problem and decision perspective in the sense of (i) what specific data-driven problem settings are in procurement and (ii) how we can optimize decisions in an analytical, data-driven and data-informed manner through advanced analytics and algorithms rather than based on gut feeling or intuition.

ChatGPT (www.chat.openai.com/chat) gives us the following definition of *procurement analytics*:

> "Procurement analytics is the use of data and analytics to improve the processes and outcomes of procurement, which is the process of acquiring goods or services. Procurement analytics involves collecting and analyzing data on procurement activities, such as spending patterns, supplier performance, and contract compliance, in order to identify trends, optimize processes, and make informed decisions.
>
> Procurement analytics can help organizations better understand their spending and make more strategic decisions about which suppliers to use and what products or services to purchase. It can also help identify opportunities for cost savings and improve the efficiency of the procurement process. Procurement analytics can be used to track key performance indicators (KPIs) such as cost per unit, on-time delivery rate, and supplier performance.
>
> Procurement analytics can be implemented through the use of specialized software and tools that enable the collection and analysis of data from multiple sources, such as financial

systems, procurement systems, and supplier databases. By using procurement analytics, organizations can gain a deeper understanding of their procurement activities and make data-driven decisions to improve their operations."

However, for many companies, it is still an open question how to effectively exploit the value of data. For instance, a procurement professional needs to decide when to buy which quantity based on a broad range of information and restrictions such as the current inventory levels, product shelf life, spot market price expectations and production plans. So she might ask herself what data is relevant for an optimal course of action. Another example is price (re-)negotiation with suppliers. Here, data analytics and artificial intelligence are able to identify price potentials based on a vast amount of internal data (e.g., results from previous tender and e-auction processes or should-cost models) and external data (e.g., raw material price developments).

In this book, we present concrete examples on how to exploit advanced analytics to quickly assess the value of available internal and external data for concrete procurement problem settings as shown in Fig. 1.3.

In this book, we focus on three dimensions of data analytics, i.e., descriptive analytics, predictive analytics and prescriptive analytics (see Chap. 2).

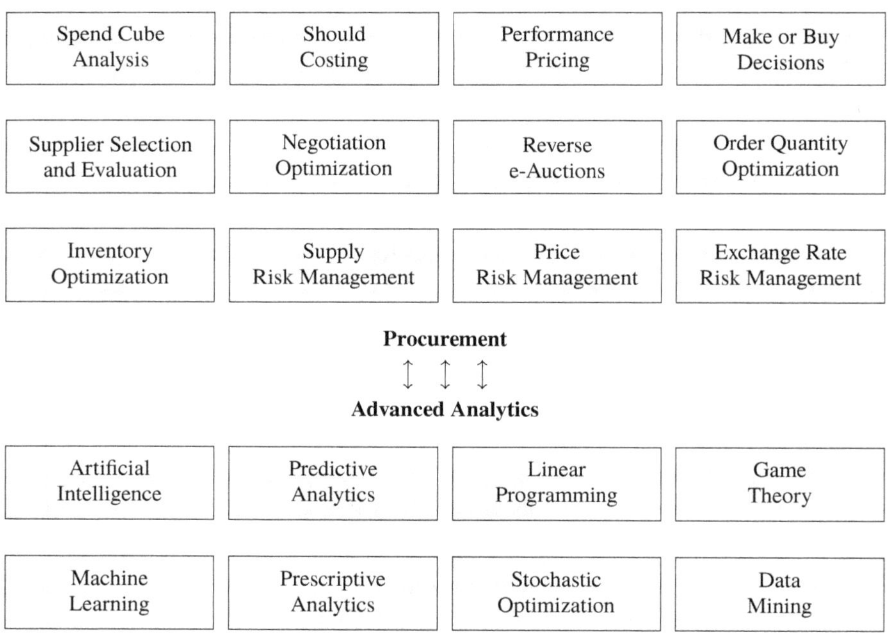

Fig. 1.3 Dimensions of procurement analytics

1.5 Structure of the Textbook

The book *Procurement Analytics* studies analytics-based procurement and therefore combines both advanced analytics methodologies and procurement applications, which is unique. On one hand, there are important textbooks that are addressing procurement from a more qualitative direction (e.g., [1, 6]). On the other hand, there are textbooks on supply chain and logistics with a strong quantitative focus but no procurement attention (e.g., [5]).

Rather than showcasing existing software from the procurement analytics field, we focus on methodology applied to procurement problem settings. The results should inspire procurement professionals to identify analytics use cases in the procurement field or frame the starting point to build and implement their own industrial decision-support tools and systems.

Each chapter of this textbook describes concepts and presents examples for application in procurement. Examples include (i) *numerical examples* and (ii) *industry examples* in order to motivate different topics based on anecdotal applications from industrial practice.

Numerical Example
Numerical examples aim at demonstrating the application and value of different procurement analytics methods.

Industry Example
Industry examples aim at motivating different topics based on anecdotal evidence from practice.

The textbook starts with a chapter on methodology and continues with several chapters on data-driven procurement applications addressing the perspectives spend management, supplier management, inventory management and risk management.

Chapter 2 lays the methodological foundation by giving an overview of relevant data analytics methods from the fields of descriptive data analytics, predictive planning and prescriptive decision-support. Even though we regard Chap. 2 as an upfront technical introduction of basic concepts, it is already connected to procurement by illustrating these methods based on procurement data. Readers, who are familiar with basic concepts from machine learning and operations research, can easily skip this chapter.

Chapter 3 covers data-driven spend management including spend data classification and spend analytics. The chapter presents the concept of spend cubes, simple and advanced AI-based methods for spend classification, procurement key performance indicators for performance measurement and spend optimization methods such as should-cost modeling and linear and nonlinear performance pricing.

Chapter 4 covers data-driven supplier management including decision-support approaches to derive optimal sourcing strategies such as make or buy or multi-sourcing, digital tender management via e-RFX and e-auctions, bid analytics, game theory in supplier negotiations, data-driven supplier selection and evaluation models, algorithms for supply network design and data-driven supply contracting and coordination.

Chapter 5 covers data-driven inventory management reviewing deterministic models such as the EOQ model and the dynamic lot sizing model and stochastic models such as the safety stock formula, different newsvendor models and different dynamic inventory control policies. It furthermore includes novel approaches from machine and deep learning that are capable of leveraging internal and external data for optimal inventory decisions.

Chapter 6 covers data-driven risk management including three risk dimensions that are particularly relevant for procurement, i.e., supply disruption risk, commodity price risk and exchange rate risk. The chapter focuses on (i) computation of the related risk and (ii) data-driven measures for risk mitigation.

Chapter 7 gives a summary and proposes an outlook on how advancements in procurement analytics might further change purchasing and supply management in the future.

References

1. Benton WC (2010) Purchasing and Supply Chain Management, 3rd edn. McGraw-Hill, New York
2. McKinsey & Company (2020) Taking Supplier Collaboration to the Next Level. https://www.mckinsey.com/capabilities/operations/our-insights/taking-supplier-collaboration-to-the-next-level/. Accessed 22 Dec 2022
3. PricewaterhouseCoopers (2022) 2022 Digital Procurement Survey. https://www.pwc.de/en/strategy-organisation-processes-systems/digital-procurement-survey.html. Accessed 14 Dec 2022
4. Roland Berger (2018) Digitalization and Beyond—The Future of Procurement in the Age of Artificial Intelligence. https://www.rolandberger.com/en/Insights/Publications/AI-and-the-future-of-procurement.html. Accessed 27 Dec 2022
5. Simchi-Levi D, Kaminsky P, Simchi-Levi E (2009) Designing and Managing the Supply Chain: Concepts, Strategies and Case Studies, 3rd edn. McGraw-Hill, New York
6. Van Weele AJ (2010) Purchasing and Supply Chain Management, 5th edn. Cengage Learning, Boston

Chapter 2
Fundamentals of Data Analytics

Abstract This chapter gives an introduction to the methodological foundations of data analytics that is required for an effective reading of the subsequent chapters of this textbook. The structure follows a widespread and accepted breakdown of analytics levels, i.e., descriptive analytics, predictive analytics and prescriptive analytics, presenting accuracy measures and methods for each field—always related to problem settings from the procurement function. The chapter covers areas such as data collection, data visualization, prediction and classification methods from machine learning, mathematical optimization, simulation and game theory. It builds the methodological basis for procurement analytics professionals that plan to develop or extend their own planning approaches. Readers who are familiar with the basics of data analytics such as correlation analysis, regression models, linear programming and classification models can easily skip this technical chapter.

Keywords Descriptive analytics · Predictive analytics · Prescriptive analytics · Machine learning · Operations research · Game theory

2.1 Introduction

Data analytics is often connected with artificial intelligence, machine or deep learning and operations research however without being precisely defined in most cases. The following brief definitions aim at highlighting the differences of those disciplines, concepts and methods.

- *Artificial intelligence (AI)* is the overall term that describes machines or systems that incorporate and reproduce human behavior and intelligence such as cognitive abilities, recognition, learning and understanding via algorithms.
- *Generative artificial intelligence (Generative AI)* is a type of AI that produces new content from training data such as images, text, audio or video. The most prominent example are chatbots such as OpenAI's ChatGPT or Google's Bard.

C. Mandl, *Procurement Analytics*, Springer Series in Supply Chain Management 22, https://doi.org/10.1007/978-3-031-43281-1_2

- *Machine learning (ML)* is a discipline of AI that comprises all methods that learn from past experience by training an analytical model on sample data. ML algorithms are typically used for prediction and classification tasks.
- *Deep learning (DL)* is an advanced machine learning technique to perform prediction or classification tasks using artificial neural networks.
- *Operations research (OR)* is a discipline at the interface of management, mathematics and computer science that comprises analytical methods for better (managerial) decision-making. This includes the domains mathematical optimization, simulation and game theory.
- *Advanced analytics (AA)* comprises all data-driven methods from statistics, machine learning and operations research in order to analyze business data, generate business insights from data and derive optimal data-driven business decisions. Advanced analytics (also often referred to business analytics) is closely related to data science, which however has a stronger scientific foundation and may be less connected to a specific business problem.

In this textbook, we focus on three dimensions of data analytics, i.e., descriptive analytics, predictive analytics and prescriptive analytics (even though there is often a fourth dimension mentioned, which is *diagnostic analytics*, which is related to investigating why something has happened). While descriptive analytics is already prevalent in many procurement departments, predictive and prescriptive analytics applications are still on an early implementation stage and hence can generate a competitive advantage if implemented quickly (Fig. 2.1).

Descriptive analytics is the systematic collection and analysis of data. This can be product data (e.g., production quantities), customer data (e.g., demand), process data (e.g., inventory levels) and environmental data (e.g., weather or macroeco-

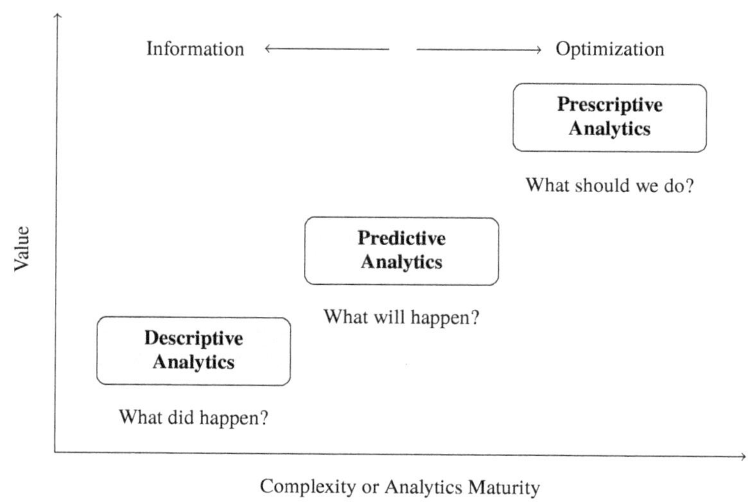

Fig. 2.1 Dimensions of advanced analytics according to Gartner

nomic data). For analysis, descriptive analytics uses data mining and visualization techniques. The goal is to create a data lake or data warehouse and to identify relationships in the data. In the procurement context, this can include a segmentation of suppliers or purchase items based on clustering techniques. Descriptive analytics is also often referred to as business intelligence and uses real-time dashboards and KPIs for managerial communication and aggregation of data-driven results. Popular software in the field of descriptive analytics is `Microsoft PowerBI`, `Tableau` or `QlikView`. The output of descriptive analytics is a data model that often defines the basis for predictive and prescriptive analytics applications.

Predictive analytics is often referred to as machine learning or data science and focuses on predictive planning. In the procurement context, this can include predictions of customer demand or prices at commodity markets. Methods applied are regression analysis, neural networks or deep learning. The goal is to predict the future as accurate as possible. Existing machine learning techniques therefore focus on prediction quality but do typically not address optimal decision-making since generic machine learning methods do typically not exploit the structure of the underlying decision problem. For instance, a forecast with a forecast error of 5% does not give any recommendations on optimal stock levels or supply network design decisions. Popular software in the field of predictive analytics is statistical software such as `R` or `SPSS` as well as programming languages such as `Python` with libraries for machine learning and data science such as `Scikit-learn`, `TensorFlow`, `Pandas`, `NumPy` and `SciPy`. The output of predictive analytics is a prediction model (or forecasting model) that may be trained on data from a data model generated via descriptive analytics and used as input for a decision model in prescriptive analytics.

Prescriptive analytics is often referred to as optimization or operations research and exploits the structure of the underlying optimization problem, focuses on business decisions and evaluates decision options and its implications with regard to cost or other objectives. It therefore defines the transition from (big) data to optimal decisions. In the procurement context, decisions can be purchasing quantities, timing of purchases, inventory levels, supplier selection, supply network design, negotiation strategies or hedging decisions for commodity risk management. Methods that are used for prescriptive analytics are mathematical optimization, simulation and reinforcement learning. The goal of prescriptive analytics is to give data-driven decision-support with a clear data-informed recommendation that is interpretable and accessible to managers in practice. Popular software packages for prescriptive analytics applications are mathematical optimization solvers, such as `Excel Solver`, `CBC COIN-OR`, `PuLP`, `Gurobi`, `FICO XPRESS` or `CPLEX`, and simulation software, such as `Plant Simulation`, `Arena` or `Anylogic`. The output of prescriptive analytics is a decision model (or decision-support model) that may be solved based on data from the data model from descriptive analytics and prediction resulting from the prediction model from predictive analytics (see [3]).

Cognitive analytics is sporadically named as a next step in advanced analytics that combines all other analytics disciplines with natural language processing

(NLP), neural programming and artificial intelligence (AI) to quickly find answers to decision problems in large data sets within minutes or even seconds.

2.2 Descriptive Analytics

Descriptive Analytics is the systematic collection and analysis of data. This can be product data (e.g., production quantities), customer data (e.g., demand), process data (e.g., inventory levels) and environmental data (e.g., weather or macroeconomic data). The objective is to create a data lake, build data transparency and identify relationships in the data. Descriptive analytics includes data aggregation and visualization, correlation analysis, seasonality analysis and data mining.

2.2.1 Data Collection and Consolidation

The basis for any analytics application is the collection and extraction of data. Therefore, a first step of procurement analytics is the development of a data lake (or big data warehouse) as a master data repository and the single source of truth. The data lake consists of internal and external data.

Internal data is all data that is generated within the firm such as spend data, inventory levels and supplier performance (e.g., delay rates). It is retrieved from transactional databases such as enterprise resource planning systems (ERP) as the backbone of procurement, customer relationship management (CRM) platforms, invoice and purchase order management solutions, accounting software, RFX management software or engineering solutions for computer-aided design (CAD). In the procurement context, internal data is typically collected in spend cubes that summarize all purchase transactions with information about, e.g., purchase date, purchase price, purchase volume and supplier. In addition, tendering processes (e.g., requests for information, requests for quotation and e-auctions) are another valuable data source. They provide information about supplier pricing, capacities and capabilities and can be used to identify price discrepancies and derive optimal data-driven supplier negotiation strategies.

External data is all data that is generated outside the organization such as market prices, exchange rates, supply data, supplier credit ratings and supply risk data. This data can either be provided by suppliers (e.g., supplier's real-time inventory levels) or retrieved from third parties like the Federal Statistical Office or database providers such as Bloomberg, Refinitiv Datastream (formerly Thomson Reuters Datastream), Refinitiv Eikon (formerly Thomson Reuters Eikon) or Economist Intelligent Unit. These databases can semiautomatically be integrated into the data lake by application programming interfaces (API). Further data sources for external data are procurement benchmarking services as provided by, for instance, consultancies or procurement associations but also through social media tracking (e.g., in terms of supply disruptions due to natural disasters).

For an effective analysis, both internal and external data needs to be combined and integrated in a data consolidation process. For instance, in order to analyze the exchange rate risk of the supplier portfolio of a procurement organization, it is essential to have an overview of negotiated currencies of supplier contracts (internal data) and to have access to financial data in order to quantify exchange rate volatility (external data). Furthermore, to efficiently work on product innovation in supplier-buyer collaborations, both parties need to exchange, for instance, CAD data. Another example is the combination of internal data on inventory levels with external data on live tracking of container locations for predictive planning against supply shortages.

2.2.2 *Descriptive Statistics*

After data collection, data cleansing and validation aims at removing irrelevant data, managing incomplete data (e.g., gaps in time series) and identifying outliers. Good data is essential for optimization and machine learning applications. In this matter, descriptive statistics helps us get a quick overview of raw data.

The *arithmetic mean* μ calculates the average over a series of $i = 1, \ldots, n$ data points x_i:

$$\mu = \frac{1}{n}\sum_{i=1}^{n} x_i = \frac{x_1 + x_2 + \ldots + x_n}{n} \tag{2.1}$$

However, the mean is very sensitive to outliers. Therefore, it is useful to additionally calculate the median, which is the value that separates the smaller half of all data points from the larger half of all data points. After ordering the data set x of n numbers from smallest to largest (x_1 is smallest value, x_n is largest value), the median is calculated by

$$\text{median(x)} = \begin{cases} x_{(n+1)/2} & \text{if n is odd,} \\ \frac{1}{2}(x_{n/2} + x_{n/2+1}) & \text{if n is even.} \end{cases} \tag{2.2}$$

The *median* is referred to as the 50th percentile (or second quartile). To get additional information about the skewness of the data, one can additionally calculate the 25th percentile (or first quartile) and 75th percentile (or third quartile). Together with the minimum and maximum values of the data set, this provides the so-called five-number-summary of data and is often visualized in box-and-whisker plots (see Sect. 2.2.5).

In practice, data sets typically exhibit fluctuation (e.g., time series data). Therefore, it is valuable to get a quick impression how large fluctuation is. Therefore, the standard deviation σ is calculated, i.e.,

$$\sigma = \sqrt{\frac{1}{n}\sum_{i=1}^{n}(x_i - \mu)^2} \tag{2.3}$$

and variance VAR(X), i.e.,

$$\text{VAR(X)} = \frac{1}{n}\sum_{i=1}^{n}(x_i - \mu)^2. \tag{2.4}$$

Both σ and VAR are the basis for volatility measures that are, for instance, relevant in commodity and exchange rate risk management (see Chap. 6).

The *mode* determines the most frequent value in a data set. In the procurement context, the *mode* is, for instance, useful in measuring how often specific suppliers occur in spend cube data.

Numerical Example: Descriptive Statistics of Delivery Delays
We track the days of delay of the last 20 purchase orders at a specific supplier, i.e., 0, 0, 0, 1, 2, 3, 1, 2, 5, 1, 8, 10, 2, 1, 0, 0, 0, 0, 0, 1.

Based on this data, we can calculate the mean as as 1.9 days, the median as 1 day, the standard deviation as 2.7 days and the mode as 0 days.

In order to assess the form of distributional data, *kurtosis* and *skewness* can be used. *Skewness* of an (empirical) distribution measures the symmetry (or asymmetry) of a probability distribution. A negative skew (left-skewed distribution) indicates that the left tail of the distribution is longer and the mass of the distribution is concentrated on the right. A positive skew (right-skewed distribution) indicates that the right tail of the distribution is longer and the mass of the distribution is concentrated on the left. *Kurtosis* measures the tailedness of a probability distribution.

Besides analyzing data via descriptive statistics, data can also be aggregated by defining business-specific key performance indicators (KPIs). Those can be absolute metrics (e.g., profit, cost) or relative metrics (e.g., return on investment defined as the profit generated divided by the cost of an investment). We give a comprehensive overview of procurement KPIs in Chap. 3 of this textbook.

2.2.3 *Correlation Analysis*

Correlation is any relationship between two variables. This relationship can but does not need to be causal, i.e., correlation does not imply causality ("A happens due to B"). However, even if there is no causality, correlations are useful because they can exhibit predictive power.

In the literature, there are different measures for correlation. The most popular metric is Pearson's correlation coefficient ρ that is based on covariance $cov(X, Y)$ between time series x_t and y_t with $t = 1, \ldots, T$ that is defined as

$$cov(X, Y) = \frac{1}{T} \sum_{t=1}^{T} (x_t - \bar{x})(y_t - \bar{y}) \tag{2.5}$$

with $\bar{x}$ and $\bar{y}$ as the arithmetic means of data series x_t and y_t, respectively. Pearson's correlation coefficient ρ normalizes covariance through standard deviations σ_X and σ_Y of the series x_t and y_t:

$$\rho = \frac{cov(X, Y)}{\sigma_X \cdot \sigma_Y} \tag{2.6}$$

ρ is a value on or between -1 and 1. $\rho = 1$ describes a perfect positive correlation between X and Y characterized by a linear equation. $\rho = -1$ describes a perfect negative correlation between X and Y characterized by a linear equation. While some textbooks define thresholds for "very strong," "strong," "medium" and "low" correlation, we want to point out that this needs to be treated very carefully. While a correlation of 0.7 may be very high for one problem setting, it can be already quite low for another.

Correlation coefficients such as ρ can be calculated by spreadsheet software `Excel` using function `CORREL()`, statistical programming language `R` using function `cor()` or `Python` using `SciPy` function `pearsonr()`.

Numerical Example: Correlation Analysis

The prices of copper (LCPCASH) and aluminum (LAHCASH) show clear positive correlation ($\rho = 0.83$), while the price of copper is negatively correlated with the copper world mine production (CUIWMPM) ($\rho = -0.70$).

That shows that if aluminum prices are high, copper prices are high as well and with increasing supply, copper prices decrease. While the first observation is an example for correlation without causality, the second observation is an example for both correlation and causality. As Fig. 2.2 shows, the prices of copper (LCPCASH and aluminum (LAHCASH)) are positively correlated ($\rho = 0.83$), while the price of copper is negatively correlated with the copper world mine production (CUIWMPM) ($\rho = -0.70$).

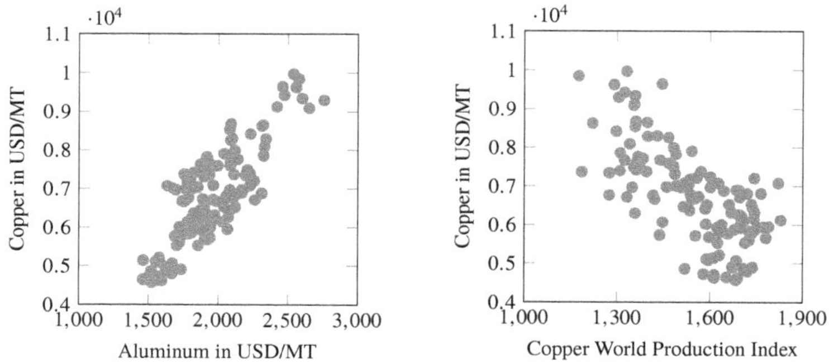

Fig. 2.2 Correlation between LME copper prices, LME aluminum prices and copper world mine production between January 2010 and January 2020 (Data source: Refinitiv)

2.2.4 Data Mining and Principal Component Analysis

The general idea behind *data mining* is to automatically identify new patterns and trends in huge data sets (big data). Therefore, data mining systematically uses different kinds of statistical methods described in this chapter (e.g., correlation and regression analysis), however in a big data context (see [1]). Data mining finds intense application in procurement in the context of spend cube analysis (see Chap. 3). A spend cube as a huge collection of transactional data builds an excellent basis for data mining applications that, for instance, identify price discrepancies and savings opportunities. Another application in the procurement context is pattern recognition in tender results in order to identify, for instance, inconsistent supplier bidding behavior.

Principal component analysis (PCA) is a method in data mining that goes beyond descriptive statistics in order to identify underlying patterns in large data sets and reduce the dimensionality of large data sets without losing valuable information. It is based on covariance matrix computation and transforms large data sets with many variables to smaller data sets with less variables by extracting important variables only (i.e., extracting uncorrelated components from correlated data). PCA can be executed using, for instance, the statistical programming language `R` (`prcomp()` function) or `Python` under the machine learning library `Scikit-learn` (`sklearn.decomposition.PCA`). In the procurement and supply management context, PCA is, for instance, used for monitoring the supply chain with regard to supply disruptions. A huge amount of data may indicate supply chain risks such as inventory levels, market demand, market supply and economic indicators. Some of these variables may be highly correlated, and PCA is able to reduce the big data set to relevant data needed for early warning of supply disruptions.

2.2.5 *Data Visualization*

To support managerial decision-making, it is helpful to visualize data. Therefore, we give a brief overview of visualization methods that are helpful for analytics dashboards and data-driven management presentations to CPOs. Many spreadsheet tools such as `Microsoft Excel`; business intelligence tools such as `Tableau`, `Microsoft PowerBI` or `QlikView`; or prevalent programming languages such as `Python` or `R` provide a wide range of chart types for visualization (see Fig. 2.3).

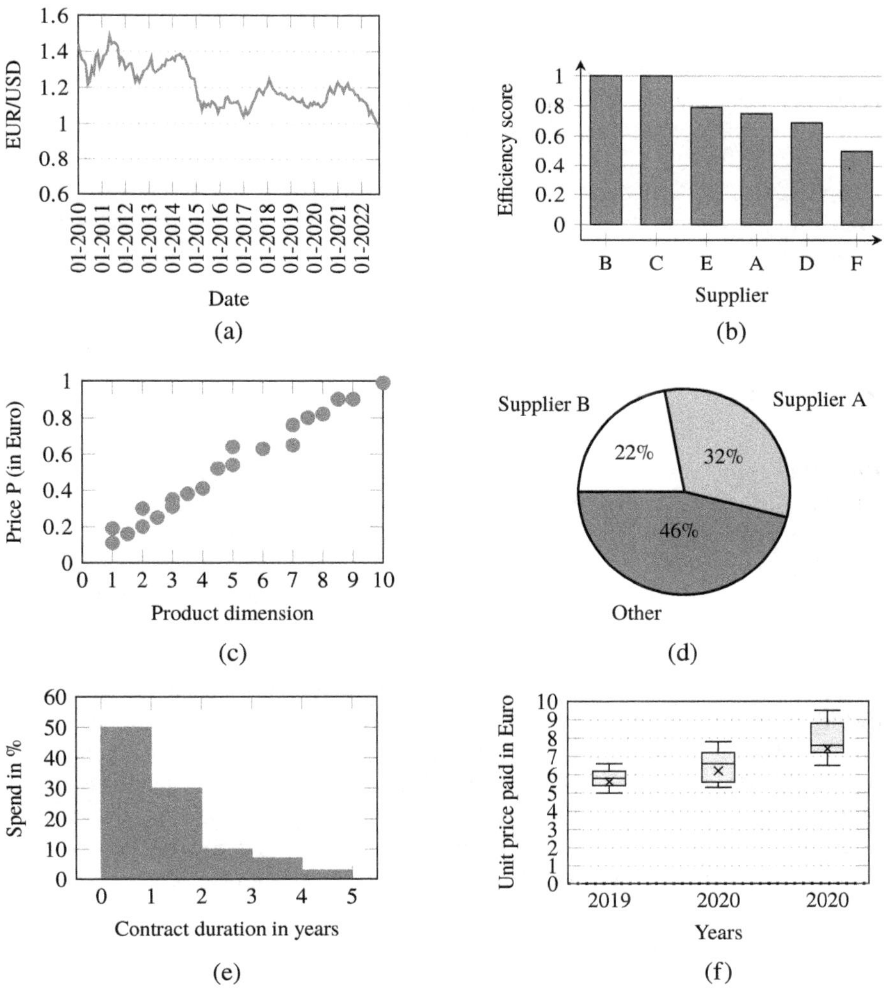

Fig. 2.3 Basic visualization techniques. (**a**) Line chart. (**b**) Bar chart. (**c**) Scatterplot. (**d**) Pie chart. (**e**) Histogram. (**f**) Box-and-whisker plot

The challenge is to select the most appropriate chart type for the corresponding data set.

A *line chart* is typically applied to time series data. It is not appropriate if there is no (time) relationship between the objects on the x-axis. In this case, a *(stacked) bar chart* is preferred. A *scatterplot* is appropriate to show correlation between two data sets (e.g., between price and performance or product characteristics). A *pie chart* gives a relative overview about the composition of data (e.g., supplier spend distribution). A *histogram* is appropriate for presenting frequencies and empirical distributions of data. A *box-and-whisker plot* gives a compact statistical overview by showing minimum and maximum values of a data set as well as the first, second and third quartile and the mean.

Further popular chart types that are considered in the `PowerBI` dashboard of Fig. 2.4 for real-time spend cube analytics are tree maps, waterfall diagrams, geospatial plots and funnel charts. Spend cube visualization is an essential part of procurement dashboards that additionally track cost performance, quality, lead time and risk.

For multi-criteria evaluation tasks (e.g., evaluation of process maturity or supplier evaluation), radar charts are a common way to illustrate the results (see Fig. 2.5). In order to derive decisions (e.g., supplier A or supplier B), we refer to analytical multi-criteria decision-making methods introduced in Chap. 4.

2.3 Predictive Analytics

Predictive analytics focuses on predictions of a variable Y_t. In the procurement context, this can be the prediction of customer demand or purchase prices at commodity markets. Applied methods are divided into traditional statistical methods such as moving averages and regression analysis and advanced machine learning models such as neural networks or deep learning. The common goal is to predict the future as accurate as possible, which is needed for adequate business decisions. For instance, accurate price forecasts are essential for price negotiations with suppliers, or a high confidence about future demand can be used for negotiating quantity discounts. And if a supply chain manager is able to accurately predict supply shortages from a specific supplier, he can take countermeasures such as dual sourcing or stockpiling. Furthermore, an adequate spend forecast (defined by future prices times volumes) supports budget and investment planning.

In the following, we give an overview on how to measure the performance of prediction models in Sect. 2.3.1 and introduce a variety of prediction and classification models in Sect. 2.3.2.

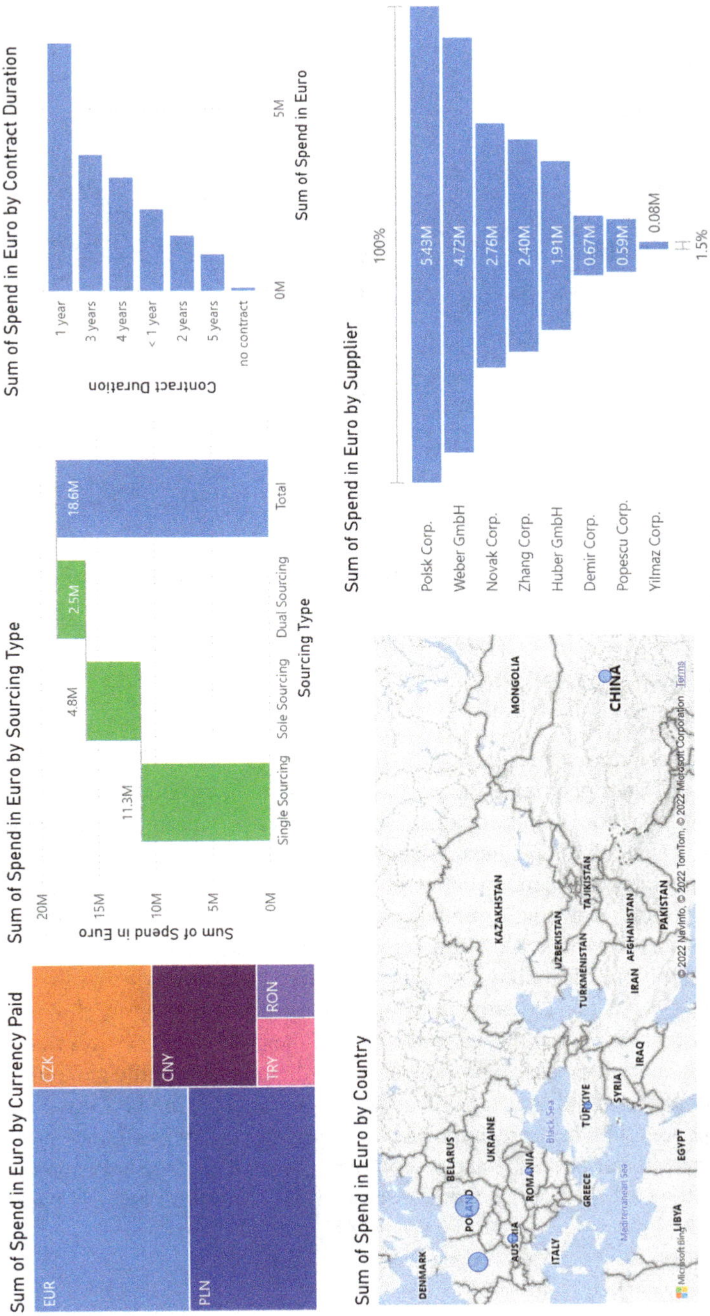

Fig. 2.4 Spend cube visualization with business intelligence dashboards (Visualization in Microsoft PowerBI)

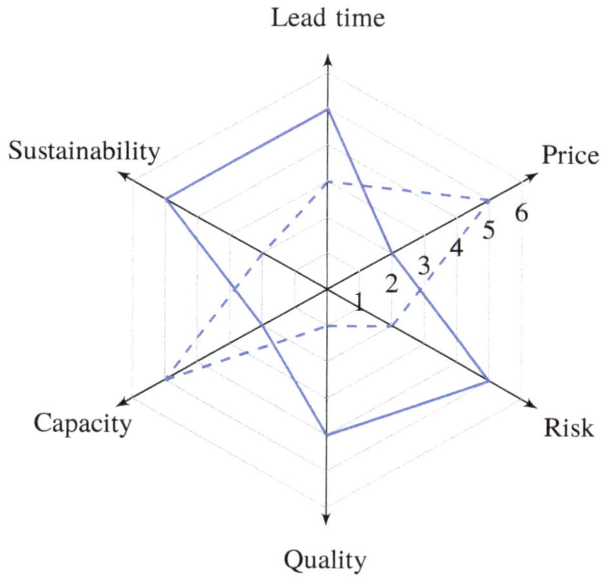

Fig. 2.5 Radar chart for criteria-based comparison of two suppliers on a six-point scale (1, very poor; 6, excellent)

2.3.1 Accuracy Measures

Prediction is very difficult, especially if it's about the future. This famous quote, attributed to different people including Nobel laureate Niels Bohr, gives important insights about the nature of predictions. Even though predictions are usually wrong, they are still essential for business planning. The much more important question is: How wrong are they, and what does wrong actually mean? In the business context, you often hear that somebody achieved a prediction accuracy of, for instance, 95%. However, what does this actually mean? Does it mean that the observed value is only 5% above or below the predicted value or that the forecast is correct in 95% of the cases or that the general direction (up or down) of the forecast is correct in 95% of the cases? In reality, there are various ways to measure accuracy of prediction models. For most of them, there is no specific and universally valid numerical threshold that signals a "good" accuracy. This is always strongly problem-dependent. It is more important to compare the performance over time ("Do our forecasts get better?") and to compare the performance between methods ("Do we use the best method?"). Consequently, it is essential to define a baseline to compare to.

In the following, we want to give a comprehensive overview of the different accuracy measures that are used in practice for calculating the performance of prediction models. The choice of the correct accuracy measure depends on the overall business objective.

Forecast Error

The *forecast error* e_t determines the delta between the forecast and the actual realized value at a certain point in time t. It is calculated by

$$e_t = |A_t - Y_t| \tag{2.7}$$

with A_t as the actual observation at time period t and Y_t as the prediction for time period t. A low forecast error indicates high precision of a prediction algorithm.

Mean Absolute Error (MAE)

The *mean absolute error (MAE)* (or mean absolute deviation (MAD)) averages the forecast error e_t over a sequence of T observations. It is calculated by

$$\text{MAE} = \frac{1}{T}\sum_{t=1}^{T} e_t. \tag{2.8}$$

MAE gives a consolidated view of forecast performance. $MAE = 0$ means that the forecast always perfectly matches the actual realizations. *MAE* is easy to interpret but problem-specific. Therefore, it does not allow to compare across different time series of different levels.

Mean Absolute Percentage Error (MAPE)

The *mean absolute percentage error (MAPE)* determines the average forecast error over a sequence of T observations as a percentage number. It is calculated by

$$\text{MAPE} = \frac{1}{T}\sum_{t=1}^{T} \left|\frac{A_t - Y_t}{A_t}\right| \cdot 100\%. \tag{2.9}$$

Therefore, it gives a standardized view on forecast errors and allows for comparisons across different time series. However, *MAPE* may underestimate large but seldom errors.

Mean Squared Error (MSE)

The *mean squared error (MSE)* determines the average squared forecast error over a sequence of T observations. It is calculated by

$$\text{MSE} = \frac{1}{T}\sum_{t=1}^{T} e_t^2. \tag{2.10}$$

Therefore, *MSE* gives more weight on larger errors or outliers that are underestimated by *MAPE*. *MSE* is used as predominant performance indicator for many algorithms in the machine learning field.

Root Mean Squared Error (RMSE)

The *root mean squared error (RMSE)* is an extension of *MSE* and determines the square root of the average squared forecast error over a sequence of T observations. It is calculated by

$$\text{RMSE} = \sqrt{\frac{1}{T}\sum_{t=1}^{T} e_t^2}. \tag{2.11}$$

RMSE is the standard measure in inventory management for quantifying forecast errors, which is required for optimal safety stock placement (see Chap. 5). Compared to *MSE*, *RMSE* is simpler to interpret as it is measured in the same unit as the predicted value.

Bias

Bias determines whether there is an(a) (consistent) over- or underestimation of an algorithm and is calculated by

$$\text{Bias} = \frac{1}{T}\sum_{t=1}^{T}(A_t - Y_t). \tag{2.12}$$

Compared to forecast error that only measures the magnitude, *bias* considers the errors' directions. If the bias is significantly positive, then there is an underestimation; if the bias is significantly negative, then there is an overestimation.

A/F Ratio (A/F)

A/F ratio is the ratio between actual observations A_t and the forecast Y_t (often described by F_t).

$$\text{A/F ratio} = \frac{A_t}{Y_t} \tag{2.13}$$

A fully accurate forecast has a A/F *ratio* of 1. If $A/F > 1$, then the forecast is too low. If $A/F < 1$, then the forecast is too high. It therefore indicates whether there are structural problems with regard to the applied prediction method (Fig. 2.6).

Tracking Signal (TS)

The *tracking signal (TS)* indicates whether a prediction is permanently above or below the actual realization (also called forecast bias). It is calculated by

$$\text{TS} = \frac{\text{Bias}}{\text{MAE}} = \frac{\sum_{t=1}^{T}(A_t - Y_t)}{\frac{1}{T}\sum_{t=1}^{T}|A_t - Y_t|}. \tag{2.14}$$

The calculated values are permanently compared to thresholds (lower and upper control limits). If $TS > 3.75$, then there is persistent underestimation, but if $TS < -3.75$, then there is persistent overestimation. Therefore, $|TS| > 3.75$ implies a

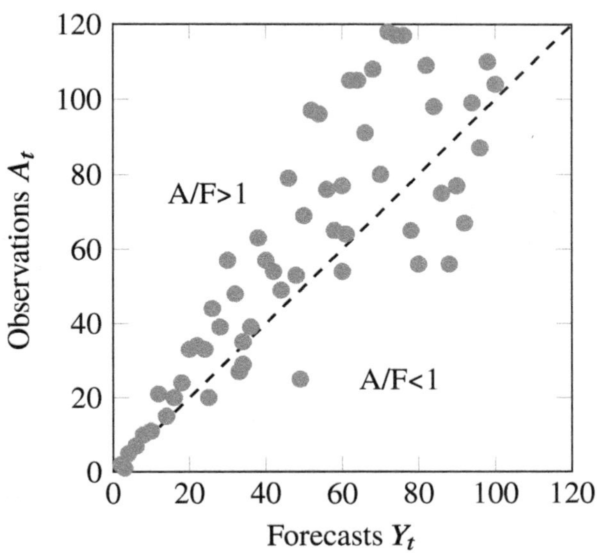

Fig. 2.6 Concept of A/F ratios

forecast bias. The threshold value 3.75 is an approximation and derived statistically based on normal distribution assumptions.

Mean Directional Accuracy (MDA)

The *mean directional accuracy* is not based on the size of the forecast error but on the direction of the error. For instance, a forecasting method that is correctly predicting commodity price increases and decreases is very valuable and often sufficient for risk management decisions such as whether to hedge or not to hedge. MDA is calculated by

$$\text{MDA} = \frac{1}{T}\sum_{t=1}^{T}\mathbf{1}_{sign(A_t-A_{t-1})=sign(Y_t-A_{t-1})}\cdot 100\% \tag{2.15}$$

where **1** is the indicator function that is 1 if the actual equals the predicted direction.

Theill's U

Theill's U is a forecast accuracy measure that compares the quality between a specific forecasting method and a naïve forecast. A naïve forecast assumes that next period's value equals today's value, i.e., $A_{t+1} = A_t$. *Theill's U* is defined as

$$U = \frac{\sqrt{\sum_{t=1}^{n-1}\left[\left(\frac{Y_{t+1}-A_t}{A_t}\right)-\left(\frac{A_{t+1}-A_t}{A_t}\right)\right]^2}}{\sqrt{\sum_{t=1}^{n-1}\left(\frac{A_{t+1}-A_t}{A_t}\right)^2}}. \tag{2.16}$$

If $U > 1$, then a naïve forecast outperforms the selected forecast method. If this is the case, the selected forecast method cannot be regarded as appropriate. In the procurement context, it turns out that naïve forecasts are not as bad as one might expect for forecasting time series data that is characterized by high volatility without clear trends (e.g., some commodity prices)

Table 2.1 Example: Prediction and realization

	$t = 1$	$t = 2$	$t = 3$	$t = 4$	$t = 5$	$t = 6$	$t = 7$	$t = 8$	$t = 9$	$t = 10$	$t = 11$
A_t	10	11	13	14	15	13	12	11	10	9	8
Y_t	9	9	11	12	14	16	13	12	12	11	9

Table 2.2 Example: Predictive performance measures

Indicator	Value
MAE	1.64
MAPE	14.52%
MSE	3.10
RMSE	1.76
Bias	−0.18
TS	−1.22
MDA	0.0%
Theill's U	1.44

Numerical Example: Predictive Accuracy Measures

Consider the following time series of actual values A_t (realizations) and predicted values Y_t (Table 2.1).

Given this data, the accuracy measures are given by the values in Table 2.2. The accuracy measures indicate that there is no persistent underestimation or overestimation (see *bias* or TS). *Theill's U* shows that a naïve forecast with $A_{t+1} = A_t$ would perform better.

Machine learning libraries such as `Scikit` in `Python` offer modules such as `sklearn.metrics` that automatically calculate prediction metrics. In R there are built-in functions for the different prediction metrics available from the package `MLmetrics`.

Accuracy, Precision, Recall, Specificity and F1 Score

Machine learning distinguishes between prediction problems and classification problems (see Fig. 2.9). While the above accuracy measures particularly address prediction, for classification problems there are different major performance metrics, i.e., accuracy, error rate, precision, recall, specificity and F1 score. The results of a binary classification algorithm can be summarized in the so-called confusion matrix (see Fig. 2.7). In the procurement context, binary classification is, for instance, relevant for predicting supplier failure or rejecting (or not rejecting) lots of incoming goods.

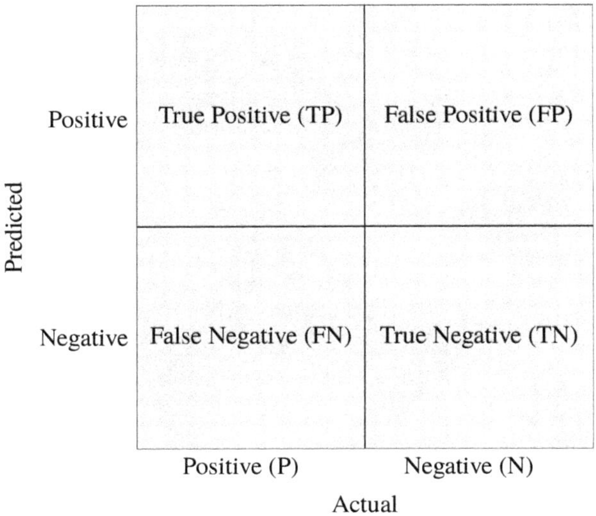

Fig. 2.7 Confusion matrix

Accuracy measures the share of correctly classified items on total items. It is calculated by

$$\text{Accuracy} = \frac{\text{TP} + \text{TN}}{\text{P} + \text{N}} = \frac{\text{TP} + \text{TN}}{\text{TP} + \text{FN} + \text{FP} + \text{TN}}. \tag{2.17}$$

The *error rate* is defined as

$$\text{Error Rate} = 1 - \text{Accuracy}. \tag{2.18}$$

Precision measures the correctly classified positive results as a percentage of all positive predictions:

$$\text{Precision} = \frac{\text{TP}}{\text{TP} + \text{FP}} \tag{2.19}$$

Recall (also called true positive rate or sensitivity) measures the correctly classified positive results as a percentage of all positive actual results:

$$\text{Recall} = \frac{\text{TP}}{\text{TP} + \text{FN}} \tag{2.20}$$

Specificity measures the proportion of negatives that are correctly classified:

$$\text{Specificity} = \frac{\text{TN}}{\text{TN} + \text{FP}} \tag{2.21}$$

The *F1 score* (also known as F-score or F-measure) is the harmonic mean of precision and recall and is calculated by

$$\text{F1 Score} = \frac{2 \cdot \text{Precision} \cdot \text{Recall}}{\text{Precision} + \text{Recall}}. \tag{2.22}$$

Further accuracy measures for classification problems are the receiver operating characteristic curve (*ROC curve*) and the area under the ROC curve (*AUC*).

Numerical Example: Accuracy of Supplier Classification
A typical task in the procurement risk management context is the classification of suppliers with regard to insolvency risk. A classification algorithm can classify suppliers in classes "low risk" (N) and "high risk" (P) based on features such as liquidity information, market outlook, etc. Suppose that the classification algorithm shows the following results for a classification of 30 suppliers: TP, 8 suppliers; FP, 2 suppliers; FN, 3 suppliers; and TN, 17 suppliers. This means that 8 suppliers that were flagged as high-risk suppliers were actually concerned with insolvency, 2 suppliers that were flagged as high-risk suppliers were actually not concerned with insolvency, 3 suppliers that were not flagged as high-risk suppliers were actually concerned with insolvency and 17 suppliers that were not flagged as high-risk suppliers were actually not concerned with insolvency. Based on these numbers, the accuracy of the classification algorithm is 0.83, the error rate is 0.17, the precision of the classification algorithm is 0.8 and the recall of the classification algorithm is 0.73. Please note that FN is the most critical classification error because it supports the selection of high-risk suppliers, while FP only leads to rejecting suppliers that are actually not concerned with insolvency, which may result in missed (savings) opportunities.

2.3.2 Methods of Predictive Analytics

Most of data-driven prediction methods are based on statistical time series analysis (see [11]) that are applied whenever (sufficient) historical data is available. In the following, we give an overview of simple rule-based forecast methods that are not trained on data, traditional statistical time-series forecast methods, advanced methods from machine learning and judgmental forecasts that are needed whenever data quality or availability is poor.

Naïve Forecast

The *naïve forecast* (or no-change forecast) is the simplest possible forecasting method. It assumes that the prediction Y_t equals the last observed realization A_{t-1}, i.e.,

$$Y_t = A_{t-1}. \tag{2.23}$$

Therefore, naïve forecasts do not require any training on historical data. In practice, it often turns out that naïve forecasts are not as bad as expected in terms of forecast accuracy, which is in line with Occam's razor (i.e., keep it simple if it performs well). This is the motivation of the introduced accuracy measure Theill's U that quantifies the performance of any prediction method relative to the naïve forecast.

Numerical Example: Naïve Forecasts
Suppose the following time series of aluminum spot prices at the London Metal Exchange from January 2021 until December 2021 quoted in USD per metric ton (MT) at the first trading day of the month. For performance evaluation, we calculate the percentage deviation by $D_t = |(A_t - Y_t)/A_t)| \cdot 100\%$, the MAPE and RMSE. In this example, a naïve one-step forecast yields a MAPE of 3.8% and a RMSE of 109.9 USD/MT (Table 2.3).

Table 2.3 Prediction of aluminum prices (in USD/MT) with naïve forecasts

Month t	Observation A_t	Prediction Y_t	Percentage deviation D_t
Jan-21	1973.60	–	–
Feb-21	1970.50	1973.60	0.2%
Mar-21	2115.00	1970.50	6.8%
Apr-21	2203.00	2115.00	4.0%
May-21	2407.50	2203.00	8.5%
Jun-21	2449.95	2407.50	1.7%
Jul-21	2495.50	2449.95	1.8%
Aug-21	2612.75	2495.50	4.5%
Sep-21	2695.25	2612.75	3.1%
Oct-21	2837.00	2695.25	5.0%
Nov-21	2705.50	2837.00	4.9%
Dec-21	2680.75	2705.50	0.9%
		MAPE (RMSE)	3.8% (109.9)

Moving Averages and Weighted Moving Averages

Moving Averages is a time series model and another simple prediction method. It extends naïve forecasts and relies on several historical observations of the variable that should be predicted (e.g., demand, price). It calculates the average over a limited selection of historical observations A_i from $i = t-n, \ldots, t-1$ and takes the result as the forecast as shown in the following equation:

$$Y_t = \frac{1}{n} \cdot \sum_{i=t-n}^{t-1} A_i \tag{2.24}$$

Therefore, naïve forecasts are a special case of *Moving Averages* with $n = 1$. Other than machine learning algorithms, moving averages do not require any training and optimization of coefficients based on historical data.

Numerical Example: Moving Averages
Table 2.4 shows the previous example for a moving average prediction of 2021 aluminum prices (in USD/MT) with $n = 3$ observations.

Often, it is valuable in terms of prediction quality to test adjustments to the standard *moving average*. For example, it can be beneficial to give higher weights to more recent observations and smaller weights to past (and outdated) observations.

Table 2.4 Prediction of aluminum prices (in USD/MT) with moving averages ($n = 3$ months)

Month t	Observation A_t	Prediction Y_t	Percentage Deviation D_t
Jan-21	1973.60	–	-
Feb-21	1970.50	–	-
Mar-21	2115.00	–	-
Apr-21	2203.00	2019.70	8.3%
May-21	2407.50	2096.16	12.9%
Jun-21	2449.95	2241.83	8.5%
Jul-21	2495.50	2353.48	5.7%
Aug-21	2612.75	2450.98	6.2%
Sep-21	2695.25	2519.40	6.5%
Oct-21	2837.00	2601.16	8.3%
Nov-21	2705.50	2715.00	0.4%
Dec-21	2680.75	2745.91	2.4%
		MAPE (RMSE)	6.6% (185.9)

In this case, the *weighted moving average* is calculated by

$$Y_t = \frac{\sum_{i=t-n}^{t-1} w_i A_i}{\sum_{i=t-n}^{t-1} w_i} \tag{2.25}$$

with w_i as the weights of historical values. Weights are, for instance, decreasing by 1 per period, i.e., $w_{t-1} = n, w_{t-2} = n - 1, \ldots, w_{t-n} = 1$.

Even though *moving averages* and *weighed moving averages* are very simple, it can be a very valuable benchmark for more sophisticated prediction methods that we introduce in the following. For example, if a machine learning algorithm does not consistently and significantly outperform simple methods, there is no reason to go for a sophisticated solution.

Moving averages can easily be implemented in any spreadsheet software or within any programming language such as `R` or `Python`. `Microsoft Excel` additionally offers an add-in under `Data` → `Data Analysis` → `Moving Average`.

Simple Exponential Smoothing

Simple exponential smoothing is an extension of *Moving Averages* and considers both historical observations A_{t-1} and historical predictions Y_{t-1} for predicting Y_t according to the following formula:

$$Y_t = \alpha \cdot A_{t-1} + (1 - \alpha) \cdot Y_{t-1} \tag{2.26}$$

α as the so-called smoothing factor is a value between 0 and 1 and determines the weight of historical observations relative to the weight of historical predictions. It is not a fixed parameter but needs to be tuned based on the data of the specific prediction problem (*parameter tuning*). For instance, α can be optimized through linear programming based on historical data by minimizing the mean squared prediction error MSE subject to $\alpha \leq 1$ (see Sect. 2.4.2 for an introduction to linear programming).

Numerical Example: Simple Exponential Smoothing
Table 2.5 shows the previous example for aluminum price predictions however via exponential smoothing with $\alpha = 0.4$. For performance evaluation, we again calculate the percentage deviation D_t, the MAPE and RMSE.

Please note that even though *naïve forecasts* and *moving averages* slightly outperform *Exponential Smoothing* in this example, this is not a general statement. There is no one-size-fits-all approach, and the best-performing

(continued)

prediction method always depends on the underlying prediction problem and data set. Furthermore, similar to *moving averages* whose results are sensitive to n, the results of *Exponential Smoothing* are sensitive to α.

Similar to *moving averages*, *exponential smoothing* is a very basic forecasting method. However, it should again be seen as a valuable natural benchmark for advanced predictive analytics techniques.

Exponential smoothing can easily be implemented in any spreadsheet software or within any programming language such as `R` or `Python`. `Microsoft Excel` additionally offers an add-in (`Data` → `Data Analysis` → `Exponential Smoothing`).

Holt's Linear Trend Model

Many time series such as price or customer demand exhibit trends. *Holt's linear trend model* (also known as double exponential smoothing or second-order exponential smoothing) is an extension of simple exponential smoothing and takes trends in the time series into account, which is not the case for simple exponential smoothing. Predictions are calculated by

$$Y_t = \alpha \cdot A_{t-1} + (1 - \alpha) \cdot (Y_{t-1} + B_{t-1}) \tag{2.27}$$

Table 2.5 Prediction of aluminum prices (in USD/MT) with exponential smoothing ($\alpha = 0.4$)

Month t	Observation A_t	Prediction Y_t	Percentage Deviation D_t
Jan-21	1973.60	2000.00	1.3%
Feb-21	1970.50	1989.44	1.0%
Mar-21	2115.00	1981.86	6.3%
Apr-21	2203.00	2035.12	7.6%
May-21	2407.50	2102.27	12.7%
Jun-21	2449.95	2224.36	9.2%
Jul-21	2495.50	2314.60	7.2%
Aug-21	2612.75	2386.96	8.6%
Sep-21	2695.25	2477.28	8.1%
Oct-21	2837.00	2564.47	9.6%
Nov-21	2705.50	2673.48	1.2%
Dec-21	2680.75	2686.29	0.2%
		MAPE (RMSE)	6.1%(182.0)

with B_t as the trend component that is calculated by

$$B_t = \beta \cdot (Y_t - Y_{t-1}) + (1 - \beta) \cdot B_{t-1} \tag{2.28}$$

with $0 \leq \beta \leq 1$ being the trend smoothing factor. Based on these formulas, Holt's linear trend model can quickly be implemented in any spreadsheet software such as `Excel`. Alternatively, the *holt* function in `R` can be used using the `R` forecast package or in `Python` using `statsmodels.tsa.holtwinters` from the `statsmodels` package using `pandas` data analysis library.

Holt-Winters' Seasonal Method

The *Holt-Winters' seasonal method* (also known as triple exponential smoothing) is a an extension of Holt's linear trend model in order to additionally capture seasonal patterns in forecasting (e.g., seasonal customer demand). We distinguish between two variations, i.e., Holt-Winters' additive method (e.g., a company sells 5000 more products in summer than in winter) and Holt-Winters' multiplicative method (e.g., a company sells 10% more products in summer than in winter). For the multiplicative method, predictions are calculated by

$$Y_t = \alpha \cdot \frac{A_{t-1}}{S_{t-l}} + (1 - \alpha) \cdot (Y_{t-1} + B_{t-1}) \tag{2.29}$$

with B_t as the trend component and S_t as the seasonal component. B_t is again calculated as

$$B_t = \beta \cdot (Y_t - Y_{t-1}) + (1 - \beta) \cdot B_{t-1} \tag{2.30}$$

and the seasonal component S_t is calculated as

$$S_t = \gamma \cdot \frac{A_{t-1}}{Y_t} + (1 - \gamma) \cdot S_{t-l} \tag{2.31}$$

with $0 \leq \gamma \leq 1$ as the seasonal change smoothing factor and l as the length of the seasonal cycle.

For implementation and testing, the `hw()` function in `R` can be used using the `R` forecast package or in `Python` using `statsmodels.tsa.holtwinters` from the `statsmodels` package using `pandas` data analysis library.

Autoregressive Integrated Moving Average (ARIMA)

ARIMA(p,q) models are composed of auto-regressive models (AR) and moving average models (MA) that are fitted to time series data.

In auto-regressive models AR(p), the values of time series can be described by linear models based on previous observations, i.e.,

$$Y_t = a + \sum_{i=1}^{p} \alpha_i \cdot Y_{t-i} + \epsilon_t \tag{2.32}$$

with an estimated level a, AR(p) coefficient α_i and a random noise term ϵ_t. The parameters are learned from historical data. Therefore, ARIMA belongs to the class of learning algorithms. In the procurement context, AR models are often used to model market rates such as commodity prices or exchange rates (see Chap. 6). The most prominent AR process is the AR(1) process, i.e., an autoregressive process of order 1. If $\alpha = 1$ and $a = 0$ ($a \neq 0$) for AR(1), the time series follows a so-called random walk (with drift).

AR(p) models can be extended to ARMA(p,q) models by adding a moving average term of the noise ϵ_t, i.e.,

$$Y_t = a + \sum_{i=1}^{p} \alpha_i \cdot Y_{t-i} + \sum_{j=1}^{q} \beta_j \cdot \epsilon_{t-j} + \epsilon_t. \tag{2.33}$$

with estimated level a, AR(p) coefficient α_i and MA(q) coefficient β_j. ARIMA(p,d,q) is a further generalization of ARMA(p,q) models. All parameters can be estimated following the Box-Jenkins approach.

Linear Regression

While *moving averages* and *exponential smoothing* do only rely on past information about the variable to be predicted, *linear regression* is a causal forecasting model and able to use further explanatory variables that are called features (e.g., weather data, macroeconomic data, sensor data) to predict a variable such as demand or price (dependent variable). Contrary to nonlinear regression, linear regression assumes a linear relationship between the dependent variable Y_t and n independent variables $X_{t,n}$ (see Fig. 2.8) according to the following formula:

$$Y_t = \beta_0 + \sum_{i=0}^{n} \beta_i X_{t,i} + \epsilon_t \tag{2.34}$$

The values β_i are the coefficients of feature i and determine the impact of $X_{t,i}$ on the dependent variable Y_t. β_0 is the feature-independent intercept and ϵ_t is the variation in dependent variable Y_t that cannot be explained by the regression model. The goal

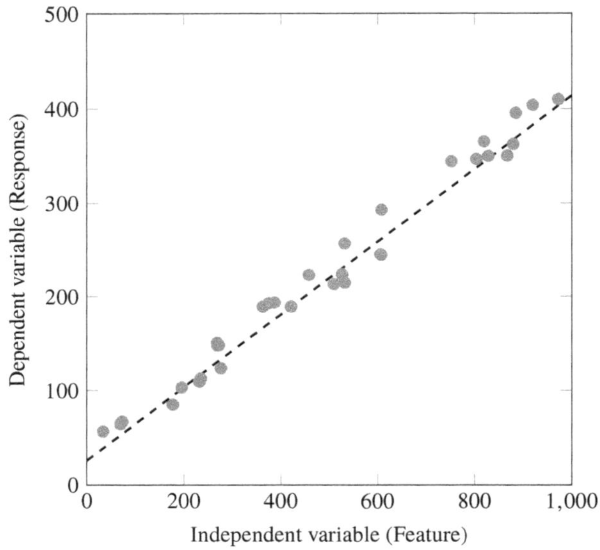

Fig. 2.8 Concept of linear regression

of linear regression is to optimize the weights β_i in a way such that

$$\min \sum_{t=1}^{T} \left(Y_t - \sum_{i=0}^{n} \beta_i X_{t,i} \right)^2 . \tag{2.35}$$

This equation is called the loss function of linear regression according to the ordinary least square (OLS) method. The difference between observed value Y_t and predicted value $\sum_{i=0}^{n} \beta_i X_{t,i}$ is called residual. Therefore, OLS sets the coefficients in a way that minimizes the square of the residuals. Alternatively to OLS, the coefficients can be estimated based on a maximum likelihood estimation, which is a probabilistic framework that maximizes the probability of observing specific data given a model and model parameters. Both approaches belong to the class of learning algorithms as the coefficients are learned from historical data.

Please note that similar to *moving averages* or *exponential smoothing*, linear regression can also use lagged observations $Y_{t-1}, Y_{t-2}, \ldots$ as additional explanatory variable, which is often quite useful in practice.

Table 2.6 shows an exemplary output of a linear regression model in `Excel`. The two most important metrics to assess the quality of regression models are the coefficient of determination R^2 and the p-value. Besides the fitted β coefficients, both are essential parts of the regression output in order to correctly interpret the relationship between dependent and independent variables.

R^2 is a metric between 0 and 1 for assessing the goodness-of-fit of a regression model. $R^2 = 0.98$ means that 98% of the variance in Y can be explained by the

Table 2.6 Linear regression: regression statistics and ANOVA

Regression statistics						
Multiple R	0.99					
R^2	0.98					
Adjusted R^2	0.98					
Standard Error	15.3					
Observations	32					
ANOVA	**df**	**SS**	**MS**	**F**	**Significance F**	
Regression	3	366382	122127	518	1.250E-24	
Residual	28	6593	235			
Total	31	372975				
	Coefficients	**Standard Error**	**t Stat**	***p*-value**	**Lower 95%**	**Upper 95%**
Intercept	25.6	8.7	2.9	0.006	7.8	43.4
X Variable 1	0.4	0.009	39.4	4.622E-26	0.37	0.41
X Variable 2	12.8	9.4	1.4	0.19	−6.51	32.08
X Variable 3	−0.003	0.1	−0.04	0.97	−0.20	0.19

fitted regression model. There is no unique answer in the literature on thresholds for a sufficient goodness-of-fit.

The *p-value* is the level of significance or probability of error, respectively, error rate, and assesses the significance of the impact of each single independent variable on the dependent variable. The smaller the p, the higher the probability that there is an actual impact. If $p < 5\%$, the result is typically seen as significant, which is not the case for variables 2 and 3 in Table 2.6.

Please note that linear regression is based on several important assumptions that need to be fulfilled in order to draw reasonable conclusions from the regression model: (i) *linearity,* there is a linear relationship between dependent variable Y and independent variables X; (ii) *absence of multicollinearity,* independent variables X should not be (highly) correlated; (iii) *normality,* all variables should be normally distributed; (iv) *homoscedasticity,* the variance σ^2 of error term ϵ that is normally distributed with $\mu = 0$ is constant; and (v) *independence,* residuals should be independent of each other, i.e., there should not be any auto-correlation. In statistics, there are various tests available to test whether these five assumptions are fulfilled or not.

Linear regression is a standard approach in statistics and machine learning and implemented in a variety of software products including spreadsheet software such as `Microsoft Excel` (`Data` → `Data Analysis` → `Regression`), statistical programming language `R` (`lm()` function) and `Python` under the machine learning library `Scikit-learn` (`sklearn.linear_model.LinearRegression`). Whenever the underlying pattern is nonlinear, we refer to nonlinear regression models such as polynomial regression that fits a polynomial equation to the data rather than a linear function.

In the procurement context, linear regression plays a crucial role for demand and price forecasting. Another application is linear performance pricing (LPP) that estimates a (linear) relationship between product characteristics and the product price from various supplier offers in order to support price negotiations (see Chap. 3). What needs to be considered whenever it comes to demand or sales forecasting is the phenomenon of *censored demand*, i.e., the divergence between sales and actual demand. If a fruit seller provides 100 apples per day and sells 100 apples per day, then 100 apples is not necessarily the actual demand for apples. The fruit seller might have sold more than 100 apples if more than 100 apples would have been available. Consequently, censored demand reduces the adequacy of the training data and can lead to a reduced prediction accuracy. For censored dependent variables, we want to refer to censored regression.

Machine Learning

Machine learning (ML) became a popular buzzword that is often misused in business practice. Therefore, Fig. 2.9 presents an overview of important machine learning methods from the three major ML classes, i.e., supervised learning, unsupervised learning and reinforcement learning.

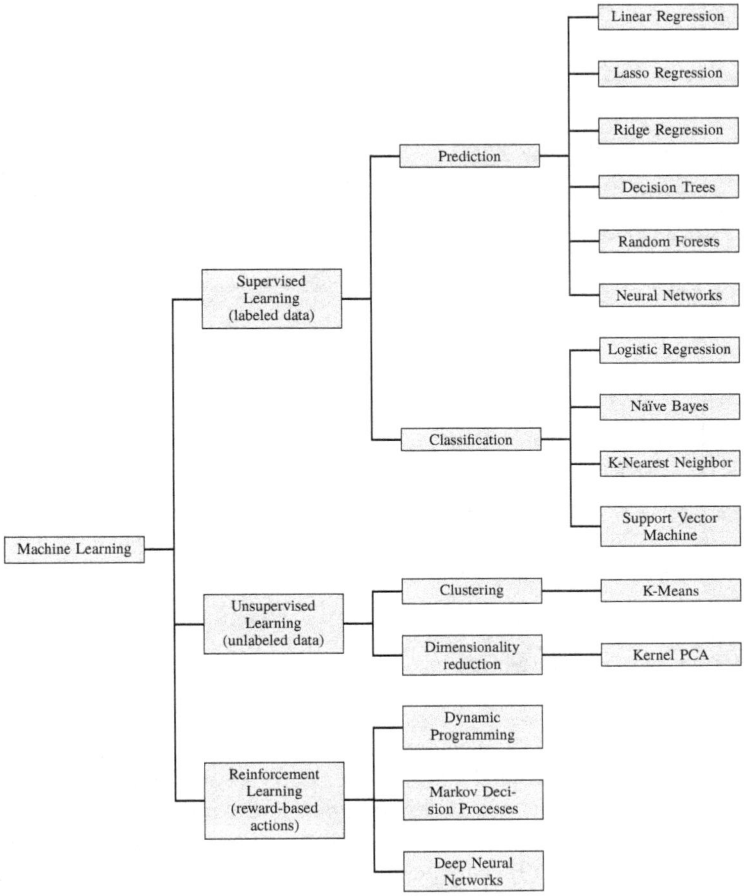

Fig. 2.9 Machine learning taxonomy

Supervised learning comprises prediction and classification algorithms. To use those, the data needs to be labeled (e.g., inputs and outputs pairs of independent and dependent variables such as price time series, demand time series or exchange rate time series). *Unsupervised learning* can also learn patterns on unlabeled data (e.g., audio recordings, photos or news articles) and comprises, for instance, clustering algorithms. *Reinforcement learning* considers interactions with the environment (e.g., customer behavior) and determines the optimal (i.e., reward-maximizing) course of action in a given state or context (e.g., purchase decision). It comprises techniques from (stochastic) optimization such as dynamic programming and Markov decision processes (see also Sect. 2.4).

Predictive analytics mainly refers to prediction methods from the field of supervised learning. The methods are based upon statistical learning theory (see

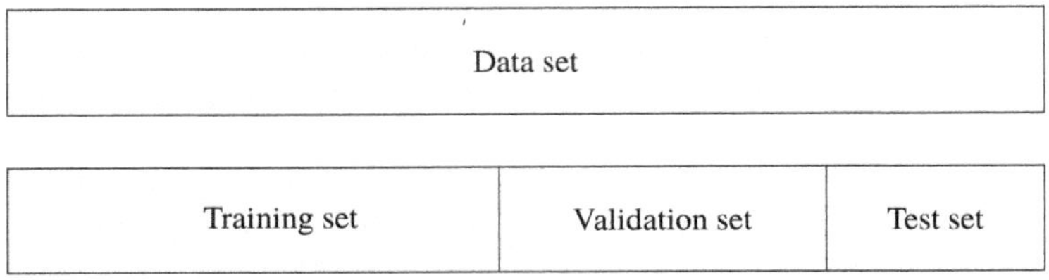

Fig. 2.10 Train-test framework in machine learning

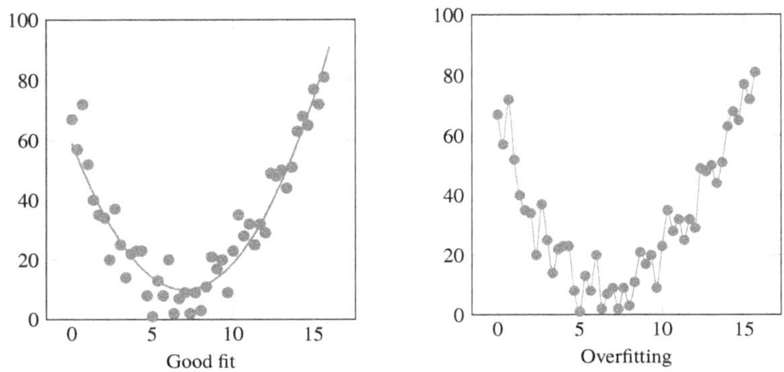

Fig. 2.11 Problem of overfitting in regression models

[12, 14, 24]). The simplest machine learning method for prediction is linear regression. More advanced methods and extensions are presented in the following. All of them follow the train-test paradigm of machine learning (see Fig. 2.10): First, the machine learning models are trained on historical training data (e.g., time series data from 2018 until 2019), parameter-tuned on historical validation data (e.g., data from 2020 until 2021) and evaluated via accuracy measures out-of-sample on historical evaluation data (e.g., data from 2022 until 2023). This procedure is called backtesting. Afterward, the best trained model is used for future predictions.

Please note that prediction via machine learning is not only about training an algorithm based on available data. It requires more more such as feature engineering, model selection and parameter fine-tuning. Otherwise, ML algorithms often perform even worse than very simple methods such as naïve or moving average forecasts.

Lasso and Ridge Regression

Standard regression models (e.g., linear regression) are often affected by *overfitting*. That means that the algorithm learns the data set (by heart) but does not recognize fundamental patterns (see Fig. 2.11). Overfitting happens, for instance, whenever there are many feature parameters estimated relative to the number of data points in the training set. The result is often a weak prediction accuracy. On the other hand, underfitting occurs whenever prediction models are too simplistic in order to capture the underlying patterns.

The goal of lasso regression (least absolute shrinkage and selection operator) and ridge regression is to reduce overfitting through *regularization*. Therefore, the linear regression model from Eq. (2.35) is extended by a penalty term weighted by a regularization parameter $\lambda \geq 0$, which is determined in a cross-validation procedure (parameter tuning). The lasso-adjusted loss function is given by

$$\min \sum_{t=1}^{T} \left(Y_t - \sum_{i=0}^{n} \beta_i X_{t,i} \right)^2 + \lambda \cdot \sum_{i=1}^{n} |\beta_i| \tag{2.36}$$

and the ridge-adjusted loss function is given by

$$\min \sum_{t=1}^{T} \left(Y_t - \sum_{i=0}^{n} \beta_i X_{t,i} \right)^2 + \lambda \cdot \sum_{i=1}^{n} \beta_i^2. \tag{2.37}$$

Please note that the first term is the loss function of the standard linear regression model. Therefore, if $\lambda = 0$, lasso and ridge regression reduce to linear regression. The effect of lasso regression is that it tends to set (many) coefficients to zero (feature selection property). This yields a simpler feature model that often generalizes better (see Occam's razor). Ridge regression on the other hand shrinks the coefficients and therefore reduces model complexity.

Elastic net regularization is a combination of both lasso and ridge regression that combines both penalty terms. It is especially useful whenever the number of observations is very small relative to the number of independent variables or whenever independent variables are highly correlated.

Regularized regression models can be fitted using standard software such as `R` with `glmnet()` function or via the `Python` library `Scikit-learn` using the class `sklearn.linear_model.Lasso` or `sklearn.linear_model.Ridge`. For further details on the methodology of lasso and ridge regression, we refer to Chapter 6 of the textbook [14] or Chapter 10 of the textbook [17] for a more theoretical discussion.

In the procurement context, regularization with lasso and ridge regression can be used for causal price and demand predictions whenever standard regression models yield weak prediction results even though there is an underlying relationship to specific features. We show an inventory management application of regularization in Chap. 5 of this textbook introducing the machine learning-enabled newsvendor model.

Logistic Regression

Linear regression models are not appropriate for processing discrete variables (e.g., binary variables). In the procurement context, this is, for instance, relevant whenever to predict whether a supplier is appropriate or not. In this case, a logistic regression model (also called Logit model) helps. It models the probability that a data sample belongs to a certain class (e.g., appropriate supplier or inappropriate supplier) using a logistic function.

There are two types of logistic regression models, i.e., binary logistic regression and multinomial logistic regression.

Binary logistic regression is used whenever there are two outcomes of the dependent variable (e.g., appropriate vs. not appropriate, on-time delivery vs. late delivery). It determines the probability $P(Y = 1)$ that the dependent variable $Y = 1$ (e.g., supplier is appropriate, delivery is on-time) given feature information X (e.g., supplier's experience in the corresponding segment in years, distance between supplier and buyer):

$$P(Y = 1) = \frac{e^{\beta_0+\beta_1 X_1}}{1 + e^{\beta_0+\beta_1 X_1}} \tag{2.38}$$

This results in the following probability function (see Fig. 2.12).

If there are more than two outcomes of the dependent variable (e.g., appropriate-partially appropriate-not appropriate), then we need to use a multinomial logistic regression model.

Logistic regression models can be fitted using standard software such as R with *glm()* function or in `Python` library `Scikit-learn` using the class `sklearn.linear_ model.LogisticRegression`. For further details on the methodology of logistic regression, we refer to Chapter 4 of the textbook [14] or Chapter 6 of the textbook [17] for a more theoretical discussion.

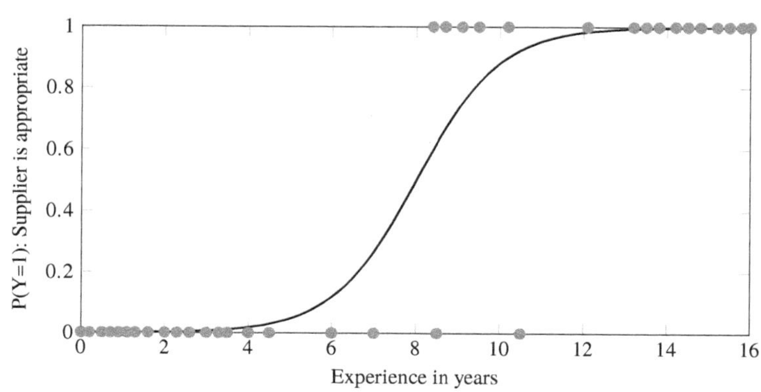

Fig. 2.12 Concept of logistic regression

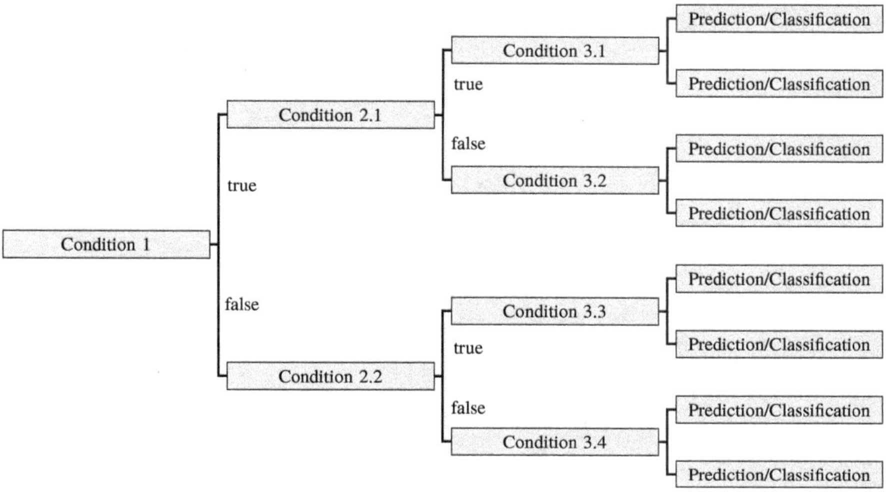

Fig. 2.13 Concept of a decision tree

Decision Trees and Random Forests

Decision trees are simple methods for classification and regression tasks. They are well-known under the term *Classification and Regression Tree (CART)* and predict or classify based on relationships between features in the data set. Figure 2.13 shows a generic decision tree with conditions that are fulfilled or not and therefore lead to a specific prediction or classification. Decision trees can be trained through the `rpart` package in `R` or `sklearn.tree` in `Python`.

Random forests are related to decision trees. They can also be used for both regression and classification and are based on several randomly generated (trained) decision trees with predictions/classifications being combined afterward. This process is also known as *ensemble learning* and can improve the prediction or classification accuracy of a single decision tree.

In the procurement context, decision trees can, for instance, be used for supplier risk classification (i.e., high supply risk, low supply risk), given financial predictors such as liquidity or revenue as illustrated in Chap. 6. For further details on the methodology of tree-based methods, we refer to Chapter 8 of the textbook [14] or Chapter 8 of the textbook [17] for a more theoretical discussion.

Artificial Neural Networks and Deep Learning

Standard regression models typically cannot learn complex nonlinear relationships and are not able to process large data sets (big data). In this case, artificial neural networks (ANN) can be used. The basic idea behind ANN is inspired by the

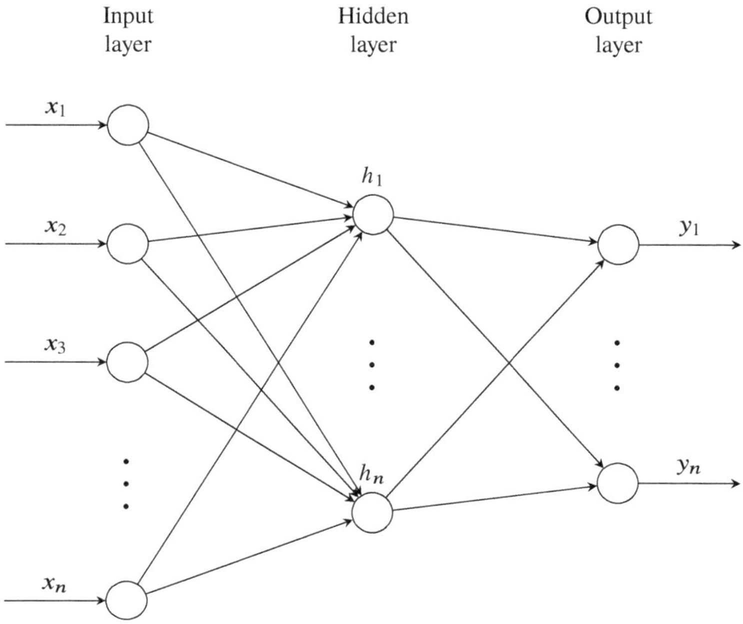

Fig. 2.14 Concept of artificial neural networks (ANN)

biological concept of neurons that collect signals (features), weight them and decide whether the signal should be sent to the human brain or not. As illustrated in Fig. 2.14, ANNs consist of an input layer (e.g., pictures, measured data, invoices), hidden layer(s) and an output layer (e.g., classification or prediction outcome). Deep learning is a methodology that is based on ANN and characterized by a high complexity regarding the hidden layer structure. To evaluate prediction quality, the mean squared error (MSE) is often calculated between the output generated by the neural network and a specified target value. Large language models (LLMs) such as OpenAI's ChatGPT or Google's Bard are based on artificial neural networks.

On the one hand, through ANNs, complex nonlinear relationships can be identified, and big data can effectively be processed. On the other hand, other than simple regression models, ANN do typically not allow for interpretability but are more like a black box. Furthermore, they require sufficient large data input (for training), high computing times and high energy consumption. A popular open-source `Python` library to train deep learning algorithms is `Keras`.

In the procurement context, ANNs are in use for spend classification tasks, i.e., classifying spend into various procurement categories (see Chap. 3), and for time series forecasting (e.g., forecasting of commodity prices or demand given input such as macroeconomic data, weather data or price and demand history). Furthermore, ANNs are also used for decision-support in inventory management under demand uncertainty as we show in Chap. 5 of this textbook where we introduce the deep learning-enabled newsvendor model.

Further Classification Algorithms

Besides logistic regression and decision trees, there are three more major classification algorithms that are heavily applied in practice to classification problems, i.e., *k-nearest neighbor*, *naïve Bayes* and *support vector machines*. For further details on the methodology of these classification methods, we refer to Chapter 4 of the textbook [14] or Chapter 8 of the textbook [17] for a more theoretical discussion.

K-Nearest neighbor (kNN) is a nonlinear and non-parametric classifier that classifies elements according to their k nearest data points based on their similarity (e.g., proximity) regarding specific features. kNN is run several times on a training data set for different k in order to reduce the number of errors on unseen data. It is a very simple algorithm and easy to implement because there is no training required but just the pre-determination of the parameter k. Figure 2.15 shows an example of kNN: While for $k = 1$, the item (Δ) is categorized to class 1, for $k = 3$, the item (Δ) is categorized to class 2.

Naïve Bayes is a linear and parametric classifier that performs robust whenever there is less training data available. Compared to kNN, it is typically much faster.

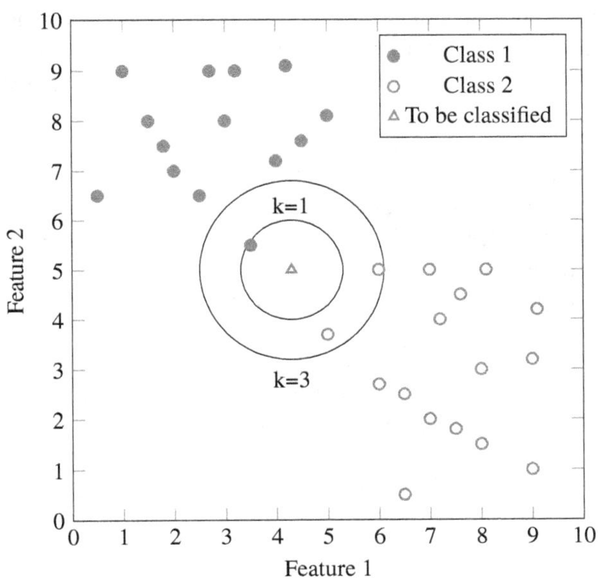

Fig. 2.15 Concept of KNN classification

Support vector machines (SVM) are classifiers that support both linear and nonlinear classification tasks with the objective to maximize separation between classes in the underlying data.

Bayesian Forecast

Forecasts are accompanied by forecast errors, and uncertainty in forecasts typically increases with forecast horizons. For instance, it is easier to forecast tomorrow's raw material price of copper than to predict the copper price one year ahead. The same is true for customer demand. Consequently, forecast accuracy for tomorrow's price or demand is typically lower if we predict today compared to predicting tomorrow's price or demand 1 year ago. The reason is that uncertainty decreases with additional information available. Therefore, it is essential to regularly update forecasts as soon as new information arrives. This can be statistically illustrated using Bayes' rule (or Bayes' theorem) from probability theory, i.e.,

$$P(A|B) = \frac{P(B|A) \cdot P(A)}{P(B)}. \tag{2.39}$$

Bayes' rule calculates the conditional probability $P(A|B)$ of an event A happening given that event B has occurred (e.g., given that we have certain new information available). This probability is called posterior probability and is determined based on the prior probabilities $P(A)$ and $P(B)$ (e.g., probability prior to new information available) that event A (B) will happen and the probability $P(B|A)$ (also called likelihood) that B will happen given evidence A has already happened.

Numerical Example: Bayesian Forecast Updating in Procurement
Suppose that a purchase manager identified that a supplier's delivery is late (L) in 1% of the cases, i.e., $P(L) = 1\%$ (prior probability). From historical data, the manager knows that there is an effect of severe weather conditions (W) on the lateness of deliveries: Whenever deliveries were late, there were severe weather conditions in 90% of the cases, i.e., $P(W|L) = 90\%$. The meteorological service analyzed that those severe weather conditions happen with a probability of $P(W) = 2\%$. One day, the purchase manager gets the information that there will be severe conditions tomorrow. Using Bayesian forecast updating, the manager adjusts its forecast of late delivery from a 1% chance (prior probability $P(L)$) to a 45% chance (posterior probability $P(L|W)$) and reacts accordingly.

In procurement practice, forecast updates are, for example, also used in the fast fashion industry. At the beginning of a season, customer demand is highly uncertain, which challenges the purchase department of fashion retailers regarding how much of a fashion collection to order in advance. The purchase department only has a prior belief about future sales over the season. After the first weeks of sales, fashion retailers get valuable information on customer satisfaction, weather developments, etc. that drives sales potential. Based on this information, the retailer can use a *quick response* system that updates its belief and triggers to accurately respond to early sales based on reduced forecast uncertainty (see [8] for an early application in the fashion skiwear industry).

Judgmental Forecast

If there is a lack of historical data or new market conditions emerge, statistical time series analysis and machine learning is not appropriate for forecasting. In this case, *judgmental forecasting* is used, which is a qualitative forecasting method that is appropriate whenever one cannot (or should not) learn from historical data. This can be due to new underlying patterns (e.g., caused by political or legislative decisions, new competitors or substitutes) or the fact that forecast horizons are too long to derive valid statistical numbers.

Judgmental forecasting is based on expert knowledge or crowd knowledge. In this case, Delphi method is used that builds on sending questionnaires to a panel of experts, aggregating their responses, sharing the results and asking for a consensus (collaborative forecasting). Judgmental forecasting is mainly applied for long-term forecasting and often results in scenarios rather than point predictions. In the procurement context, this may include the forecast of political decisions or climate change in different geographic supply regions and its effect on medium- or long-term supply disruption risk.

2.4 Prescriptive Analytics

Prescriptive analytics is referred to as optimization or operations research and focuses on making optimal business decisions. It typically relies on the results of descriptive analytics and predictive analytics that provide the input for optimization models or decision-support. In the procurement context, prescriptive analytics can, for instance, answer the question whether or when it is reasonable to reduce risk by additional cost from inventories, second sources or localization.

2.4.1 Accuracy Measures

As prescriptive analytics focuses on decisions rather than predictions, it requires different accuracy or performance measures. A decision-maker in practice typically does not primarily aim at making the perfect prediction but wants to take optimal decisions or actions with the best possible effect on cost, profit, revenue or efficiency. An interesting observation in commodity procurement, for instance, is that optimal hedging decisions (e.g., price lock via futures contracts) does not require optimal (i.e., perfect) price forecasts. It is often sufficient to correctly forecast the direction of price movements. On the other hand, perfect price predictions as input for optimization models for sure yield optimal decisions. Therefore, it is worth evaluating the relationship between forecast performance (predictive accuracy measures) and operational performance (prescriptive accuracy measures) for each decision problem. A 5% improvement on forecast accuracy (e.g., MAPE) does typically not translate into a 5% improvement of operational performance (e.g., cost savings).

Therefore, we want to present the following accuracy measures for prescriptive analytics models that are typically also compared to a specific predefined baseline, which can be, for instance, the status quo of the company.

Cost

For many years, procurement was mainly cost-centered. For cost-minimizing decisions, it is important to consider all cost dimensions that are affected by a specific business decision. This is related to the concept of *total cost of ownership* that states that an investment decision cannot only focus on investment cost but needs to consider cost of usage, shipping cost, recycling cost, energy cost and opportunity cost. The delta between the cost resulting from optimized decisions and the current cost of the company (baseline) defines the savings potential.

Revenue

For revenue-maximizing decisions, it is important to consider the overall revenue generated by decisions. This includes immediate revenue but also expected future revenues. In the context of procurement, purchasing managers increasingly have the task not to only cut cost but also take the right decisions (e.g., in terms of supplier and technology selection) to drive innovation and therefore future revenues.

Profit

For profit-maximizing decisions, both the overall cost and overall revenues need to be evaluated simultaneously. Note that there might also be interactions between revenue and cost. For example, a machine with a higher cost might be able to generate more revenue, or a purchase component of higher quality can generate more revenue.

Efficiency

Contrary to profit that addresses the delta between revenue and cost, efficiency addresses the ratio between input (e.g., cost) and output (e.g., revenue). In the context of procurement, efficiency scores are calculated, for instance, for supplier selection and evaluation problems via *data envelopment analysis (DEA)* (see Sect. 4.5).

Multi-Objective

Traditionally, the main objective of procurement was to minimize cost under securing short-term supply. Today, it is rather a mix of objectives including cost, risk, sustainability, innovation, quality and customer satisfaction that need to be addressed by procurement decision-makers. Typically, there is a significant trade-off between these goals that needs to be addressed by prescriptive analytics models. For example, sustainability and risk minimization come at a specific cost.

2.4.2 Methods of Prescriptive Analytics

In the following, we give an overview of generic methods to optimize business decisions and relate each method to the procurement context.

Linear and Mixed-Integer Linear Programming

Linear and mixed-integer linear programming dates back to 1939. It is the most important and widely used method for combinatorial optimization problems in order to derive optimal decisions (in the sense of minimal cost or maximal revenue or profit) for a specific business problem that is somehow restricted in resource (e.g., in machine capacity, personnel capacity or monetary capacity). The following lines show the structure of a typical linear programming model.

Example: General Structure of Linear Programming Models

$$\text{minimize} \quad c_1 \cdot x_1 + c_2 \cdot x_2 \tag{2.40}$$

$$\text{subject to (s.t.)} \quad a_{11} \cdot x_1 + a_{12} \cdot x_2 \geq b_1 \tag{2.41}$$

$$a_{21} \cdot x_1 + a_{22} \cdot x_2 \geq b_2 \tag{2.42}$$

(continued)

$$a_{31} \cdot x_1 + a_{32} \cdot x_2 \geq b_3 \tag{2.43}$$

$$x_1, x_2 \geq 0 \tag{2.44}$$

A linear program (LP) or mixed-integer linear program (MILP) is characterized by three objects:

- Objective function (see Eq. (2.40))
- Constraints (see Eqs. (2.41)–(2.44))
- Decision variables (see variables x_1 and x_2)

(i) The *objective function* defines the goal that we want to achieve with our decision. It can be a maximization function or a minimization function depending on whether we address, for example, a profit maximization problem, a revenue maximization problem, a cost minimization problem or a time minimization problem. The resulting optimized value of the objective function is the so-called objective value. In the procurement context, for a long time, cost-cutting was the focus, and therefore procurement analytics focused on cost minimization problems. However, with increasing responsibility of procurement functions for innovation management, procurement analytics additionally focuses on profit maximization. With an increasing interest in non-monetary objectives (e.g., sustainability), there is also an increasing interest in multi-objective optimization that optimizes decisions under at least two objectives in the objective function (e.g., maximizing profit plus minimizing the ecological footprint).

(ii) The *constraints* consider limitations that any decision problem has and that limit a company in decreasing its cost to zero or increasing its revenue or profit to infinity. In the procurement context, this can be capacity limitations in the sense of limited raw material availability, limited storage space or limited financial resources. Another constraint can be customer demand needs to be satisfied. This restricts the decision space with regard to buying too less in order to minimize cost.

(iii) The *decision variables* describe the optimal course of actions the decision-maker should take in order to optimize the objective function subject to the restrictions defined by the constraints. Therefore, it is the output of the prescriptive analytics model. In the procurement context, this can be decision-support with regard to purchase quantity, inventory level or supplier selection. A linear program becomes a mixed-integer linear program as soon as (some) decision variables are restricted to integers (e.g., binary variables of selecting a supplier A or not).

Table 2.7 Input data

Consumption in min	Product 1	Product 2	Product 3	Product 4	Maximum capacity in min
Machine 1	4	4	4	4	120
Machine 2	4	2	0	0	80
Machine 3	2	5	0	0	60
Machine 4	0	0	5	3	60
Machine 5	0	0	5	6	75

Numerical Example: Linear Programming

Suppose that based on the following data, a manager needs to decide on production quantities (in liters) of product 1 to 4. From the sales department, the manager gets profit forecasts per production unit of product 1 to 4, i.e., 10 Euro (Product 1), 15 Euro (Product 2), 10 Euro (Product 3) and 15 Euro (Product 4). Production of product 1 to 4 requires five machines with machine capacity limited in time. The manager additionally receives the following data from operations (see Table 2.7). How much to produce from product 1 to 4 in order to maximize the profit and ensure efficient use of resources?

The decision problem can be modeled via a linear program. The objective function maximizes the profit, and constraints ensure capacity limits at each of the machines.

$$\text{maximize} \quad 10 \cdot x_1 + 15 \cdot x_2 + 10 \cdot x_3 + 15 \cdot x_4 \tag{2.45}$$

$$\text{s.t.} \quad 4x_1 + 4x_2 + 4x_3 + 4x_4 \leq 120 \tag{2.46}$$

$$4x_1 + 2x_2 + 0x_3 + 0x_4 \leq 80 \tag{2.47}$$

$$2x_1 + 5x_2 + 0x_3 + 0x_4 \leq 60 \tag{2.48}$$

$$0x_1 + 0x_2 + 5x_3 + 3x_4 \leq 60 \tag{2.49}$$

$$0x_1 + 0x_2 + 5x_3 + 6x_4 \leq 75 \tag{2.50}$$

$$x_1, x_2, x_3, x_4 \geq 0 \tag{2.51}$$

Solving the linear program gives us the optimal production quantities $x_1 = 9.2$, $x_2 = 8.3$, $x_3 = 0$ and $x_4 = 12.5$ that yield an optimal profit of 404.2.

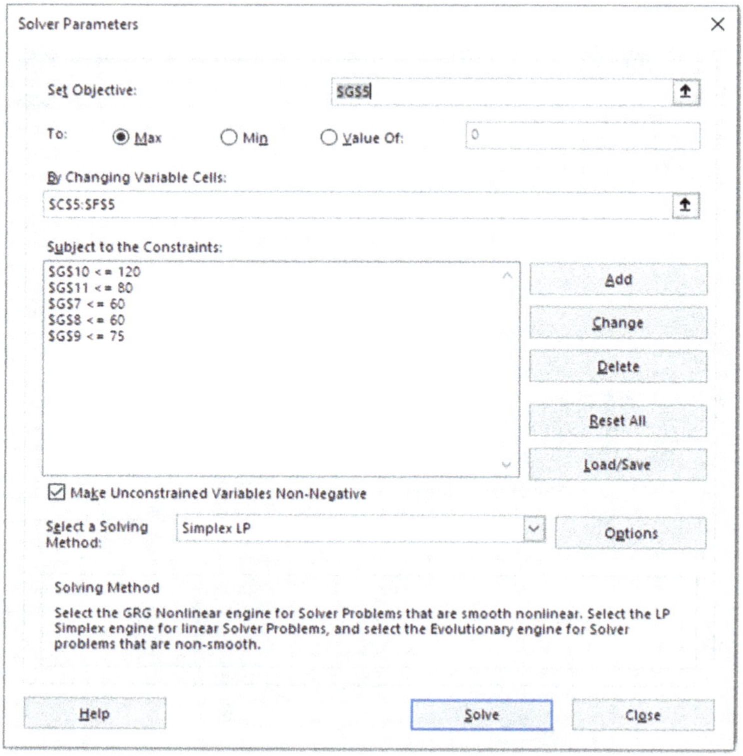

Fig. 2.16 Linear programming via Excel solver

Linear and mixed-integer linear programs can be solved (i.e., decision variables can be derived) by using mathematical solvers. Besides powerful commercial solvers (e.g., `Gurobi`, `FICO XPress`, `IBM ILOG CPLEX`) that can be used to solve problems with thousands of decision variables and constraints, open-source solvers are available for smaller problem instances (e.g., `PuLP` in `Python` or `Coin-OR CBC`). Widely used spreadsheet software such as `Microsoft Excel` has solver add-ins, too (see Fig. 2.16). It needs to be activated in the `Excel` options and can be found under the tab `Data` → `Solver`. However, the `Excel` solver is limited to 200 decision variables and therefore not appropriate for optimization problems of real-world size.

Note that there is a range of standard optimization problems that are solved using linear and mixed-integer linear programming and that build the algorithmic basis for many practical optimization problems. We will introduce some of the most important problem classes at the end of this chapter.

Linear programming is heavily used in industrial planning tools. In the procurement context, it is, for example, applied to tenders and auctions to solve the *Winner Determination Problem* (see Chap. 4), to several supplier selection and evaluation models (see Chap. 4), to supply network optimization models (see Chap. 4) and to several data-driven inventory optimization models (see Chap. 5). For a deep-dive into linear and mixed-integer linear programming, we refer to the standard textbook [25].

Scenario Planning and Stochastic Programming

Business decisions (particularly in the procurement field) are usually decisions under uncertainty that require predictive planning and probabilistic thinking of purchasing managers. For example, the decision-maker needs to make a purchase decision without knowing how the raw material prices might evolve, whether there are supply disruptions or how customer demand will develop. Standard linear programming as presented in Eqs. (2.40)–(2.44) does not explicitly address uncertainty in its parameters but rather optimizes based on expected values (e.g., point forecasts) without considering that the future cannot be perfectly predicted.

This is where scenario planning and stochastic programming come into play that becomes more and more important as business volatility and uncertainty increase and ask for resilient decisions. Scenario planning calculates optimal decisions for different scenarios of input parameters (e.g., demand or prices) such as best-case, average-case and worst-case scenarios (what-if analysis). For instance, what is the effect on cost, risk and sustainability if we use supplier A rather than supplier B? Stochastic programming considers uncertainty about the future and optimizes decisions accordingly. Therefore, it requires a stochastic model to represent uncertainty. This can, for instance, be a probability distribution function (see Fig. 2.17).

Because linear or mixed-integer linear programming models cannot directly process continuous distribution functions as shown in Fig. 2.17, discrete values are sampled from distributional information through sampling methods such as Monte Carlo sampling, descriptive sampling or Latin Hypercube sampling. The result can be illustrated in scenario trees (see Fig. 2.18). Rather than giving recommendations about what to do in each of the scenarios (which is a deterministic scenario

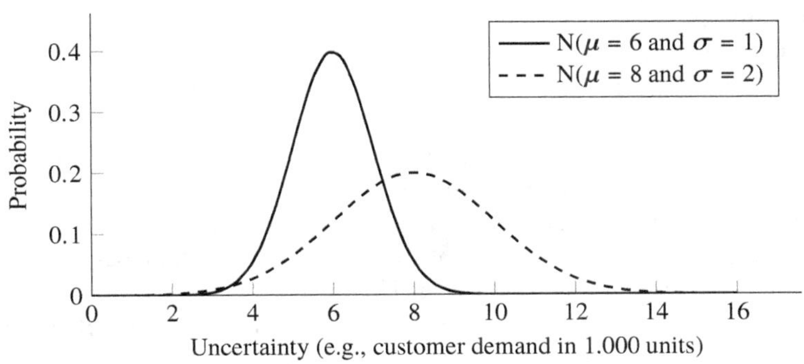

Fig. 2.17 Normal distributions with different mean μ and standard deviation σ

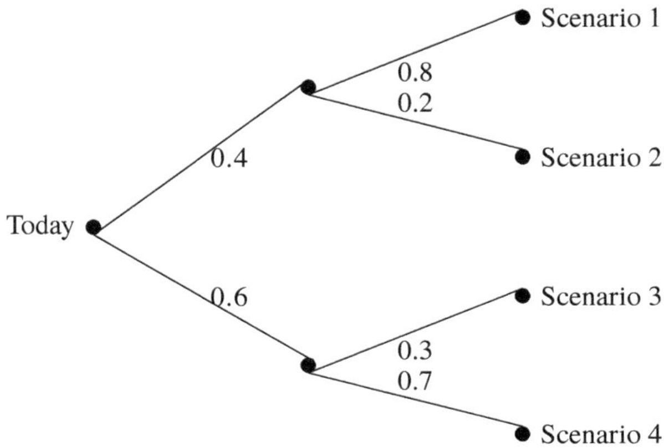

Fig. 2.18 Multi-stage scenario tree with probabilities

optimization or what-if analysis, which gives interesting insights but is not very helpful to take optimal actions under uncertainty), stochastic programming gives recommendations what to do here and now (i.e., today) without knowing which scenario will happen but only under consideration of scenario probabilities. The objective of stochastic programming is to find a decision that works well in all potential future scenarios. It therefore is an important method in risk management (see Chap. 6).

In the procurement context, we present a stochastic programming approach for supply network design in Sect. 4.6 and for commodity purchasing under price risk in Sect. 6.3. For further details on stochastic programming, we refer to the textbooks [4, 15] and [22].

Markov Decision Processes and Reinforcement Learning

A *Markov decision process (MDP)* is another stochastic method where the agent (decision-maker) learns a strategy (policy) based on data or probability distributions. An example from the procurement context is the computation of optimal inventory control policies. The decision-maker follows a specific strategy in order to control the stock level. For instance, for a (s, S) policy, inventory is filled up to a base-stock level S, whenever the inventory level reaches a certain reorder point s (see Chap. 5 for more details). This strategy including the optimal parameters for s and S can be determined by solving the *MDP* via dynamic programming (see [2]). Another example is the computation of optimal supply contracting strategies in commodity procurement under price uncertainty (see [21]) (Fig. 2.19).

Reinforcement learning as a major machine learning class is related to MDP however with unknown probabilities or rewards that directly need to be learned from historical data. The major drawback of MDPs is the so-called curse of

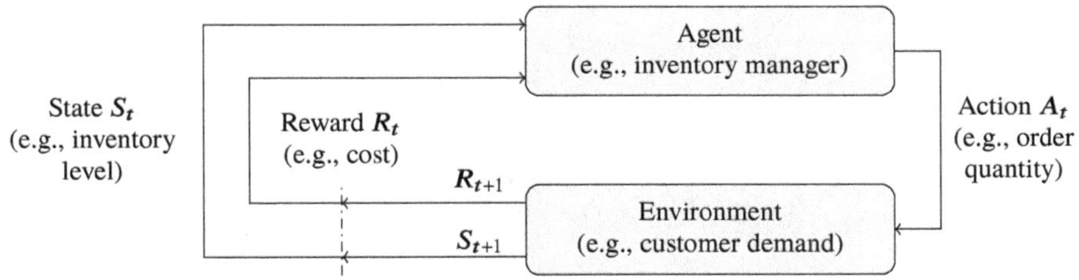

Fig. 2.19 Concept of MDP and reinforcement learning

dimensionality that yields high computing effort. This asks for approximations (e.g., approximate dynamic programming). For further details, we refer to the textbooks of [19, 20, 23] and [21].

Data-Driven and Machine Learning-Enabled Optimization

In data-driven and learning-enabled optimization, methods from machine learning and optimization are combined in order to derive the best possible decision under uncertainty. Therefore, prediction and optimization are often not separated anymore but integrated. In the procurement context, it is more relevant for decision-makers to train decisions (e.g., inventory levels or purchase quantity) as a function of features rather than deriving a perfect demand or price forecast. This interplay between machine learning and optimization is explained in, e.g., [3, 6] and [7].

Heuristics and Metaheuristics

Many optimization problems of realistic size (in terms of decision variables and constraints) cannot be solved to optimality due to limited computational power. This asks for computable approaches in practice that find "good" (near-optimal) solutions in a reasonable amount of time. Those approaches are called heuristics or metaheuristics that are often based on (simple) decision rules and are widespread in practical prescriptive analytics applications.

A heuristic is a solution approach designed or developed for a specific problem setting, while metaheuristics are generic heuristic methods that are applicable to a variety of problem settings. The most important metaheuristics in practice are *genetic algorithms*, *simulated annealing*, *tabu search* and *ant colony optimization*. For further details, we refer to the excellent textbook of [10].

A widely applied heuristic in transportation analytics is the nearest-neighbor heuristic for planning cost- or distance-minimal tours in networks (see Traveling Salesman Problem). This heuristic chooses the nearest location that was not visited yet as the location to be visited next. The following example shows that appropriate heuristics can perform near optimal.

Table 2.8 Distance matrix

	D	L1	L2	L3	L4	L5	L6	L7	L8	L9	L10	L11
Depot (D)	–	8	13	26	25	41	45	54	29	23	35	41
L1	8	–	5	18	17	33	37	46	21	15	27	33
L2	13	5	–	15	12	28	32	41	16	10	22	28
L3	26	18	15	–	11	27	32	41	31	25	37	39
L4	25	17	12	11	–	16	21	30	28	22	31	28
L5	41	33	28	27	16	–	5	14	30	27	15	12
L6	45	37	32	32	21	5	–	9	25	22	10	7
L7	54	46	41	41	30	14	9	–	34	31	19	16
L8	29	21	16	31	28	30	25	34	–	10	15	21
L9	23	15	10	25	22	27	22	31	10	–	12	18
L10	35	27	22	37	31	15	10	19	15	12	–	6
L11	41	33	28	39	28	12	7	16	21	18	6	–

Numerical Example: Nearest-Neighbor Heuristic

Suppose that you need to plan a tour starting and ending at a depot (D) while visiting 11 different locations (L). The distances between locations are shown in Table 2.8. What is the tour according to the nearest-neighbor heuristic, and what is the optimal tour under the objective to minimize overall distance?

The nearest-neighbor heuristic leads to the following tour: D-L1-L2-L9-L8-L10-L11-L6-L5-L7-L4-L3-D with corresponding overall transportation distance of 147. The optimal tour D-L1-L3-L4-L5-L6-L7-L11-L10-L8-L9-L2-D leads to an overall transportation distance of 137. Therefore, the heuristic performs 7% worse than optimum.

In the procurement context, the reoptimization heuristic (also known as rolling intrinsic policy), which is introduced in Chap. 6, is used in commodity storage optimization under price uncertainty.

Simulation

While optimization is the identification of the decision with the best outcome, simulation compares outcomes of different decisions. This becomes increasingly important whenever the future is highly uncertain or one wants to compare the implications of different decisions. In this case, simulation can be used for what-if analysis, sensitivity analysis and scenario analysis (e.g., best-case, average-case, worst-case scenarios).

The benefit of simulation is that it does not require any analytical model, which is advantageous because many real-world systems cannot or can only hardly be

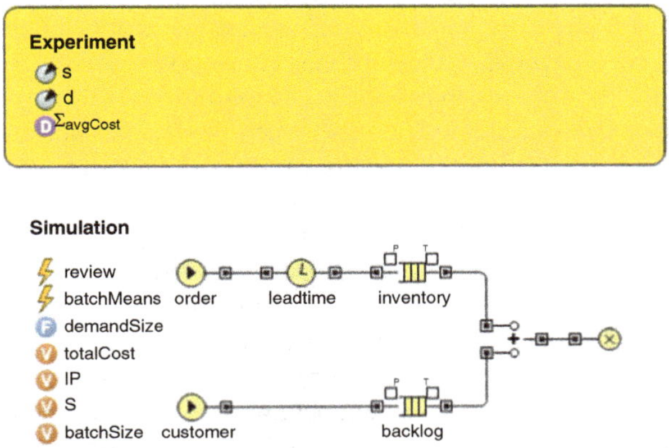

Fig. 2.20 Example of a simple inventory simulation implemented in AnyLogic

described analytically. Furthermore, simulation allows for simple and quick modifications and also for simple execution of experiments. Compared to optimization, it is often more accessible to users without a strong analytics background.

On the other hand, simulation produces stochastic outcomes and therefore requires many simulation runs to draw significant conclusions or even derive decision-support. In addition, simulation has high data requirements with regard to data availability and quality. If historical data is available for only a limited time, synthetic data needs to be used. Furthermore, many simulation applications require (expensive) software, and the results are often difficult to interpret.

Major software products for simulation are Arena, Anylogic (Fig. 2.20), Plant Simulation, Matlab-Simulink and many more. For further details on simulation optimization, we refer to the textbook of [16].

In the procurement context, Monte Carlo simulation is frequently used. Monte Carlo simulation is a simulation method that randomly selects samples (e.g., prices) from a probability distribution or stochastic process. It therefore can be used to generate scenarios about the evolution of commodities or energy prices. It can easily be implemented in any spreadsheet software or within any statistical programming language. For instance, one can sample a value from the well-known normal distribution with mean μ and standard deviation σ by using the `Excel` function `NORM.INV(RAND(),`μ`,`σ`)` with the `RAND()`-function returning a random value between 0 and 1. We demonstrate Monte Carlo simulation for commodity price modeling in Chap. 6 of this textbook.

Game Theory

All decision models that were introduced above have in common that they do not address interactions between decision-makers. However, in many practical situations, the actions of other decision-makers (e.g., competitors, suppliers or customers) might affect the own optimal course of action. Game theory is a mathematical and analytical framework that allows to model situations whenever there are interactions between individuals or organizations (i.e., players) and where the outcome of a decision depends on the action of all other players. It is divided into cooperative game theory and non-cooperative game theory depending on the player's preference. Furthermore, there is a distinction between simultaneous games and sequential games depending on the timing of the player's decisions. While the standard (analytical) game theory is mainly based on the concept of *homo economicus*, i.e., all players are rational, behavioral game theory additionally uses experiments to capture players' potential irrationalities.

In the procurement context, game theory plays a particularly important role in supplier negotiations and optimized contract awarding where suppliers and buyers interact (see Sect. 4.4) but also in situations of horizontal cooperation where two or more individual buyers interact (e.g., purchasing conglomerates) (see Sect. 4.7).

Games are illustrated by trees or payoff matrices (see Fig. 2.21 and Table 2.9). Each player has decision options and can choose from a set of *strategies*. Player 1 can decide for "A" (e.g., reduce prices) or "B" (e.g., keep prices), and player 2 can decide for "C" (e.g., reduce prices) or "D" (e.g., keep prices). The combination of player 1 and player 2's strategies defines the *outcome*. For each outcome, both players receive a *payoff* (e.g., profit). For instance, if player 1 chooses "A" and player 2 chooses "C," then this results in a payoff of "a" for player 1 and "a" payoff of b for player 2.

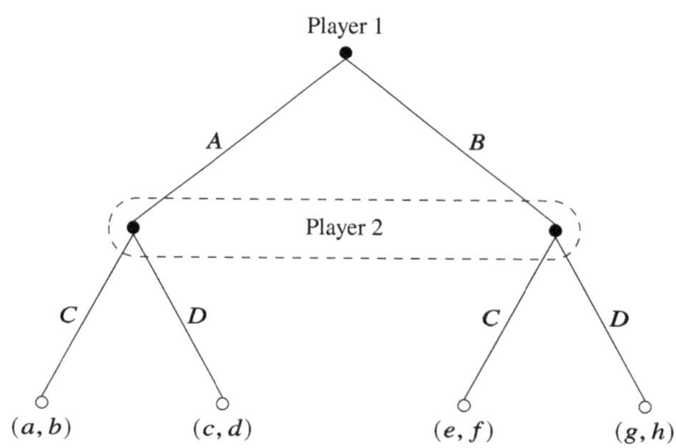

Fig. 2.21 Tree illustration of a game

Table 2.9 Payoff matrix of a game

	Player 2: C	Player 2: D
Player 1: A	(a,b)	(c,d)
Player 1: B	(e,f)	(g,h)

Table 2.10 Pareto-optimality, Nash equilibria and dominant strategies

Game 1	Player 2: C	Player 2: D
Player 1: A	(1,1)	(-4,2)
Player 1: B	(2,-4)	(-2,-2)

Game 2	Player 2: C	Player 2: D
Player 1: A	(1,1)	(-1,-1)
Player 1: B	(-1,-1)	(-2,-2)

A *dominant strategy* is a player's strategy that always outperforms all other available strategies no matter which strategy the opponent player follows.

An outcome is called *Pareto-optimal* if there is no other outcome in which both players have a higher payoff, i.e., there is no outcome in which a player can improve its payoff without making the other player worse off.

An outcome is a *Nash equilibrium* where no player improves its payoff by changing its strategy assuming it knows the equilibrium strategy of the other player. In a pure strategy Nash equilibrium, each player's strategy must be the dominant strategy to the other player's dominant strategy.

Game 1 from Table 2.10 illustrates a game where the outcome (1,1) is Pareto-optimal but no Nash equilibrium as there is an incentive for both players to change their strategy. The dominant strategy of player 1 is B because it maximizes his payoff no matter how player 2 decides. The dominant strategy of player 2 is D because it maximizes her payoff no matter how player 1 decides.

Game 2 from Table 2.10 illustrates a game where the outcome (1,1) is both Pareto-optimal and a Nash equilibrium as there is no incentive to change strategy. The dominant strategy of player 1 is A because it maximizes his payoff no matter how player 2 decides. The dominant strategy of player 2 is C because it maximizes her payoff no matter how player 1 decides.

Important games are *zero-sum games*, *prisoner's dilemma*, *chicken game*, *ultimatum game* and *battle of sexes* (see Sect. 4.4 in the context of supplier negotiations). Game theory has many applications in economics. For a comprehensive introduction to game theory, we refer to [9, 18]. For a review of game theory in the supply chain context, we refer to the tutorial of [5].

2.4.3 Fundamental Optimization Problems

In the following, we give an overview of standard optimization problems from operations research. A majority of optimization problems in practice are derivatives of one (or more) of these optimization problems and can be solved using the techniques introduced above (in particular linear and mixed-integer linear programming). For a detailed description of operations research problems, we refer to the textbook [13].

Knapsack Problem

The *knapsack problem* finds the optimal subset of objects to be selected in the presence of resources with limited capacity. The problem dates back to 1897 (T. Dantzig) and can be formulated as a mixed-integer linear programming model as follows:

$$\text{maximize} \quad \sum_{i=1}^{N} c_i \cdot x_i \tag{2.52}$$

$$\text{s.t.} \quad \sum_{i=1}^{N} a_i \cdot x_i \leq W \tag{2.53}$$

$$x_i \in \{0, 1\} \qquad \forall i = 1, \ldots, N \tag{2.54}$$

The decision variable x_i is about selecting or not selecting a specific object $i = 1, \ldots, N$ that is characterized by a specific value c_i and requires specific resource capacity a_i. The objective is to maximize the overall value of selected objects under consideration of capacity limit W.

Numerical Example: Knapsack Problem
Suppose we need to pack a knapsack with a capacity of 15 kg ($W = 15$) with different objects that are characterized by an individual value and weight. We can find the data in Table 2.11. Which objects should be packed into the knapsack in order to maximize its value?

Solving the knapsack problem with the data above, the decision-maker would decide to consider objects 1, 2, 4, 6, 7 and 8, which yields an overall value of 1375 Euro with a total weight of 14.5 kg.

Table 2.11 Data

Object i	Value in Euro	Weight in kg
1	375	3.5
2	300	2.5
3	100	2.0
4	225	3.0
5	50	1.0
6	125	1.75
7	75	0.75
8	275	3.0
9	150	2.5
10	50	2.25

The knapsack problem has a broad range of applications in business: from optimal truck load and optimal packaging to optimal project selection under budget constraints. In the procurement context, the knapsack problem is relevant, for instance, for transportation service procurement.

Assignment Problem

The assignment problem finds the optimal assignment of competencies (workers) to tasks with workers having individual time requirements for specific tasks. The objective is to minimize the overall completion time, respectively, the overall cost. The problem can be formulated as a mixed-integer linear program as follows:

$$\text{minimize} \quad \sum_{i=1}^{N}\sum_{j=1}^{N} c_{ij} \cdot x_{ij} \tag{2.55}$$

$$\text{s.t.} \quad \sum_{j=1}^{N} x_{ij} = 1 \qquad \forall i = 1, \ldots, N \tag{2.56}$$

$$\sum_{i=1}^{N} x_{ij} = 1 \qquad \forall j = 1, \ldots, N \tag{2.57}$$

$$x_{ij} \in \{0, 1\} \qquad \forall i, j = 1, \ldots, N \tag{2.58}$$

The decision variable x_{ij} is about assigning workers $i = 1, \ldots, N$ to tasks $j = 1, \ldots, N$. Each worker has an individual cost c_{ij} for each task (e.g., time) and needs to be assigned to exactly one task and vice versa. The objective is to minimize the overall cost (or overall completion time).

Numerical Example: Assignment Problem
Six tasks should be assigned to six workers that have different time requirements (in minutes) to complete those tasks. You can find the data in Table 2.12. Which person should work on which task in order to minimize the overall completion time?

Solving the assignment problem with the data input above, the decision-maker would decide for the following task-worker assignment, which yields a minimum completion time of 260 minutes: 1–3, 2–1, 3–6, 4–2, 5–5, 6–4.

Table 2.12 Data: Completion times

Worker i	Task 1	Task 2	Task 3	Task 4	Task 5	Task 6
1	40	47	80	80	80	80
2	72	36	58	44	45	58
3	24	61	66	71	75	71
4	24	86	84	84	65	56
5	72	55	97	56	46	77
6	45	63	43	53	63	54

The assignment has a range of applications in business: from production planning to human resources planning. In the procurement context, the assignment problem is, for instance, relevant for assigning contracts to bidders by systematic bid evaluation (see *Winner Determination Problem* in Sect. 4.3.1).

Bin Packing Problem

The bin packing problem aims at finding the optimal assignment of objects to bins (e.g., containers, vessels, tanks, pallets, etc.). The objective is to minimize the number of required bins. The problem can be formulated as a MILP model as follows:

$$\text{minimize} \quad \sum_{i=1}^{M} y_i \tag{2.59}$$

$$\text{s.t.} \quad \sum_{i=1}^{M} x_{ij} = 1 \qquad \forall j = 1, \ldots, N \tag{2.60}$$

$$\sum_{j=1}^{N} a_j \cdot x_{ij} \leq K_i \cdot y_i \qquad \forall i = 1, \ldots, M \tag{2.61}$$

$$y_i, x_{ij} \in \{0, 1\} \qquad \forall i = 1, \ldots, M, j = 1, \ldots, N \tag{2.62}$$

The decision variable y_i states whether a bin $i = 1, \ldots, M$ is used or not and the decision variable x_{ij} assigns objects $j = 1, \ldots, N$ to bins $i = 1, \ldots, M$. The objective function minimizes the number of required bins under the constraints that all objects are assigned to a bin and that the capacity K_i of a bin $i = 1, \ldots, M$ is not exceeded.

Table 2.13 Data: completion times

Object	A	B	C	D	E	F	G	H	I	J
Size	3	6	4	5	4	12	8	2	13	6

Table 2.14 Optimal assignment

Object	A	B	C	D	E	F	G	H	I	J
Bin	1	1	2	3	2	4	3	4	5	1

Numerical Example: Bin Packing Problem
Ten objects of different size (e.g., heights) should be packed into bins of of size 15 (e.g., heights). Data on object size is summarized in Table 2.13. How many bins are required under the objective to use as little bins as possible?

Solving the bin packing problem, we get the result of a minimum number of 5 bins. Please note that there are different assignment decisions possible that yield an optimal solution. A possible assignment decision looks as shown in Table 2.14.

The bin packing problem can be extended to two and three dimensions (2D and 3D bin packing) and has its main applications in packaging procurement and logistics.

Transportation Problem

The transportation problem aims at finding optimal transportation plans between a number of sources (e.g., supplier sites) and a number of destinations (e.g., production sites). The objective is to minimize total transportation cost. The problem can be formulated as a LP model as follows:

$$\text{minimize} \quad \sum_{i=1}^{N}\sum_{j=1}^{M} c_{ij}x_{ij} \tag{2.63}$$

$$\text{s.t.} \quad \sum_{j=1}^{M} x_{ij} \leq k_i \qquad \forall i = 1, \ldots, N \tag{2.64}$$

$$\sum_{i=1}^{N} x_{ij} = d_j \qquad \forall j = 1, \ldots, M \tag{2.65}$$

$$x_{ij} \geq 0 \qquad \forall i = 1, \ldots, N, j = 1, \ldots, M \tag{2.66}$$

Table 2.15 Data: unit transportation cost, demand and capacities

	Production facilities					
Suppliers	A	B	C	D	E	Capacity
1	100	50	500	400	100	900
2	500	500	100	200	50	800
3	200	400	300	50	200	600
Demand	400	400	400	400	500	

The decision variable x_{ij} determines the transportation quantity from source $i = 1, \ldots, N$ to destination $j = 1, \ldots, M$. The objective function minimizes the total transportation cost subject to capacity restriction k_i at sources $i = 1, \ldots, N$ and satisfaction of demand d_j at destinations $j = 1, \ldots, M$.

Numerical Example: Transportation Problem
Suppose that five production facilities (A–E) with specific demand need to be served from three potential suppliers (1,2,3) with limited capacity. Unit transportation cost between supply locations and production facilities are summarized in Table 2.15. Which supplier should be selected for which production site in order to minimize the overall transportation cost (e.g., with regard to sustainability goals)?

By solving the transportation problem, we get the cost-optimal (and sustainable) transportation network with production site D served by supplier 3, production site C served by supplier 2 and production sites A and B served by supplier 1. Production site E is served from both supplier 1 (with quantity 100) and supplier 2 (with quantity 400). This results in overall transportation cost of 150,000.

The transportation problem builds the basis for many problems in transportation optimization (e.g., traveling salesman problem, vehicle routing problem). In the procurement context, the transportation problem is particularly relevant for the procurement of transportation capacities or supply network optimization that is described in Chap. 4.

References

1. Aggarwal C (2015) Data Mining: The Textbook, 1st edn. Springer, Berlin
2. Bertsekas D (1995) Dynamic Programming and Optimal Control, 1st edn. Athena Scientific, New York
3. Bertsimas D, Kallus N (2019) From predictive to prescriptive analytics. Manage Sci 66(3):1025–1044

4. Birge JR, Louveaux F (2011) Introduction to Stochastic Programming, 2nd edn. Springer, Berlin
5. Cachon GP, Netessine S (2006) Game theory in supply chain analysis. *Tutorials in Operations Research*. INFORMS 2006:200–233
6. Curtis FE, Scheinberg K (2017) Optimization methods for supervised machine learning: from linear models to deep learning. *Tutorials in Operations Research*. INFORMS 2017:89–113.
7. Elmachtoub AN, Grigas P (2021) Smart Predict, then optimize. Manage Sci 68(1):9–26
8. Fisher M, Raman A (1996) Reducing the cost of demand uncertainty through accurate response to early sales. Oper Res 44(1):87–99
9. Fudenberg D, Tirole J (1991) Game Theory, 1st edn. MIT Press, New York
10. Gendreau M, Potvin JY (2019) Handbook of Metaheuristics, 3rd edn. Springer, Berlin
11. Hamilton J (1994) Time Series Analysis, 1st edn. Princeton University Press, Princeton
12. Hastie T, Tibshirani R, Friedman J (2013) The Elements of Statistical Learning: Data Mining, Inference, and Prediction, 1st edn. Springer Series in Statistics, Berlin
13. Hillier FS, Lieberman GJ (2014) Introduction to Operations Research, 10th edn. McGraw-Hill, New York
14. James G, Witten D, Hastie T, Tibshirani R (2021) An Introduction to Statistical Learning—with Applications in R, 2nd edn. Springer, Berlin
15. King AJ, Wallace S (2012) Modeling with Stochastic Programming, 1st edn. Springer, Berlin
16. Kleijnen JPC (2015) Design and Analysis of Simulation Experiments, 2nd edn. Springer, Berlin
17. Mohri M, Rostamizadeh A, Talwalkar A (2018) Foundations of Machine Learning, 2nd edn. MIT Press, New York
18. Von Neumann J, Morgenstern O, Rubinstein A (1944) Theory of games and economic behavior. In: 60th Anniversary Commemorative Edition. Princeton University Press, Princeton
19. Powell W (2011) Approximate Dynamic Programming: Solving the Curses of Dimensionality, 2nd edn. Wiley, New York
20. Powell W (2022) Reinforcement Learning and Stochastic Optimization: A Unified Framework for Sequential Decisions, 1st edn. Wiley, New York
21. Powell W (2022) Sequential Decision Analytics and Modeling: Modeling with Python, 1st edn. now Publishers
22. Shapiro A, Dentcheva D, Ruszczynski A (2009) Lectures on Stochastic Programming: Modeling and Theory, 1st edn. SIAM Series on Optimization, New York
23. Tijms HC (2003) A First Course in Stochastic Models, 1st edn. Wiley, New York
24. Vapnik VN (1998). Statistical Learning Theory, 1st edn. Wiley, New York
25. Wolsey L, Nemhauser G (1998) Integer and Combinatorial Optimization, 1st edn. Wiley, New York

Chapter 3
Data-Driven Spend Management

Abstract This chapter targets the analysis of a company's spend cube, which builds the data basis for data-driven optimization in procurement. We present standard and advanced spend classification methods from the field of machine learning, major key performance indicators for spend control from different dimensions (e.g., cost, time, risk and sustainability) as well as spend analytics and spend intelligence methods such as should-cost analysis or linear and nonlinear performance pricing for spend optimization through finding price inconsistencies and discrepancies in supplier data.

Keywords Spend cube · Spend intelligence · Spend classification · Should-cost analysis · Linear performance pricing

3.1 Introduction

Spend management is a major task of every purchasing organization and includes spend classification, performance measurement and spend optimization. The major goals of spend management are (i) to establish spend transparency across the entire organization; (ii) to benchmark procurement performance over time, between internal entities and against the external market; and (iii) to identify optimization potential with regard to the dimensions cost, time, quality, risk and sustainability.

In order to establish spend transparency across the entire organization, spend data classification is essential. The basis builds the spend cube where all spend data is saved and consolidated. This data lake builds the input for basic and advanced classification methods such as ABC analysis with regard to purchase items or suppliers, XYZ analysis, Kraljic classification, geospatial classification or AI-based classification (see Sect. 3.2).

The spend cube additionally builds the basis for data-driven performance measurement of the procurement function. While over many decades cost objectives were predominant, this recently shifted toward a strong focus on risk and sustainability goals. Therefore, in order to assess procurement performance holistically, it

C. Mandl, *Procurement Analytics*, Springer Series in Supply Chain Management 22, https://doi.org/10.1007/978-3-031-43281-1_3

is essential to develop a balanced scorecard with key performance indicators from various dimensions (see Sect. 3.3).

In a last step, internal spend cube data and data from further sources such as RFQs or e-auctions together with external data from market databases is used to optimize purchasing and spend management in order to improve KPIs. Spend analytics methods such as should-cost analysis and linear or nonlinear performance pricing identify optimization potential and give data-driven decision-support and recommendations regarding, for example, supplier selection and price (re-) negotiations (see Sect. 3.4).

3.2 Spend Classification

3.2.1 Spend Cube

A company's *spend cube* is a collection of spend data in the form of line items, i.e., purchase orders classified into several categories. The basis of a spend cube is a relational database. Standard spend cube dimensions (also called spend taxonomy) are (i) spend category, (ii) supplier and (iii) cost center (Fig. 3.1).

The **spend category dimension** often contains the classes *direct material* and *indirect material* and builds the basis for category management. Direct material includes all items required for the production of the actual product or service. It can further be split into the categories such as raw materials, semi-finished products or components and finished products. Indirect procurement includes all products and services that support production or service creation but are not directly involved in the manufacturing or creation process. Indirect material categories include operating resource management (ORM) and maintenance, repair and operations (MRO).

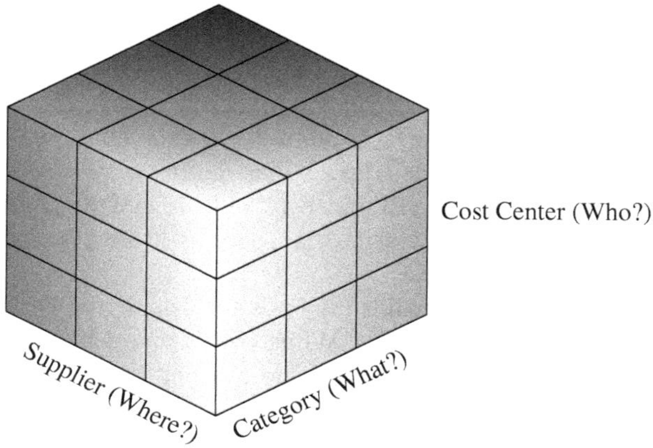

Fig. 3.1 Concept of spend cubes in procurement

ORM again includes facility management including office supplies, IT (hardware and software), travel management, fleet management, HR services, legal services, consulting services and marketing services. MRO includes capital goods (plant and machinery) and utilities (gas, electricity, water). Practical evidence shows that indirect procurement accounts for around 15 to 30% of a company's overall spend depending on the industry.

The **supplier dimension** contains information such as supplier name, supplier location, geographical region, transportation agreements (e.g., incoterms) and payment agreements (e.g., currencies).

The **cost center dimension** contains information about the business unit, the plant location and therefore together with supplier information provides additional information on transportation distance, potential supply risks, etc.

Therefore, a spend cube builds the basis for descriptive analytics in order to answer the following questions:

- What items are we buying?
- How many items have we bought?
- When did we buy the items?
- How often did we buy the items?
- From whom did we buy the items?
- Who bought the items?
- How much have we paid per item?

Industry Example: Spend Cube in Practice

In practice, spend cubes are huge data pools. German carmaker Porsche has around 7000 direct suppliers such as Bosch. The spend cube of Bosch again includes 24,000 suppliers, 225 plants, 43 billion Euro purchase volume from which there are 64% direct material, 28% indirect material and services and 8% trading goods. The spend cube of the US agricultural machinery manufacturer AGCO includes 54 plants, several thousand direct suppliers and above 14,000 transportation relations.

Table 3.1 shows a standard spend cube extract. An extended spend cube may also include information such as incoterms to specify whether the published price includes or excludes transportation fees.

Therefore, the spend cube is a valuable data lake and (enriched with external data such as commodity market prices or exchange rates) the basis for spend analysis with the objective to categorize spend, increase spend transparency, identify deficiencies (e.g., price inconsistencies across suppliers, plants or time or maverick buying) and derive optimization potential (e.g., economies of scale through volume bundling over time and plant locations, volume re-allocation between suppliers, data-informed price re-negotiations or switching from buy to make for specific items if less costly).

Table 3.1 Spend cube extract

Date	Item	Category	Supplier	Plant	Unit price	Volume	Spend in mUSD
…	…	…	…	…	…	…	…
Jan-23	Al-2359	Raw Materials	Supply Ltd.	Bremen	2254 USD/MT	421 MT	0.949
Feb-23	Al-2359	Raw Materials	Supply Ltd.	Bremen	2410 USD/MT	421 MT	1.015
Mar-23	Al-2359	Raw Materials	Supply Ltd.	Bremen	2353 USD/MT	421 MT	0.991
Jan-23	Service A-2	Facility Mgmt	Clean Corp.	Plzen	10.432 USD	1	0.010
Feb-23	Service A-2	Facility Mgmt	Clean Corp.	Bremen	20.652 USD	1	0.021
Feb-23	Al-2359	Raw Materials	Metal Corp.	Plzen	2000 USD/MT	510 MT	1.020
Mar-23	Al-2359	Raw Materials	Metal Corp.	Plzen	2000 USD/MT	11 MT	0.022
Mar-23	FKS-20	Finished Goods	Novia Corp.	Plzen	959 USD/unit	400 units	0.384
Jan-23	Bubble foil	Packaging	4Pack	Bremen	0.52 USD/sqm	80000 sqm	0.042
Mar-23	Bubble foil	Packaging	OptPack	Bremen	0.3 USD/sqm	50000 sqm	0.015
…	…	…	…	…	…	…	…

Industry Example: Spend Cube Analysis
During a consulting project, the following cost drivers could be identified through a descriptive analysis of the company's spend cube: (i) high number of suppliers relative to number of purchase items (e.g., on average 4.4 suppliers per item), (ii) high number of orders per item (e.g., 200 orders per item per year), (iii) high rate of maverick buying (e.g., 23% of items, 9% of spend), (iv) price inconsistency over time for a specific material from the same supplier (see also Table 3.1 for Al-2359), (v) price inconsistency between suppliers for a specific material (see also Table 3.1 for bubble foil) and (iv) price inconsistency for a specific material across plants (see also Table 3.1 for Service A-2).

3.2.2 ABC-XYZ Classification

ABC and XYZ analysis are simple standard methods for classification that are particularly applied in inventory management (see Chap. 5). In the procurement context, ABC-XYZ analysis can be used to classify spend with regard to suppliers or SKUs.

ABC Analysis

ABC analysis is a standard method in order to classify or segment spend cube items. It is often one of the first steps of descriptive analytics. The general idea follows the pareto principle (or 80/20 rule), i.e., 80% of consequences come from 20% of causes, and therefore 20% of consequences come from 80% of causes.

In procurement, we typically distinguish between supplier pareto and item pareto depending on the focus of the analysis, i.e., supplier classification/segmentation or SKU classification/segmentation. It states that x% of spend results from y% of SKUs or suppliers. ABC classification divides SKUs or suppliers into three groups A, B and C depending on their spend contribution. The thresholds for classification can vary from industry to industry and need to be selected individually per company. In many cases, companies follow the standard 80/20 rule, i.e., A suppliers are those who contribute to 80% of the cumulative spend. In other industries, A suppliers are defined as those who account for 50% of the procurement budget, while B suppliers account for 35% and C suppliers for the rest.

In the example from Fig. 3.2, 20% of items (or suppliers) contribute to 80% of the spend (A items or suppliers), while 30% of items (or suppliers) contribute to 15% of the spend (B items or suppliers), and 50% of items (or suppliers) contribute to only 5% of the spend (C items or suppliers).

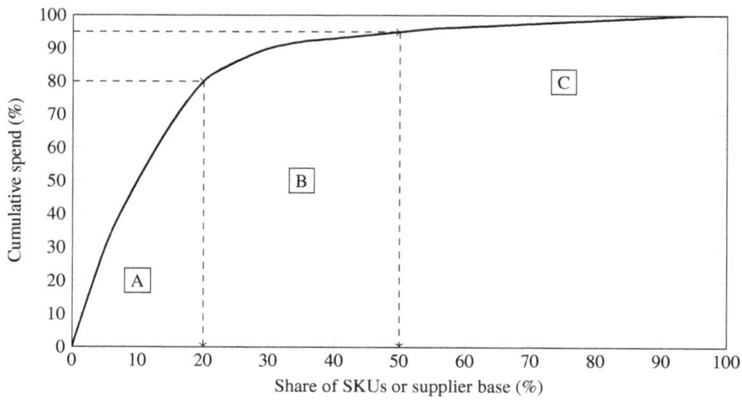

Fig. 3.2 Output of an ABC analysis

In purchasing, A is often referred to as the core spend, while B and C are referred to as the tail spend. Tail spend is characterized by a large number of SKUs/suppliers/purchase transactions (80%) with a rather small spend volume (20%). In terms of supplier pareto, tail spend often corresponds to fragmented local or regional suppliers; in terms of item pareto, tail spend often refers to SKUs with low order frequency.

For spend optimization, most companies mainly focus on their A items/suppliers, which is reasonable because (i) of A's high contribution to total spend and (ii) reduced complexity because of the lower number of items/suppliers. Due to its rather low spend volume, its high complexity and its low order frequency, tail spend is often not managed appropriately by procurement organizations, which yields a significant untapped savings potential. It can be dangerous to decrease attention for C items/suppliers for two different reasons: (i) There typically is a lot of optimization potential for C, while A and B classes are often already effectively optimized (e.g., in terms of price negotiations), and (ii) a failure or shortage of C items or suppliers can lead to a failure of the entire production system.

XYZ Analysis

In comparison to ABC analysis, XYZ analysis does not focus on item/supplier classification based on spend contribution or value but rather on classification based on demand patterns. In the procurement context, XYZ analysis is useful for evaluating the number of interactions with suppliers or the frequency of purchase orders (regular, irregular or sporadic). The coefficient of variation (CV) is used as a classification criterion, i.e.,

$$CV = \frac{\sigma}{\mu} = \frac{\sqrt{\frac{\sum_{i=1}^{n}(d_i-\mu)^2}{n-1}}}{\frac{\sum_{i=1}^{n}d_i}{n}} \tag{3.1}$$

with d_i as (historical) demand observations $i = 1, \ldots, n$, σ as the demand standard deviation and μ as the average demand over all (historical) observations.

X items (or X suppliers) are those with a regular demand and small demand variation over time (high runners). They are characterized by a high demand predictability as they are demanded daily or at least frequently. Those products are typically classified by a coefficient of variation of smaller than 0.25.

Y items (or Y suppliers) are those with fluctuating demand and significant demand variation over time (e.g., seasonal behavior or trends). They are characterized by a more complex demand predictability. Those products are typically classified by a coefficient of variation between 0.25 and 0.5.

Z items (or Z suppliers) are those with a irregular or sporadic demand that is characterized by a significant number of periods without any demand (low runners) and a coefficient of variation of above 0.5. Z items typically have a low demand predictability as they are demanded very irregularly or sporadically. An example is spare parts (Fig. 3.3).

ABC-XYZ Analysis

A combination of the results from ABC and XYZ analysis allows to classify each item within two dimensions, i.e., value (ABC) and uncertainty (XYZ) (Fig. 3.4).

Based on that, strategic recommendations can be derived for the different classes. For example, in inventory management (see Chap. 5), for AX products, small safety stocks are appropriate, while for CZ items, large safety stocks are required and appropriate as they do not lock too much capital.

ABC-XYZ analysis is sometimes extended to a third dimension, i.e., physical item volume (large-volume, medium-volume, small-volume).

3.2.3 *Kraljic Classification and Derivatives*

The Kraljic classification was introduced by Peter Kraljic in 1983 (see [1]) and classifies purchase items according to the two dimensions *profit impact* and *supply risk* (Fig. 3.5). Both dimensions need to be quantified for each of the purchase items.

Profit impact can be calculated by, e.g., the total spend of the specific item relative to the total spend or total revenue of the firm, by the impact of the item on the

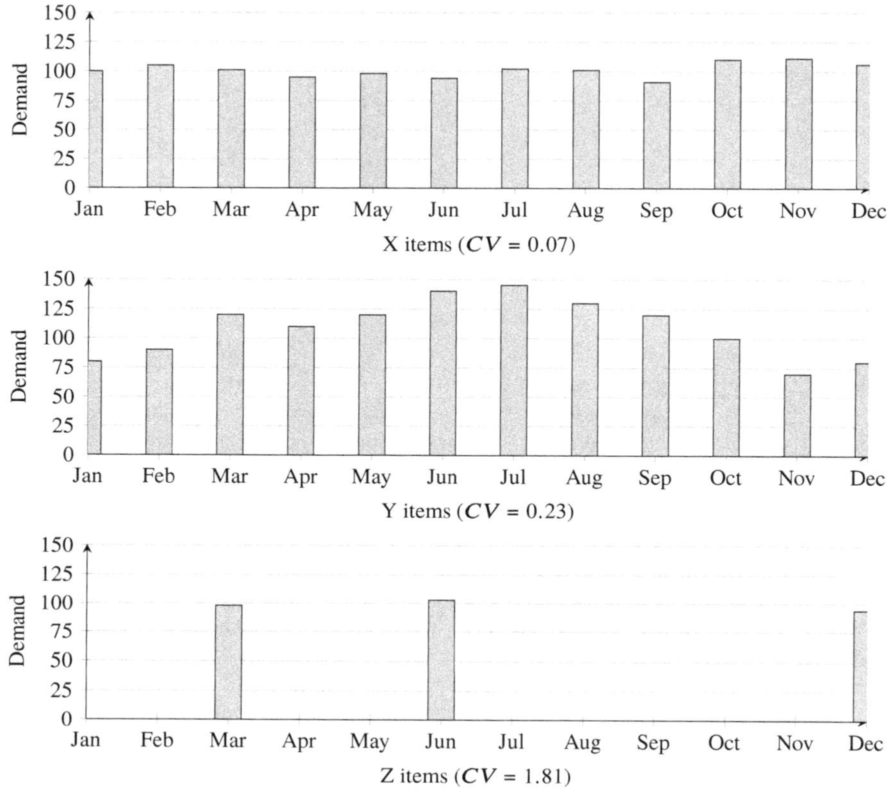

Fig. 3.3 Output of a XYZ analysis

firm's profit or by price elasticity or cost savings potential, i.e., change of supply and demand after a price change.

Supply risk can be determined by the reliance on the supplier of the item (calculated by, e.g., number of item suppliers available, length of supply contracts, the firm's contribution to the total revenue of the supplier, financial figures of the supplier, availability of substitutes, patent and license status of the item).

Using two attributes per dimension (e.g., high and low), this results in four item classes, i.e., strategic items, leverage items, bottleneck items and non-critical items. For each of the four classes, strategic implications and recommendations are defined.

Strategic items are characterized by a high supply risk (e.g., few suppliers available) and a high profit impact. Examples are automotive battery supplies or semiconductors for the automotive industry. For these items, long-term supplier relationship should be well-kept and intensified. Strategic partnerships should be developed, and make-or-buy decisions carefully need to be elaborated in order to be prepared for any supply disruption scenario.

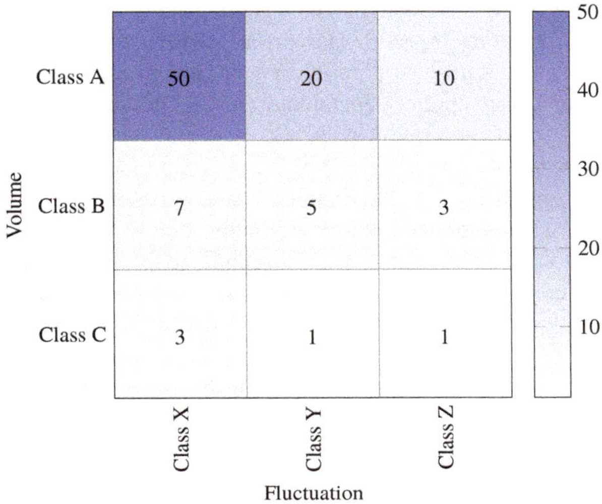

Fig. 3.4 Output of an ABC-XYZ analysis (with item or supplier shares in percent)

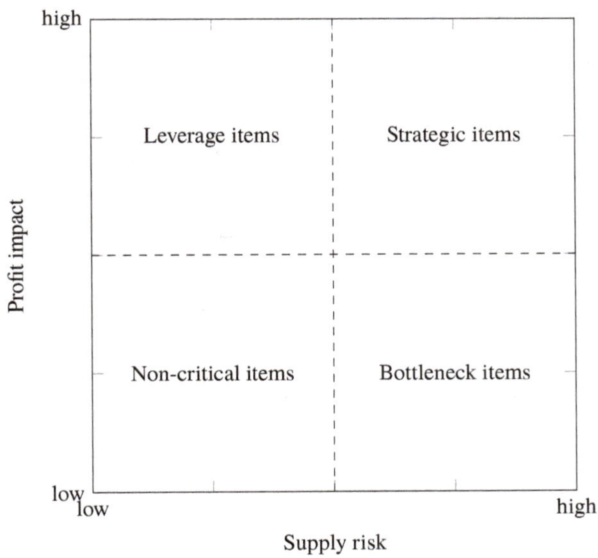

Fig. 3.5 Kraljic matrix for purchase item classification

Leverage items are characterized by a low supply risk (e.g., many suppliers available) and a high profit impact. Examples are hardware, heating oil or electric motors. For these items, procurement organizations should leverage their strength by frequent supplier negotiations or the use of digital tools such as e-auctions in order to fuel price competition.

Bottleneck items are characterized by a high supply risk (e.g., few suppliers available) and a low profit impact. Examples are catalyst materials or specific electronic parts. For these items, medium-term contractual agreements or inventories can guarantee supply, or supplier dependency can be limited by product substitution if possible.

Non-critical items are characterized by a low supply risk (e.g., many suppliers available) and a low profit impact. Examples are office supplies. For these items, products should be standardized, and order volume should be optimized (bundling).

It is essential to update the item categorization from time to time in order to apply the right measures. During the COVID-19 crisis, companies needed to recognize that originally non-critical items became bottleneck items (e.g., pulp and toilet paper).

The Kraljic classification is the starting point for several advancements such as the Wildemann portfolio or the purchasing chessboard.

Wildemann (see [5]) combines the Kraljic portfolio for items with the same classification for suppliers and derives strategic implications (see Fig. 3.6). The international consulting company Kearney provides a *Purchasing Chessboard* with

	Standard supplier	Bottleneck supplier	Core supplier	Strategic supplier
Strategic item			Partnership	Partnership
Core item			Partnerships	Partnership
Bottleneck item		Secure supply		
Standard item	Purchase efficiently			

Fig. 3.6 Wildemann portfolio for spend classification

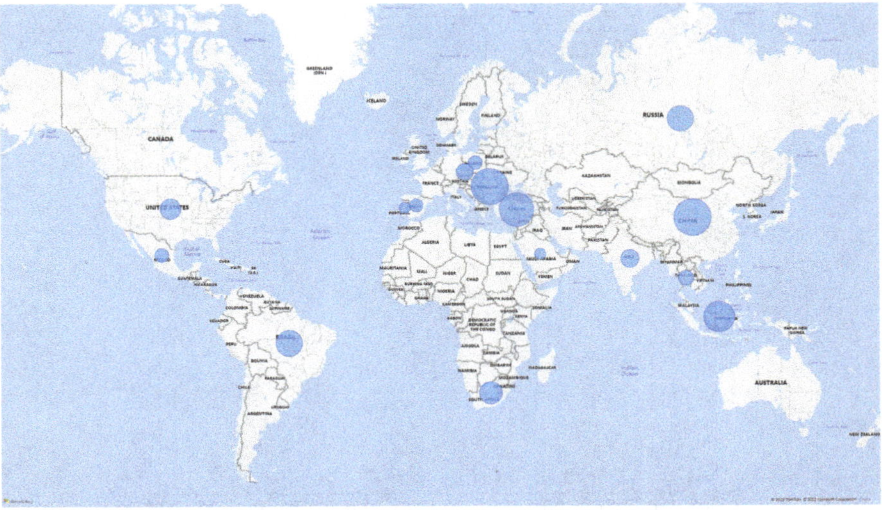

Fig. 3.7 Geospatial classification: Spend per country (Visualization in `Microsoft PowerBI`)

the dimensions supply power and demand power that define 64 purchasing strategies (see [3]).

3.2.4 Geospatial Classification

The spend cube can also serve as a data basis for geospatial classification analysis. This can help identify high-risk spend versus low-risk spend due to geographical risk. It is also used to identify cluster risk. For instance, in 2022–2023, geopolitical risk in Ukraine, Russia and Taiwan was tremendously high and asked procurement managers to develop contingency plans. Figure 3.7 shows an example of a geospatial classification for a (real-time) risk dashboard implemented in `Microsoft PowerBI`.

3.2.5 AI-Based Classification

Artificial intelligence in the sense of machine learning is increasingly used to detect patterns in spend data in order to remove repetitive classification tasks. Therefore, different supervised learning algorithms based on labeled data such as k-nearest neighbor (kNN), naïve Bayes and support vector machines (SVM) (see Chap. 2) are used for feature-based, data-driven classification. The following example from Fig. 3.8 illustrates kNN classification applied to spend cube data.

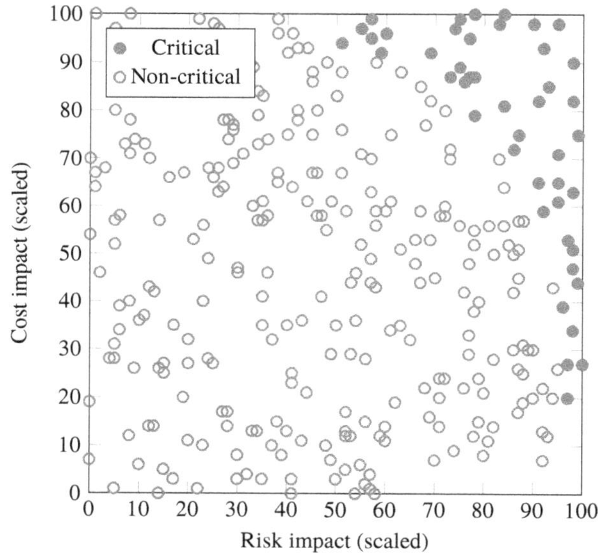

Fig. 3.8 Supplier spend classification

A concrete application of classification in procurement is *invoice line classification* where spend is (correctly) and automatically classified from invoice to the correct spend cube classes via text-mining technology.

3.3 Procurement Performance Indicators

While spend data classification increases procurement transparency, it does not per se measure procurement performance. However, as the economist Peter Drucker already said: "If you cannot measure it, you cannot manage or improve it." Therefore, performance measurement with procurement performance indicators is essential. Procurement controlling (spend control) is responsible for planning, monitoring and controlling of the procurement function based on a set of metrics that are calculated on the basis of data that is collected from different sources such as accounting, logistics and external data providers. An adequate procedure can look as follows:

- **Step 1:** Definition of adequate KPIs based on overall firm objectives. KPIs should preferably be ratios or percentages for comparison reasons.
- **Step 2:** Determination of target values per KPI. Thresholds can help define intuitive performance classes such as *strong*, *medium* and *weak*.
- **Step 3:** Calculation of KPIs for the status quo and compared to a defined baseline.

- **Step 4:** Benchmarking of KPIs across time, competitors and business units or departments.
- **Step 5:** Tracking and visualization of KPIs with interactive and real-time BI dashboards.

Those steps can be executed on different levels, e.g., spend categories (category management), suppliers (spend management) or geography (location management), in order to measure the procurement performance in different product categories, for different suppliers or in different locations and markets. This also allows to compare procurement performance across company departments, which is often relevant for compensation and budgeting decisions. Reports such as the benchmarking study of the *German Association Materials Management, Purchasing and Logistics* help obtain numbers for best-in-class and industry averages.

In the procurement controlling context, different perspectives are regarded in the sense of a balanced scorecard. In the following, we distinguish between the perspectives *cost*, *quality*, *time*, *supplier*, *risk*, *organization* and *sustainability*. Table 3.2 gives an overview of important procurement performance indicators per dimension that are mainly defined as ratios.

From a **cost perspective**, *cost reduction* quantifies the percentage price change from the previous price paid to the currently paid price and is calculated by

$$\text{Cost Reduction} = \frac{\text{Current unit price - Previous unit price}}{\text{Previous unit price}} \cdot 100\%. \tag{3.2}$$

Table 3.2 Collection of procurement performance indicators

Metric	Unit
1. Cost Perspective	
Cost Reduction	%
Cost Avoidance	%
Price Benchmark Ratio	–
Purchase Price Variance	–
Adherence to Budget	%
Deviation from Target Cost	%
Procurement Return on Invest	%
Cost per Order Process	Euro
Average Discount Rate	%
Days Payable Outstanding	Days
Negotiation Success Rate	%
Frequency of Price Change	Months
2. Quality Perspective	
Defect Rate	Parts per million (ppm)
Rejection Rate	%
Certification Rate	%

(continued)

Table 3.2 (continued)

Metric	Unit
3. Lead Time Perspective	
Average Lead Time	Days
PO Cycle Time	Days
Delay Rate	%
Delivery in Full (DIF)	%
Delivery on Time (DOT)	%
Delivery in Full on Time (DIFOT)	%
4. Supplier Perspective	
Total Number of Suppliers	#
Relative Number of Suppliers	# per mn Euro
Supplier-Spend Allocation	Euro
Supplier Availability	%
Share of New Suppliers	%
5. Risk Perspective	
Single Source Rate	%
Sole Source Rate	%
Global Sourcing Rate	%
Forward Sourcing Rate	%
Index-based Contract Ratio	%
Foreign Currency Rate	%
6. Organizational Perspective	
Spend under Management	%
Maverick Buying Rate	%
Emergency Purchase Ratio	%
Personal Purchase Volume	Euro
Personal Purchase Orders	#
Spend under Contract	Euro
Contracting Rate	%
Communication Time Lag	Hours
Training Budget per Employee	Euro
Compliance Rate	%
7. Sustainability Perspective	
Supplier Transportation Distance	km
Supplier Carbon Footprint	Tons CO2e
Supplier Sustainability Audit Rate	%
Supplier Sustainability Certification Rate	%

Cost reduction has an immediate effect on the profit and loss (P&L) and can have different reasons such as successful (re-)negotiations with suppliers, supplier switches, economies of scale from quantity discounts, drops in raw material or energy prices or in general economic deflation. In order to assess the positive effects of cost-cutting programs via this KPI, external market effects (such as deflation) need to be excluded from calculation.

Cost avoidance is another metric that has no immediate observable effect on the P&L. Therefore, opposed to the hard KPI cost reduction, *cost avoidance* as a soft KPI is often not systematically tracked, which is problematic particularly in inflationary market phases where procurement departments are often not able to reduce cost but at least can avoid cost increases. Approaches to quantify *cost avoidance* can be to compare cost effects without action and cost effects through cost avoidance actions such as long-term contracts (Table 3.3).

Numerical Example: Cost Avoidance

Table 3.3 Cost avoidance based on the example of natural gas price contracting in Europe (Data source: FRED Economic Data)

Date	Market price in USD/mmbtu	Contracted price in USD/mmbtu	Cost avoidance in USD/mmbtu
Jan-2022	27.89	30.00	−2.11
Feb-2022	26.98	30.00	−3.02
Mar-2022	41.73	30.00	+11.73
Apr-2022	31.98	30.00	+1.98
May-2022	27.46	30.00	−3.54
Jun-2022	32.91	30.00	+2.91
Jul-2022	51.15	30.00	+21.15
Aug-2022	69.98	30.00	+39.98
Sep-2022	55.18	30.00	+25.18
Oct-2022	20.80	30.00	−9.20
Nov-2022	28.79	30.00	−2.21
Dec-2022	35.37	30.00	+5.37
Average			+7.52

Price Benchmark Ratio compares the current purchase price with a benchmark price and is calculated as

$$\text{Price Benchmark Ratio} = \frac{\text{Current purchase price}}{\text{Benchmark price}}. \tag{3.3}$$

The benchmark price can be the price offer from another supplier or an external price benchmark such as an market index or average market price. A *Price Benchmark Ratio* above 1 indicates that there is a savings potential from switching supplier or from price (re-) negotiation. For instance, a ratio of 1.2 indicates that the current price paid is 20% above the benchmark price. This metric is particularly relevant for commodities with a transparent market pricing (e.g., exchange-traded raw materials).

Purchase Price Variance compares the actual spend with the budgeted spend based on the standard price and is calculated as

$$\text{Purchase Price Variance} = (\text{Actual price} - \text{Standard price}) \cdot \text{Volume}. \quad (3.4)$$

A negative purchase price variance indicates that the actual spend is below budget, which is favorable and can have different reasons such as successful price negotiations or favorable raw material and energy cost developments. During 2022, energy cost increased significantly and raised purchase price variance tremendously for those companies without long-term energy purchasing contracts. Purchase price variance is also referred to the KPIs *Adherence to Budget* or *Deviation from Target Cost*.

The *Procurement Return on Invest (ROI)* is a popular metric from finance applied to the procurement function whenever investment decisions become relevant. It is calculated as follows and quantifies the profitability of procurement departments:

$$\text{Procurement ROI} = \frac{\text{Realized annual purchase cost savings}}{\text{Total annual purchase cost}} \cdot 100\% \quad (3.5)$$

It can also be used to evaluate the benefit of introducing new procurement (software) tools. In general, the ROI should exceed the return of alternative investment options such as financial investments in company stocks or the interest rate provided by financial institutions. For instance, if a new employee in the purchasing department costs 100,000 USD per year but generates savings through negotiations of 300,000 USD per year, then the ROI is 300%. This can be compared to the ROI of a new AI software tool that can also help purchasing to save cost.

Cost per Order Process quantifies the total cost per order including IT system cost, labor cost and other administrative cost. This KPI is only effective if regarded relative to previous values (i.e., does the order process become cheaper) or between business units or departments.

Days Payable Outstanding (DPO) indicates the average time in number of days it takes for payment of suppliers. It is calculated as follows:

$$\begin{aligned}&\text{Days Payable Outstanding}\\&\quad= \frac{\text{Accounts payable of the period} \cdot \text{Number of days}}{\text{Total purchase cost or COGS of the period}} \cdot 100\%\end{aligned} \quad (3.6)$$

Purchasers aim for a high DPO in order to keep liquidity high. A high number of days payable outstanding indicates that the buyer is in a dominant position relative to the corresponding supplier and also gives an indication about the success of a negotiation process where typically also payment terms are agreed. A typical value for DPO in practice is between 30 and 40 days. A value that is significantly higher than 40 days indicates a strong market position.

Negotiation Success Rate quantifies the price change during a supplier negotiation from the supplier's first offer until the final purchase price. It is calculated by

$$\text{Negotiation Success Rate} = \frac{\text{First offer - Final price}}{\text{First offer}} \cdot 100\%. \tag{3.7}$$

Negotiation Success Rate is sometimes also referred to as *Average Discount Rate* that also gives an indication about the success of the negotiation process. In practice, it is not uncommon to reduce the initial price during negotiation by 10–20%. E-auctions can additionally lower the price.

Frequency of Price Change is an indicator for uncertainty in budget planning. It strongly depends on contract duration and negotiated pricing mechanism. In terms of index-based contracts, the price varies continuously (beneficial if it decreases, unfavorable if it increases), while fixed-price contracts provide price certainty.

From a **quality perspective**, *Defect Rate* is the major metric and calculated by

$$\text{Defect Rate} = \frac{\text{Number of defective units}}{\text{Number of units tested}} \cdot 100\%. \tag{3.8}$$

It is also often measured in parts per million (ppm) rather than percentage. A ppm measures the number of defective units per 1 million units. Consequently, a ppm defective rate of 10,000 means that the defect rate is $<1\%$. Many industries ask for defect rates smaller than 25 ppm. However, it needs to be considered that *Defect Rate* is a statistical measure based on a sample that does not necessarily reflect the population. Two potential errors need to be considered: (i) Type I error (alpha error) is the error of rejecting a supplier lot that is actually of good quality. (ii) Type II error (beta error) is the error of accepting a supplier lot that is actually of bad quality.

Rejection Rate is related to Defective Rate and defined as

$$\text{Rejection Rate} = \frac{\text{Number of supplies rejected}}{\text{Total number of supplies}} \cdot 100\%. \tag{3.9}$$

Another quality metric is *Certification Rate* that is calculated by

$$\text{Certification Rate} = \frac{\text{Number of ISO-9000-certified suppliers}}{\text{Total number of suppliers}} \cdot 100\%. \tag{3.10}$$

Alternatively, quality can also be measured by the share of audited or assessed suppliers.

From a **lead time perspective**, the most important metric is *Average Lead Time* that is calculated by

$$\text{Average Lead Time} = \text{Delivery time} - \text{Order time}. \tag{3.11}$$

The average lead time is critical because it affects business decisions such as safety stock placements (see Chap. 5) as observed during the early 2020s where companies increased their safety stocks as a reaction on lead time increases, for instance, in semiconductors where delivery times increased from around 10 weeks to 30 weeks. In general, average lead times strongly depend on the corresponding industry and geographical location with the Supply Delivery Time Index giving an indication (see Chap. 6).

Purchase Order (PO) Cycle Time is the cumulative time in days from supplier request until supplier confirmation. It therefore focuses on the purchase order process rather than the delivery process.

Delivery in Full (DiF) is a quantity-oriented measure and addresses whether delivery quantity matches with order quantity. It is calculated by

$$\text{Delivery in Full (DiF)} = \frac{\text{Delivery quantity}}{\text{Order quantity}} \cdot 100\%. \tag{3.12}$$

A related measure is *Delivery on Time (DoT)* that is not quantity- but time-oriented calculated by

$$\text{Delivery on Time (DoT)} = \frac{\text{Number of on-time deliveries}}{\text{Total number of deliveries}} \cdot 100\%. \tag{3.13}$$

A best-in-class DoT rate could be, for instance, >90%. *Delay Rate* is calculated as 100 % - DoT.

Delivery in Time on Full (DiFoT) (also known as purchase order (PO) accuracy, perfect order rate or on-time-in-full (OTIF)) addresses both on-time delivery and correct delivery quantity with regard to the right item and the right time and without any incident. It is calculated by

$$\text{DiFoT} = \frac{\text{Number of correctly fulfilled POs}}{\text{Total number of POs}} \cdot 100\%. \tag{3.14}$$

DiFoT can however be interpreted by supply chain participants in different ways and ask for clear upfront definition. For instance, *on-time* may mean *within a specific time window* or *latest at a certain point in time.*

From a **supplier perspective**, the *relative number of suppliers* gives insights about the supplier structure. It is defined as follows and can be calculated in number of suppliers per Euro spent, per product category or per region:

$$\text{Relative Number of Suppliers} = \frac{\text{Number of suppliers}}{\text{1 mn Euro purchase volume}} \tag{3.15}$$

Supplier-Spend Allocation is related to the relative number of suppliers and calculated by

$$\text{Supplier-Spend Allocation} = \frac{\text{Total spend (per category, region)}}{\text{Total number of suppliers (per category, region)}}. \tag{3.16}$$

Supplier Availability is an event-based metric that quantifies how many of the orders were immediately available. It is related to the metric fill rate from inventory management (see Chap. 5) and calculated by

$$\text{Supplier Availability} = \frac{\text{Number of orders available}}{\text{Total number of orders}}. \tag{3.17}$$

The *Share of New Suppliers* is another metric that measures the results of supplier scouting activities considering that disruptive innovations often come from young companies such as start-ups. It is calculated by

$$\text{Share of New Suppliers} = \frac{\text{Number of suppliers with} < 1 \text{ year of interaction}}{\text{Total number of suppliers}}. \tag{3.18}$$

From a **risk perspective**, the *single source rate* as a risk score gives an indication about the dependence on single suppliers. It is an indicator for supply (disruption) risk and calculated as

$$\text{Single Source Rate} = \frac{\text{Single source spend}}{\text{Total spend}} \cdot 100\% \tag{3.19}$$

with the single source spend defined as the spend for purchase items and services that are purchased at a single supplier even though further suppliers exist.

The *Sole Source Rate* is defined as

$$\text{Sole Source Rate} = \frac{\text{Sole source spend}}{\text{Total spend}} \cdot 100\%. \tag{3.20}$$

with the sole source spend defined as the spend for purchase items or services that are purchased at a single supplier because no second supplier exists. While the single source rate can easily be reduced by a dual- or multisourcing strategy, this is not the case for the sole source rate that can only be reduced by product substitution or through a make rather than buy strategy.

The *Global Sourcing Rate* may also be an indicator for supply disruptions. It is defined as

$$\text{Global Sourcing Rate} = \frac{\text{Globally sourced purchase volume}}{\text{Total purchase volume}} \cdot 100\%. \tag{3.21}$$

For effectively using this KPI, it is essential to define the word *global* that can, for instance, be "sourcing from a foreign country" or "sourcing from another continent."

The *Forward Sourcing Rate* addresses both supply (disruption) risk and commodity price risk. It quantifies the share of purchase volume that is secured over a longer period of time through forward contracts rather than short-term spot purchases. The forward sourcing rate is calculated by

$$\text{Forward Sourcing Rate} = \left(1 - \frac{\text{Spot purchase volume}}{\text{Total purchase volume}}\right) \cdot 100\%. \tag{3.22}$$

The *Index-Based Contract Rate* is also related to price risk. The rate defines how many purchase contracts are linked to a price index and therefore risky (if price increases) or beneficial (if price decreases). The metric is calculated as follows:

$$\text{Index-Based Contract Ratio} = \frac{\text{Index-based purchase volume}}{\text{Total purchase volume}} \cdot 100\% \tag{3.23}$$

Foreign Currency Rate measures the share of purchase volume linked to a foreign currency and therefore addresses exchange rate risk. It is calculated as

$$\text{Foreign Currency Rate} = \frac{\text{Non-Euro purchase volume}}{\text{Total purchase volume}} \cdot 100\%. \tag{3.24}$$

From an **organizational perspective**, the metric *Spend under Management* defines the spend that is actively managed and approved through the purchasing department through, for instance, standardized supplier contracts. It is calculated by

$$\text{Spend under Management} = \frac{\text{Spend controlled and regulated}}{\text{Total spend}} \cdot 100\%. \tag{3.25}$$

A low spend under management metric indicates ill-defined procurement processes, a high potential for cost optimization through spend analytics and a high risk of maverick buying.

The *Maverick Buying Rate* is defined as

$$\text{Maverick Buying Rate} = \frac{\text{Purchase volume outside of formal purchase process}}{\text{Total purchase volume}}. \tag{3.26}$$

A high maverick buying rate can be the consequence of a lack of understanding internal procurement processes and a high share of indirect purchasing. In practice, we observe that maverick buying rates are often around 25% and above, which indicates huge optimization potential through order bundling.

The *Emergency Purchase Ratio* gives an indication about the quality of planning as emergency orders are typically (much) more expensive. The ratio is calculated by

$$\text{Emergency Purchase Ratio} = \frac{\text{Number of emergency orders}}{\text{Total number of orders}} \cdot 100\%. \tag{3.27}$$

Personal Purchase Volume is the purchase volume per employee in Euro per year, while *Personal Purchase Orders* refers to the number of purchase orders per employee and month. Both give indication on whether there is an overload of single employees or whether there is a certain dependency of single buyers within the organization. On the other hand, if the volume is too small, there might be no leverage for supply negotiations.

Contracting Rate gives an overview about the share (with regard to spend) of short-term ($<$1 year), medium-term ($<$3 years) and long-term ($>$3 years) contracts. It is related to *Spend under Contract* (in Euro) and also often referred to as contract coverage or contract loyalty and calculated by the spend through a contract divided by the total spend.

Communication Time Lag (or quick response) quantifies the average supplier response time in hours.

Training Budget per Employee quantifies the budget spent per employee for training of skills related to the procurement function. This can also include training in procurement analytics.

Compliance Rate covers the legal side of procurement activities. It is calculated as

$$\text{Compliance Rate} = \frac{\text{Disputed invoices}}{\text{Total invoices}} \cdot 100\%. \tag{3.28}$$

Alternatively, it can also be calculated as the difference between the price paid and the price quoted.

From a **sustainability perspective**, the definition of adequate KPIs is more challenging. This is especially because (i) sustainability is a broad term and difficult to measure and (ii) each supplier may measure sustainability in a different way. Nevertheless, there are several ESG metrics conceivable that may give an indication for sustainability performance such as *Supplier Transportation Distance* between suppliers and buyers assuming that a local sourcing supply network would ceteris paribus (i.e., all other things being equal) generate less CO2 emissions due to reduced transportation. Another possibility is to directly measure the *Supplier Carbon Footprint* of the supply network, i.e., measuring the upstream scope 3 emissions in tons of CO2 equivalent (CO2e). Furthermore, during the last years, sustainability ratings were developed that can also be used for sustainability assessment. For instance, purchasing can use a *Supplier Sustainability Audit* or *Supplier Sustainability Certification Rate* in order to measure the share of suppliers that were audited/certified with focus on sustainability. Furthermore, organizations can measure the percentage of suppliers that use a code of conduct that is in accordance with their own code of conduct. Other companies measure their ecological footprint in procurement by calculating the use of recycled packaging material in percent of the purchase volume for packaging.

3.4 Spend Optimization

While procurement KPIs measure the procurement performance, they do not per se optimize procurement results. In this chapter, we present two methods for spend optimization. Both methods are used for data-driven supplier negotiations and an effective RFI/RFQ design. We start with the bottom-up approach of should-cost analysis and conclude with the top-down approach of linear and nonlinear performance pricing.

3.4.1 Should-Cost Analysis

Should-cost analysis is the bottom-up process of identifying a reasonable price for a purchase item or service under the requirement to reach an expected target profit. Based on target cost and target profit, a target price can be calculated (target pricing). For should-cost modeling, it is important to consider total cost of ownership, i.e., all life cycle costs of a product or service need to be evaluated. Therefore, should-cost modeling is an instrument of cost engineering that uses cost breakdown analysis (also known as clean sheet analysis, shadow costing, cost structure analysis, true cost analysis, factor cost analysis or cost-based pricing) in order to identify major cost drivers and derive an adequate should-cost as presented in Fig. 3.9.

Cost engineering breaks the product down into its components and sub-components and therefore is able to estimate the supplier's material cost under consideration of product weight and the current material price. Supply chain cost can be approximated by fuel cost or quoted freight rates. Manufacturing costs are all supplier cost related to labor, energy and capital expenditure (CapEx). Labor costs are derived from working hours and country-specific wages under consideration of the supplier's production footprint. Energy costs are all cost related to electricity, natural gas or crude oil required for the manufacturing process. CapEx are all costs related to investment in plants, buildings, technology, machinery and tools. Manufacturing cost plus overhead cost for administrative tasks plus a reasonable profit margin results in a product's or service's should-cost.

The delta between estimated should-cost and the quoted supplier price is the monetary value that can be negotiated in supplier negotiations. Therefore, a detailed cost breakdown and should-cost model is a strong argument and basis for successful supplier negotiations and therefore industrial standard even apart from the automotive industry where it originally was developed. Furthermore, should-cost modeling can also be used to discuss the supplier's individual space for productivity

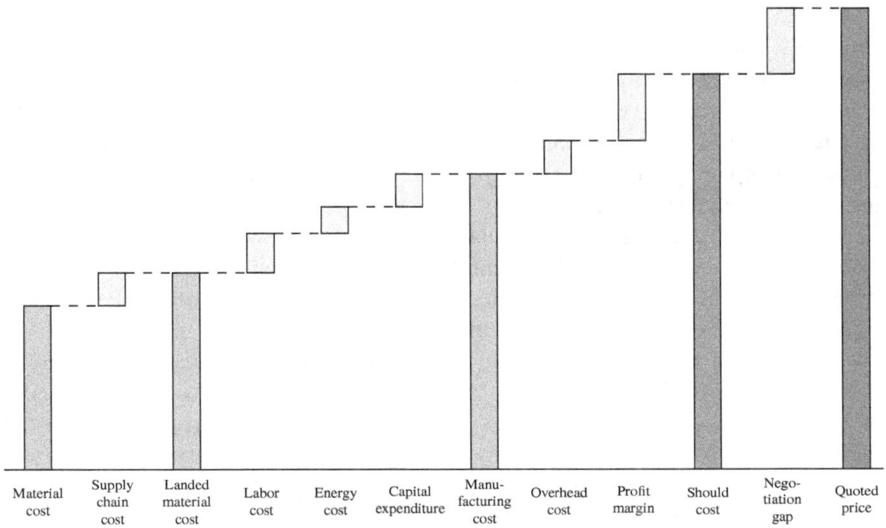

Fig. 3.9 Cost breakdown in should-cost modeling

improvement. For instance, high supply chain cost can recommend an optimization of the supply network, labor cost deltas can recommend the relocation of production facilities and high energy cost can recommend financial hedging or long-term contracting.

On the other hand, should-cost analysis is associated with a very high effort, expertise and cost to build up the bottom-up cost model on the greenfield if the cost breakdown cannot be requested from suppliers during the RFQ, which typically is only realistic if the buyer is in a strong negotiation position.

3.4.2 Linear Performance Pricing (LPP)

Linear performance pricing (LPP) that is sometimes also called linear price performance measurement (LPPM) or cost regression analysis is a popular method in spend analytics in order to identify savings potential, price inconsistencies or outliers across suppliers, for instance, in preparation of supplier negotiations (see [2]). In opposite to the bottom-up approach of should-cost modeling, LPP follows a top-down approach starting at the quoted price and the performance specifications of a product or a service rather than with an (estimated) cost breakdown. While a detailed cost breakdown is hardly accessible from suppliers in practice, quoted price and performance specifications are easily obtainable as a result of RFQ processes that provide a huge data lake for LPP applications.

LPP is closely related to target pricing or target costing concepts and was originally introduced by the management consulting firm McKinsey & Company (see [4]) for short-term cost cutting. Today, LPP is positioned as an industrial standard and part of the toolbox of nearly every procurement consulting firm. LPP is also related to invoice price variance (IPV) analysis, which analyzes discrepancies between supplier prices or agreed purchase prices and invoice prices. This can uncover hidden overpayments.

While ABC analysis typically classifies items or suppliers with a focus on price or spend, the general idea behind LPP is to compare different offers (from different suppliers) with regard to price and performance. Therefore, LPP (i) creates transparency, (ii) identifies price inconsistencies (e.g., outliers), (iii) calculates an adequate target price and (iv) triggers data-driven supplier (re-)negotiations. A requirement for LPP is that performance of a product or service is measurable (e.g., via technical parameters such as weight, lifetime, dimensions, electrical performance in Watt, fuel consumption or torque or service parameters such as lead time, delay, complaint rate, etc.). Technically, LPP compares a large number of price quotes through a linear regression model that fits the functional relationship $P(X)$ between those performance parameters X and the price offers P of the suppliers with a and b_i being the estimated regression coefficients and ϵ_t being the error term.

$$P(X) = a + \sum_{i=1}^{n} b_i X_i + \epsilon_t \tag{3.29}$$

Based on the LPP formula, one can calculate the target price for any combination of product or service specification. If the product price is driven by one major performance parameter, a simple regression model with a single explanatory variable can be used. For instance, the target price $P(X)$ of packaging material might mainly depend on the surface (in square meters). If the product price is driven by several performance parameters, a multiple regression model is needed. For instance, the target price of a battery might, for example, be characterized by several factors such as charging time, life time and capacity. The target price of a robot might be expressed by the features arm length and load-carrying capacity, and the price of a ride service might depend on distance, type of car and time.

Figure 3.10 illustrates the general idea behind LPP for a product with one major performance parameter. Each dot represents a supplier offer for an item characterized by a specific performance or technical product value. LPP is characterized by two regression lines: the market line P^M and the benchmark line P^B.

P^M represents the average market price curve over all price quotes available (across all suppliers). In this example, it is characterized by $P^M(X) = 5.98 + 3.36 \cdot X$ with regression statistics $R^2 = 0.75$ and $p < 0.01$ for all fitted parameters, which indicates statistically significant results.

P^B as the benchmark line determines the price benchmark and represents the target price. There are three approaches to determine P^B: (i) P^B can be represented

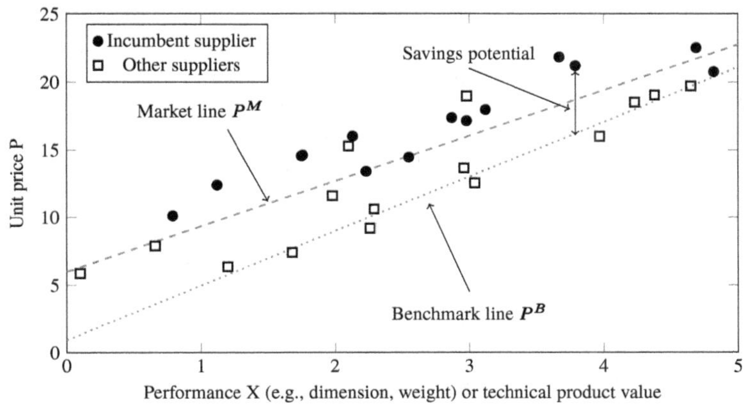

Fig. 3.10 Concept of LPP

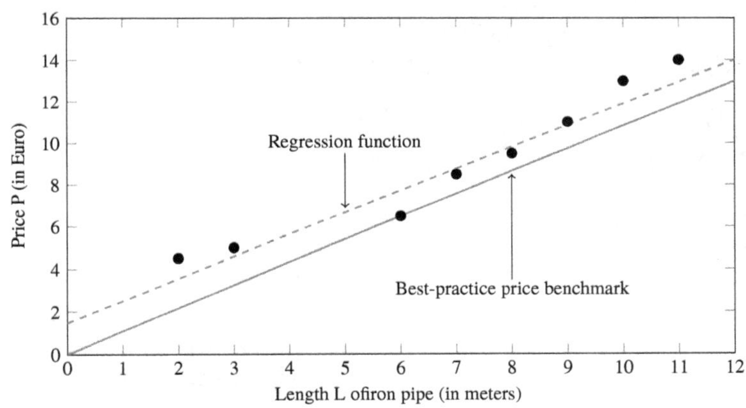

Fig. 3.11 LPP results

as the regression line of a subset of price points. For instance, in Fig. 3.10, P^B is represented by the regression line of the top 33% price offers, i.e., the top 33% of prices with highest savings potential compared to the market line P^M. In this example, it is fitted by $P^M = 0.92 + 4.04 \cdot X$. Alternatively, P^B can also be calculated through (ii) a shift of the market line toward the offer with the best price-performance ratio (see example from Fig. 3.11) or (iii) by fitting a line between the two offers with the best price-performance ratio.

From the example from Fig. 3.10, it gets obvious that the price quotes of the incumbent supplier are significantly above the market level and not competitive with price offers from other suppliers, which may have different reasons such as higher production cost, higher raw material cost, higher profit margins or over-engineering and over-specification.

An effective LPP procedure follows the subsequent steps: (i) Identify potential cost drivers; (ii) collect price and specification data (e.g., from an RFQ, the ERP system or the engineering department); (iii) fit a regression model (market line) over all data points and interpret output under consideration of R^2 and p values (see Chap. 2); (iv) fit another regression line (benchmark line) based on a reduced data set that represents, for instance, 33% of the top price offers relative to the market line; (v) calculate cost savings potential per supplier based on the price deviation to the benchmark line multiplied by purchase volumes; and (vi) use the LPP results of items with high savings potential for data-driven supplier negotiations with incumbent and potential suppliers and for supplier awarding decisions under consideration of supplier switching and ramp-up cost.

Numerical Example: LPP with Single Performance Parameter
A purchase manager wants to apply LPP for her preparation of price negotiations of iron pipes. LPP should identify an accurate target price for iron pipes with a length of 4 meters. The purchase manager does not have historical price offers for 4m-pipes but has access to supplier offers for other pipe length that are summarized in Table 3.4.

All pipes have the same caliber (10 cm) and wall thickness (2 mm) and only differ in length. What is an appropriate target price for the upcoming supplier negotiations?

Leveraging LPP with a linear regression model over all data points, we obtain the linear relationship between pipe length (L) and price (P) by $P^M = 1.465 + 1.076 \cdot L$ ($R^2 = 0.94$). Inserting a length of $L = 4$ meter into the regression function, we obtain a price of $P^M = 5.77$ Euro. However, we might not want to use this price for supplier negotiations as we observe that there is a best practice price benchmark of 6.5 Euro for 6 meters that gives us a best practice price benchmark function of $P^B = 6.5/6 \cdot L = 1.083 \cdot L$. Inserting a length of $L = 4$ meter into the best practice benchmark, we receive a price of $P^B = 4.33$ Euro that we would use as a data-driven starting point for supplier negotiations.

Table 3.4 Data: Pipe length and corresponding supplier price

Pipe length in m	2	3	6	7	8	9	10	11
Supplier price in Euro	4.5	5	6.5	8.5	9.5	11	13	14

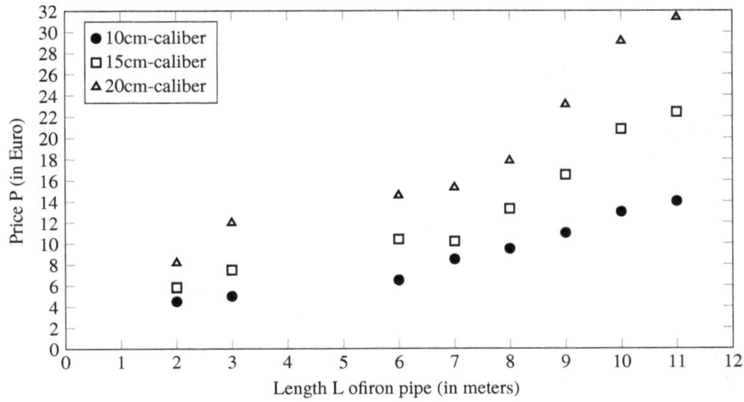

Fig. 3.12 LPP input: Supplier price offers

Numerical Example: LPP with Multiple Performance Parameters
The results from the previous example are valuable for iron pipes of a caliber of 10 cm, however do not help for calibers of 12 cm. For identifying a data-driven target price for calibers of 12 cm, additional data for calibers of 15 cm and 20 cm is available as summarized in Fig. 3.12.

Given the additional data, a multiple linear regression model with the factors pipe length (L) and caliber (C) is calculated resulting in price formula $P^M(L, C) = -13.43 + 1.76 \cdot L + 0.99 \cdot C$ ($R^2 = 0.88$, $p < 0.001$). This yields a target price of 5.49 Euro for a pipe length of 4 m and a caliber of 12 cm.

A major benefit of LPP is that it creates price transparency and quickly identifies and quantifies price inconsistencies. It is therefore another method for supplier classification (e.g., suppliers above market price level versus suppliers below market price level) and supplier evaluation (high performers versus low performers). If inconsistencies come from incumbent suppliers, LPP allows to quickly calculate savings potential by either re-negotiating prices with the inconsistent supplier or switching from the inconsistent supplier to another supplier. Even though there might be reasons for price deltas, LPP generates a shifting of the burden of proof toward the supplier, who now needs to argue where the price delta to the market or benchmark prices come from. The buyer should prioritize those items that yield the highest savings potential, i.e., price inconsistency multiplied by the purchase volume of this item. Furthermore, LPP is able to analyze the potential of supplier bundling or consolidation as it uncovers whenever two or more identical items are purchased from different suppliers at different prices. Another advantage of LPP is that it is simple and therefore easy to communicate and execute. LPP results can be updated very quickly as soon as the general database is available. Compared to the bottom-up approach of should-cost modeling, LPP is associated with significantly less effort, know-how and cost as there is no disassembly of the product required. Furthermore, LPP is also beneficial from a supplier perspective as it generates price transparency across competitors and is therefore a useful (and free of charge) benchmark.

The main challenge of LPP is to correctly quantify and assign performance. There might be product characteristics that drive the price but are difficult to specify and measure (e.g., design). In general, LPP is only applicable if product and parts have clear and measurable cost drivers. Second, LPP is based on historical values; however, price levels change over time due to inflation, deflation or learning curve effects at suppliers. Therefore, the time dimension of price quotes may be crucial to be considered. Additionally, dumping prices or temporary price discounts skew the input data. Moreover, LPP is based on regression analysis and therefore requires that all regression assumptions are met by the underlying price-performance data (see Chap. 2 for technical details). Furthermore, LPP is a very simplistic method that gives a first impression about the market potential. For complex products, it may only be applicable in combination with cost engineering. In this case, X represents the technical product value resulting from should-cost modeling, and subsequently LPP analyzes whether the quoted supplier price represents the technical value of the product or not. Last but not least, LPP assumes a linear relationship between price and performance parameters, which is often not true in practice. In this case, nonlinear performance pricing (NLPP) can help.

3.4.3 Nonlinear Performance Pricing (NLPP)

In many real-world applications, the general assumptions of linear regression and therefore LPP are not fulfilled (see Chap. 2). For instance, the relationship between price and product characteristics can also be nonlinear, i.e.,

$$P(X) = a + \sum_{i=1}^{n} b_i f_i(X_i) + \epsilon \tag{3.30}$$

with $f_i(X_i)$ as a nonlinear function. A nonlinear function between price and features is, for instance, reasonable assuming that the marginal price is increasing with performance. Another reason could be that there are fewer manufacturers and therefore fewer competition in high-performance environments, which allows the few available suppliers to ask for relatively high prices at high-performance segments. This can be modeled by an exponential function of the following form and refers to nonlinear performance pricing:

$$P(X) = e^{a+b_1X_1+b_2X_2+b_3X_3+...+b_nX_n} \tag{3.31}$$

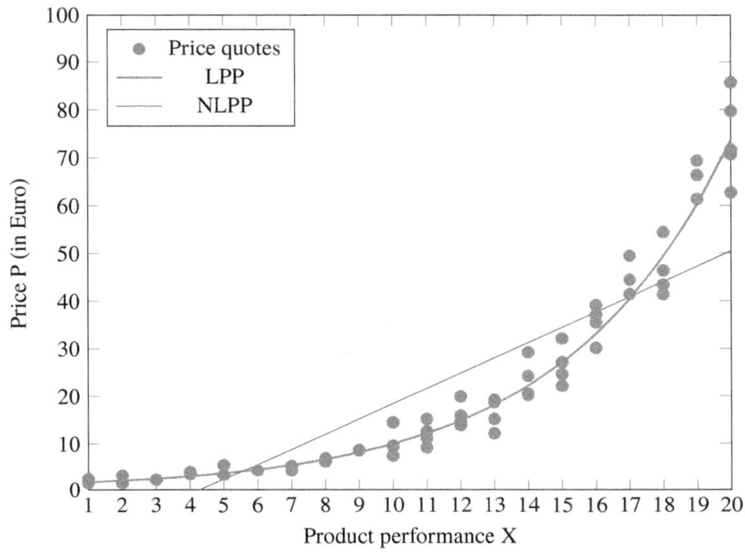

Fig. 3.13 Concept of nonlinear performance pricing

Figure 3.13 shows a nonlinear relationship between the price and product performance that is fitted by a nonlinear regression approach with $P = e^{0.3+0.2 \cdot X}$. A LPP approach would fit a relationship $P = -13.8 + 3.2 \cdot X$ and would not correctly represent the underlying pattern. This yields non-adequate target prices. While LPP that is based on linear regression can even be executed via spreadsheet software such as Excel, NLPP requires the execution of nonlinear regression (e.g., polynomial regression) via, for example, the statistical programming language `R` using function `nls()` or `Python` using `sklearn` function `PolynomialFeatures()`.

References

1. Kraljic P (1983) Purchasing must become supply management. Harvard Business Review 09/10:109–117.
2. Newman WR, Krehbiel TC (2007) Linear performance pricing: a collaborative tool for focused supply cost reduction. J Purch Supply Manag 13(1):152–165
3. Schuh C, Raudabaugh JL, Kromoser R, Strohmer MF, Triplat A, Pearce J (2017) The Purchasing Chessboard—64 Methods to Reduce Costs and Increase Value with Suppliers, 3rd edn. Springer, Berlin
4. McKinsey & Company (2003) McKinsey & Company details linear performance pricing. Automotive OE Supplier News 6:5–8
5. Wildemann H (2006) Global Sourcing—Erfolg versprechende Strategieableitung. In: Blecker T (ed) Wertschöpfungsnetzwerke, 1st edn. Erich Schmidt, New York

Chapter 4
Data-Driven Supplier Management

Abstract This chapter presents analytical models and use cases for data-driven decision-making in buyer-supplier relationships. It covers standard sourcing strategies (e.g., make or buy), digital tender management, auction theory, bid analytics, game theory in supplier negotiations and multi-criteria supplier selection and evaluation techniques. It furthermore addresses analytical methods for supply network optimization under cost, sustainability, risk and resilience aspects and data-driven planning approaches for supply contracting and supply chain coordination.

Keywords Tender management · Bid analytics · Auction theory · Negotiation games · Multi-criteria decision-making · Supply network optimization · Supply chain coordination

4.1 Introduction

A major field of procurement is supplier management, which covers a broad range of topics such as tender management, supplier negotiations, supplier selection and evaluation, supplier contracting and coordination as well as supplier relationship management.

Apart from that, spend management heavily depends on selected sourcing strategies: Make versus buy decisions determine whether suppliers are needed at all. Global versus local sourcing decisions determine the geographical radius for supplier scouting, and multi-sourcing versus single-sourcing decisions determine the number of suppliers that need to be identified and awarded as well as order allocation, i.e., how much volume to allocate to the primary source and how much to the dual (or multi) source. In Sect. 4.2 we provide data-driven and analytical models to support those strategic decisions.

After having defined the direction with regard to strategic sourcing decisions, the natural next step is to start a tender with supplier scouting via an RFI process, supplier bidding via an RFQ process and potentially an auction mechanism. Today, these steps are typically executed via digital tools. This allows to effectively and efficiently consider a huge number of potential suppliers and analyze results via bid

C. Mandl, *Procurement Analytics*, Springer Series in Supply Chain Management 22, https://doi.org/10.1007/978-3-031-43281-1_4

analytics and scenario techniques for an optimal awarding decision. In Sect. 4.3, we give an overview of digital tender management including RFX analysis, bid analytics and auction design covering both single-item procurement auctions (sealed-bid first and second price auctions, English auctions, Dutch auctions and Japanese auctions) and multi-item procurement auctions (combinatorial auctions).

Tenders often result in a pre-selection of three to five suppliers that are invited to supplier negotiations. Today, negotiations are widely supported by data and data analytics that provide a fact-based and quantitative argumentation including market developments, analysis of the supplier's historical performance, analysis of reservation prices and benchmark analysis including offers from competitors. The results of data analysis help derive optimal negotiation strategies based on psychological and game-theoretic concepts that are introduced in Sect. 4.4.

After being selected, supplier's performance needs regularly to be evaluated relative to its competitors and over time across various criteria such as cost, quality or lead time. Methods from multi-criteria decision-making (MCDM) offer concrete and objectified data-driven decision support for supplier selection evaluation. In Sect. 4.5 we illustrate simple MCDM methods such as the weighted sum model and the analytic hierarchy process as well as more advanced methods based on mathematical optimization such as data envelopment analysis and problem-specific linear programming formulations.

Given the huge amount of suppliers along the supply chain, supply network design and optimization is a complex task that is not manageable without analytical models and tools. In today's VUCA[1] world, deterministic planning approaches that do not account for uncertainty are typically not appropriate anymore. Stochastic models based on scenarios and probabilities are required for deriving robust supply networks under risk aspects such as demand risk, supply disruption risk or exchange rate risk. In addition, network design decisions require a multi-objective approach that addresses cost, resilience and sustainability goals simultaneously and potentially leads to significantly different supply networks (e.g., multi-sourcing networks or local-for-local networks) compared to a pure cost-centric focus that typically yields a global single-source footprint. In Sect. 4.6, we cover data-driven and analytical methods for deterministic and stochastic supply network planning and also address how resilience and sustainability aspects can be considered in quantitative decision models.

Another task in supplier management is supply contracting and supply chain coordination, which is addressed in Sect. 4.7. This includes decisions on contract parameters with regard to pricing schemes (e.g., linear pricing scheme or two-part tariffs), quantity flexibility and buy-back conditions or revenue-sharing mechanisms between the buyer and the supplier (i.e., vertical purchasing agreements). Furthermore, horizontal purchasing agreements and cooperative sourcing between several buyers (e.g., through purchasing conglomerates) provide additional savings potential that can be assessed through the use of analytical models. Subsequently,

[1] Volatility, Uncertainty, Complexity, Ambiguity.

benefit allocation mechanisms such as the Shapley value allow to allocate savings between the cooperating parties in a fair way.

4.2 Sourcing Strategies

4.2.1 Make or Buy

Make or buy is an essential strategic decision that determines responsibilities, i.e., whether it is a procurement or a production topic. While a *make* decision guarantees independence and fosters internal knowledge building, *buy* reduces fixed cost, opens doors to supplier innovations and often provides a better price due to economies of scale and learning curve effects at suppliers that produce high volumes for a variety of customers.

Industry Example: Make or Buy in the Automotive Industry
With the political decision to switch to electric cars in the future, automotive OEMs needed to decide whether to produce battery cells on its own or purchase them from suppliers. While an own production would guarantee independence for these strategic items (in particular from leading Asian cell suppliers such as Panasonic, CATL, BYD and LGChem), it would also require high investment cost and the buildup of deep expertise and know-how. The make-or-buy decisions of some major OEMs show that this is not a trivial decision. While German carmaker Volkswagen decided for producing batteries, Daimler and BMW decided to *buy* rather than *make*. However, the market is continuously monitored, and to switch from *buy* to *make* is not a completely unrealistic scenario for the future.

Another example is automotive software. Most OEMs strive for (more) independence of tech giants such as Apple, Google or Microsoft and therefore focus on software engineering rather than outsourcing. For instance, Volkswagen established the software brand CARIAD in 2019 with the objective to increase the in-house engineering rate for automotive software from 10% to at least 60%.

Various frameworks and methods are available for supporting the decision. In the following, we present the cost-based break-even analysis, the net present value analysis from cost accounting, a linear programming approach and qualitative make-or-buy portfolio techniques.

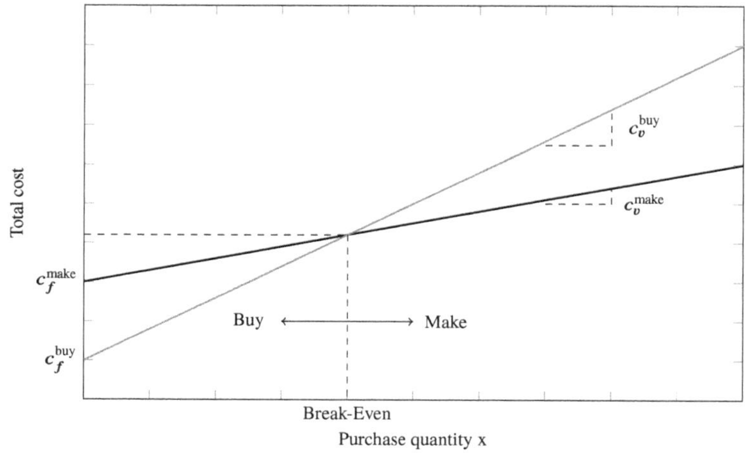

Fig. 4.1 Break-even analysis for make-or-buy decisions

Break-Even Analysis

Traditionally, the decision between make (own production capacities) and buy (outsourcing) was mainly driven by cost. In this case, a break-even analysis gives a recommendation between make or buy by comparing the total cost of both options (see Fig. 4.1). While building own production capacities (make) is typically favorable if production or purchase quantities are sufficiently large due to high investments (fixed cost), outsourcing (buy) is favorable whenever purchase quantities are small, which makes higher variable cost acceptable. For an accurate break-even analysis, it is essential to follow a total cost of ownership approach that captures all cost that occur including transaction costs such as search and information cost for supplier screening, bargaining cost and enforcement cost to make sure that suppliers fulfill contractual agreements. Those costs are aggregated into fixed cost c_f and variable cost c_v such that total cost of both options is given by

$$C^{\text{buy}} = c_f^{\text{buy}} + x \cdot c_v^{\text{buy}} \tag{4.1}$$

and

$$C^{\text{make}} = c_f^{\text{make}} + x \cdot c_v^{\text{make}} \tag{4.2}$$

respectively. x is the purchase or production quantity. Typically, $c_f^{\text{make}} > c_f^{\text{buy}}$ and $c_v^{\text{make}} < c_v^{\text{buy}}$ as shown in Fig. 4.1.

Based on the general relationships between fixed cost c_f and variable cost c_v, the break-even analysis derives a make recommendation if one of the following three cases applies:

$$c_f^{\text{make}} \leq c_f^{\text{buy}} \text{and } c_v^{\text{make}} \leq c_v^{\text{buy}} \tag{4.3}$$

independent of purchase quantity x or

$$c_f^{\text{make}} \leq c_f^{\text{buy}} \text{and } c_v^{\text{make}} > c_v^{\text{buy}} \tag{4.4}$$

if

$$x < \frac{c_f^{\text{buy}} - c_f^{\text{make}}}{c_v^{\text{make}} - c_v^{\text{buy}}} \tag{4.5}$$

or

$$c_f^{\text{make}} \geq c_f^{\text{buy}} \text{and } c_v^{\text{make}} < c_v^{\text{buy}} \tag{4.6}$$

if

$$x > \frac{c_f^{\text{make}} - c_f^{\text{buy}}}{c_v^{\text{buy}} - c_v^{\text{make}}}. \tag{4.7}$$

Net Present Value Analysis

The *net present value (NPV) analysis* is a dynamic method from cost accounting for decision-making whenever to choose between several (investment) options or whenever to evaluate whether a decision option is economically beneficial. The NPV is calculated by

$$\text{NPV} = \sum_{t=1}^{T} CF_t \cdot (1+i)^{-t} - I_0 \tag{4.8}$$

with CF_t as the cash flow in period t (e.g., year), i as the market interest rate and I_0 as the initial investment. NPV allows a simple interpretation. If $NPV > 0$, then the decision option is economically beneficial (with a return above market return). If $NPV < 0$, then a decision option is economically not beneficial (with a return below market return). Whenever two options have a positive NPV, then the decision option with higher NPV is preferable.

In the context of make or buy, NPV requires to estimate (predict) cash flows over a specific planning horizon for both decision options, i.e., make and buy. This requires to follow the concept of *Total Cost of Ownership* in order not to miss important cost implications. Opposed to break-even analysis, NPV also considers revenues, which might differ between the two options, make and buy, due to different capacity restrictions or different productivity. Therefore, the make option should include revenue estimates under consideration of capacity restrictions, initial and follow-up investment cost, maintenance cost, labor cost and energy cost. The buy option should include revenue estimates under consideration of supply capacity restrictions, unit purchase cost (excluding discounts), transportation cost, customs, duties and inventory cost (due to required safety stock).

Linear Programming

Linear programming is adequate for make-or-buy decisions whenever break-even analysis or standard cost accounting methods are not sufficient due to, for example, capacity restrictions and bottlenecks. In this case, a linear programming model for a make-or-buy decision problem under cost minimization objectives can look as follows:

$$\text{minimize} \quad \sum_{i=1}^{I} c_i^b \cdot x_i^b + c_i^m \cdot x_i^m \tag{4.9}$$

$$\text{s.t.} \quad x_i^b + x_i^m = d_i \qquad \forall i = 1, \ldots, I \tag{4.10}$$

$$\sum_{i=1}^{I} a_{ij} \cdot x_i^m \leq A_j \qquad \forall j = 1, \ldots, J \tag{4.11}$$

$$x_i^m, x_i^b \geq 0 \qquad \forall i = 1, \ldots, I \tag{4.12}$$

The decision-maker needs to decide about quantities for make x_i^m and purchase quantities x_i^b of products $i = 1, \ldots, I$. c_i^m is the unit cost for the make option, while c_i^b is the unit cost for the buy option. Product demand d_i needs to be satisfied either by the make option x_i^m or by the buy option x_i^b. The make option requires machine capacity a_{ij} on machines $j = 1, \ldots, J$. Resources for in-house production are restricted by A_j.

Numerical Example: LP for Make-or-Buy Decision-Support
Assume that a company needs to decide for make or buy for three components $i = 1, 2, 3$. Demand data d_i is given in units ($d_1 = 5{,}000$, $d_2 = 2{,}500$, $d_3 = 3{,}000$). Unit cost c_i^m for *make* is given by $c_1^m = 6$, $c_2^m = 8$ and $c_3^m = 9$. Unit cost c_i^b for *buy* is given by $c_1^b = 6$, $c_2^b = 10$ and $c_3^b = 11$. Therefore,

(continued)

the option to *make* is in general favorable (except for component 1 where the decision-maker is indifferent between the two options). However, resources for in-house production are restricted. For producing components $i = 1, 2, 3$, two manufacturing steps on machines $j = 1, 2$ are required with machine 1's capacity being limited to 10,000 hours, while machine 2's capacity is limited to 5,000 hours. Each component i requires a different machine capacity in minutes that is given by $a_{11} = 2$, $a_{12} = 1$, $a_{21} = 2$, $a_{22} = 2$, $a_{31} = 3$ and $a_{32} = 1$.

Solving the model with any optimization solver results in a minimum total cost of 80,500 with component 1 fully being sourced from suppliers, component 2 50% being sourced and 50% being manufactured and component 3 with 500 units being sourced and 2,500 units being manufactured.

Make-or-Buy Portfolio

While break-even analysis, NPV analysis and linear programming mainly rely on cost or revenue figures, the make-or-buy portfolio addresses another relevant dimension, which is risk in terms of market availability.

The make-or-buy portfolio as illustrated in Fig. 4.2 recommends to build own production capacities if the strategic relevance of the product or service is high and at the same time market availability is low, which is the case, for example, for electric vehicle batteries. On the other hand, if strategic relevance is rather low

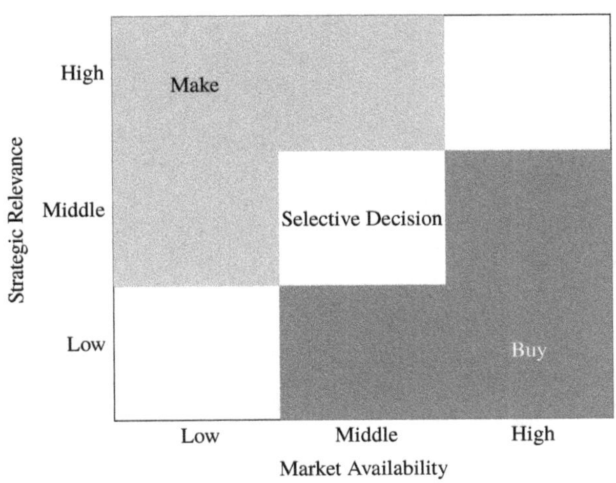

Fig. 4.2 Make-or-buy portfolio

and market availability is high (e.g., screws), it is recommended to outsource and leverage negotiation power at the supplier markets.

The buy decision in make or buy is also related to the terms *outsourcing*, i.e., moving internal processes to a third party; *offshoring*, i.e., moving internal processes to a foreign country; and *friendshoring*, i.e., restricting trade (e.g., with suppliers) to countries with common values.

4.2.2 Supplier Partnerships

Besides *make* or *buy*, there is also the option to *cooperate* with suppliers in the form of supplier partnerships. Partnerships can be characterized by long-term contracts, exclusive supply or even vertical integration of the supplier. Deep collaboration with selected suppliers is expected to increase in the future with regard to supplier-driven innovation that buyers want to have (exclusive) access to.

To support the decision between the three options, *make*, *buy* and *cooperate*, transaction cost theory can be used, which distinguishes between the two dimensions, asset specificity and uncertainty (Fig. 4.3). Asset specificity means that a product, process or location is configured to a specific supplier. Transaction cost theory states that the higher the asset specificity and uncertainty, the higher the probability that companies source their input within their own organization. Make and cooperate decreases the incentives for opportunistic behavior of suppliers.

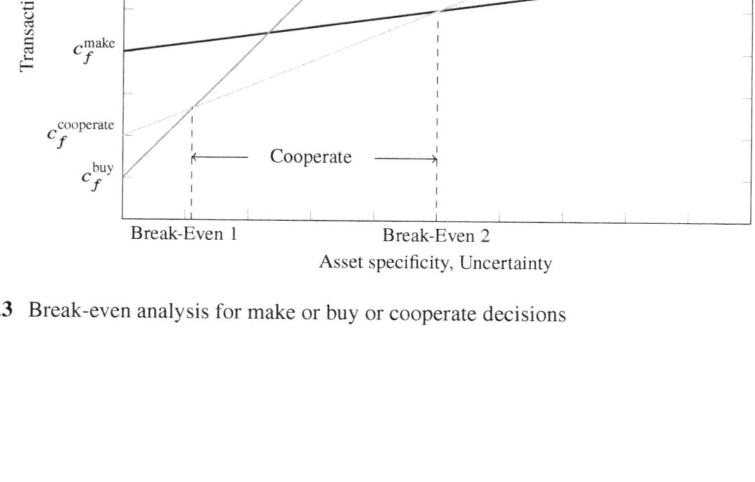

Fig. 4.3 Break-even analysis for make or buy or cooperate decisions

Industry Example: Supplier Collaborations at Volkswagen
In 2015, Volkswagen introduced the FAST (Future Automotive Supply Tracks) program to intensify collaboration with around 50 strategic suppliers in selected areas of competence (e.g., SAP for process digitization, Bosch for control devices or Schaeffler for couplings). The goal is to better align processes through standardization and collaboratively drive innovations. For battery supply, Volkswagen goes even one step further and invested in the battery start-up Northvolt in 2019.

4.2.3 Global Sourcing Versus Local Sourcing

The decision between global sourcing and local sourcing is mainly a geography-driven decision.

Reasons for **global sourcing** are lower purchase cost due to significantly lower labor cost (low-cost country sourcing, best-cost country sourcing), access to an extended supplier base, access to limited resources (e.g., rare-earth elements), development of new (sales) markets, cost and performance pressure on local suppliers, exchange rate benefits and lower environmental protection standards.

Reasons for **local sourcing** are lower transportation cost and lead times, lower logistical risk, reduced number of transportation modes required, lower transaction cost (e.g., communication, order process), higher flexibility (rush orders, small orders, after-sales service) and a positive image in the region.

A recent trend is **local for local sourcing**, i.e., a geographical conglomeration of suppliers, production sites and customers. It requires the development of autonomous supply chains in the target region and has the following benefits: lower transportation cost, higher flexibility, lower lead times, higher security of supply, lower safety stocks, elimination of exchange rate risk and satisfaction of local content requirements. On the other hand, it increases administrative effort and may reduce economies of scale through local sourcing in smaller lot sizes.

However, what is the right balance between local and global sourcing? From an analytical perspective, cost-based and risk-based supplier selection and supply network design models can support the decision between global and local sourcing (see Sect. 4.6). Same is true for simple allocation rules and tailored base-surge policies (see Sect. 4.2.4). While pure cost minimization objectives typically yield a global sourcing footprint and pure risk minimization objectives typically yield a local sourcing footprint, a multi-objective focus on both cost and risk leads to a combination of global and local sourcing through, for instance, multi-sourcing that is addressed in the next section.

4.2.4 Multi-sourcing Versus Single Sourcing

Multi-sourcing versus single sourcing differs in the number of utilized suppliers. While multi-sourcing states that there is more than one supplier used for a specific item or service, single sourcing states that there is one supplier used even though more than one supplier is available for the corresponding item or service. Sole sourcing on the other hand states that a single source is used because only one supplier offers the corresponding item or service, i.e., there is no alternative supplier.

The benefits of **multi-sourcing** are supplier competition with potentially lower purchase cost, risk diversification and reduction of dependencies, higher flexibility and satisfaction of local content requirements.

The benefits of **single sourcing** are economies of scale through higher lot sizes, higher negotiation power, development of long-term supplier partnerships and reduction of process complexity and cost (i.e., process cost, logistics cost, negotiation cost, communication cost).

Whenever a company follows a multi-sourcing strategy (e.g., dual sourcing), the procurement function needs to decide on how to allocate demand to the different sources (*order allocation problem*). To support this decision, different simple rules of thumb are applied, but also more advanced allocation policies are available (e.g., tailored base-surge policies).

Rules of Thumb for Order Allocation

In order to allocate orders to suppliers, practice typically uses simple rules of thumb. The simplest rule is the *1/N rule* that allocates supply equally across N suppliers (with $N = 2$ for dual sourcing).

Another rule often applied in practice is the 70-20-10 rule, i.e., allocating 70% of the demand to the cheapest source, 20% to the less risky source and 10% to any other source(s).

In the context of dual sourcing under uncertain demand, the three-quarters allocation rule is applied (see, e.g., [1]), i.e., allocating roughly 75% to a global low-cost source that is slow and 25% to a flexible but more expensive local source.

Tailored Base-Surge Policy for Order Allocation

Dual sourcing is a complex management task. Effective dual sourcing uses suppliers with different strengths. This can be a low-cost source (e.g., offshoring, global sourcing) that is less flexible and far away and a responsive source (e.g., nearshoring, local sourcing) that is more expensive but can react quickly to surges in demand (see, e.g., [1, 2]).

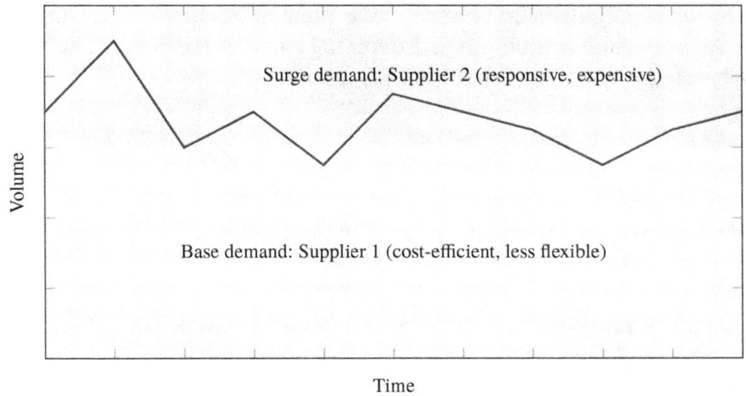

Fig. 4.4 Base-surge policy for dual sourcing

The presented rules of thumb do not consider the impact of system parameters such as holding cost, cost differentials between suppliers and supply-demand volatility on the optimal allocation decision.

In this case, mathematical optimization helps derive optimal dual-sourcing policies that optimally allocate a base demand to the cost-efficient but high-risk and less-flexible global source and the surge demand to a local source that is highly flexible, low risk and highly responsive (see Fig. 4.4).

Base and surge demand are determined under the objective to minimize total landed cost (TLC), i.e., the end-to-end cost from source to sold, which is the sum of cost of goods sold (COGS) including material cost, labor cost and overhead cost, plus supply chain cost (i.e., shipping cost, duties, customs and taxes), plus working capital (e.g., inventory safety stocks depending on service level requirements, lead time and demand-supply volatility).

However, the computation of optimal dual-sourcing policies via dynamic programming is computationally complex due to the well-known curse of dimensionality. Therefore, a good approximation in practice is the tailored base-surge policy (TBS) introduced by [1, 2]. This policy yields a near-optimal solution where inventory is replenished at a constant rate (base allocation) from the high-risk supply location, and surges in demand are covered from the expensive location according to the following formula:

$$\text{Base Allocation} \simeq 1 - \sigma \cdot \sqrt{\frac{h}{2\Delta c\lambda}} \tag{4.13}$$

with σ as the supply-demand volatility, h as the unit holding cost including cost of capital, Δc as the unit sourcing cost differential and λ as the demand rate. If there is no supply but only demand volatility, TBS reduces to

$$\text{Base Allocation} \,\tilde{=}\, 1 - \sqrt{\frac{h}{2\Delta c}} \cdot COV_D \tag{4.14}$$

with COV_D as the coefficient of variation of the demand distribution.

Numerical Example: Drivers of Demand Allocation in Dual Sourcing
In the following, we use a simulation experiment in order to showcase the effect of the allocation drivers presented in the equation above. Therefore, we vary unit holding cost h, demand rate λ, supply-demand volatility σ and sourcing cost differential Δc (Fig. 4.5).

The results show that allocation to the low-cost supplier (base supplier) is high when (i) the holding cost is low, the expected demand rate is high, supply-demand volatility is low and sourcing cost differential is high. This is reasonable because TBS evaluates the monetary trade-off between the sourcing cost differential and inventory holding cost. If the ratio $\Delta c/h$ is large, one should allocate more to the low-cost source.

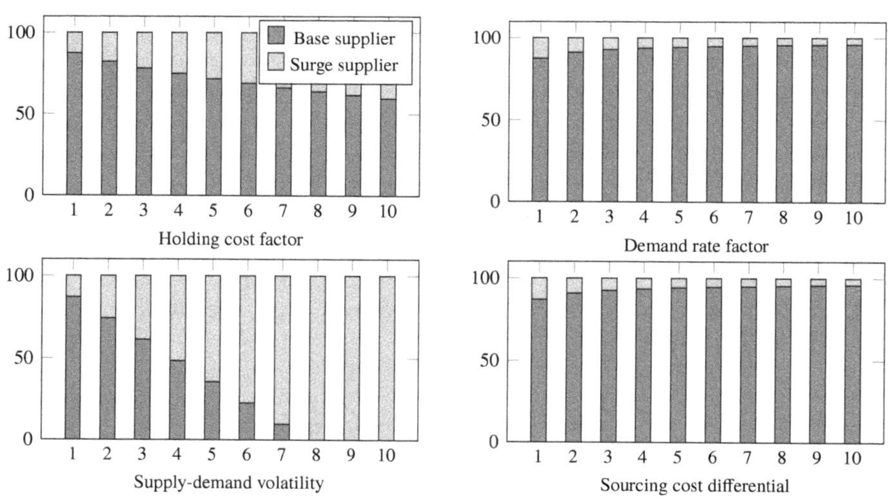

Fig. 4.5 Drivers of demand allocation in dual sourcing

4.3 Tender Management

After taking strategic sourcing decisions, suppliers are typically scouted and invited to a tender. This section covers request-for-X, reverse auctions and combinatorial auctions and gives an overview of how to use bid analytics to set up and analyze tender results for data-driven awarding decisions. This relates to the *mechanism design problem* that studies how to optimally set up tenders to achieve the best price, the *market design problem* that sets the rules and incentives to control the suppliers' behavior in order to obtain the desired results and the *winner determination problem* that derives the optimal awarding decisions in order to obtain the best possible tender results.

4.3.1 Request-for-X (RFX)

Request-for-X is the overall term for the tender processes *Request for Information (RFI)*, *Request for Quotation (RFQ)* and *Request for Proposal (RFP)*. All processes have the overall goal to optimally allocate items (products or services) to suppliers (awarding). In addition, electronic RFX processes also generate valuable external data from suppliers with regard to price quotations, lead time quotations, capacities and capabilities. This data pool is the basis for AI- and analytics-driven procurement optimization and applications such as should-cost modeling or linear and nonlinear performance pricing (see Chap. 3).

An *RFI* consists of a market screening and invitation of potential suppliers that are requested to provide information about relevant company data (contact persons, financial figures, capacity, experience). The goal of an RFI is to generate a long list of suppliers that are in general able to supply specific products or services (line items). Therefore, product specification is often already provided to suppliers during RFI. For a high supplier attraction rate, an RFI needs to be as simple as possible with drop-down queries rather than free-text queries. Digital platforms for supplier screening can support this process.

After RFI completion, an *RFQ* consolidates all potential suppliers that are able to deliver the specific product or service. The supplier pool for a RFQ consists of new suppliers with a successful RFI completion and incumbent suppliers. The buyer offers a detailed product or service specification including technical requirements and demand volumes, and the suppliers are asked to submit price offers (bids). An RFQ generates a supplier short list and typically goes over several rounds (see Fig. 4.6) with feedback and supplier shortlisting in between. An RFP is often used interchangeably with RFQ, but in case of an RFP, offers (bids) are more concrete and binding. From a game-theoretic perspective, a RFQ/RFP is a simultaneous game where each supplier considers its own dominant strategy but also anticipates the dominant strategies of the other participating suppliers. A dominant strategy is the

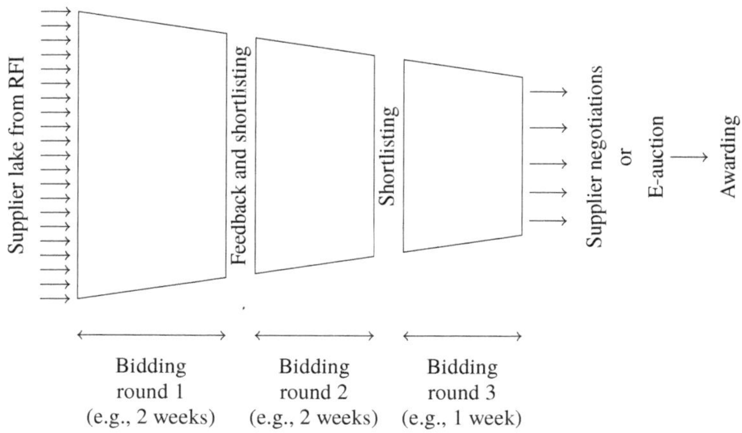

Fig. 4.6 Concept of multi-round RFQs: the RFQ funnel

utility-maximizing strategy of a player independent of the other player's actions (see Chap. 2 for details).

After typically two to three rounds of RFQ including a best and final offer (BAFO) round, there often follows either an invitation to personal supplier negotiations (see Sect. 4.4) or to a subsequent electronic auction (see Sect. 4.3.2).

During the process of RFI and RFQ, bid analytics comes into play in particular for live tracking of results. Dashboards help for real-time monitoring of savings compared to a baseline, bid coverage and implications for the profit and loss based on expected volumes.

While traditional procurement organizations used email and `Excel`, digital procurement can choose from a wide range of market offers to run a fully digitized and automated process (e.g., with Coupa, SAP Ariba, etc.). This allows to handle hundreds of suppliers for hundreds of items simultaneously. A high number of (invited) bidders and a high number of items to bid for are beneficial in terms of bidding competition and bundling potential. Furthermore, software providers also offer software to manage quick RFQs that allow to generate savings within a couple of days.

An important analytics feature of RFX processes is scenario analysis (or scenario allocation). It may be very interesting for the purchaser to understand the savings potential compared to the baseline scenario (i.e., status quo) for different supplier constellations. Therefore, one may analyze real-time savings for several relevant scenarios:

- **Best bid scenario:** Scenario that evaluates savings versus the status quo (baseline) if the best bidding supplier per line item is awarded (cherry-picking scenario). In a typical RFX process with hundreds or thousands of items, this typically leads to a large number of suppliers that are difficult to handle.

- **Incumbent bid scenario**: Scenario that evaluates savings versus the status quo (baseline) if only incumbent suppliers are awarded. Neglecting new suppliers increases reliability (in terms of supplier capabilities) and avoids implementation effort and supplier switching cost but generates the risk of missing additional savings potential.
- **Minimum number of suppliers scenario (or single award scenario):** Scenario that evaluates savings versus the status quo (baseline) generated by a minimum number of suppliers (i.e., one supplier if there is a single supplier that bids for all items). Even though a minimum number of suppliers might yield higher bid prices for items, it can be reasonable because it reduces administrative cost in the sense of supplier handling cost.
- **Supplier bundling scenario:** Limiting awarding to a specific number of suppliers only (e.g., five in total). This scenario is a compromise between the scenario with a minimum number of suppliers and the best bid scenario.

Numerical Example: RFX Bid Analytics

Suppose a company is tendering office material (i.e., printing paper, ballpoint pens and folders). The company's incumbent supplier of printing paper is supplier 3, the incumbent supplier of ballpoint pens is supplier 1 and the incumbent supplier of folders is supplier 2.

Based on the supplier bids from Table 4.1, the best bid scenario results in a purchase price of 1.870 Euro with two suppliers being awarded. The incumbent bid scenario results in a purchase price of 1.980 Euro (+5.9% compared to the best bid scenario) with three suppliers being awarded. The minimum number of suppliers scenario results in awarding supplier 3 with a resulting purchase price of 1.940 Euro (+3.7% compared to the best bid scenario). Based on a total cost of ownership approach under consideration of supplier switching cost and administrative cost for supplier handling, the purchasing manager needs to decide for awarding.

Awarding decisions are typically calculated based on the *Winner Determination Problem*, which is a mixed-integer linear program that is particularly relevant for combinatorial auctions (see Sect. 4.3.3).

Table 4.1 RFQ results for office material with bids in Euro

Item	Demand	Supplier 1	Supplier 2	Supplier 3	Supplier 4
Printing paper	50.000 sheets	650	800	700	850
Ballpoint pen	1.000 units	300	–	320	380
Folder	1.000 units	1.000	980	920	–

4.3.2 Reverse Auctions

Digital procurement leverages different auction formats that increase competition between suppliers that can bid for contracts (B2B auctions). This typically requires a high volume in order to compensate auctioning cost, sufficient competition between suppliers and the same baseline for all suppliers. Our experience shows that the direct competition between suppliers during auctions typically leads to cost savings of 5 up to 40% compared to the standard RFX process.

In procurement, we typically speak about reverse auctions (also known as buyer-determined auctions or procurement auctions) that fundamentally differ from the more common forward auction format as we know it from platforms such as eBay. A forward auction is characterized by several buyers and one seller with the seller's objective to maximize his revenue. The seller determines the starting price with prices increasing during the auction process. In contrast, a reverse auction is characterized by one buyer and several sellers with the buyer's objective to minimize her cost. The buyer determines the starting price with the price bids decreasing during the auction process.

In the procurement practice, software companies provide tools to the buyer for an efficient operation of reverse auction including different auction formats that can easily be combined with the standard RFX process. Examples are SAP Ariba (www.ariba.com), Coupa (www.coupa.com), Jaggaer (www.jaggaer.com) and Market Dojo (www.https://marketdojo.com/) among others. Most of the providers also allow for auctions-as-a-service, where the auctioning infrastructure is only used when needed. From the supplier perspective, auction bots are increasingly used for automated bidding with predefined parameters that determine the bidding strategy.

In the following, we introduce the most important reverse auction formats and mechanisms in procurement. For a detailed discussion of auctions and quantitative auction theory, we refer to the textbooks of [19, 20] and [22].

Sealed-Bid First-Price and Second-Price Auctions (Reverse)

In sealed-bid auctions, bids are made privately and simultaneously by all bidders. Bidders typically provide a single bid. In reverse sealed-bid first-price auctions, the lowest bid wins, and the awarded supplier receives the bid price. In a reverse sealed-bid second-price auction (Vickrey auctions), the bidder with the lowest bid wins and receives the second lowest bid price (Fig. 4.7). This encourages lower bidding. Game-theoretic analysis shows for second-price auctions, it is optimal for suppliers to set their bids equal to their reservation prices. However, Vickrey auctions are still not very common in practice.

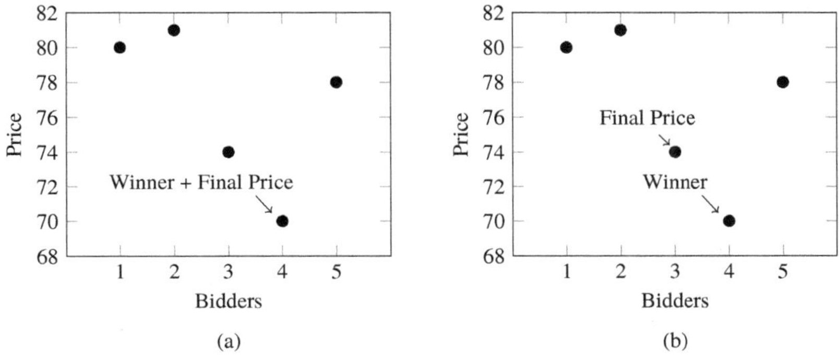

Fig. 4.7 Concept of reverse first- and second-price sealed bid auctions. (**a**) First-price auction. (**b**) Second-price auction

English Auction (Reverse)

An English auction is not private but open (public-bid), i.e., bids are transparent and can be adjusted over time. The buyer sets a specific starting price. This can be, for instance, the buyer's reservation price, i.e., the highest price the buyer is able or willing to pay. Invited suppliers alternately undercut their prices. All suppliers are free in their bids as long as the currently lowest bid is undercut (open outcry auction). Consequently, the bidding in English auctions is referred to as dynamic reverse bidding. Therefore, the suppliers observe the current best bid or at least the rank. The lowest (last) bid wins the auction. The benefit of an English auction is the game character that motivates suppliers to go (a bit) further than originally planned. Please note that English forward auctions are increasing in price.

Consequently, the buyer (or auctioneer) needs to solve the following optimization problem similar to the assignment problem (see Chap. 2) in order to derive awarding decision x_i with parameter v_i as the minimum price that bidders $i = 1, \ldots, N$ are willing to accept for the item or service.

$$\text{minimize} \quad \sum_{i=1}^{N} v_i \cdot x_i \tag{4.15}$$

$$\text{s.t.} \quad \sum_{i=1}^{N} x_i \geq 1 \tag{4.16}$$

$$x_i \in \{0, 1\} \qquad \forall i = 1, \ldots, N \tag{4.17}$$

The objective is to minimize total cost with (typically) one supplier being awarded. In case of multi-unit auctions, we refer to combinatorial auctions that are described in detail in Sect. 4.3.3.

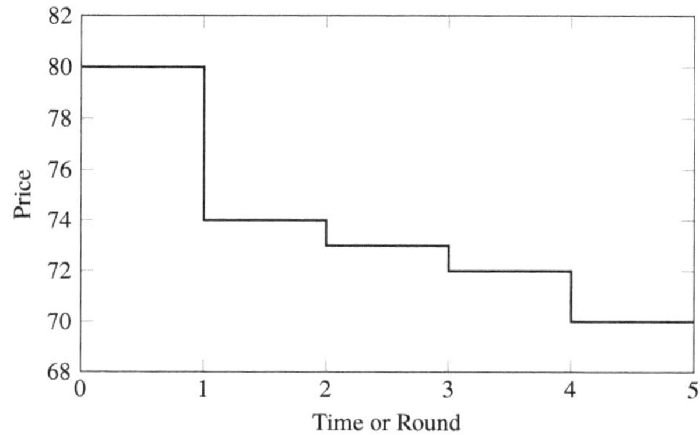

Fig. 4.8 Bid progression chart of a reverse English auction

Numerical Example: Reverse English Auction
The buyer (or auctioneer) determines a starting price of 80. Supplier A accepts. Supplier B bids 74. Supplier A bids 73. Supplier B bids 72. Supplier A bids 70. Price of 70 is not undercut. Therefore, supplier A gets awarded and receives a price of 70 (first-price auction) or 72 (second-price bid auction, Vickrey auction) (Fig. 4.8).

Dutch Auction (Reverse)

Dutch auctions are another form of public-bid auctions. The buyer sets a specific (low) starting price, which is increased stepwise until a specified reservation price is reached. The time interval between automatic constant price changes (absolute or in percent) needs to be specified by the buyer and can be, for instance, 30 seconds. Invited suppliers can bid on each step for the corresponding quoted price. Consequently, bidding in Dutch auctions is referred to as structured progressive bidding. The first (lowest) bid wins the auction (sudden death option) or if at least two suppliers accept a price level simultaneously, then a subsequent sealed-bid first price auction can follow (full step option). Dutch auctions are public-bid auctions. The benefit of a Dutch auction is that it puts maximum psychological pressure on (incumbent) suppliers, which can lead to purchase prices that are significantly better than the market price. Please note that Dutch forward auctions are decreasing in price.

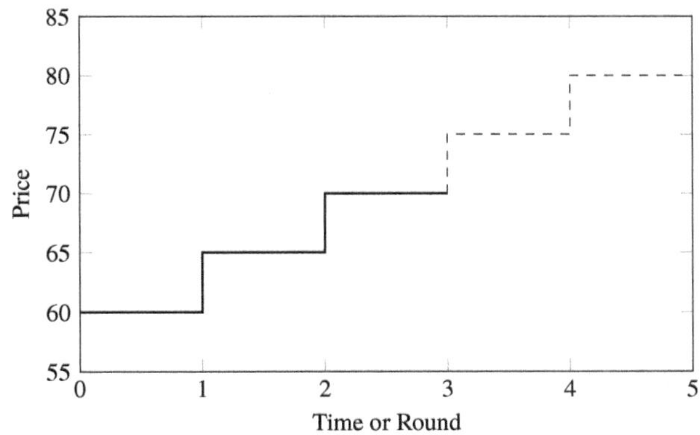

Fig. 4.9 Bid progression chart of a reverse Dutch auction

Numerical Example: Reverse Dutch Auction
Consider a reverse Dutch auction with a starting price of 60 and price increments of 5. At a price of 60, no supplier accepts. The price increases to 65. No supplier accepts. The price increases to 70. Supplier A bids and wins the auction. Supplier A gets awarded and receives a price of 70 (Fig. 4.9).

Japanese Auction (Reverse)

In Japanese auctions, the buyer sets a specific (high) starting price, which is reduced stepwise. The price needs to be confirmed by the invited suppliers at each step. Consequently, bidding in Japanese auctions is referred to as structured reverse bidding. Suppliers who do not accept need to leave the auction. The last remaining supplier wins the auction. The benefit (or drawback from a buyer's perspective?) of a Japanese auction is that suppliers get a greater transparency about the market by being able to observe how many competitors leave the auction at which price. Game theory shows that the supplier's optimal bidding behavior for Japanese auctions is to participate as long as the price is above the reservation price of the supplier. Therefore, the resulting bids from a Japanese auction may lay open the cost structure of suppliers, which can be used for bid analytics and the preparation of supplier negotiations and as a benchmark data set for should-cost analysis.

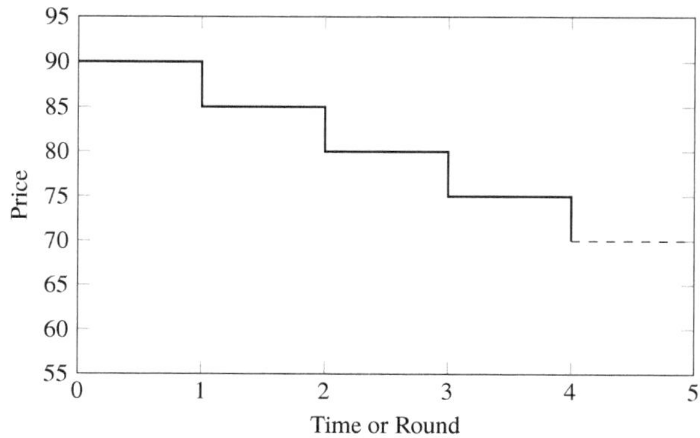

Fig. 4.10 Bid progression chart of a reverse Japanese auction

Numerical Example: Reverse Japanese Auction

Consider a reverse Japanese auction with a starting price of 90 and price decrements of 5. At a price of 90, suppliers A,B,C and D accept the price level. The price is reduced to 85. Suppliers A, B and C accept, and supplier D leaves the auction. The price is reduced to 80. Suppliers B and C accept, and supplier A leaves the auction. The price is reduced to 75. Supplier B accepts, and C leaves. Supplier B wins the auction and is awarded at a price of 75 (Fig. 4.10).

Auction Design

In addition to auction formats, the auctioneer also needs to decide on further details regarding the auction design. An auction is a *mechanism design problem* where the auctioneer aims at designing the auction in a way that minimizes its expected purchase cost. The design can be optimized based on data from historical observations or behavioral experiments.

The auctioneer needs to determine the following *auction parameters*:

- **Number of participants:** The number of participants should not be too high due to complexity reasons and not too low due to competition reasons.
- **Starting price:** For reverse English auctions and Japanese auctions, the starting price is often set to the buyer's reservation price, i.e., the highest possible price the buyer is willing/able to pay. Alternatively, if the auction follows an RFQ process, the best bid price of the RFQ can be used as starting price. For reverse Dutch auctions, the starting price can be set to an experience-based best-case price or to material cost of the item without consideration of processing, logistics cost and supplier margins. In general, it should be a realistic starting price in

order not to displease suppliers. A realistic starting price shows that the buyer knows the market.

- **Termination price:** The auctioneer can (but does not have to) determine a termination price that marks the price where the auction ends.
- **Auction duration:** The right duration of an auction strongly depends on the number of line items and the number of suppliers that are invited to bid. There can be a random stop, a hard stop (e.g., 30 minutes after the start) or a soft stop (e.g., 10 minutes after the last offer). The stopping criterion needs to be communicated upfront.
- **Time steps:** Time steps define the time interval within that the bidders need to place their bids (e.g., 30 seconds). Live auctions allow for real-time participation and bidding.
- **Price steps:** Optimizing ürice decrements (for Japanese auctions) and price increments (for Dutch auctions) is essential as too small increments/decrements can reduce supplier's motivation and too large increments/decrements can reduce competition quickly. Typically, percentage increments and decrements are reasonable (e.g., 2–4% steps). For English auctions, minimum price reductions might be defined, e.g., bidders need to bid at least 2% lower than the current lowest bid. In the following, we want to illustrate the effect of different price decrements on the final price in Japanese auctions.

Numerical Example: Effect of Price Decrements in Japanese Auctions

Suppose a Japanese reverse auction with a starting price of 10,000 EUR and two bidding suppliers (A and B). The reservation price of supplier A is 5,000 EUR, i.e., supplier A would no go below 5,000 EUR. We consider two scenarios with regard to supplier B's reservation price: 7,200 EUR (scenario 1) and 5,050 EUR (scenario 2). Table 4.2 shows the auction results for different price decrements.

The example shows that the final price (and number of rounds) can vary significantly depending on the choice of the price decrements. It furthermore shows that the Japanese auction is not recommended if suppliers' reservation prices are very different (scenario 1), which can result in a final price that is significantly above the best price achievable, i.e., 5,000 EUR in this example.

Table 4.2 Effect of different price decrements in Japanese auctions

Scenario	Price decrements	1	10	100	1,000
Scenario 1	Final price (EUR)	7,199	7,190	7,100	7,000
	No. of rounds	2,802	282	30	4
Scenario 2	Final price (EUR)	5,049	5,040	5,000	5,000
	No. of rounds	4,952	497	51	6

The example shows that it is essential for the auctioneer to better understand reservation prices of suppliers. Tools such as should-cost analysis (see Sect. 3.4.1) and linear performance pricing (see Sect. 3.4.2) can help get insights into the suppliers' cost structure and therefore can derive probabilistic information about reservation prices. In a next step, the auction designer can use simulation techniques (e.g., Monte Carlo simulation) to derive approximate optimal price decrements (or increments) by varying simulation parameters such as the number of bidders, the probability distribution of reservation prices and the starting price.

The auctioneer also needs to determine the *feedback mechanism*:

- **Blind bidding or blind auctions:** Only the bidder with the best bid is informed about his leading position. Blind auctions are recommended whenever the number of suppliers and the heterogeneity of the suppliers' cost structures is high.
- **Leading price bidding or best bid auctions:** All bidders get (permanent) feedback regarding the value of the best bid (lowest bid) but not about the identity of the best bidder. This feedback mechanism is recommended whenever the number of suppliers is high and the heterogeneity of the suppliers' cost structure is low.
- **Positional bidding or rank auctions:** All bidders get (permanent) feedback regarding the rank of their bids (e.g., first, second, third) but not about the value of other bids. This is an effective feedback mechanism particularly if there are more than five suppliers bidding. This feedback mechanism is recommended whenever the number of suppliers is low and the heterogeneity of the suppliers' cost structures is high.
- **Positional and leading price bidding or English rank auctions:** All bidders get (permanent) feedback regarding the value of the best bid and their rank. This feedback mechanism is particularly effective if there are many (e.g., more than 30) suppliers bidding. This feedback mechanism is recommended whenever the number of suppliers and the heterogeneity of the suppliers' cost structure is low.
- **All price auction:** All bidders get (permanent) feedback about the size of all current bids (i.e., full transparency).

Furthermore, the auctioneer determines the *bidding mechanism or format*:

- **Open auction:** An open auction refers to an auction where bids of other bidders are public and visible to other bidders.
- **Sealed bid auction:** A sealed bid auction refers to a closed auction format where bids of other bidders are hidden. The bids are only known by the auctioneer.

Optimal Supplier Bidding in Reverse Auctions

It can be beneficial for a buyer to understand the optimal bidding strategy of the suppliers. Therefore, we analytically want to derive optimal supplier bidding strategy for different auction types in the following.

In general, each supplier $i = 1, \ldots, n$ aims at maximizing its expected utility (or expected payoff) $E[U_i]$ that is calculated by

$$E[U_i] = P_i(w) \cdot (b_i - c_i)_i^{\alpha}. \tag{4.18}$$

with $P_i(w)$ as the supplier i's probability to win the auction, b_i as the bid of supplier i, c_i as the supplier's internal cost to offer the product or service and α_i as the risk aversion coefficient. Therefore, the supplier's bid b_i is a function of the supplier's probability $P_i(w)$ to win the auction and the supplier's margin $b_i - c_i$. However, there exists the following trade-off in maximizing $E[U_i]$: If the supplier's bid b_i is (too) small, then the supplier's probability to win the auction $P_i(w)$ is high, but at the same time, the supplier's margin $b_i - c_i$ is small. If the supplier's bid b_i is (too) large, then $P_i(w)$ is small, but margin $b_i - c_i$ is high.

For *second-price sealed-bid auctions*, *English auctions* and *Japanese auctions*, the supplier's optimal bid b_i only depends on the supplier's reservation price. For *Japanese auctions*, if the auction price is above the reservation price, then the supplier should accept the price and bid, otherwise not. Consequently, the supplier with the lowest reservation price typically wins the auction. Therefore, the final price of a *Japanese auction* is determined by the second-lowest reservation price from the supplier pool and the price decrement of the auction.

For *first-price sealed-bid auctions* and *Dutch auctions*, the supplier's optimal bid b_i is more difficult to derive as it depends on the cost structure of the other suppliers participating in the auction. However, the cost structure of other suppliers is typically unknown to its competitors. Therefore, we model production cost c_i of supplier $i = 1, \ldots, n$ by a uniform distribution, i.e., $c_i \sim U[c_i^L, c_i^U]$ with a lower cost bound c_i^L and an upper cost bound c_i^U. Consequently, the cumulative distribution function $F(x)$ of the cost distribution is characterized by

$$F(x) = \begin{cases} 0 \text{ if } x < c^L \\ \frac{x - c^L}{c^H - c^L} \text{ if } c^L \leq x \leq c^U \\ 1 \text{ if } x > c^U. \end{cases} \tag{4.19}$$

Therefore, the probability $P_i(w)$ of supplier i to win the auction can be expressed by

$$P_i(w) = P(b_i < b_{-i}) = \left(\frac{c^U - b_i}{c^U - c^L} \right)^{n-1} \tag{4.20}$$

with b_{-i} as the lowest bid across all other suppliers. Therefore, if c_i is normalized to a value between 0 and 1 (i.e., $c_i^L = 0$ and $c_i^U = 1$), then the expected payoff $E[U_i]$ can be expressed by

$$E[U_i] = \max \left(0, (1 - b_i) \cdot (b_i - c_i)_i^{\alpha} \right) \tag{4.21}$$

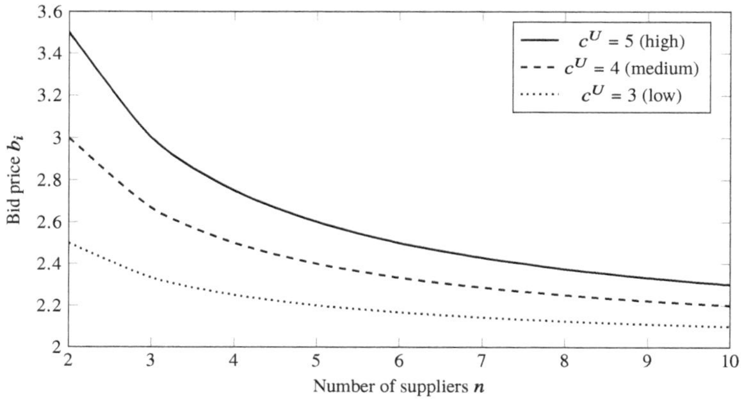

Fig. 4.11 Optimal auction bid price b_i of supplier i with production cost $c_i = 1$ as a function of participating suppliers for different maximum production cost expectations c^U

Therefore, the optimal bid b_i of supplier i can be derived through

$$\frac{\partial U_i}{\partial b_i} \stackrel{!}{=} 0 \leftrightarrow b_i(c_i) = \frac{\alpha_i + c_i \cdot (n-1)}{\alpha_i + n - 1}. \tag{4.22}$$

The optimal bid formula shows that a higher risk aversion (i.e., a higher α) of the supplier toward a zero utility induces lower bids. For risk-neutral suppliers ($\alpha = 0$) and without normalizing c_i^L and c_i^U, the optimal bid b_i is given by

$$b_i(c_i) = \frac{(n-1) \cdot c_i + c^U}{n}. \tag{4.23}$$

Figure 4.11 shows the optimal bid price b_i as a function of the number of participating suppliers n. This result showcases valuable insights for buyers how to set up the auction: (i) The more suppliers participating, the lower the bid because suppliers need to decrease their bids significantly to have a fair chance to win the auction if n is large. (ii) The largest price decrease effect comes from 2 to 3 participating suppliers. (iii) The lower the suppliers expectation about maximum production cost c^U of its competitors, the lower their own bid.

4.3.3 Combinatorial Auctions

Combinatorial auctions or multi-lot auctions are applied to multi-item settings (i.e., lots) with a number of heterogeneous items to be assigned to suppliers. This is the standard case for e-tendering processes as described in Sect. 4.3.1. In combinatorial auctions, suppliers can bid on a combination of line items (i.e., bundles), which creates attractive packages for suppliers but makes the buyer's allocation problem much more complex compared to the single-item case. In practice, this can be reasonable if the buyer wants to bundle demand for its different geographical locations in expectation of getting better supplier bids (economies of scale). For products with similar characteristics such as office supply, chemicals, transportation services or package material, combinatorial auction may also be effective.

In combinatorial auctions, the auctioneer needs to solve two major problems, i.e., the *mechanism design problem* and the *winner determination problem (WDP)*. The *mechanism design problem* considers how to bundle items suppliers can bid for in combinatorial auctions. This drives complexity as 20 items already lead to more than one million possible combinations and 30 items even lead to more than one billion possible combinations.

The *winner determination problem (WDP)* or the *combinatorial auction problem (CAP)* is a special case of the assignment problem (see Chap. 2) and optimally assigns bundles of items to bidders (awarding). Bundles give incentives to bidders that are not willing to bid for single items. Assume that the set of bidders is defined as $i = 1, \ldots, N$ and the set of items is defined as $m = 1, \ldots, M$. As it is not practical for RFX processes of real-world size for suppliers to bid for any combination of item bundles, i.e., $2^M - 1$ possible bundles, the buyer typically defines an appropriate number of bundles $s \in S$ as subsets of items $m = 1, \ldots, M$. v_{is} is the bid of bidder i for bundle s. The decision variable x_{is} is a binary variable that indicates whether bundle s is assigned to bidder i or not.

$$\text{minimize} \quad \sum_{i=1}^{N} \sum_{s \in S} v_{is} \cdot x_{is} \tag{4.24}$$

$$\text{s.t.} \quad \sum_{i=1}^{N} \sum_{s|m \in s} x_{is} \geq 1 \qquad \forall m = 1, \ldots, M \qquad (XOR) \tag{4.25}$$

$$\sum_{s \in S} x_{is} \geq 1 \qquad \forall i = 1, \ldots, N \qquad (OR) \tag{4.26}$$

$$x_{is} \in \{0, 1\} \qquad \forall i = 1, \ldots, N, s \in S \tag{4.27}$$

The objective is to minimize total purchase cost of the buyer by assigning bundles to bidders. The first constraint is a XOR constraint where bidders only want to win exactly one bundle or only one bid can be accepted. Alternatively, the OR constraint is used if bidders are indifferent to win more than one bundle or the buyer accepts an arbitrary number of bids.

Additionally, further constraints are possible such as a minimum number of winners (suppliers). This makes the problem a computationally complex problem to solve.

Table 4.3 Bid results of a combinatorial procurement auction with all-or-none

Item	Demand	Supplier 1	Supplier 2	Supplier 3	Supplier 4
Printing paper	50,000 sheets	1	1	1	0
Ballpoint pen	1,000 units	0	1	1	0
Folder	1,000 units	1	1	0	1
Bid price (in Euro)		1,500	1,750	650	1,000

Numerical Example: Combinatorial Auction with All-or-None

Consider a combinatorial procurement auction of all-or-none type, i.e., each supplier of a reverse auction has provided a bundled all-or-nothing bid (all-or-none) and a price for the bundle of items. The bid results are summarized in Table 4.3. For instance, supplier 1 offers the bundle of 50,000 sheets of printing paper and 1,000 folders for 1,500 EUR.

Based on this simple example, the purchaser would award supplier 3 (for paper and pens) and supplier 4 (for folders) with a minimum purchase cost of 1,650 Euros. Please note that the cost-optimal solution can theoretically provide more items than demanded. For instance, if supplier 1 would bid 950 Euros rather than 1,500 Euros for its bundle (for paper and folders), the optimal solution would award supplier 1 (for paper and folders) and supplier 3 (paper and pens) with resulting purchase cost of 1,600 Euros.

Combinatorial auctions can also deal with subsets of demanded items. Referring to the example above, a supplier could define a bundle that offers 20,000 sheets of papers. This requires slight adjustments to the mixed-integer linear programming formulation of the *winner determination problem (WDP)* as illustrated based on the following example.

Numerical Example: Combinatorial Auction with Partial Fill

Consider a combinatorial procurement auction with partial fill. Rather than all-or-none bids, each supplier of a reverse auction has provided a bundled partial fill bid and a price for the bundle of items. Partial fill means that the supplier does not need to bid for the entire size of demand. For instance, Table 4.4 shows that supplier 1 offers 30,000 sheets of printing paper and 600 units of folders for 1,200 Euro.

Based on the data from Table 4.4, *the winner determination problem (WDP)* can be modeled by the following mixed-integer linear programming model where x_i represents a binary decision variable that indicates whether supplier i is awarded or not. The buyer's purchase cost is minimized under

(continued)

Table 4.4 Bid results of a combinatorial procurement auction with partial fill

Item	Demand	Supplier 1	Supplier 2	Supplier 3	Supplier 4
Printing paper	50,000 sheets	30,000	30,000	40,000	0
Ballpoint pen	1,000 units	0	1,000	500	0
Folder	1,000 units	600	500	0	500
Bid price (in Euro)		1,200	1,600	850	500

the constraints that all demand is fulfilled:

$$\text{minimize} \quad 1{,}200 \cdot x_1 + 1{,}600 \cdot x_2 + 850 \cdot x_3 + 500 \cdot x_4 \tag{4.28}$$

$$\text{s.t.} \quad 30{,}000 \cdot x_1 + 30{,}000 \cdot x_2 + 40{,}000 \cdot x_3 + 0 \cdot x_4 \geq 50{,}000 \tag{4.29}$$

$$0 \cdot x_1 + 1{,}000 \cdot x_2 + 500 \cdot x_3 + 0 \cdot x_4 \geq 1{,}000 \tag{4.30}$$

$$600 \cdot x_1 + 500 \cdot x_2 + 0 \cdot x_3 + 500 \cdot x_4 \geq 1{,}000 \tag{4.31}$$

$$x_1, x_2, x_3, x_4 \in \{0, 1\} \tag{4.32}$$

This mixed-integer linear programming formulation results in awarding decisions for supplier 1 and supplier 2 with a total cost of 2,800 Euros and a purchase of 60,000 sheets of printing paper, 1,000 ballpoint pens and 1,100 folders.

In the procurement context, combinatorial auctions are, for instance, widely used for purchasing transportation services, which is motivated by the fact that certain routes can be provided at a cheaper price if there are no unloaded (return) trips. This is illustrated in the following example.

Numerical Example: Combinatorial Auction for Transportation Services
Assume that a major German car manufacturer invites shippers for tendering transportation services between its major German plants in Wolfsburg (WOB), Ingolstadt (IN) and Kassel (KS). Therefore, the OEM defines bundles to bid for. Table 4.5 shows the 11 transportation bundles that are defined and the corresponding bids of two shippers. The data shows that the shippers bid better prices for bundles of two or three routes, which allows them to avoid unloaded trips. For instance, transportation from Ingolstadt to Wolfsburg is part of three bundles (i.e., 1, 7, 10). Shipper 1 offers transportation between those two locations for 319 EUR/ton for one way and 542 EUR/ton for the round trip.

(continued)

Table 4.5 Results of a combinatorial auction for transportation services

	Transportation bundles										
Connection	1	2	3	4	5	6	7	8	9	10	11
IN-WOB (527 km)	1						1			1	
WOB-IN (527 km)		1					1				1
WOB-KS (184 km)			1					1		1	
KS-WOB (184 km)				1				1			1
IN-KS (403 km)					1				1		1
KS-IN (403 km)						1			1	1	
Shipper 1 (EUR/ton)	319	319	218	218	268	268	542	370	455	724	724
Shipper 2 (EUR/ton)	332	350	202	210	290	280	613	350	513	691	722

The corresponding combinatorial auction is of all-or-none type and can be solved via the WDP with the objective to minimize the purchase price of transportation across all routes. The optimal solution suggests to award bundle 7 and 9 to shipper 1 and bundle 8 to shipper 2. This yields total cost of 1,347 Euro per ton and savings of 15.1% compared to single-route bidding with total cost of 1,586 Euro per ton.

In practice, there are software providers such as CombineNet (www.combinenet.com), NetExchange (www.netex.com), Quintagroup (https://quintagroup.com/) and Trade Extensions (www.tradeextensions.com) that provide tools for solving combinatorial auction problems in the procurement context. For further details on combinatorial auctions, we refer to the textbook of [10].

Other Auction Formats

Furthermore, *Total-Cost-of-Ownership (TCO) or Total-Cost-of-Acquisition (TCA) auctions* allow to tender several cost components (e.g., separately for items and transportation services). The results of the auction are determined by the sum of all cost.

For non-monetary factors, the auctioneer can either use quality gates or a bonus/minus approach. Quality gates determine the minimum requirements with regard to a supplier's quality, lead time or financial situation that are needed to be permitted to an auction. The bonus/minus approach adjusts the supplier's price offers in accordance with their quality or lead time performance (Fig. 4.12).

A related concept that, besides the price, allows the consideration of further bid variables such as lead time, service level or quantity discount is *expressive bidding*, which is often combined with combinatorial auctions. This allows to integrate further rules of *if-then* type. For instance, *if the supplier is awarded part A and*

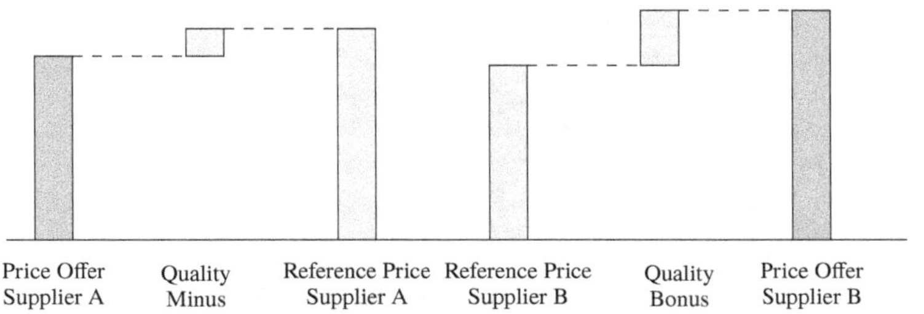

Fig. 4.12 Bonus and minus approach for tender result analysis

Table 4.6 Ausubel auction for printing paper (Bid prices in Euro)

Demand	Supplier 1	Supplier 2	Supplier 3	Supplier 4
50,000 sheets	500	610	450	500
100,000 sheets	890	1100	900	1000
150,000 sheets	1269	1617	1350	1400

B, then the supplier accepts to reduce the price for A by 10% compared to A-only awarding. Expressive bidding makes bid analysis and awarding decisions very complex if there are many if-then conditions open to the suppliers, which makes it difficult to identify the maximum amount of savings without optimization and bid analytics.

A special case of expressive bidding is the *Ausubel auction* that considers economies of scale due to fixed cost degression. In Ausubel auctions (see Table 4.6), the supplier's bid is a price-quantity combination, i.e., the supplier is asked for price offers for several quantities.

Average price auctions are used to reduce the price pressure from suppliers by awarding at the average of prices (e.g., average of lowest bid and second-lowest bid) with the objective to avoid situations of insolvencies or unplanned cost increases.

4.4 Supplier Negotiations

After the completion of a RFX process and alternatively to e-auctions, suppliers can be invited to buyer-supplier negotiations. This chapter gives an overview of approaches for supplier negotiation and bargaining including psychological and game-theoretic concepts that are often applied after a supplier shortlisting during an RFQ.

4.4.1 Basic Terms in Negotiations and Bargaining

Supplier negotiations are a complex task for procurement professionals that is increasingly supported by data and data analytics in order to derive optimal

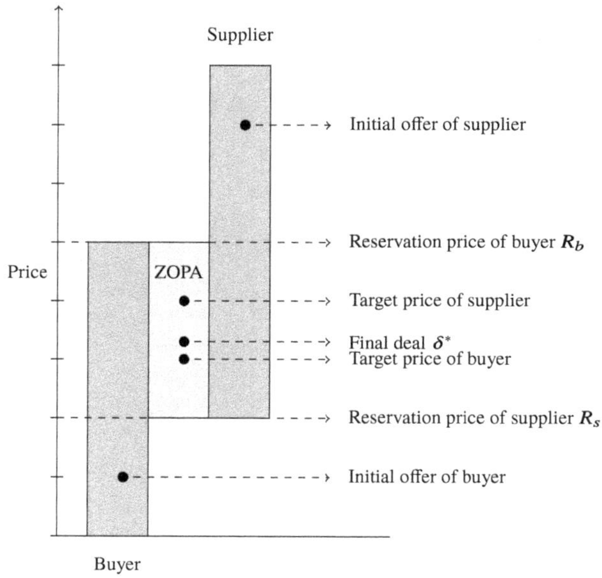

Fig. 4.13 Basic terms in supplier negotiations and bargaining

data-driven negotiation strategies. The general objective is to find a price that is (subjectively) adequate for both parties, i.e., for the buyer and for the supplier. This price is located in the zone of possible agreements (ZOPA) (also called bargaining zone) that is bounded by the reservation price of the supplier R_s and the reservation price R_b of the buyer (see Fig. 4.13). R_s is the lowest price that the supplier is able to accept under consideration of its cost structure plus expected profit margins. R_b is the maximum price that the buyer is able to accept under consideration of the price sensitivity of its own customers, its best alternative to a negotiated agreement (BATNA), i.e., the best price offer of an alternative supplier or the price for the *make* rather than the *buy* option. If the final negotiated price is above R_b, then the buyer would be better off with no agreement.

The challenge of negotiation or bargaining games is that buyer and supplier might not agree to an even split of the ZOPA with a price of $(R_b + R_s)/2$ and that both players typically do not know the size of the ZOPA $R_b - R_s$ as they do not exactly know the counter-party's reservation price. The counter-party's reservation price can only be estimated prior or during a negotiation game. Two analytical methods to estimate the supplier's reservation price R_s as part of the negotiation preparation are should-cost modeling that includes cost breakdowns (see Sect. 3.4.1) and linear performance pricing (see Sect. 3.4.2).

Sequential bargaining starts with an initial offer of the supplier or an initial offer of the buyer. If the supplier (or buyer) accepts the offer, the bargaining game ends with a deal. If the supplier (buyer) rejects the offer, both can make a counteroffer. However, offers can be beyond the ZOPA. However, an agreement can only be achieved anywhere within the ZOPA, i.e., the bargaining zone is defined by the interval $[R_s; R_b]$. If $R_b < R_s$, no bargaining zone exists. Based on the individual negotiation power, buyer or supplier reach or do not reach their target prices. Given that δ^* is the final deal, the buyer's marginal gain is defined by $R_b - \delta^*$ (buyer's surplus), and the supplier's marginal gain is defined by $\delta^* - R_s$ (supplier's surplus). Please note that the ZOPA can be increased if the buyer identifies potential cost improvements of the supplier in the course of a should-cost analysis (see Chap. 3). In addition, the BATNA can be improved through parallel negotiations with several suppliers.

4.4.2 Contingency Compensation in Distributive Bargaining

Behavioral economics shows that there is a significant effect of contingency compensation of both buyers and suppliers on the outcome of negotiation or bargaining games. A typical compensation scheme looks as follows: The sales person of a supplier is compensated by a base salary plus a commission that is based on her selling effectiveness. The purchase manager of a buyer is compensated by a base salary plus a commission that is based on her purchase effectiveness.

Numerical Example: An Experiment in Purchasing Negotiations

An experiment at Ohio State University that already dates back to 1983 (see [21]) wanted to evaluate the effects of contingency compensation of buyers and suppliers on the negotiation results. Therefore, buyers were told in an experiment that they are hired to represent a person who wants to purchase an office building for a maximum price of 150,000 USD. And sellers (suppliers) were told that they are hired to represent a person who wants to sell an office building with the restriction that the minimum selling price is 100,000 USD. Therefore, the bargaining zone is defined by $R_s = 100{,}000$ USD and $R_b = 150{,}000$ USD with a range of 50,000 USD (Fig. 4.14). There is a time limit of 25 minutes for the negotiation process. Sellers are divided into two groups: 50% are informed that they are contingently compensated with 1 USD for each 5,000 USD by which the final price exceeds 100.000 USD up to a maximum of 10 USD. The other 50% are paid 10 USD regardless of whether a deal happens or not. Buyers are also divided into two groups: 50% are informed that they are contingently compensated with 1 USD for each 5,000 USD by which the final price is lower than 150,000 USD up to a maximum of 10 USD. The other 50% are paid 10 USD regardless of whether a deal happens or not.

The statistically significant results are presented in Table 4.7 and show that contingently rewarded suppliers open with higher initial offers than non-

(continued)

contingently rewarded suppliers. They also show that the initial offer of the buyers is always above the supplier's reservation price. Furthermore, the way how negotiation outcomes are paid affects the outcome significantly. If both players are contingently rewarded, then the negotiation time is significantly longer.This yields the conclusion that reward systems are essential in bargaining.

Negotiation research furthermore distinguishes between psychological negotiation approaches (*integrative negotiations*) and analytical negotiation approaches (*distributive negotiations*) that are rooted in game theory. While psychological approaches aim at maximizing the own utility under causing lowest possible cost for the opponent (win-win situations), game theory also addresses win-lose situations with the objective to maximize the own utility under causing highest possible cost for the opponent. We give an overview of both approaches in the following.

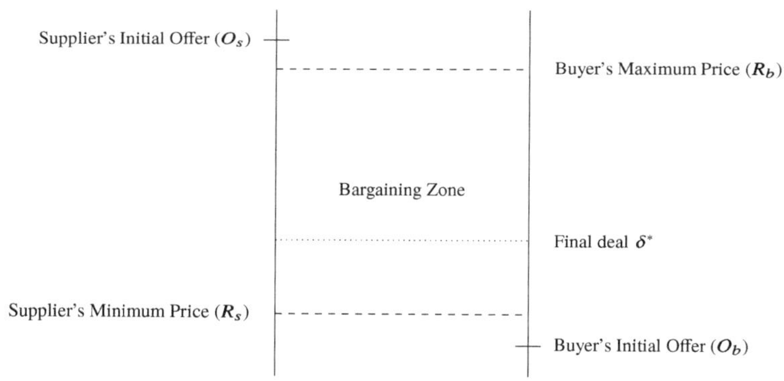

Fig. 4.14 Bargaining zone for negotiations (see [21])

Table 4.7 Experiment outcome

Supplier	Buyer	O_b	O_s	δ^*	Negotiation time [min]
Contingent	Contingent	114,150	160,300	129,607	20.07
Contingent	Noncontingent	117,944	173,052	135,446	16.57
Noncontingent	Contingent	110,895	155,500	128,019	17.14
Noncontingent	Noncontingent	118,111	149,500	132,036	14.79

4.4.3 Psychological Negotiation Design

While standard (analytical) game theory tries to explain the decisions of negotiation parties based on analytical models, psychological approaches focus more on behavioral factors corresponding to behavioral economics or behavioral game theory.

An important psychological effect is the *anchoring effect* that states that players' decisions are affected by environmental information. In the context of supplier negotiations, this anchor can be the placement of an extreme claim at the beginning of a negotiation. For instance, a supplier that initially planned to push for a 20% price increase is less willing to push for 20% after the buyer pushed for a 20% price decrease at the beginning of the negotiation.

The most popular psychological concept of supplier negotiations is the *Harvard Approach of Principled Negotiation* introduced by Roger Fisher and William Ury in 1981. In this context, the *Harvard Negotiation Project* was founded to improve negotiation techniques. The approach of principled negotiation states that positional bargaining where each party starts with their relatively fixed position and tries to defend it is not very efficient for reaching agreements because it neglects the other player's interests and involves ego and is harming the players' relationship. The Harvard approach states that principled negotiations offer a better way of reaching a good agreement. Principled negotiations are based on four prescriptions:

- Separate the people from the problem.
- Focus on interests not positions.
- Invent options for mutual gain.
- Insist of using objective criteria.

For further information on psychological approaches for negotiation optimization, we refer to [13].

4.4.4 Game-Theoretic Negotiation Design (Negotiation Games)

Game theory is a mathematical discipline that leverages analytical methods to model conflicts and cooperation between decision-makers (see [7, 15, 29]). A *game* is an interaction between at least two players that act as strategic decision-makers with individual objectives (e.g., buyer vs. supplier). Therefore, they follow an individual strategy, i.e., a plan of action in order to achieve the objectives. A common objective is to maximize the individual payoff (e.g., to maximize cost savings). Consequently, game theory tries to determine optimal strategies through mathematical rigor in order to anticipate the other player's choices and probabilities.

There are around 30 different games considered in game theory. In the following, we focus on those games (i.e., negotiation games) that are particularly relevant for negotiations between buyers and suppliers (vertical negotiations) or between two buyers (horizontal negotiations). For a detailed review of game theory for negotiations (also known as negotiation games), we refer to the textbook of [5].

Table 4.8 Zero-sum games: payoff matrix for player A and player B

	B: Scissors	B: Rock	B: Paper
A: Scissors	(0,0)	(−1,1)	(1,−1)
A: Rock	(1,−1)	(0,0)	(−1,1)
A: Paper	(−1,1)	(1,−1)	(0,0)

Zero-Sum Game

Zero-sum games are games where the payoff of a player equals the loss of the other player (see *distributive bargaining*). The famous game *rock, paper, scissors* is an illustrative example for a simultaneous zero-sum game where the players' decisions are taken simultaneously, i.e., players have no knowledge of the opponent's strategy. Rock dominates scissors, scissors dominates paper and paper dominates rock. There is no option that both players win but only a win-lose situation as the game's payoff matrix of Table 4.8 shows.

At the *rock, paper, scissors* game, there is no dominant strategy for each of the players and no pure Nash equilibrium because no player improves its payoff by changing its strategy assuming it knows the equilibrium strategy of the other player.

In the procurement negotiation context, zero-sum games occur whenever there is asymmetric information with one player having sufficiently higher bargaining power. This is, for instance, the case in the automotive industry (e.g., OEMs versus small suppliers) or in the food industry (e.g., discount supermarket chains versus farmers). Please note that pure zero-sum games where one party wins all and the other loses all are typically not existent in buyer-supplier negotiations.

Prisoner's Dilemma

The probably most well-known game in game theory is the prisoner's dilemma, which is also a simultaneous game. Two prisoners (A and B) are indicted for crime. Both are separately interrogated and cannot communicate with each other. Each of the prisoners can follow two different strategies: "Cooperate (keep silent)" or "Do not cooperate (confess)" with the following consequences: If one player confesses, she gets a lower punishment (e.g., 1 year in prison), while the silent player gets maximum punishment (e.g., 6 years in prison). If both prisoners confess, both get high punishment (e.g., 4 years in prison), and if both prisoners keep silent, both get low punishment (e.g., 2 years in prison). This is illustrated in the payoff matrix in Table 4.9.

Table 4.9 Prisoner's dilemma: payoff matrix for player A and player B

	B cooperates	B does not cooperate
A cooperates	(−2,−2)	(−6,−1)
A does not cooperate	(−1,−6)	(−4,−4)

Table 4.10 Stag hunt: payoff matrix for player A and player B

	B hunts stag	B hunts hare
A hunts stag	(10,10)	(1,8)
A hunts hare	(8,1)	(5,5)

What is the best possible strategy now not knowing how the other player decides? Game theory determines that not to cooperate is the dominant strategy for both players because it maximizes their payoff independently of what the other player does. There is one pure Nash equilibrium, i.e., both players do not cooperate, which yields 4 years of prison for both even though both would go to jail for 2 years if both would cooperate.

In the procurement context, this is prevalent in supplier negotiations whenever two parties have an agreement and decide now whether they honor the agreement or not.

Stag Hunt

In game theory, stag hunt (also called assurance game, trust dilemma or common interest game) illustrates the conflict between safety and (social) cooperation. It is also considered as a simultaneous game. Two hunters in a forest hunt either for a hare or a stag. A hunt provides lower payoff than a stag. One hunter can only hunt for a hare because a stag is difficult to hunt alone. A stag can be hunted in cooperation with the other hunter, however requires to share the stag. A hunter can hunt a hare with less effort and time if not cooperating. Table 4.10 shows a payoff matrix for this type of game.

There is no dominant strategy of player A and B. However, there are two pure-strategy Nash equilibria where no player improves its payoff by changing its strategy assuming it knows the equilibrium strategy of the other player: Either both players cooperate or both players do not.

In the procurement context, stag hunt is widely used in contract negotiations where cooperation can increase benefits but benefits need to be shared so that the individual party can get less or greater benefit at the end compared to no cooperation. An example is purchasing conglomerates that aim at reducing transaction cost (e.g., setup cost) and potentially getting better unit prices due to economies of scale. Stag hunt is also relevant for negotiations in the fields of M&A, joint ventures or strategic partnerships.

Chicken Game

Another simultaneous game is chicken game. Two car drivers (A and B) move toward each other at high speed. The player who avoids the other car loses the game. Therefore, there are two strategies each player can follow: Avoid the other car or do not avoid. According to the payoff matrix from Table 4.11, if both avoid each other, there is a draw, and both players achieve a payoff of 4. If A avoids B,

Table 4.11 Chicken game: payoff matrix for player A and player B

	B avoids A	B does not avoid A
A avoids B	(4,4)	(2,6)
A does not avoid B	(6,2)	(0,0)

Table 4.12 Battle of sexes: payoff matrix for player A and player B

	B chooses soccer	B chooses concert
A chooses soccer	(3,1)	(0,0)
A chooses concert	(0,0)	(1,3)

then A loses with a payoff of 2, while B gets a payoff of 6. If both players do not avoid each other, both players die, which equals a payoff of 0.

This game does not have any dominant strategies but two pure Nash equilibria (i.e., avoid/not avoid and not avoid/avoid).

In the procurement context, chicken game is a common game played during supplier negotiations that are characterized by dominance and coercion. Unless one of the parties capitulate, the negotiation can yield serious damage or harm (for both parties). An example is a negotiation between a buyer and a supplier about an item that is critical for the buyer (e.g., because there is no further supplier on the market) but where the supplier also does not have alternative customers. This can be special purpose machinery manufacture or customized software.

Battle of the Sexes

Battle of the sexes is a simultaneous game of coordination. Player A and B want to spend the evening together. Both forgot to agree on a location. A prefers a soccer match, while B prefers to visit a concert. Both need to decide independently now where to go in to meet and spend the evening. If B (A) chooses soccer, it would be the best strategy for A (B) to go for soccer as well. If A (B) chooses concert, it would be the best strategy for B (A) to choose concert as well. However, if both choose their preference, there would not be any date. If both choose the preference of the other, there would not be any date, too (Table 4.12).

There are no dominant strategies—neither for player A nor for player B. However, there are two pure Nash equilibria: one where both players go to the soccer match and one where both choose concert.

In procurement negotiations, battle of the sexes points out the problem of coordination between two or more parties (e.g., buyer and supplier or members of purchasing consortia).

Ultimatum Game

The ultimatum game is a sequential game where the players' decisions are taken sequentially. Player A gets a budget of 100 Euro from which she needs to give a

Table 4.13 Ultimatum game: payoff matrix for player A and player B

	B accepts offer	B rejects offer
Offer of A	(100-s,s)	(0,0)

Table 4.14 Trust game: payoff matrix for player A and player B

	A does not trust B	A trusts B, B abuses trust	A trusts B, B honors trust
Payoff for A	0	−1	1
Payoff for B	0	2	1

specific share $0 \leq s \leq 100$ to player B. If B accepts the offer, then B gets an amount s, while player A gets an amount 100-s. If B rejects the offer, then both do not get any budget. Player A wants to maximize her budget, while A does not know about the objective of B (Table 4.13).

The game-theoretic approach derives a solution of $s = 0.01$ Euros if players are rational and profit-maximizing. In empirical experiments, we however observe that player B typically rejects the offer for $s < 15$ Euros because she does not perceive it as fair.

In procurement negotiations, the ultimatum game and ultimatum bargaining plays a major role whenever fairness is an important factor. This is relevant for savings allocation generated through vertical collaborations (e.g., revenue-sharing contracts between buyer and supplier) or horizontal collaborations (e.g., purchasing consortia).

Trust Game

The trust game characterizes a sequential game between two players where one party is the trust giver (A) and the other party is the trust taker (B). A gives a task to B and has two decision options: She can either trust B or not. If A does not trust B, there is no deal, and both parties have a zero payoff. If A trusts B, then B has two decision options: He can either honor the trust of A or abuse it. The consequences of decisions are summarized in the payoff matrix in Table 4.14. Any rational player A would abuse the trust of A in order to maximize its own payoff. As player A knows that, she would never trust B, which leads to a dilemma with zero payoffs for both. To solve this dilemma, there are two instruments available: (i) A can control B and threaten B with punishment for abusing her trust, or (ii) A only gives trust to players with positive experience in the past. Both instruments can lead to the scenario that A trusts B and B honors the trust, which results in a positive payoff for both.

In the procurement context, the trust game points out the value of positive buyer-supplier relationships, with player A representing the buyer and player B representing the supplier. A strong relationship based on past experience in combination with a trustworthy negotiation setup can yield a win-win situation.

4.4.5 Negotiation Strategies and Technology

Game theory is able to derive and evaluate several negotiation strategies that buyers can follow. Please note that it is sometimes recommended to change strategies over time. The following list highlights a selection of strategies (or tactics) that are commonly used in negotiation practice:

- **Take-it-or-leave-it strategy (TIOLI):** The buyer provides one offer and communicates not to change this offer anymore. This strategy is particularly effective if the buyer's negotiation power is high and if the supplier's BATNA is known. In this case, a TIOLI offer that is fractionally above the supplier's reservation price may be accepted by the supplier. TIOLI can be combined with a budget tactic, i.e., the TIOLI offer can be justified by internal budget limits or company policies that, for instance, do not allow to accept a deviation from specific contract forms with regard to payment terms and lead times.
- **Threat strategy:** The buyer threatens the supplier with breakup of negotiations or with a switch of supplier. The threat strategy is risky and should only be applied if buyer has an adequate option (e.g., a supplier with similar or better price and quality or capacities and capabilities for make rather than buy).
- **Benchmarking strategy:** The buyer highlights the weaknesses (and strengths) of the supplier relative to best-practice benchmarks. This is particularly effective for products and services that are standard and equal or at least similar across suppliers. The benchmarking strategy can also effectively be used if the price components (e.g., raw material cost, energy cost, logistics cost) are known from a precise should-cost analysis or from supplier communication. In this case, a comparison with transparent market prices is possible. For instance, the buyer can emphasize that the supplier's logistics cost is 10% above the market price as quoted at specific platforms or the quoted raw material cost is 5% above the spot market price.
- **Cherry-picking strategy:** The buyer leverages the best offer per criteria (e.g., price, warranty, lead time) across suppliers and asks suppliers to adjust their offers accordingly. For instance, supplier A offers a price of 5 USD per unit and a lead time of 1 week, and supplier B offers a price of 3 USD per unit and a lead time of 2 weeks. In this case, supplier A is confronted with an existing price offer of 3 USD per unit, and supplier B is confronted with an existing lead time offer of 1 week. Supplier A is given the opportunity to adjust the price offer, and supplier B is given the opportunity to adjust the lead time offer.
- **Bluff strategy:** The buyer uses fictive arguments such as a competitor's offer that is, for instance, 5% below the supplier's offer. A bluff strategy is risky and only recommended if the buyer has a sufficient understanding about the cost structure of the corresponding product or service. For instance, if the bluff price is even below the raw material price of the product, the supplier will quickly identify the bluff. Furthermore, the buyer needs to be sure that there is no full transparency about price offers between the supplier and its competitors.

- **Grim-trigger strategy:** The grim-trigger strategy relies on history and is therefore only applicable for repeated negotiations. The buyer starts with cooperation and continues with cooperation if and only if the supplier cooperated in the past. A single defect by the supplier triggers punishment forever (*strictly unforgiving*). Grimm-trigger strategy is related to the win-stay-lose-shift strategy where the buyer starts kind and stays with the strategy if the supplier cooperates and shifts if not.
- **Tit-for-tat strategy:** The buyer starts with cooperation and continues with the last round's strategy of the supplier. This is similar to grim-trigger strategy but less punishing with one punishment for each defection. As soon as the supplier cooperates again, the buyer cooperates as well. Tit-for-tat is effective due to four reasons: (i) It is comprehensive, and both parties can quickly adjust their behavior accordingly, (ii) it is decent as it starts with cooperation, (iii) it is forgiving and not resentful and (iv) it is cautionary because it punishes deviations immediately.

Negotiations are increasingly supported by technology. Data analytics can help prepare negotiations in a data-informed manner, for instance, analyzing massive amounts of RFI/RFQ datasets and external market data (e.g., raw material prices) in order to derive an adequate target price. In addition, technology in the sense of chatbots can also execute negotiations without human support, which eliminates human emotions that can lead to non-optimal behavior in negotiations and also reduces the need personnel resources.

Industry Example: Automated Procurement Negotiations at Walmart
The US retailer Walmart needs to deal with a supplier base of 100,000+ direct suppliers. This makes human-led negotiations impossible. Therefore, since 2021, Walmart uses an artificial intelligence-powered software with a chatbot for automated negotiations with its tail-end suppliers. The AI-driven negotiations are based on structured scripts that guide the supplier through the negotiation and could achieve 1.5% savings on the spend negotiated and an extension of the payment terms of on average 35 days (see [28]).

4.5 Supplier Selection and Evaluation Models

In practice, suppliers regularly need to be evaluated and potentially being replaced by new (better) suppliers. However, supplier selection and evaluation is a complex task as there are typically (i) multiple options (suppliers) available and (ii) there are multiple selection and evaluation criteria that need to be considered. While for a long time cost and quality were the major drivers of supplier selection and evaluation decisions, today, there is also a service, risk and sustainability perspective that needs to be addressed. Even though the definition of appropriate supplier selection criteria

Table 4.15 A categorization of supplier selection criteria

Cost	Quality and sustainability	Service and risk
Price	Reputation	Lead time
Discount	Certification (e.g., ISO 9000)	Supply reliability
Payment terms	Packaging	Supply capacity
Switching cost	Sustainability	Flexibility
Exchange rate risk	Defect rate (ppm)	Responsiveness
Total cost of ownership		Additional service
		Communication

can be (and typically is) very industry-specific (e.g., software procurement vs. commodity procurement), we categorize the most important criteria in Table 4.15. The idea follows the TCO approach, i.e., in the cost category, the entire life cycle related to a supplier needs to be considered. This also includes cost for switching from an existing supplier to a new one, which can be significant. Furthermore, with companies defining their path to net zero emissions, sustainability gets more and more important (keywords *Act on Corporate Due Diligence Obligations in Supply Chains*, *Internal Carbon Pricing* and *Environmental Social Governance (ESG)*) and can, e.g., be measured by transportation distance, carbon emissions in CO2 equivalents or available sustainability certifications of suppliers.

The idea of data-driven supplier selection and evaluation models is to connect criteria and suppliers as illustrated in Fig. 4.15. However, as we see, some criteria favor supplier A, and other criteria favor supplier B, which makes an appropriate selection decision difficult. Typically, there are various trade-offs possible: For instance, a supplier that offers rather poor quality, should offer a better price, while a high-quality supplier is more pricey. A supplier with a high production capacity may yield a lower supply risk compared to suppliers with low production capacities.

The following approaches that refer to multi-criteria decision-making (MCDM) with S alternatives (i.e., suppliers) and K decision criteria help derive an optimal selection and evaluation decision based on an aggregated level. Please note that these methods are not only applicable for supplier selection and evaluation but to any multi-criteria decision problem. They are therefore also relevant for other problem settings in procurement.

4.5.1 *Weighted Sum Model (WSM)*

The weighted sum model (WSM), also referred to as scoring method, weighted score method, weighted linear combination (WLC), simple additive weighting

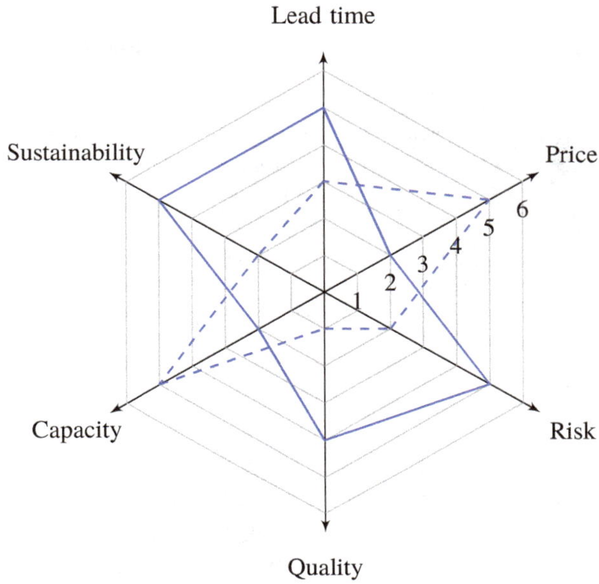

Fig. 4.15 Criteria-based supplier evaluation for two suppliers on a 6-point scale (1, poor; 6, excellent)

(SAW) or linear averaging, is the simplest method for solving a multi-criteria decision problem. It follows the following steps:

- **Step 1:** Definition of decision criteria $k = 1, \ldots, K$
- **Step 2:** Definition of relative criteria weights w_k with $w_k = \sum_{k=1}^{K} w_k = 1$
- **Step 3:** Definition of an evaluation scale (e.g., a 5-point scale)
- **Step 4:** Definition of criteria fulfillment $p_k(s)$ per supplier $s = 1, \ldots, S$
- **Step 5:** Calculation of supplier scores $N(s) = \sum_{k=1}^{K} w_k \cdot p_k(s)$
- **Step 6:** Selection of supplier with the highest score

Even though WSM is still the standard method in most industries due to its simple application, it comes with some severe drawbacks. The most important drawback is its vulnerability to manipulation due to the determination of w_k and $p_k(s)$ that often happens on a very subjective basis.

Numerical Example: WSM for Supplier Selection and Evaluation

Table 4.16 WSM with a three-point scale

Criterion	Weight	Supplier A	Supplier B
Supply capacity	0.1	Very good (5)	Very weak (1)
Quality	0.2	Very weak (1)	Very good (5)
Switching cost	0.1	Moderate (3)	Very weak (1)
Unit price	0.3	Very good (5)	Moderate (5)
Lead time	0.2	Moderate (3)	Very good (5)
Supply distance	0.1	Moderate (3)	Very good (5)
Supplier score		3.4	4.2

The example from Table 4.16 highlights the drawback of WSM, which is the high sensitivity of selection decisions to very small changes in the input. This opens the place for manipulation. Simply by switching the weights for supply capacity and quality, WSM would recommend to go for supplier A rather than supplier B.

Therefore, WSM is a good starting point to think about relevant criteria, suppliers, weights and evaluation, but its output should be interpreted carefully especially whenever the resulting supplier scores are very close to each other. In this case, a scenario analysis can help analyze the switching behavior. To avoid that evaluators set weights in favor of their preferred supplier(s), it is essential that criteria weights are determined a priori to receiving proposals from suppliers.

4.5.2 *Weighted Product Model (WPM)*

The weighted product model (WPM) is an extension of the weighted sum model with a focus on multiplication rather than summation. The procedure equals step 1 to 6 of WPM with the slight difference that the score $N(s)$ in step 5 is calculated as follows:

$$N(s) = \prod_{k=1}^{K} p_k(s)^{w_k} \tag{4.33}$$

Numerical Example: WPM for Supplier Selection and Evaluation
Applied to the example from WSP, WPM would yield a supplier score of 2.95 for supplier A and 3.62 for supplier B.

4.5.3 Analytic Hierarchy Process (AHP)

The analytic hierarchy process (AHP) is a significant extension of WSM with the main objective to systemize and structure the decision process of weight choice w_k and evaluation $p_k(s)$ through pairwise comparisons. The method dates back to R.W. Saaty [25] and follows the following five steps.

Step 1: Development of a Hierarchy

Similar to WSM and WPM, AHP builds a hierarchy of relevant criteria and alternatives (i.e., potential suppliers) (Table 4.17).

Step 2: Pairwise Comparison of Criteria and Standardization

Rather than selecting criteria weights arbitrarily, AHP uses a more structured approach through pairwise comparisons. Therefore, all criteria are compared in 1-on-1 comparisons with regard to what criterion is more important and how much more important.

In the example from Table 4.18, the pairwise comparison of quality and price shows that the decision-maker regards quality twice as important as price. Therefore, price is half as important as quality. In order to derive criteria weights w_k, AHP standardizes by calculating the average that equals the criteria weights w_k that sum up to 1.0 (see Table 4.19).

The benefit of pairwise comparisons is that it asks for explicit evaluations rather than abstract weight definitions. It makes people think about the relative importance and gives a good basis for discussions in workshops. In general, the objective is to get more consistent evaluations.

Table 4.17 Step 1 of AHP: hierarchy building

	Quality	Price	Service	Lead time
Supplier 1				
Supplier 2				
Supplier 3				
Supplier 4				

Table 4.18 Step 2 of AHP: pairwise comparisons

	Quality	Price	Service	Lead time
Quality	1	2	4	3
Price	1/2	1	3	3
Service	1/4	1/3	1	2
Lead time	1/3	1/3	1/2	1
Total	25/12	11/3	17/2	9

Table 4.19 Step 2 of AHP: standardization

	Quality	Price	Service	Lead time	Average
Quality	12/25	6/11	8/17	3/9	0.457
Price	6/25	3/11	6/17	3/9	0.300
Service	3/25	1/11	2/17	2/9	0.138
Lead time	4/25	1/11	1/17	1/9	0.105
Total					1.00

Table 4.20 Step 3 of AHP: pairwise comparison and standardization (1)

Quality	Supplier 1	Supplier 2	Supplier 3	Supplier 4	Score
Supplier 1	1	5	6	1/3	0.297
Supplier 2	1/5	1	2	1/6	0.087
Supplier 3	1/6	1/2	1	1/8	0.053
Supplier 4	3	6	8	1	0.563
Total					1.00

Table 4.21 Step 3 of AHP: pairwise comparison and standardization (2)

Price	Supplier 1	Supplier 2	Supplier 3	Supplier 4	Score
Supplier 1	1	1/3	5	8	0.303
Supplier 2	3	1	7	9	0.573
Supplier 3	1/5	1/7	1	2	0.078
Supplier 4	1/8	1/9	1/2	1	0.046
Total					1.00

Table 4.22 Step 3 of AHP: pairwise comparison and standardization (3)

Service	Supplier 1	Supplier 2	Supplier 3	Supplier 4	Score
Supplier 1	1	5	4	8	0.597
Supplier 2	1/5	1	1/2	4	0.140
Supplier 3	1/4	2	1	5	0.214
Supplier 4	1/8	1/4	1/5	1	0.050
Total					1.00

Step 3: Pairwise Comparison of Suppliers and Standardization

In step 3, step 2 is repeated, but for suppliers rather than criteria. Therefore, suppliers $s = 1, \ldots, S$ are compared pairwise for each single criterion $k = 1, \ldots K$. For instance, based on Table 4.20, supplier 1 outperforms supplier 2 with regard to quality by factor 5. After standardization, each supplier gets a single score per criterion (the higher, the better) (Tables 4.20, 4.21, 4.22, and 4.23).

Table 4.23 Step 3 of AHP: pairwise comparison and standardization (4)

Lead time	Supplier 1	Supplier 2	Supplier 3	Supplier 4	Weight
Supplier 1	1	3	1/5	1	0.151
Supplier 2	1/3	1	1/8	1/3	0.060
Supplier 3	5	8	1	5	0.638
Supplier 4	1	3	1/5	1	0.151
Total					1.00

Table 4.24 Step 4 of AHP: calculation of final supplier scores and ranking

	Quality	Price	Service	Lead time	Score (rank)
Supplier 1	0.457 × 0.297	0.300 × 0.303	0.138 × 0.597	0.105 × 0.151	0.325 (1)
Supplier 2	0.457 × 0.087	0.300 × 0.573	0.138 × 0.140	0.105 × 0.060	0.237 (3)
Supplier 3	0.457 × 0.053	0.300 × 0.078	0.138 × 0.214	0.105 × 0.638	0.144 (4)
Supplier 4	0.457 × 0.563	0.300 × 0.046	0.138 × 0.050	0.105 × 0.151	0.294 (2)
Total					1.00

Step 4: Calculation of Final Supplier Scores

In step 4, the criteria weights from step 2 and supplier scores per criteria from step 3 are combined to get a single score per supplier that determines the rank to other suppliers. For example, according to Table 4.24, supplier 1 ranks first, followed by supplier 4, supplier 2 and supplier 3.

Step 5: Consistency Check

A final step is typically to check consistency of the pairwise comparisons. For instance, if a decision-maker regards criterion A twice as important as criterion B and B twice as important as criterion C, then criterion A should be four times as important as criterion C. For this, AHP uses a consistency ratio (CR). If CR is smaller than a value L, then consistency is existent. CR is defined as

$$CR = \frac{CI}{RI} \tag{4.34}$$

with RI as a random index and CI as a consistency index that is defined as follows:

$$CI = \frac{\lambda_{max} - n}{n - 1} \tag{4.35}$$

with λ_{max} as the maximum eigenvalue and n as the number of suppliers. Eigenvalues can be calculated via matrix multiplication in spreadsheet software (e.g., `mmult` function in `Excel`), via `Python` function `linalg.eig()` or via `R` function `eigen`.

Table 4.25 Values for random index RI

n	1	2	3	4	5	6	7	8	9	10
RI	0.00	0.00	0.58	0.90	1.12	1.24	1.32	1.41	1.45	1.49

Table 4.26 Values for parameter L

n	3	4	>4
L	0.05	0.09	0.1

Table 4.27 Step 5 of AHP: consistency check

	All criteria	Quality	Price	Service	Lead time
λ_{max}	4.13	4.12	4.11	4.14	4.05
CI	0.045	0.041	0.038	0.045	0.017
RI	0.9	0.9	0.9	0.9	0.9
CR	0.050	0.045	0.042	0.050	0.019

Parameters RI and L need to be read from Tables 4.25 and 4.26. Saaty's consistency ratio condition is given by

$$CR \leq L, \tag{4.36}$$

i.e., if $CR > L$ it is required to revise and evaluate the results from pairwise comparison until $CR \leq L$ is fulfilled. Table 4.27 shows that consistency is fulfilled in our numerical example.

Over the years, AHP was extended in several ways. For instance, the analytic network process (ANP) allows for inter-dependencies between decision criteria or AHP for group decision-making focuses on an aggregation of individual preference rankings in a consensus ranking. For further details, we refer to [4].

4.5.4 Technique for Order Preference by Similarity to Ideal Solution (TOPSIS)

The Technique for Order Preference by Similarity to Ideal Solution (TOPSIS) is another multi-criteria decision-making method introduced by Hwang and Yoon in 1981 (see [18]). It measures the geometric distance to the ideal solution per criterion $k = 1, \ldots, K$, i.e., the solution with the best score for a specific criterion.

In the supplier selection and evaluation process, the method follows the following seven steps.

Table 4.28 Evaluation matrix

	Quality	Price	Service	Lead time
Supplier 1	$x_{11} = 9$	$x_{12} = 6$	$x_{13} = 9$	$x_{14} = 8$
Supplier 2	$x_{21} = 5$	$x_{22} = 10$	$x_{23} = 7$	$x_{24} = 5$
Supplier 3	$x_{31} = 6$	$x_{32} = 7$	$x_{33} = 4$	$x_{34} = 7$
Supplier 4	$x_{41} = 7$	$x_{42} = 7$	$x_{43} = 7$	$x_{44} = 7$

Table 4.29 Normalized matrix

	Quality	Price	Service	Lead time
Supplier 1	$r_{11} = 0.65$	$r_{12} = 0.39$	$r_{13} = 0.64$	$r_{14} = 0.59$
Supplier 2	$r_{21} = 0.36$	$r_{22} = 0.65$	$r_{23} = 0.50$	$r_{24} = 0.37$
Supplier 3	$r_{31} = 0.43$	$r_{32} = 0.46$	$r_{33} = 0.29$	$r_{34} = 0.51$
Supplier 4	$r_{41} = 0.51$	$r_{42} = 0.46$	$r_{43} = 0.50$	$r_{44} = 0.51$

Step 1: Evaluation Matrix

Draw a matrix of $s = 1, \ldots, S$ suppliers and $k = 1, \ldots, K$ decision criteria. This results in an evaluation matrix as shown in Table 4.28 with scores x_{sk} based on a scale from 1 (bad) to 10 (very good).

Step 2: Normalization

Normalize the evaluation matrix from step 1 using the following formula for all combinations of suppliers $s = 1, \ldots, S$ and decision criteria $k = 1, \ldots, K$:

$$r_{sk} = \frac{x_{sk}}{\sqrt{\sum_{i=1}^{S} x_{ik}^2}} \tag{4.37}$$

See Table 4.29.

Step 3: Weighted Normalized Decision Matrix

Calculate the weighted normalized decision matrix for all combinations of suppliers $s = 1, \ldots, S$ and decision criteria $k = 1, \ldots, K$ by

$$v_{sk} = w_k \cdot r_{sk} \tag{4.38}$$

with w_k as the criterion weight with $\sum_{k=1}^{K} w_k = 1$. Table 4.30 shows the results in case all criteria have the same weight (i.e., 0.25). Please note that the weights are obtained more objectively as discussed for AHP.

Table 4.30 Weighted normalized matrix

	Quality	Price	Service	Lead time
Supplier 1	$v_{11} = 0.16$	$v_{12} = 0.10$	$v_{13} = 0.16$	$v_{14} = 0.15$
Supplier 2	$v_{21} = 0.09$	$v_{22} = 0.16$	$v_{23} = 0.13$	$v_{24} = 0.09$
Supplier 3	$v_{31} = 0.11$	$v_{32} = 0.11$	$v_{33} = 0.07$	$v_{34} = 0.13$
Supplier 4	$v_{41} = 0.13$	$v_{42} = 0.11$	$v_{43} = 0.13$	$v_{44} = 0.13$

Table 4.31 Positive and negative ideal solutions

	Quality	Price	Service	Lead time
v_k^+	0.16	0.16	0.16	0.15
v_k^-	0.09	0.10	0.07	0.09

Step 4: Positive and Negative Ideal Solutions

Determine the positive ideal solution v_k^+ and the negative ideal solution v_k^-, i.e., the best and worst supplier per criterion $k = 1, \ldots, K$:

$$v_k^+ = \max_s v_{sk} \tag{4.39}$$

$$v_k^- = \min_s v_{sk} \tag{4.40}$$

See Table 4.31.

Step 5: Separation Measure

Calculate the separation measure *Delta* by calculating the distance between a supplier $s = 1, \ldots S$ and the best condition v_k^+ by

$$\Delta_s^+ = \sqrt{\sum_{k=1}^{K} \left(v_{sk} - v_k^+\right)^2}, \tag{4.41}$$

and by calculating the distance between a supplier $i = 1, \ldots, m$ and the worst condition v_j^- by

$$\Delta_s^- = \sqrt{\sum_{k=1}^{K} \left(v_{sk} - v_k^-\right)^2}. \tag{4.42}$$

See Table 4.32.

Table 4.32 Separation measures

	Supplier 1	Supplier 2	Supplier 3	Supplier 4
Δ^+	0.07	0.10	0.12	0.07
Δ^-	0.13	0.08	0.04	0.08

Table 4.33 Relative closeness

	Supplier 1	Supplier 2	Supplier 3	Supplier 4
C_s^*	0.66	0.46	0.27	0.51

Step 6: Relative Closeness

Calculate a score for each supplier, i.e., the relative closeness C_s^* to the ideal solution by

$$C_s^* = \frac{\Delta_s^-}{\Delta_s^+ + \Delta_s^-} \tag{4.43}$$

with $0 \leq C_s^* \leq 1$. $C_s^* = 1$ if and only if supplier s performs best across all criteria $k = 1, \ldots, K$ and $C_s^* = 0$ if and only if supplier s performs worst across all criteria $k = 1, \ldots, K$. For the example from Table 4.33, supplier 1 would get a relative closeness of 1 if price would be evaluated with a *10* rather than a *6*.

Step 7: Ranking and Decision

Rank all suppliers according to C_s^*, and select the supplier with C_s^* closest to 1. Consequently, Table 4.33 recommends to select supplier 1.

4.5.5 *Outranking Method (OM)*

The general idea behind outranking methods such as ELECTRE (ÉLimination Et Choix Traduisant la REalité or Elimination and Choice Translating Reality) and PROMETHEE (Preference Ranking Organisation Method for Enrichment Evaluations) is to consider the complex and unstructured nature of many decision problems. In practice, the decision problem is often not precisely defined, consequences are undetermined or preferences of decision-makers are unknown and/or inconsistent. Under these environments, outranking methods optimize decisions based on concordance and discordance sets. While the method dates back to Bernhard Roy (see [24]), De Boer et al. (see [11]) applied the method systematically to supplier selection and evaluation. The procedure follows four main steps that we want to illustrate based on the following example.

Table 4.34 Data input for outranking method

	Supplier A	Supplier B	Supplier C	Supplier D	Supplier E
Turnover in Mio. Euro	7.5	8	11	9	8
Distance in km	50	500	900	200	550
Cost level in Euro	20	15	18	25	11
Quality image	Moderate	Excellent	Good	Good	Bad

Numerical Example: Outranking for Supplier Selection and Evaluation
A company searches for a backup supplier to guarantee supply for essential components. The management agrees on the following (vague) criteria for supplier selection and collects related data:

- The supplier should be a relevant player, but not too big. The turnover should be around 9.5 million Euro.
- The supplier location should be close to the production site (just-in-time delivery).
- The cost should not be too large.
- The supplier should have a strong quality image.

See Table 4.34.

Step 1: Determination of Criteria Weights

Determine weights w_k for all decision criteria $k = 1, \ldots, K$. This can happen via an AHP process as described in Sect. 4.5.3. We skip this step and continue with the following weights for the criteria *Turnover* (0.2), *Distance* (0.15), *Cost* (0.3) and *Quality* (0.35).

Step 2: Determination of Discordance Sets

Define discordance sets, i.e., when to reject an outranking of supplier X by supplier Y. In our case, we define the following two discordance sets:

- Cost level of supplier Y is at least two times as high as cost level of supplier X.
- Quality image of supplier Y is bad while quality image of supplier X is excellent.

(continued)

Step 3: Determination of Concordance Index

Calculate concordance indices $conc(X, Y)$ between all supplier pairs. The concordance index is calculated by

$$conc(X, Y) = \sum_{k=1}^{K} z \cdot w_k \tag{4.44}$$

with

$$z = \begin{cases} 1, & \text{if supplier X dominates supplier Y} \\ 0, & \text{otherwise.} \end{cases} \tag{4.45}$$

This yields the concordance indices presented in Table 4.35.

Step 4: Determination of Concordance Threshold

Based on a concordance threshold, we can evaluate dominance or outranking relations. For example, given a concordance threshold of 0.8, supplier B outranks suppliers A and C, while supplier C outranks supplier A. However, a concordance threshold of 0.8 does not allow a comparison of suppliers B, D and E. Therefore, we adjust the concordance threshold to 0.7. Now, supplier B outranks suppliers A, C and E, supplier C outranks supplier A and supplier D outranks supplier C. Outranking of supplier E by supplier D is rejected because the cost level of supplier D is more than twice as high as the cost level of supplier E. Consequently, suppliers B and D are most promising and should be considered for further analysis.

Table 4.35 Resulting concordance indices

	Supplier A	Supplier B	Supplier C	Supplier D	Supplier E
Supplier A	–	0.15	0.15	0.45	0.50
Supplier B	0.85	–	1.00	0.65	0.70
Supplier C	0.85	0.20	–	0.65	0.55
Supplier D	0.55	0.35	0.70	–	0.70
Supplier E	0.50	0.50	0.65	0.30	–

4.5.6 Decision Trees (DT)

The decision tree is a powerful method to structure decision problems. Therefore, it can also support supplier selection decisions. We want to illustrate this in the following simplistic example.

Numerical Example: Decision Tree for Supplier Selection
Suppose that there are three potential suppliers (A,B,C). Each supplier has a specific structure of fixed cost c_F and variable cost c_v. The $(c_F; c_v)$ pairs of the three suppliers are as follows: A (100,000; 25), B (60,000; 40) and C (170,000; 15). Therefore, given a unit selling price of 60 Euro, it is easy to identify the most appropriate supplier via break-even analysis (see Sect. 4.2.1). However, this is only true if we know the customer demand. In our example, customer demand is uncertain and modeled by three scenarios: A pessimistic scenario (scenario 1) with a demand of 4,000 and a probability of occurrence of 20%, an average scenario (scenario 2) with a demand of 8,000 and a probability of 50% and an optimistic scenario (scenario 3) with a demand of 12,000 and a probability of 30%. Based on this data, we can draw a decision tree calculating scenario profits π (Fig. 4.16).

We observe that scenario 1 favors supplier A, while scenario 2 and 3 favor supplier C. Because we do not know which scenario will happen but we know (or think we know) scenario probabilities, we can follow an expected value approach by weighting profits by scenario probabilities. Therefore, we get an expected profit of $\pi = 194{,}000$ if we select supplier A, an expected profit of $\pi = 108{,}000$ if we select supplier B and an expected profit of $\pi = 208{,}000$ if we select supplier C. This yields a selection decision for supplier C.

4.5.7 Data Envelopment Analysis (DEA)

Data envelopment analysis is another standard method in multi-criteria decision-making based on efficiency scores of decision-making units (DMUs) using multiple inputs and outputs. Originally developed by Charnes, Cooper and Rhodes in 1978 (see [8]), it was applied to various settings such as university rankings, efficiency measurement of ports and hospitals as well as performance evaluation of bank branches. The general idea is to identify the so-called efficiency frontier (see Fig. 4.17). Suppliers at this efficiency frontier are so-called efficient suppliers and potential candidates for supplier selection; others are not.

A main characteristic of DEA is not giving any a priori weights to criteria. Determining criteria weights after suppliers have been scored provides an advantage

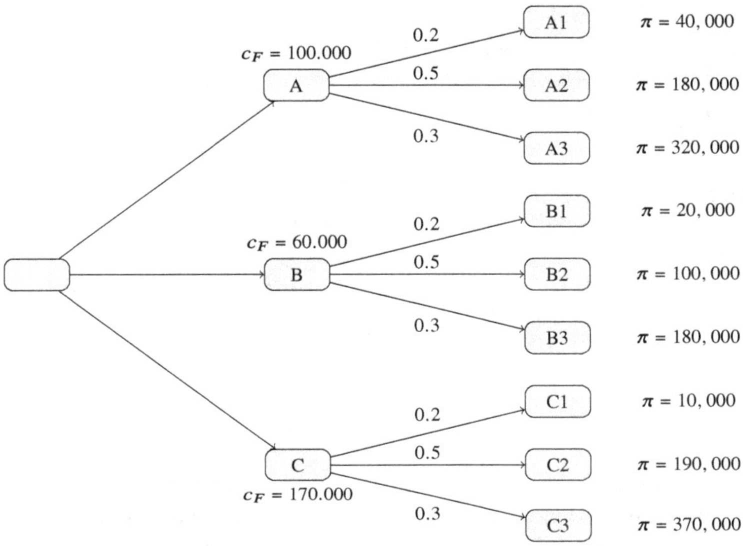

Fig. 4.16 Decision tree

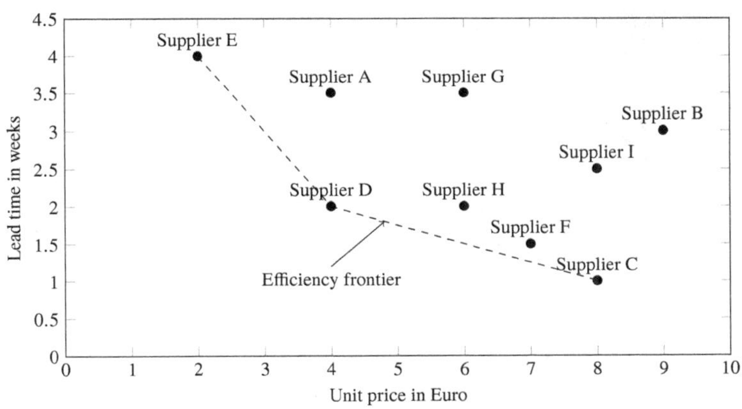

Fig. 4.17 Concept of DEA

from a fairness perspective over WSM or AHP where the selection results can easily be manipulated by (slightly) changing the criteria weights in favor of their preferred supplier(s).

For a simple setup with two selection criteria, the graphical method works as illustrated in Fig. 4.17. However, if there are more than two criteria, an analytical model is needed. Therefore, DEA mathematically defines efficiency Δ as the sum of weighted outputs divided by the sum of weighted inputs. Inputs $i = 1, \ldots, I$ are all criteria with "the lower the better" (e.g., price, lead time, probability of failure). Outputs $j = 1, \ldots, J$ are all criteria with "the higher the better" (e.g., quality, service, supply capacity). This is determined by a nonlinear optimization problem with input weights u_i and output weights v_j that are not predetermined but optimized per supplier $s_1, \ldots, S$:

$$\text{maximize} \quad \Delta_{s=1} = \frac{\text{Output}}{\text{Input}} = \frac{\sum_{j=1}^{J} v_j \cdot y_{s=1,j}}{\sum_{i=1}^{I} u_i \cdot x_{s=1,i}} \tag{4.46}$$

$$\text{s.t.} \quad \frac{\sum_{j=1}^{J} v_j \cdot y_{sj}}{\sum_{i=1}^{I} u_i \cdot x_{si}} \leq 1 \qquad \forall s = 1, \ldots, S \tag{4.47}$$

$$v_j, u_i \geq 0 \qquad \forall i = 1, \ldots, I, j = 1, \ldots, J \tag{4.48}$$

All efficient suppliers $s = 1, \ldots, S$ get an efficiency score $\Delta = 1$, while inefficient suppliers have an efficiency score $\Delta < 1$. In order to solve the problem by standard solvers (e.g., `Excel Solver`), it needs to be linearized:

$$\text{maximize} \quad \Delta_{s=1} = \sum_{j=1}^{J} v_j \cdot y_{s=1,j} \tag{4.49}$$

$$\text{s.t.} \quad \sum_{i=1}^{I} u_i \cdot x_{s=1,i} = 1 \tag{4.50}$$

$$\sum_{j=1}^{J} v_j \cdot y_{sj} = \sum_{i=1}^{I} u_i \cdot x_{si} \qquad \forall s = 1, \ldots, S \tag{4.51}$$

$$v_j, u_i \geq 0 \qquad \forall i = 1, \ldots, I, j = 1, \ldots, J \tag{4.52}$$

This optimization model needs to be solved independently for each supplier $s = 1, \ldots, S$ and optimized input and output weights u_i and v_j such that the supplier's efficiency score Δ is maximized under the restriction that efficiency is limited by 1. This captures the idea that each supplier would be willing to set the weights of criteria in a way that favors its own performance. If a supplier is not efficient (i.e., efficiency score $\Delta < 1$) even when being able to set its individual weights, it should not be considered for selection. Nevertheless, DEA results can also provide a strong data-driven basis for negotiation with inefficient suppliers in order to improve their performance in specific dimensions.

Table 4.36 Data input for DEA

Suppliers	A	B	C	D	E	F
Unit price in Euro	0.31	0.12	0.10	0.17	0.78	0.41
Avg. Lead time in weeks	1.03	0.77	0.95	1.16	0.97	1.54
Probability of failure in %	0.02	0.01	0.01	0.03	0.02	0.04

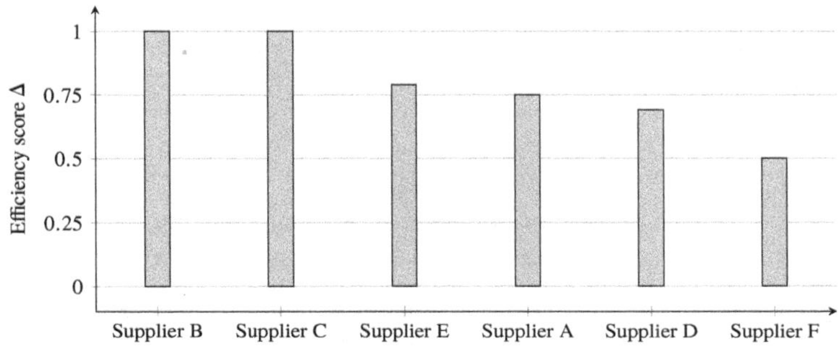

Fig. 4.18 Output of DEA model for supplier selection

Numerical Example: DEA for Supplier Selection and Evaluation
Prior to supplier selection decision, criteria data is collected as presented in Table 4.36. All criteria are of input type (the lower the better). Therefore, output can be normalized to 1 for all suppliers A–F.

Solving the DEA-LP, we obtain the results that are illustrated in Fig. 4.18 that show that two suppliers are categorized as efficient (Supplier B and C). The recommendation is to consider those two suppliers in the further process and decide for one of them based on individual preferences (e.g., high cost sensitivity favors C, while high time sensitivity favors B). For those suppliers with an efficiency score lower than 1, it may be valuable to inform them about percentage deviations to "best in class" and give them the chance to update their offers. Therefore, DEA is an effective data-driven basis for supplier (re-)negotiations based on efficiency scores (Fig. 4.18).

4.5.8 Linear Programming (LP)

Problem-tailored linear programming algorithms can also be used for optimal supplier selection decisions (see [17] for an overview). The advantage of an LP approach is that different (operational) restrictions can easily be incorporated through constraints. In the following, we describe a combined supplier selection and order allocation problem where suppliers $s = 1, \ldots, S$ need to be selected for delivering different input materials $i = 1, \ldots, I$ to different production sites $j = 1, \ldots, J$ from where the company serves its customers with its final products $k = 1, \ldots, K$. For a data-driven supplier selection, we have the following data available:

- Demand and capacity parameters
  - D_{kj}: Demand for product k at production site j
  - A_{ik}: Required units of input material i per unit of product k
  - K_{is}: Capacity of supplier s for supply of input material i
- Cost parameters
  - C_{is}: Unit cost of input material i at supplier s
  - L_{sj}: Logistics cost for transportation of one unit from supplier s to site j
  - F_{is}: Fixed cost per supplier s for delivery of input material i

The objective is to select the suppliers and determine the order quantities at each supplier in order to minimize the total cost via the following LP:

$$\text{minimize} \quad \sum_{s=1}^{S} \sum_{i=1}^{I} F_{is} \cdot y_{is} + \sum_{j=1}^{J} (C_{is} + L_{sj}) \cdot x_{isj} \tag{4.53}$$

$$\text{s.t.} \quad \sum_{s=1}^{S} x_{isj} = A_{ik} \cdot D_{kj} \qquad \forall i, j, k \tag{4.54}$$

$$\sum_{j=1}^{J} x_{isj} \leq K_{is} \cdot y_{is} \qquad \forall i, s \tag{4.55}$$

$$y_{is} \in \{0, 1\}, x_{isj} \geq 0 \qquad \forall i, s, j \tag{4.56}$$

The binary decision variable y_{is} indicates whether a supplier s is selected for delivering input material i or not (supplier selection). The decision variable x_{isj} defines the order quantity of input material i at supplier s for production site j (order allocation). The first constraint ensures demand satisfaction, and the second considers limitations in supply capacity.

Numerical Example: LP-Based Supplier Selection

A company needs to purchase three different materials from four potential suppliers (A, B, C, D) in order to manufacture three products (Standard, Premium, Exclusive) in two production sites (Berlin, Munich). The input data is shown in Tables 4.37 and 4.38.

The optimal LP solution shows that material 1 is sourced from supplier A, C and D; material 2 is sourced from supplier A, B and D; and material 3

(continued)

is sourced from supplier B only. This minimizes the total cost of 1,346,000 including fixed cost of 710,000, logistics cost of 147,500 (Munich) and 200,000 (Berlin) as well as purchase cost of 121,500 (Munich) and 167,000 (Berlin).

Table 4.37 Input data for supplier selection LP

	Material 1	Material 2	Material 3
Quantity *A*			
Standard	1	2	1
Premium	2	1	1
Exclusive	3	1	0
Capacity *K*			
Supplier A	30	10	20
Supplier B	30	30	30
Supplier C	30	10	20
Supplier D	30	20	10
Unit price *C*			
Supplier A	1	2	3
Supplier B	1.5	2.5	2.5
Supplier C	1.6	1.2	2
Supplier D	1.9	1	2
Fixed cost *F*			
Supplier A	100	90	80
Supplier B	110	100	90
Supplier C	120	110	100
Supplier D	110	100	100

Table 4.38 Input data for production sites

	Munich	Berlin
Demand D		
Standard	5.000	10.000
Premium	10.000	5.000
Exclusive	5.000	5.000
Unit logistics cost L		
Supplier A	1	1.5
Supplier B	4	3.5
Supplier C	1.5	2
Supplier D	2	1.5

Table 4.39 Method comparison: supplier selection and evaluation

Method	Benefits	Limitations
WSM/WPM	Simple methodology	Subjective weight determination
	Fast implementation	Subjective criteria determination
AHP	Qualitative and quantitative	Relatively high effort
	Consistency check	Still subjective evaluation
TOPSIS	Many criteria possible	No consistency check
	Many suppliers possible	Relatively high effort
Outranking	High stability	Higher complexity
	Suitable for fuzzy setups	Subjective thresholds
Decision Tree	Very illustrative	Only quantitative
	Probability-based	Prone to forecast error
DEA	High modeling flexibility	High complexity
	Objective evaluation	Opt solver required
LP	High modeling flexibility	High complexity
	Objective evaluation	Opt solver required

4.5.9 Method Comparison

Table 4.39 gives a brief comparison of benefits and limitations of the different multi-criteria decision-making methods (MCDM) introduced in this chapter. Please note that there is no one-size-fits-all approach, and the most appropriate method for supplier selection and evaluation needs to be selected carefully based on the comparison of those benefits and limitations. It needs to be considered that while WSM, WPM and AHP are quite intuitive and simple to explain, this is not necessarily true for more advanced linear programming-based methods such as DEA and LP, which can limit the acceptance of those methods in practice.

For most of the methods such as AHP, TOPSIS and Outranking methods, there is software available as part of broader supplier management software where the user enters its data and gets the evaluation (i.e., supplier ranking) subsequently. However, following Sect. 4.5, a proprietary development in spreadsheet or advanced software is also possible. For a further deep dive into supplier selection methods, we refer to the systematic reviews of [12, 17] and [3].

4.6 Supply Network Design

Supply networks are complex systems with many stages (tiers) and interactions (see Fig. 4.19). Therefore, supplier selection (see Sect. 4.5) also affects strategic objectives regarding the optimal design of supply chains or networks (also known as supply footprint). While over decades cost objectives were predominant for supply network design decisions, not since the COVID-19 pandemic showed that today's

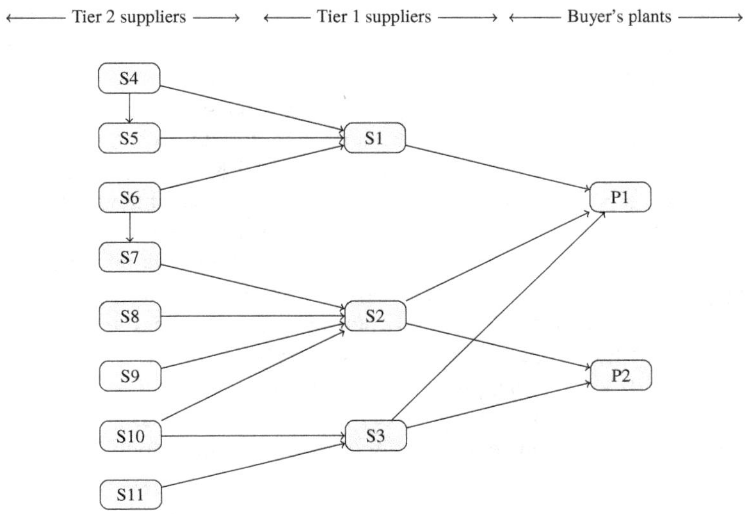

Fig. 4.19 Multi-tier supply network

supply chain planning requires to solve a multi-objective optimization problem with additional risk, resilience and sustainability goals. While cost-optimized supply networks typically yield a global footprint due to significant geographical labor cost differentials, sustainability and resilience aspects often recommend a supply chain reconfiguration with local-for-local networks or dual sourcing with an additional local source that reduces supply disruption risk and the carbon emissions generated by long-distance transportation and less ecological production facilities in low-cost countries.

4.6.1 Supply Chain Mapping

In order to evaluate the sub-optimality of the status quo supply network with regard to the cost-risk-resilience-sustainability trade-offs, it is essential to map the current supply network. This becomes even more important with regard to *Supply Chain Acts* that requires end-to-end transparency along the supply chain from tier-1 upstream to tier-n. However, according to the Deloitte 2021 Global Chief Procurement Officer Survey, while around 70% of CPOs mentioned that they have high visibility with regard to tier-1 suppliers, only 15% of CPOs currently have visibility into tier-2 suppliers and beyond, which already makes supply chain mapping a tremendously complex task.

Why is this the case? Supply chain mapping is typically not as simple as illustrated in Fig. 4.19, given that automotive manufacturers such as Porsche handle around 7,000 first-tier suppliers. First-tier suppliers, such as Bosch or Continental, again work with several thousand suppliers (second-tier suppliers). [16] empirically analyzed the complexity of automotive semiconductor supply chains between five major chip manufacturers and seven automotive OEMs. They found that there are on average 416 intermediary suppliers, 11,533 supply chain links and 3,589 source-destination links. Furthermore, supply networks are dynamic and change frequently after supplier selection processes. This immense complexity in supply chain mapping asks for prioritization and a focus on the most critical suppliers. These can be suppliers with high spend contribution or high-risk suppliers.

Depending of the scope of the analysis, supply chain mapping distinguishes between demand density mapping, sales territory mapping, isochrone mapping, center of gravity mapping (supply or demand) and gross margin mapping. Furthermore, software solutions exist for digital and real-time supply chain mapping, for instance, Sourcemap, SupplyChainMapper, Chainpoint, Sedex and Loghub. Furthermore, digital twins of supply chains using simulation models recently become increasingly popular. BMW, for instance, also uses blockchain technology to increase transparency along the supply chain and leverages media analysis for auditing suppliers between tier 1 and raw materials suppliers.

However, supply chain mapping does not per se give any decision-support for supply chain re-design/re-configuration in order to optimize the supply base footprint. Therefore, in the following, we present approaches for supply network optimization focusing on different aspects.

4.6.2 Deterministic Supply Network Optimization

Data-driven decision-support in supply network design is typically based on a fundamental optimization problem, i.e., the warehouse location problem (WLP), which is an extension of the transportation problem introduced in Chap. 2. While WLP is often used for distribution network design, it also builds the analytical basis for supply and production network optimization considering the trade-off between variable cost (e.g., transportation cost) and fixed cost (e.g., labor cost, lease cost).

The warehouse location problem (WLP) (often also referred to as facility location problem) aims at finding the optimal warehouse or supply location(s) to satisfy geographically distributed demand under capacity restrictions (capacitated WLP). The objective is to minimize the total network (or supply chain) cost consisting of fixed cost (e.g., for supply or warehouse rents) and variable cost (e.g., transportation cost from suppliers to production facilities). The problem can be formulated as a MILP model as follows:

$$\text{minimize} \quad \sum_{i=1}^{I} f_i \cdot y_i + \sum_{i=1}^{I}\sum_{j=1}^{J} c_{ij} \cdot x_{ij} \tag{4.57}$$

$$\text{s.t.} \quad \sum_{i=1}^{I} x_{ij} = d_j \qquad \forall j = 1, \ldots, J \tag{4.58}$$

$$\sum_{j=1}^{J} x_{ij} \leq k_i \cdot y_i \qquad \forall i = 1, \ldots, I \tag{4.59}$$

$$x_{ij} \leq y_i \qquad \forall j = 1, \ldots, J \tag{4.60}$$

$$y_i \in \{0, 1\}, x_{ij} \geq 0 \qquad \forall i = 1, \ldots, I, j = 1, \ldots, J \tag{4.61}$$

The decision variable y_i determines whether a supply location $i = 1, \ldots, I$ with specific fixed cost f_i should be selected or not. The decision variable x_{ij} determines the transportation quantity from supply location $i = 1, \ldots, I$ to demand location $j = 1, \ldots, J$ under consideration of variable transportation cost c_{ij}. The overall objective is to minimize the total supply chain cost as sum of fixed and variable cost. The constraints ensure that demand d_j is satisfied from one or more supply locations and that supply capacity k_i is not exceeded at any of the supply locations.

Numerical Example: Warehouse Location Problem

Suppose a company needs to decide about 5 potential supply locations (S1–S5) in order to serve 14 demand locations (D1–D14) that are geographically distributed over South Germany. The WLP determines which locations to choose and from where to serve the different demand locations in order to minimize total fixed and transportation cost given the data in Table 4.40.

Solving the WLP shows that the cost-optimal supply network uses all five supply options, which yields overall cost of 8.1 mn (3.1 mn fixed cost and 5.0 mn variable cost). All demand locations are served from one (typically close) supplier except of D7, which needs to be served from S4 and S5 due to limited supply capacity (Fig. 4.20).

The WLP is a simplified model considering one supply chain stage and does not address uncertainty in supply, demand or prices. Therefore, there are several extensions available such as a stochastic version for risk-robust location decisions (see Sect. 4.6.3), multi-echelon settings with n-tier supply chains (see Sect. 4.6.4) or multi-objective formulations considering resilience and sustainability aspects (see Sect. 4.6.5).

Table 4.40 Data: unit transportation cost between potential supply and demand locations, supply fixed cost, capacities and demand

Transportation cost per ton	S1	S2	S3	S4	S5	Demand in ton
D1	196	155	42	109	138	3.000
D2	90	80	180	108	144	4.000
D3	147	107	136	65	84	9.000
D4	72	32	126	20	64	5.000
D5	252	211	57	165	231	9.000
D6	146	105	62	60	125	14.000
D7	180	178	223	152	110	9.000
D8	54	92	240	140	121	4.000
D9	62	58	200	90	120	3.000
D10	11	36	189	84	78	2.000
D11	74	76	178	85	10	12.000
D12	170	123	125	128	194	3.000
D13	34	40	194	88	47	4.000
D14	157	172	256	136	85	2.000
Supply capacity in ton	10.000	20.000	27.000	22.000	15.000	
Fixed cost	225.000	652.500	720.000	922.500	562.500	

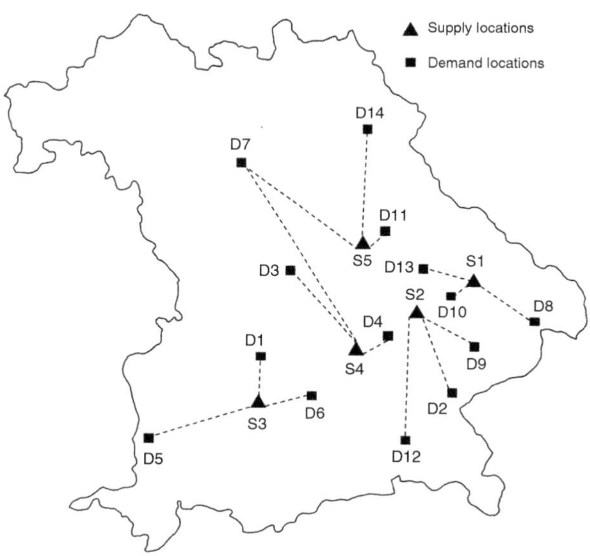

Fig. 4.20 Solution of warehouse location problem

4.6.3 Stochastic Supply Network Optimization

In this section, we present stochastic programming approaches to derive resilient supply networks under demand, supply or cost (e.g., exchange rate) uncertainty. The formulations are based on the generic form of the deterministic warehouse location problem as presented in Sect. 4.6.2.

Stochastic Supply Network Optimization Under Demand Risk

If demand is uncertain, the supply network optimization model can be formulated as a scenario approach with scenarios $s = 1, \ldots, S$ for demand d_{js} of demand location j and scenario probabilities P_s with $\sum_{s=1}^{S} P_s = 1$. This allows to model, for instance, a best case (high-demand) scenario, average-case (medium-demand) scenario and worst-case (low-demand) scenario. While scenario optimization calculates the optimal supply network decisions for each single scenario s, a stochastic programming approach finds one optimal supply network that performs well in each demand scenario. The stochastic programming model is represented by the following mixed-integer linear program:

$$\text{minimize} \quad \sum_{i=1}^{I} f_i \cdot y_i + \sum_{s=1}^{S} P_s \cdot \sum_{j=1}^{J} c_{ij} \cdot x_{ijs}$$

$$\text{s.t.} \quad \sum_{i=1}^{I} x_{ijs} = d_{js} \qquad \forall j = 1, \ldots, J, s = 1, \ldots, S$$

$$\sum_{j=1}^{J} x_{ijs} \le k_i \cdot y_i \qquad \forall i = 1, \ldots, I, s = 1, \ldots, S$$

$$x_{ijs} \le y_i \qquad \forall j = 1, \ldots, J, s = 1, \ldots, S$$

$$y_i \in \{0, 1\}, x_{ijs} \ge 0 \qquad \forall i = 1, \ldots, I, j = 1, \ldots, J, s = 1, \ldots, S$$

The objective function minimizes the total cost, which includes fixed cost f_i at supply location i and probability-weighted variable cost c_{ij} (e.g., transportation cost between supply location i and demand location j), by simultaneously determining the supply network design y_i (here-and-now decision, first-stage decision) and transportation decisions x_{ijs} (wait-and-see decision, second-stage decision) from supply location i to demand location j in demand scenario s. The first constraint ensures that demand d_{js} is met in all demand scenarios s for all demand locations j (robust network). The second constraint refers to capacity restriction k_i at supply location i, and the third constraint ensures that only selected operating supply locations i can provide supply.

Table 4.41 Supply network location: input data

Transportation cost per ton	S1	S2	S3	S4	S5
D1	1675	1460	1925	380	922
D2	700	1940	2400	1355	1646
D3	685	970	1425	699	700
D4	1630	400	655	1045	508
D5	1160	600	950	665	311
D6	2800	1200	800	2321	1797
Capacity (ton)	60	45	20	20	40
Fixed cost	8000	4000	5000	4000	2000

Table 4.42 Demand scenarios

Demand in tons	Low-demand scenario	Average-demand scenario	High-demand scenario
D1	9	12	15
D2	7	10	13
D3	13	16	19
D4	5	8	11
D5	6	9	12
D6	10	13	16
Scenario probability	0.3	0.4	0.3

Numerical Example: Stochastic Supply Network Design under Demand Risk

Suppose the following supply network planning problem with five potential supply locations (S1–S5) with limited capacities and fixed cost that can be selected to satisfy the demand at six demand locations (D1–D6) (Table 4.41).

Demand at the demand locations is fluctuating and not known with certainty. Therefore, demand is modeled by a scenario approach with a low-demand scenario, an average-demand scenario and a high-demand scenario (Table 4.42).

Based on the data given, the stochastic programming approach for supply network modeling selects suppliers 1, 3, 4 and 5. This yields expected supply network cost of 58,783 under consideration of the given scenario probabilities. Deterministic supply network design under the average-demand scenario (expected value scenario) would select suppliers 3, 4 and 5, which is a supply network that is not feasible under the high-demand scenario with a cumulative demand of 86 that exceeds the available capacity at supplier locations 3, 4 and 5. Therefore, the deterministic planning approach would not yield a resilient and robust supply network that is able to operate in high-demand scenarios, which shows the necessity and value of stochastic planning approaches in practice.

Stochastic Supply Network Design Under Exchange Rate Risk

If there is currency exchange rate risk between supply locations $i = 1, \ldots, I$ and demand locations $j = 1, \ldots, J$, a scenario-based stochastic programming approach can help find a supply network that is robust toward exchange rate fluctuations. Therefore, different scenarios $s = 1, \ldots, S$ of exchange rates e_{ijs} are calculated (e.g., best case scenario, average case scenario, worst case scenario) and together with scenario probabilities P_s included into the standard formulation of the warehouse location problem. For scenario generation, we refer to standard stochastic processes such as random walk or mean-reverting models that are also used for modeling commodity prices (see Sect. 6.3.2).

Stochastic Supply Network Design Under Supply Disruption Risk

In practice, suppliers might be (temporarily) disrupted by labor strikes, natural disasters or simply unfavorable weather conditions. During the COVID-19 pandemic, we have seen random supply chain disruptions across industries due to (temporary) production shutdowns. This can significantly increase the supply network cost as buyers need to go for backup suppliers with higher transportation cost. A probabilistic network design can help simultaneously minimize (operating) cost and disruption (penalty) cost in order to maximize reliability. Disruption cost therefore needs to be quantified as lost sales cost of not serving demand location j or the cost of serving demand location j from an expensive emergency supply location.

The *reliable capacitated facility location problem (RCFLP)* uses a stochastic programming approach in order to develop a resilient supply network under supply disruption risk scenarios. In the following, we present the $RCFLP$ approach that follows [26].

The $RCFLP$ uses a two-stage stochastic programming approach with strategic first-stage decisions (i.e., supplier location selection) and tactical/operational second-stage decisions (i.e., supply quantities). While the standard WLP formulation minimizes the sum of fixed cost and variable cost, the RCFLP additionally considers a penalty cost for unmet demand due to supply disruptions. Let $i = 1 \ldots, I$ be potential supply locations with supply capacity k_i and fixed cost f_i and $j = 1, \ldots, J$ as the demand locations with demand d_j. Unit transportation costs are denoted as c_{ij}, and unit penalty cost for unmet demand at demand location j is given by o_j. Random supply disruptions are modeled by disruption scenarios $s = \{s_1, \ldots, s_I\}$ with $s_i = 1$ if supply location i is not disrupted and $s_i = 0$ if supply location i is disrupted. P_s is the probability that disruption scenario s occurs.

This yields the following mixed-integer linear programming formulation with decision variable $y_i \in \{0, 1\}$ as the supply location selection decision and $x_{ijs} \geq 0$ as the fraction of demand from demand location j satisfied by supply location i in scenario s. Additionally, z_{js} defines the fraction of demand from demand location j that is not satisfied in scenario s due to disruptions and therefore penalized.

$$
\begin{aligned}
\text{minimize} \quad & \sum_{i=1}^{I} f_i \cdot y_i + \sum_{s=1}^{S} P_s \left(\sum_{i=1}^{I} \sum_{j=1}^{J} d_j \cdot c_{ij} \cdot x_{ijs} + \sum_{j=1}^{J} d_j \cdot o_j \cdot z_{js} \right) \\
\text{s.t.} \quad & \sum_{i=1}^{I} x_{ijs} + z_{js} = 1 \quad \forall j = 1, \dots, J, s = 1, \dots, S \\
& \sum_{j=1}^{J} x_{ijs} \cdot d_j \leq k_i \cdot s_i \cdot y_i \quad \forall i = 1, \dots, I \\
& x_{ijs}, z_{js} \geq 0 \quad \forall i = 1, \dots, I, j = 1, \dots, J, s = 1, \dots, S \\
& y_i \in \{0, 1\} \quad \forall i = 1, \dots, I
\end{aligned} \tag{4.62}
$$

The objective function minimizes the sum of fixed cost and probability-weighted variable cost including penalty cost for unmet demand. The first constraint guarantees that customer demand is either assigned to a supply location or unmet and therefore penalized. The second constraint ensures that operation only can take place from non-disrupted supply locations up to its capacity limit. Therefore, supply location decisions y_i are taken in order to increase reliability or resilience of the supply network.

4.6.4 Multi-echelon Supply Network Optimization

Supply network optimization is based on multi-echelon (or multi-stage) and multi-product (or multi-commodity) facility or warehouse location models. A typical model can look as follows as adapted from [27].

$$
\begin{aligned}
\min \quad & \sum_{s=1}^{S} g_s \cdot z_s + \sum_{i=1}^{I} f_i \cdot y_i + \sum_{p=1}^{P} \sum_{s=1}^{S} \sum_{i=1}^{I} c_{psi} \cdot x_{psi} + \sum_{p=1}^{P} \sum_{i=1}^{I} \sum_{j=1}^{J} d_{pij} \cdot w_{pij} \\
\text{s.t.} \quad & \sum_{i=1}^{I} w_{pij} = d_{pj} \quad \forall j = 1, \dots, J; p = 1, \dots, P \\
& \sum_{j=1}^{J} \sum_{p=1}^{P} a_p \cdot w_{pij} \leq A_i \cdot y_i \quad \forall i = 1, \dots, I
\end{aligned}
$$

$$\sum_{i=1}^{I}\sum_{p=1}^{P} a_p \cdot x_{psj} \leq B_s \cdot z_s \quad \forall s = 1, \ldots, S$$

$$\sum_{s=1}^{S} x_{psi} = \sum_{j=1}^{J} w_{pij} \quad \forall i = 1, \ldots, I;\ p = 1, \ldots, P$$

$$z_s, y_i \in \{0, 1\} \quad \forall s = 1, \ldots, S;\ i = 1, \ldots, I$$

$$x_{psi}, w_{pij} \geq 0 \quad \forall p = 1, \ldots, P;\ s = 1, \ldots, S;\ i = 1, \ldots, I;\ j = 1, \ldots, J$$

g_s is the fixed (annual) cost to contract supplier $s = 1, \ldots, S$ at a specific location. z_s is a binary decision variable that indicates whether a supplier s is selected or not. y_i is a binary decision variable that indicates whether a production facility $i = 1, \ldots, I$ is used at an (annual) fixed cost f_i or not. x_{psi} is the number of units of product p shipped from supplier s to production facility i at a unit cost of c_{psi}. w_{pij} is the number of units of product p shipped from production plant i to customer $j = 1, \ldots, J$ at a unit cost of d_{pij}. The first constraint guarantees demand satisfaction for demand d_{pj} at each customer j for each ordered product p. The second (third) constraint restricts capacity A_i (B_s) of production site i (supplier s) given the units of capacity consumed a_p by one unit of product p. The fourth constraint ensures that everything shipped into a production plant needs to be shipped out again.

4.6.5 Multi-objective Supply Network Optimization

Suppose there are ten potential suppliers geographically distributed and ten buyer plants. There can be different objectives for supply network design: (a) cost-optimized design, (b) resilience-optimized design or (c) sustainability-optimized design.

For **cost-optimized supply network design**, the decision is about selecting suppliers with minimal setup and transportation cost (see *Warehouse Location Problem*). Cost-optimized supply network design typically does not take other objectives into account such as supply resilience and sustainability except both are quantified as cost and added to the objective function. In practice, this typically leads to a global supply network accepting higher transportation cost due to significantly lower labor cost in low-cost countries.

For **resilience-optimized supply network design**, various approaches are possible. One can either extend the standard WLP by restricting distances between supply and demand locations under the assumption that the probability of supply disruptions increases with transportation distance. This favors local sourcing rather than global sourcing. Another approach is to force dual sourcing of critical items or for critical supply and demand locations. This can be achieved by additional dual-sourcing constraints. However, a resilience-optimized supply network is typically not cost optimal as resilience comes with a specific cost. The optimization model allows to quantify this cost, i.e.,

$$\text{Total Cost of Resilience} = \frac{\text{Cost}_R - \text{Cost}_C}{\text{Cost}_C} \cdot 100\% \tag{4.63}$$

with Cost_R as the total cost of a resilience-optimized supply chain and Cost_C as the total cost of a cost-optimized supply chain.

For **sustainability-optimized supply network design**, additional constraints related to the environmental impact are included to the standard WLP, or environmental costs are explicitly considered in the objective function. This can be cost for scope-1 emissions, which include emissions resulting from own production sites and the own vehicle fleet, and scope-3 emissions, which summarize all emissions generated along the value chain (upstream and downstream) including emissions from purchasing goods and services, transportation and capital goods (upstream) as well as product distribution, use, and disposal (downstream). To deal with environmental impact in supply network design, different approaches are possible that all address the path to net zero emissions or the minimization of the carbon footprint that many companies define as new major business objective.

For instance, transportation cost can get a higher weight in the objective function of the WLP that balances fixed cost and transportation cost. This would yield supply networks with rather more supply locations that are closer to the demand locations.

As carbon prices will increasingly become a significant cost factor for companies (below 10 Euro per ton in 2017, 85 Euro per ton in December 2022), another approach is to explicitly add a carbon price component (per tons CO2 equivalent) to the objective function of the WLP. This approach can be combined with an additional decision to choose the optimal transportation mode $m = 1, \ldots, M$ (e.g., rail, street, water) with each transportation mode between supply location i and demand location j getting an individual cost c_{ijm} (i.e., transportation cost including CO2 cost). The decision variable related to transportation quantities x_{ij} therefore needs to be adjusted to x_{ijm}.

Another approach is to limit the distance d_{ij} between a supply location i and a demand location j to d^{max} by either not generating decision variables x_{ij} where $d_{ij} > d^{max}$ or by adding another constraint, i.e.,

$$d_{ij} - M \cdot y \leq d^{max} \tag{4.64}$$

where M is a sufficiently big number and y is a binary auxiliary variable with $y = 1$ if $d_{ij} > d^{max}$. The following constraint sets x_{ij} to 0 if $y = 1$:

$$x_{ij} \leq (1 - y) \cdot M \tag{4.65}$$

4.7 Supply Contracting and Coordination

Supply contracts legally determine basic business conditions between buyers and suppliers through standard contract parameters that need to be negotiated. Parametrization includes:

- *Price structure* $p = a + b \cdot Q$ with a and b as price parameters and Q as the order quantity. A linear pricing scheme is characterized by $a = 0$, while a two-part tariff pricing scheme is characterized by $a > 0$, and a discount pricing scheme is characterized by $p = b(Q) \cdot Q$ with $b(Q)$ as a decreasing function in Q. We distinguish between all-unit discounts that apply to all units and incremental discounts that apply to those units only that are above defined breakpoints q_i (see Sect. 5.3.2).
- *Order quantity-related conditions* such as a minimum order quantity Q_{min} or quantity flexibility within an interval $[Q_{min}, Q_{max}]$.
- *Product return-related conditions* such as buy-back prices.
- *Delivery-related conditions* such as lead time, incoterms, contract horizon, order frequency and priority rules in shortage scenarios.
- *Quality-related conditions* such as dimensional tolerances.
- *Sustainability-related conditions* such as sustainability clauses that claim that suppliers measure their CO2 emissions and take actions to reduce them by, for instance, contracting a green energy provider.
- *Risk-related conditions* such as risk clauses that claim that the supplier develops effective disaster recovery plans for risks such as cyberattacks, floods and earthquakes or force majeure clauses that exempt contract parties from rights and obligations. This can also be price escalation clauses for raw material items or energy-intense production processes with heavy price fluctuations (see Chap. 6).

On the other hand, supply contracts are also used for supply chain coordination in order to maximize the profit of the entire supply chain. This is related to game theory with the goal to change the structure of the payoffs in a way that Nash equilibria are also pareto-optimal (see Chap. 2). In this section, we want to give an overview on how vertical (between buyer and supplier) and horizontal (between buyers) purchasing agreements can be set up in order to maximize benefits for all supply chain participants based on collaboration and coordination.

4.7.1 Consequences of Lacking Supply Chain Coordination

The most famous example in order to illustrate the consequences of a missing coordination between supply chain tiers is the *bullwhip effect* that was initially described by Jay Forrester in 1961 (see [14]).

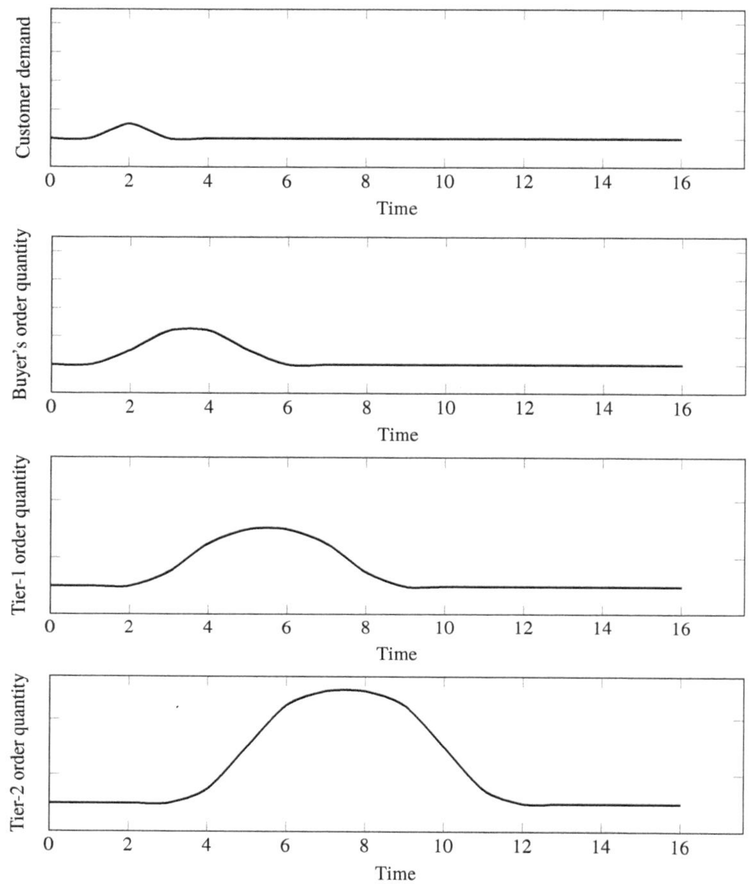

Fig. 4.21 Bullwhip effect

The bullwhip effect states that in supply chains, small fluctuations in demand at the customer level can lead to progressively larger fluctuations at the buyer's, tier-1 supplier's and tier-n supplier's level (see Fig. 4.21).

This leads to biased demand information because each stage of the supply chain derives different demand estimates and places (wrong) orders accordingly. The consequences of this lack in coordination are high inventory cost, high lead times and high transportation costs.

Industry Example: Bullwhip Effect during COVID-19
During the COVID-19 pandemic, industry observed panic buys for toilet papers, which led to empty shelves at supermarkets. As a consequence, toilet paper manufacturers ramped up production significantly without considering that the demand peak was a short-term event. Similar observations were made for other industries where companies raised orders as a consequence of container and harbor shortages.

A countermeasure against the bullwhip effect is information sharing through real-time data exchange between the different stages of the supply chain and subsequently collaborative capacity and inventory planning (*collaborative supply chains*). This can be achieved through, for instance, vendor-managed inventory (VMI) systems with both manufacturers and suppliers exchanging various information such as demand, inventory data as well as promotion and sales that lead to demand peaks. Another countermeasure is order smoothing in order to reduce demand peaks that might give a wrong signal to supply chain partners. In the extreme case, this can be achieved through just-in-time (JIT) replenishment.

4.7.2 *Vertical Purchasing Agreements*

Supply contracts between suppliers and buyers are a powerful instrument to maximize supply chain profit (see also Sect. 4.2.2 on supplier partnerships). In the following, we want to illustrate the value of vertical cooperation (or even integration) of supply chain entities. The following analytical model helps quantify the value of coordinated procurement decisions in a buyer-supplier relationship. Therefore, we assume a three-stage supply chain as illustrated in Fig. 4.22.

The supply chain in Fig. 4.22 consists of three decision-makers with individual preferences. Without coordination, all aim at maximizing their individual profits and act accordingly. The supplier chooses its unit selling price p_S considering its own production cost c_S. The buyer reacts with order quantity Q and selects its own selling price p_B based on the customer's price response function $p_B = a - bQ$ where a and b are non-negative parameters. The following analysis is based on the

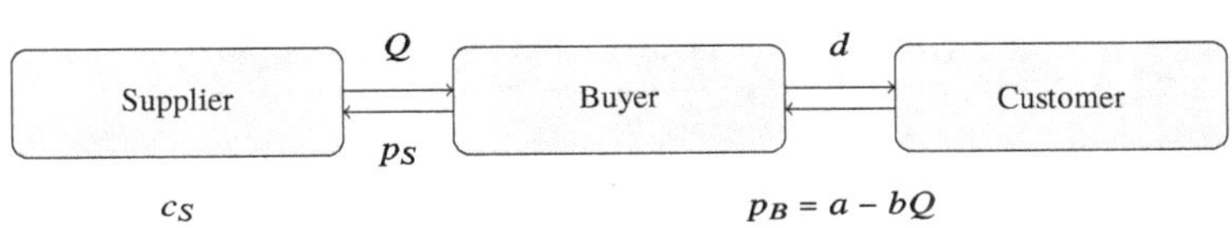

Fig. 4.22 Three-stage supply chain

assumption that the customer's demand d is known. We extend the analysis the setting where customer's demand d is unknown in Sect. 4.7.3.

Decentralized Planning

Without vertical cooperation and decentralized planning, the buyer and the supplier take their decisions in order to maximize their individual profits π_b and π_s.

The buyer's profit function is given by

$$\pi_B = (a - bQ) \cdot Q - p_s \cdot Q. \tag{4.66}$$

This yields the optimal (profit-maximizing) order quantity Q^*, i.e.,

$$Q^* = \frac{a - p_S}{2b} \tag{4.67}$$

and an optimal buyer's profit π_B^* of

$$\pi_B^* = \frac{(a - p_S)^2}{4b}. \tag{4.68}$$

The supplier maximizes its profit through optimized pricing p_S by anticipating the buyer's order quantity Q. The supplier's profit function is given by

$$\pi_S = (p_S - c_S) \cdot Q = (p_S - c_S) \cdot \frac{a - p_S}{2b}. \tag{4.69}$$

This yields an optimal (profit-maximizing) supplier's pricing of

$$p_S^* = \frac{a + c_S}{2} \tag{4.70}$$

and results in an optimal supplier's profit π_S^* of

$$\pi_S^* = \frac{(a - c_S)^2}{8b}. \tag{4.71}$$

Consequently, the total supply chain profit under decentralized planning is

$$\pi_S^* + \pi_B^* = \frac{(a - c_S)^2}{8b} + \frac{(a - p_S)^2}{4b} = \frac{3}{16} \cdot \frac{(a - c_S)^2}{b}. \tag{4.72}$$

Centralized Planning

Centralized planning aims at maximizing the profit of the entire supply chain under the supply chain's profit function π_{SC} rather than individual profits π_S and π_B. π_{SC} is calculated by

$$\pi_{SC} = (p_B - c_S) \cdot Q = (a - bQ - c_S) \cdot Q. \tag{4.73}$$

This yields an optimal (profit-maximizing) order quantity of

$$Q^*_{SC} = \frac{a - c_S}{2b} \tag{4.74}$$

and consequently an optimal supply chain profit π^*_{SC} of

$$\pi^*_{SC} = \frac{(a - c_S)^2}{4b}. \tag{4.75}$$

Double Marginalization

The analytical analysis shows that

$$\pi^*_{SC} = \frac{(a - c_S)^2}{4b} > \pi^*_S + \pi^*_B = \frac{3}{16} \cdot \frac{(a - c_S)^2}{b}, \tag{4.76}$$

i.e., the overall profit of centralized planning π^*_{SC} is 33.3% higher than the profit $\pi^*_S + \pi_B$ under decentralized planning. Therefore, there is a significant benefit of centralized planning because the buyer's order quantity is smaller than optimal because the buyer does not incorporate the supplier's profit under decentralized planning. This phenomenon is called *double marginalization*. The additional profit of 33.3% can be allocated between the supply chain entities (benefit allocation). For a fair allocation of profits, there exist several economic concepts such as bargaining solutions (e.g., Nash bargaining solution, Rubinstein bargaining solution), game-theoretic solutions (e.g., the Shapley value) and simple allocation rules (e.g., allocation proportional to quantity or cost). We illustrate the concept of Shapley value in Sect. 4.7.6.

Double marginalization can be avoided through different instruments such as (i) vertical integration of suppliers that increasingly becomes relevant when additionally supply risks play a role, (ii) marginal cost pricing (i.e., zero manufacturer profit) or (iii) nonlinear pricing schemes such as two-part tariffs and (iv) quantity discounts.

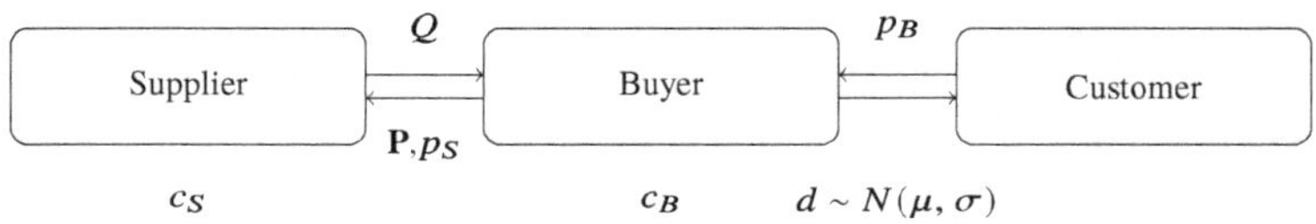

Fig. 4.23 Three-stage supply chain: customer's demand unknown

4.7.3 Supply Contracting Under Demand Risk

In practice, the customer's demand is often not known with certainty, which affects the buyer's purchasing decisions. In order to analyze the effects, we adjust the setup from Sect. 4.7.2 as follows based on the well-known newsvendor problem from inventory management (see Chap. 5).

According to Fig. 4.23, the customer's unknown demand d is modeled as a normal distribution $N(\mu, \sigma)$ with mean μ and standard deviation σ. The demand distribution function is denoted by $f(d)$ in the following. In case of stochastic demand, the buyer can only sell a quantity $\min[Q, D(p_B)]$ with $D(p_B)$ as the price-sensitive demand realization. Similar to the previous setup, c_S is the supplier's unit production cost, c_B is the buyer's marginal cost per unit and p_B is the retail price. Additionally, there is a unit salvage value g for each additional unit the buyer purchases but cannot sell to the customer. We introduce $\mathbf{P}$ as the total transfer payment from buyer to supplier that is specified by the corresponding form of the supply contract, while p_S is the defined unit price. Please note that in the following, we assume the simplest contract form of linear wholesale price contracts that defines transfer pricing as $\mathbf{P} = p_S \cdot Q$.

Decentralized Planning

Under decentralized planning, just like in Sect. 4.7.2, the buyer and the supplier take their decisions (pricing decision of the supplier, purchase decision of the buyer) individually in order to maximize their (expected) profits π_b and π_s (please note that we refer to expected profits because the optimization happens under uncertain demand environment). First, the supplier sets its price p_S. Based on the supplier's pricing, the buyer determines its optimal order quantity Q that maximizes its expected profit given by

$$\pi_B = -p_S \cdot Q + \int_0^Q (p_B \cdot d + g \cdot (Q - d)) \cdot f(d) \partial d + \int_Q^\infty p_B \cdot Q \cdot f(d) \partial d. \qquad (4.77)$$

The profit function includes expected lost sales are calculated by $ELS(Q) = \int_Q^\infty (d - Q) \cdot f(d) \partial d$, expected sales are given by $ES(Q) = E[d] - ELS(Q)$ and expected leftovers are given by $ELO(Q) = Q - ES(Q)$.

To derive the buyer's optimal order quantity Q^*, we use the newsvendor model from inventory theory (see Chap. 5). Therefore, the optimal order quantity Q^* is given by

$$Q^* = F^{-1}\left(\frac{p_B - p_S}{p_B - g}\right) \tag{4.78}$$

with F^{-1} as the inverse of the cumulative demand distribution function. The resulting profit of the supplier is given by

$$\pi_S = (p_S - c_S) \cdot Q^* \tag{4.79}$$

Centralized Planning

Under centralized planning, the expected supply chain profit is optimized, i.e.,

$$\pi_{SC} = -c_S \cdot Q + \int_0^Q (p_B \cdot d + g \cdot (Q - d)) \cdot f(d) \partial d + \int_Q^\infty p_B \cdot Q \cdot f(d) \partial d \tag{4.80}$$

with the supply chain-optimal order quantity Q^* again being derived by leveraging the newsvendor model from Sect. 5.5, i.e.,

$$Q^* = F^{-1}\left(\frac{p_B - c_S}{p_B - g}\right) \tag{4.81}$$

It turns out that due to double marginalization, the overall supply chain profit is larger in case of centralized planning. This is quantified by the performance indicator *price of anarchy (POA)* that is calculated by

$$\text{POA} = \frac{\pi_{SC}}{\pi_B + \pi_S}, \tag{4.82}$$

i.e., the overall supply chain profit under centralized planning divided by the individual profits of buyer and supplier under decentralized planning.

Numerical Example: Double Marginalization
Suppose that a three-stage supply chain is characterized by the following cost and demand structure. Under decentralized planning, the supplier sets a price $p_S = 150$ Euros. The buyer sells its product for a unit price of $p_B = 200$ Euros to its customer. The customer's demand d is uncertain and modeled by a normal distribution $N(\mu, \sigma)$ with mean $\mu = 1{,}000$ units and a standard

(continued)

deviation $\sigma = 400$ units. There is no salvage value for overage (i.e., $g = 0$). The supplier's unit cost is $c_S = 20$ Euros.

If both supplier and buyer plan independent of each other (decentralized planning), then the buyer would order $Q_B^* = 730$ units, which maximizes the buyer's expected profit of $\pi_B = 24{,}578$ Euros. The expected profit of the supplier is $\pi_S = 94{,}927$ Euros. Therefore, the total supply chain profit is $24{,}578 + 94{,}927 = 119{,}504$ Euros.

Under centralized supply chain planning, the optimal order quantity is $Q_{SC}^* = 1{,}513$ (and therefore more than 100% larger than the buyer's order quantity under decentralized planning), which yields an expected supply chain profit of $\pi_{SC} = 165{,}960$ Euros, which translate into a profit increase of almost 40% compared to the supply chain profit of decentralized planning.

The price of anarchy (POA) is 1.39.

In the analysis above, we assumed a linear pricing scheme $\mathbf{P} = p_S \cdot Q$. However, in practice, there is a variety of buyer-supplier contracts available that differ in the supplier's pricing structure. We analyze those contracts and its coordination effects in the following.

Wholesale Price Contract (WPC)

A wholesale price contract is the simplest form of supply contracts and determines that the buyer pays the supplier a given price p_S per unit Q ordered plus (if agreed) a fixed fee F (also called franchise fee), which results in the following transfer payment of the buyer:

$$\mathbf{P}^{\text{WPC}} = F + p_S \cdot Q. \tag{4.83}$$

The case $F = 0$ refers to a linear WPC pricing scheme, while $F > 0$ refers to a two-part tariff pricing scheme.

Wholesale price contracts do typically not optimize the supply chain profit and therefore do not coordinate the supply and yield double marginalization and price of anarchy as shown in the previous numerical examples. In the following, we present three contract types that differ from the standard non-coordinating *wholesale price contract (WPC)*. These contract types trigger the buyer to order a quantity that optimizes the profit of the supply chain without incentive for any supply chain member to deviate from the supply chain-optimal decision. They can be used to reduce double marginalization and increase overall supply chain performance by triggering more offensive purchasing behaviors at buyers through limitation of risk. For more information, we refer to the seminal work of [6] and [9].

Quantity-Flexibility Contracts (QFC)

A quantity flexibility contract (or contract with purchase volume flexibility) allows to flexibly adjust the purchase quantity Q after realization of the customer's demand. The contract contains a minimum and maximum quantity in between, and adjustment is possible anytime. The minimum order quantity is given by

$$Q_{min} = (1 - \beta) \cdot Q \tag{4.84}$$

and the maximum order quantity is given by

$$Q_{max} = (1 + \alpha) \cdot Q. \tag{4.85}$$

The supplier sets its price p_S and the limit parameters α and β, and the buyer optimizes its purchase decision Q^* based on the supplier's contract parameters (p_S,α,β). This reduces the buyer's risk of overage and leads to a more optimistic purchase decision.

Another variant of a QFC is that the suppliers charge a price p_S per unit and additionally compensate losses of unsold units up to a specific quantity $a \cdot Q$ with $0 \leq a \leq 1$. In this case, the transfer payment from buyer to supplier is given by

$$\mathbf{P}^{\text{QFC}} = p_s \cdot Q - (p_s + c_B - g) \cdot min\{ELO, a \cdot Q\}, \tag{4.86}$$

i.e., the buyer pays p_s per unit but gets compensated for unsold products. In practice, quantity-flexibility contracts are predominant for energy purchasing between companies and energy providers but also in dairy farming between creameries and farmers.

Buy-Back Contracts (BBC)

A buy-back contract allows buyers to buy a quantity Q at a price p_S and return overage $Q - d$ to the supplier at a predetermined unit refund $r < p_S$. Therefore, the transfer payment from buyer to supplier is characterized by

$$\mathbf{P}^{\text{BBC}} = p_s \cdot Q - r \cdot ELO(Q) \tag{4.87}$$

Consequently, in buy-back contracts, the buyer optimizes its order quantity Q to maximize the refund-adjusted expected profit:

$$\pi_B = -p_S \cdot Q + \int_0^Q (p_B \cdot d + r \cdot (Q - d)) \cdot f(d) \partial d + \int_y^\infty p_B \cdot Q \cdot f(d) \partial d \tag{4.88}$$

The optimal purchase decision Q^* can again be derived via the newsvendor model.

The supplier also maximizes its profit π_S and sets its price p_S and the refund r accordingly:

$$\pi_S = (p_S - c_S) \cdot Q - (r - g) \cdot \int_0^Q (Q - d) \cdot f(d)\partial d. \tag{4.89}$$

Numerical Example: Concept of Buy-Back Contracts
The buyer is a merchant and buys swimsuits at a supplier for a unit price of 20 Euro in order to sell them for 30 Euro each. A buy-back contract could specify that the supplier repurchases overage swimsuits that the buyer cannot sell for 10 Euro at the end of the season.

Similar to the quantity-flexibility contract, buy-back contracts also reduce the buyer's risk of overage and lead to a more optimistic purchase decision. The incentive for the supplier is that there is (i) a higher purchase quantity, (ii) a profit even from repurchased items, (iii) additional potential profit from re-selling repurchased items and (iv) an avoidance to lose image in case the buyer is a merchant and sells overage at a bargain price.

In practice, buy-back contracts are available in the fashion industry between retailers and manufacturers but also for book sales between publishers and booksellers.

Revenue-Sharing Contracts (RSC)

A revenue-sharing contract is an agreement that ensures that revenues generated from the customer are shared between the buyer and the supplier. The transfer payment between buyer and supplier is characterized by

$$\mathbf{P}^{\mathrm{RSC}} = p_S \cdot Q + \phi \cdot p_B \cdot ES(Q) \tag{4.90}$$

with a per unit payment and a payment depending on the buyer's revenue $p_B \cdot ES(Q)$ with $ES(Q)$ as the expected sales.

Consequently, the buyer sets its order quantity Q under profit maximization objectives based on the supplier's contract parameters p_S and ϕ, which is the revenue fraction for the supplier, while $1 - \phi$ is the revenue fraction for the buyer. The buyer's profit function is given by

$$\pi_B = -p_S \cdot Q + \int_0^Q ((1 - \phi)(p_B \cdot d) + g \cdot (Q - d)) \cdot f(d)\partial d$$
$$+ \int_y^\infty (1 - \phi) \cdot p_B \cdot Q \cdot f(d)\partial d \tag{4.91}$$

The supplier optimized pricing p_S and determines the fraction ϕ for revenue-sharing. The supplier's profit function is given by

$$\pi_S = (p_S - c_S) \cdot Q + \int_0^Q \phi \cdot p_B \cdot d \cdot f(d) \partial d + \int_y^\infty \phi \cdot p_B \cdot Q \cdot f(d) \partial d. \quad (4.92)$$

Numerical Example: Concept of Revenue-Sharing Contracts
The buyer purchases items at a supplier for a unit price of 20 Euro and resells them after a manufacturing or finishing process at a price of 40 Euro. The supplier offers to reduce the buyer's purchase price from 20 Euro to 17 Euro if the buyer shares 10% of its revenue.

The idea of a revenue-sharing contract to avoid double marginalization differs from quantity-flexibility contracts and buy-back contracts. The goal of revenue-sharing contracts is that the supplier sets smaller prices p_S and therefore triggers a more optimistic buyer's purchase decision Q. While the buyer has the incentive of a reduced purchase price p_S to order more, the supplier is incentivized by increased sales quantities Q and additionally a share ϕ of the buyer's revenue.

Revenue-sharing contracts are increasingly used in the automotive industry between OEMs and semiconductor or IT suppliers. For instance, the German carmaker Daimler announced that they sign a revenue-sharing contract with the supplier Nvidia that produces graphics processing units and system on a chip units. Nvidia participates in Daimler's revenue and therefore provides a strategic partnership and prioritized supply.

Sales Rebate Contracts (SRC)

In sales rebate contracts, the supplier charges the buyer a wholesale price p_S per unit and gives the buyer a rebate r per unit sold above a threshold T. The transfer payment between buyer and supplier is therefore characterized by

$$\mathbf{p}^{\text{SRC}} = \begin{cases} p_S \cdot Q, & \text{for } Q < T \\ (p_S - r) \cdot Q + r \cdot (T + \int_T^Q F(y)dy), & \text{for } Q \geq T \end{cases} \quad (4.93)$$

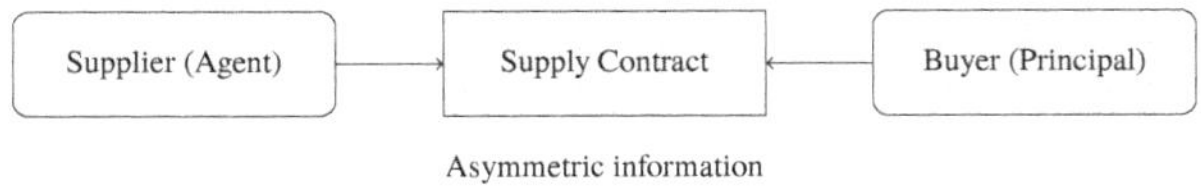

Fig. 4.24 Principal-agent setup in procurement

Quantity Discount Contract (QDC)

In quantity discount contracts, the supplier charges the buyer a price $p_S(Q)$ per unit that is decreasing in Q. The transfer payment between buyer and supplier is therefore characterized by

$$\mathbf{P}^{\mathrm{QDC}} = p_S(Q) \cdot Q \tag{4.94}$$

4.7.4 Supply Contracting Under Asymmetric Information

Contracts between buyers and suppliers are typically characterized by asymmetric information. This refers to the *Principal-Agent-Theory (PAT)* that aims to model the situation of asymmetric information in a buyer-supplier relationship (Fig. 4.24).

The supplier (agent) has an information advantage compared to the buyer (principal). Asymmetric information results from hidden characteristics (e.g., private information about supplier's cost structure or supplier's capacities, investments and available know-how), hidden action (e.g., private information about work effort after signing the contract) or hidden information (e.g., superior information of the supplier about input markets). The buyer has high transaction cost to collect information in order to decrease information asymmetry.

According to PAT, there occur three problems from contracting under asymmetric information:

(i) *Adverse selection* states that the buyer is not able to observe characteristics of the supplier ex ante (hidden characteristics), which can lead to the selection of undesirable suppliers. For instance, the buyer does not know whether the communicated cost breakdown (see should-cost model from Sect. 3.4.1) of the supplier is true and therefore whether the supplier's quoted price is fair or not.

(ii) *Moral hazard* states that the buyer is not able to observe or evaluate activities (e.g., quality inspection, use of adequate input material) of the supplier after contracting, i.e., ex post (hidden action), or does not have all necessary information about the supplier (hidden information). Hidden actions can be that the supplier uses confidential information that the buyer provides for collaboration with the buyer's competitor or that the supplier selects low-quality second-tier suppliers.

(iii) *Hold-up problem* states that hidden intentions of the supplier lead to opportunistic behavior of the supplier.

The resulting problems of asymmetric information in buyer-supplier relationships can be avoided by signaling (e.g., the supplier signals high-quality by certifications or willingness to include penalties to contracts), screening (e.g., buyer conducts quality inspections or searches for alternative suppliers) or self-selection (e.g., buyer is offering different contract options with specific performance-based incentives for the supplier) but also through information systems (controlling, project management with milestones, time recording).

4.7.5 Service-Level Agreements (SLA)

Service-level agreements (SLA) are frame contracts that guarantee a prespecified service over a pre-specified contract duration. Service levels can address versatile perspectives, from quality objectives over (reaction) time objectives to availability objectives. For instance, an IT service should be available in 99.99% of the time. SLAs have in common that the level of service should be measurable via KPIs (see Sect. 3.3).

For instance, inventory management (see Chap. 5) distinguishes between two major service levels that are often used in SLAs: (i) alpha service level and (ii) beta service level. The alpha service level is an event-oriented service level that compares the number of periods without shortfall with the total number of periods. A alpha service level of 95% means that a product or service is available in 95% of the time. The beta service level is a quantity-oriented service level and compares the demand that can immediately be served with the total demand. A beta service level of 95% means that 95% of an order can immediately be satisfied, while for 5%, the customer has to wait.

4.7.6 Horizontal Purchasing Agreements

Besides a contractual collaboration between buyers and suppliers (vertical cooperation), there is also the opportunity for horizontal cooperation between companies of the same supply chain stage (Fig. 4.25).

In the procurement context, this is often referred to as cooperative sourcing through, for instance, purchasing conglomerates (also known as cartels coopetition if partners are competitors).

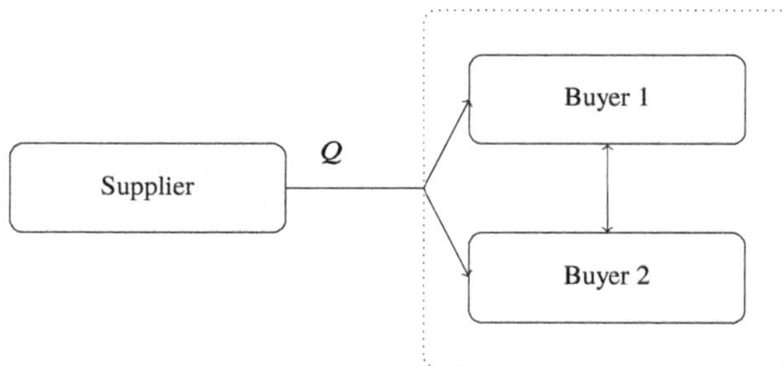

Fig. 4.25 Concept of horizontal purchasing agreements

Industry Example: Purchasing Conglomerates
In 2008, a prominent purchasing conglomerate was established between the automotive OEMs BMW and Daimler for components that are not related to brand identity. But also automotive suppliers collaborate in purchasing as the example of Vitesco and Schaeffler shows. Another example is RTG Retail Trade Group, a joint venture between the German retailers Rossmann, METRO, Globus and others that was founded in 2017. The main goal of RTG is to bundle purchase volumes for food and non-food products in order to leverage economies of scale. Germany breweries Warsteiner and Karlsberg also decided to source cooperatively as a reaction to significantly increased prices and supply risk for agricultural commodities, packaging material and energy in 2022.

Value of Cooperative Sourcing

In order to quantify the value of cooperative sourcing, we present an analytical model based on the well-known economic order quantity approach from inventory management (see Sect. 5.3). The following analysis is based on [23].

The EOQ model is the most basic inventory model and solves the trade-off between the setup cost (e.g., administrative cost of the order process) and inventory holding cost (see Fig. 4.26). The higher the purchase quantity Q, the higher the inventory holding cost, but the lower the order frequency and therefore the setup cost. In Chap. 5, we show that given setup cost A (per order, not per unit), unit inventory holding cost h, unit purchase cost c and demand d_i of company i, the EOQ model derives the optimal (cost-minimizing) order quantity Q_i for each company i by

$$Q_i = \sqrt{\frac{2d_i A}{hc}}. \tag{4.95}$$

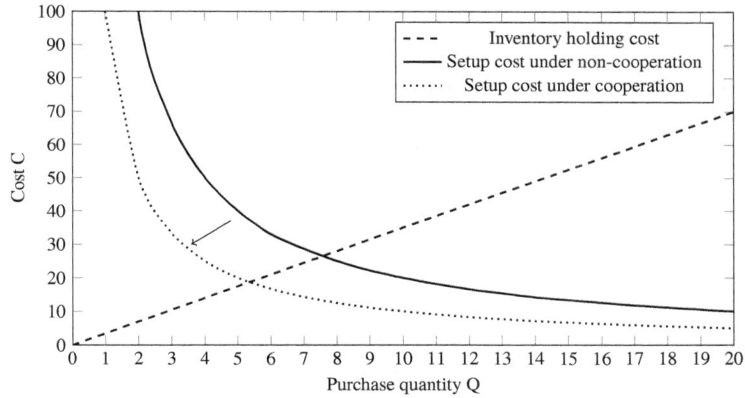

Fig. 4.26 Effect of cooperative sourcing

Now, suppose that two companies build a purchasing conglomerate. Then, the optimal joint replenishment quantity is

$$Q^{co} = \sqrt{\frac{2(d_1 + d_2)A}{hc}} \tag{4.96}$$

with individual order quantities under cooperation given as

$$Q_i^{co} = \frac{d_i}{d_1 + d_2} Q^{co}. \tag{4.97}$$

Given the EOQ cost function $C(Q)$, i.e.,

$$C(Q) = \frac{d}{Q} \cdot A + \frac{h}{2} \cdot Q + c \cdot d, \tag{4.98}$$

we can calculate the cost savings potential through cooperative sourcing by comparing total cost of non-cooperative sourcing, i.e.,

$$C^{non-co} = \sqrt{2 \cdot d_1 \cdot h \cdot A} + \sqrt{2 \cdot d_2 \cdot h \cdot A} + c \cdot (d_1 + d_2) \tag{4.99}$$

with the total cost of cooperative sourcing, i.e.,

$$C^{co} = \sqrt{2 \cdot (d_1 + d_2) \cdot h \cdot A} + c \cdot (d_1 + d_2) \tag{4.100}$$

This is also referred to as the square root effect of cooperative sourcing. It can easily be shown that $C^{co} < C^{non-co}$.

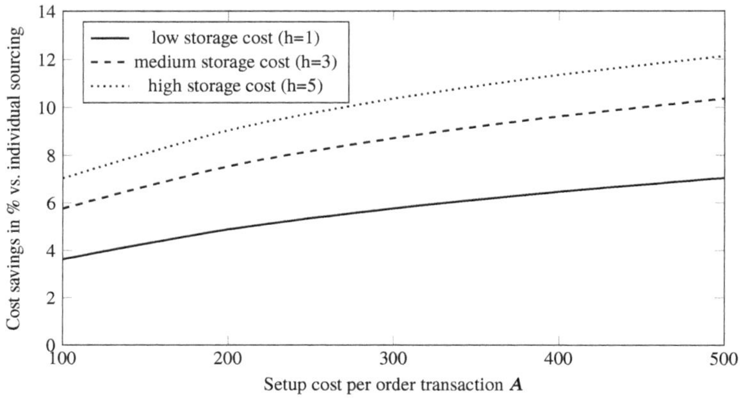

Fig. 4.27 Cost savings through cooperative sourcing

A second savings component of purchasing conglomerates that is not even quantified here may also be better unit purchase cost c due to an increase in negotiation power.

Numerical Example: Savings Through Cooperative Sourcing
Suppose two companies with an individual demand of $d = 100$ units. Unit purchase costs are $c = 10$. Currently, both companies source individually (baseline scenario). Now, both plan to build a purchasing conglomerate in order to share setup cost per order transaction A that can be significant in practice. Based on the presented modeling approach, cooperative sourcing leads to a significant cost savings potential as shown in Fig. 4.27.

We observe that the savings potential of cooperative sourcing increases with setup cost A and inventory holding cost h, however in a logarithmic manner.

For benefit (or savings) allocation, the purchasing partners need to a priori specify a corresponding mechanism. This can be simple allocation rules such as allocation proportional to quantity or cost, game-theoretic concepts such as the Shapley value or bargaining solutions (e.g., Nash or Rubinstein bargaining solution). In the following, we illustrate the Shapley value for savings allocation in collaborative purchasing.

Shapley Value for Benefit Allocation

The Shapley value was developed in 1953 by 2012 Nobel laureate Lloyd S. Shapley. It is a concept from cooperative game theory where different players $i = 1, \ldots, n$ (e.g., companies) can enter different coalitions (e.g., purchasing consortia). The objective of this cooperative game (or coalitional game) is a fair allocation of gains or cost savings, which is a difficult task and often lacks in practice why purchase consortia often fail due to missing trust. The Shapley value helps find a coalition where the profit or cost is shared in a fair way based on each company's contribution to the coalition such that there is no coalition that is more favorable for any player.

Numerical Example: Shapley Value in Cooperative Sourcing
Consider the following cooperative purchasing game. Due to economies of scale, three companies, A, B and C ($n = 3$), can reduce their purchase prices by forming coalitions (purchasing conglomerates). In this case, three setups are possible: (i) no coalition ($n = 1$), i.e., A, B and C do not enter any coalition and purchase their demand individually; (ii) coalition of two ($n = 2$), i.e., a coalition between A and B, A and C or B and C; and (iii) coalition of three (*grand coalition*), i.e., a coalition between A, B and C ($n = 3$). The purchase prices affect the coalition's profit that is presented in Table 4.43.

Without purchasing coalition, company A generates a profit of 200,000 Euros, company B of 100,000 Euros and company C of 200,000 Euros. A coalition of company A and B results in a total profit of 320,000 Euros, a coalition of company A and C in 420,000 Euros and a coalition of company B and C in a profit of 360,000 Euros. A three-party coalition generates a profit of 600,000 Euros, which is above the sum of profits of the three companies if those purchase individually.

Table 4.44 shows the logic behind the Shapley value calculated for company A.

Consequently, the Shapley value of company A is calculated as the average marginal contribution of company A to the coalition, i.e.,

$$SV_A = \frac{1}{6} \cdot \left(200 + 200 + 220 + 240 + 220 + 240\right) = 220. \tag{4.101}$$

Shapley values for company B and C are calculated accordingly, i.e., $SV_B = 140$ and $SV_C = 240$. The sum of the three Shapley values equals 600, which is the profit of the three-company coalition ($n = 3$).

In a next step, the Shapley values are calculated for all other coalition sizes. The results are presented in Table 4.45. They show that no company is better off in another coalition or purchasing at its own. Therefore, a three-company coalition between A, B and C is optimal where the coalition profit of 600.000 Euro is splitted as follows: A receives 220,000 Euros, B receives 140,000 Euros and C receives 240,000 Euros.

Table 4.43 Profits of different purchase conglomerates

Coalition	A	B	C	A,B	A,C	B,C	A,B,C
Profit π[1,000 Euro]	200	100	200	320	420	360	600

Table 4.44 Shapley value calculation for company A

Sequence	Profit of company left to A	Profit of company left to A plus A	Marginal contribution of A for a three-company coalition
A,B,C	0	200	200
A,C,B	0	200	200
B,A,C	$\pi(B) = 100$	320	220
B,C,A	$\pi(B, C) = 360$	600	240
C,A,B	$\pi(C) = 200$	420	220
C,B,A	$\pi(C, B) = 360$	600	240

Table 4.45 Shapley values for different coalition constellations

Coalition	SV_A	SV_B	SV_C
{A,B,C}	220	140	240
{A,B} and {C}	210	110	200
{A,C} and {B}	210	100	210
{A} and {B,C}	200	130	230
{A} and {B} and {C}	200	100	200

Please note that there are alternatives to the Shapley value for benefit allocation in cooperative games (e.g., cooperative purchasing games) such as the compromise value or nucleolus.

References

1. Allon G, Van Mieghem J (2010) Global dual sourcing: tailored base-surge allocation to near- and offshore production. Manage Sci 56(1):110–124
2. Allon G, Van Mieghem J (2010) The Mexico-China sourcing game: teaching global dual sourcing. INFORMS Trans Educ 10(3):105–112
3. Aouadni S, Aouadni I, Rebai A (2019) A systematic review on supplier selection and order allocation problems. J. Ind. Eng. Int. 15(1):267–289
4. Basak I, Saaty T (1993) Group decision making using the analytic hierarchy process. Math. Comput. Model. 17(4–5):101–109
5. Brahms SJ (2003) Negotiation Games – Applying Game Theory to Bargaining and Arbitration, 2nd edn. Routledge, Milton Park
6. Cachon GP (2003) Supply chain coordination with contracts. Handbooks Oper Res Manage Sci 11:227–339
7. Cachon GP, Netessine S (2006) Game theory in supply chain analysis. Tutorials Oper Res INFORMS 2006:200–233
8. Charnes A, Cooper W, Rhodes E (1978) Measuring the efficiency of decision making units. Eur J Oper Res 2(6):429–444

9. Chopra S, Meindl P (2015) Supply Chain Management: Strategy, Planning and Operation, 6th edn. Pearson, London
10. Cramton P, Shoham Y, Steinberg R (2006) Combinatorial Auctions, 1st edn. MIT Press, Cambridge
11. De Boer L, van der Wegen L, Telgen J (1998) Outranking methods in support of supplier selection. Eur J Purchasing Supply Manage 4(2–3):109–118
12. De Boer L, Labro E, Morlacchi P (2001) A review of methods supporting supplier selection. Euro J Purchasing Supply Manage 7(1):75–89
13. Fisher R, Ury W (1981) Getting to Yes – Negotiating an Agreement without Giving In, 1st edn. Houghton Mifflin, Boston
14. Forrester J (1961) Industrial Dynamics. MIT Press, Cambridge
15. Fudenberg D, Tirole J (1991) Game Theory, 1st edn. MIT Press, Cambridge
16. Gaur V, Osadchiy N, Udenio M (2022) Why it's so hard to map global supply chains. Harvard Business Review. https://hbr.org/2022/10/research-why-its-so-hard-to-map-global-supply-chains. Accessed 22 Feb 2023
17. Ho W, Xu X, Dey PK (2010) Multi-criteria decision making approaches for supplier evaluation and selection: a literature review. Euro J Oper Res 202(1):16–24
18. Hwang CL, Yoon K (1981) Multiple Attribute Decision Making: Methods and Applications, 1st edn. Springer, Berlin
19. Klemperer P (2004) Auctions: Theory and Practice, 1st edn. Princeton University Press, Princeton
20. Krishna V (2009) Auction Theory, 2nd edn. Academic Press, Cambridge
21. McFillen J, Reck R, and Benton Jr. WC (1983) An experiment in purchasing negotiations. J Purchasing Mat Manage 19(2):155–162
22. Milgrom P (2004) Putting Auction Theory to Work, 1st edn. Cambridge University Press, Cambridge
23. Minner S (2007) Bargaining for cooperative economic ordering. Decis Support Syst 43:569–583
24. Roy B (1968) Classement et Choix en Présence de Points de Vue Multiples (la Méthode ELECTRE). La Revue d'Informatique et de Recherche Opérationelle 8:57–75
25. Saaty RW (1987) The analytic hierarchy process – what it is and how it is used. Math Modell 9(3–5):161–176
26. Shen M, Zhan R, Zhang J (2011) The reliable facility location problem: formulations, heuristics, and approximation algorithms. Informs J Comput 23(3):331–492
27. Snyder LV, Shen M (2011) Fundamentals of Supply Chain Theory, 1st edn. Wiley, Hoboken
28. Van Hoek R, DeWitt M, Lacity M, Johnson T (2022) How walmart automated supplier negotiations. Harvard Business Review. https://hbr.org/2022/11/how-walmart-automated-supplier-negotiations. Accessed 17 Jul 2023
29. Von Neumann J, Morgenstern O, Rubinstein A (1944) Theory of Games and Economic Behavior. 60th Anniversary Commemorative Edition. Princeton University Press, Princeton

Chapter 5
Data-Driven Inventory Management

Abstract Over the last decades that were characterized by just-in-time supply chains, inventories were highly unpopular and avoided wherever possible in order to reduce capital lockup to a minimum. However, severe supply disruptions and inflation risk in the early 2020s showed that inventories can be of strategic importance in times of high volatility and economic uncertainty. This chapter focuses on single-item inventory optimization and addresses both deterministic and stochastic models as well as single-period and multi-period approaches to optimally control stock levels in a data-driven manner. The chapter introduces important inventory metrics for performance management, analytical safety stock planning models and latest developments in machine learning and deep learning for inventory management applications.

Keywords EOQ model · Safety stock · Newsvendor · Data-driven inventory control · Machine learning-enabled inventory control · Deep learning-enabled inventory control

5.1 Introduction

While inventories and hence inventory optimization have not been prioritized in the just-in-time economy, recent supply disruptions put again attention to inventories that are regarded as strategically important in order to increase resilience. While on the one hand inventories secure supply, on the other, they cost a significant amount of money especially in times of increasing interest rates at financial markets.

Inventories can be classified into raw material inventories, work in process inventories and finished goods inventories. They have five different functions: first, the *transaction function*, i.e., building lot sizes in order to reduce fixed order costs that occur per order process; second, the *safety function*, i.e., building safety stocks in order to reduce the consequences of supply shortage or unexpected customer demand spikes; third, the *balancing function*, i.e., building buffers between two non-synchronous material flows (decoupling inventory); fourth, the *speculation function*, i.e., building speculative stocks in expectation of significant price increases; and

C. Mandl, *Procurement Analytics*, Springer Series in Supply Chain Management 22, https://doi.org/10.1007/978-3-031-43281-1_5

fifth, the *refinement function*, i.e., building inventories as part of the production process (e.g., for wine, timber and cheese).

In the following, we introduce important inventory metrics to monitor the performance of an inventory system in Sect. 5.2 and present analytical models to optimally plan inventories in Sects. 5.3 to 5.6. We distinguish between deterministic planning models, where all parameters are known, and stochastic planning models, where certain parameters such as demand or supply are unknown. This chapter is limited to single-echelon inventory models and does not address multi-echelon inventory optimization along the entire supply chain.

5.2 Inventory Metrics

In order to assess the status quo of a company's inventory system, several metrics are applied in practice (see Table 5.1).

Inventory turnover ratio is a metric that quantifies how often inventory is replaced (per year). It is calculated by

$$\text{Inventory Turnover Ratio} = \frac{\text{COGS}}{\text{Average inventory}}. \tag{5.1}$$

COGS are cost of goods sold and typically measured in USD or EUR. In some cases, COGS are replaced by net sales in inventory turnover ratio calculations. The average inventory is specified as the average yearly inventory, i.e., the sum of inventory at beginning of year and inventory at end of year divided by two or simply by the inventory at the end of the year. It is also measured in EUR or USD multiplying the inventory level with the inventory sales price. Adequate inventory turnover ratios lie between 5 and 10, which means that the stock is replenished 5 up to 10 times per year, i.e., every 1–2 months. While automotive suppliers exhibit an inventory turnover ratio of around 4 to 6, restaurants can have a ratio of around 20 to 40.

Table 5.1 Important inventory metrics

Metrics	Unit
Inventory turnover ratio	–
Inventory days	Days
Inventory coverage	Days
Inventory accuracy ratio	–
Inventory to sales ratio	–
Service level (α, β, γ)	%

Table 5.2 Inventory turnover ratios at different companies for fiscal year 2022 (Source: https://www.alphaquery.com/)

Metric	Unit
McDonald's	191.83
Microsoft	16.74
Ford	8.94
Walmart	7.59
Tesla	4.72
Pfizer	3.82
Johnson & Johnson	2.49

Industry Example: Inventory Turnover Ratios in Different Industries
Inventory turnover ratios are strongly industry-, company- and time-dependent. Table 5.2 shows ratios of major companies of different branches for the fiscal year of 2022. The numbers show a high inventory turnover ratio for the fast-food company McDonald's, while pharmaceutical companies such as Pfizer and Johnson & Johnson have a rather low ratio.

Related to the inventory turnover ratio, the KPI *inventory days* (or days in inventory, inventory days of supply, days inventory outstanding, inventory period) quantifies the average number of days a company holds its inventory before selling it. It is calculated by

$$\text{Inventory Days} = 365 \cdot \frac{\text{Average inventory}}{\text{COGS}} = \frac{365 \text{ days}}{\text{Inventory turnover ratio}}. \tag{5.2}$$

Inventory coverage is an indicator that measures the number of days customers can be served by the current physical inventories and the outstanding orders from suppliers.

Inventory to sales ratio determines the number of time periods (e.g., months) that can be covered with the current level of inventory. It is calculated as

$$\text{Inventory to Sales Ratio} = \frac{\text{Average inventory}}{\text{Net sales}}. \tag{5.3}$$

Figure 5.1 presents the development of the inventory-to-sales ratio in the US. It shows a spike at the beginning of the corona pandemic and a sharp decrease a few months later.

Inventory accuracy ratio is a metric that gives insights regarding the accuracy of a company's inventory data by comparing the actual inventory level with the

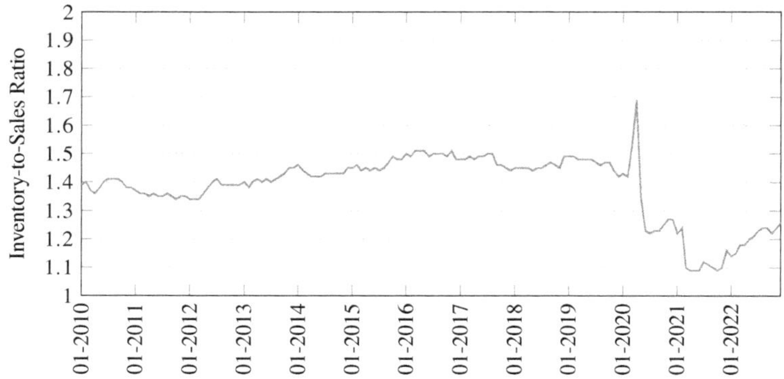

Fig. 5.1 Inventory-to-sales ratio in the USA from January 2010 until December 2022 (Source: US Census Bureau)

inventory that is recorded in the company's IT system. It is calculated as

$$\text{Inventory Accuracy Ratio} = \frac{\text{Actual inventory level}}{\text{Recorded inventory level}}. \tag{5.4}$$

The ratio gives an indication for damage, system errors or even thefts.

In inventory management, we distinguish between two major *service levels*: the α service level and the β service level.

The α service level is the non-stockout probability (type 1 service level) and an event-oriented service level:

$$\alpha = \frac{\text{Number of periods without shortfall}}{\text{Total number of periods}} \cdot 100\% \tag{5.5}$$

The β service level is the fill rate (type 2 service level) and a quantity-oriented service level:

$$\beta = \frac{\text{Demand that can immediately be satisfied from stock}}{\text{Total demand}} \cdot 100\% \tag{5.6}$$

In practice, it is important to track both KPIs because a high non-stockout probability does not necessarily indicate a high fill rate and the other way around. Therefore, a multi-dimensional KPI dashboard can help.

Numerical Example: Service-Level Calculation
Based on the data from Table 5.3, the alpha service level is 57.1%, while the beta service level is 96.2%.

Table 5.3 Data: service level calculations

Months	Jan	Feb	Mar	Apr	May	Jun	Jul
Customer demand [1,000 units]	10	11.2	13.4	12.1	11.3	15.2	13.12
Satisfied demand [1,000 units]	10	11.0	12.3	12.1	11.3	13.2	13.12

In contrast to α- and β-service levels, the γ-service level, which is sporadically used in industrial practice, addresses both performance in time and quantity. In addition to the amount of back orders, γ also addresses the waiting time, i.e., how long customers need to wait for their back-ordered demands. The γ service level is defined as

$$\gamma = \left(1 - \frac{\text{Backlog per period}}{\text{Period demand}}\right) \cdot 100\%. \tag{5.7}$$

For inventory classification, i.e., classification of SKUs, we refer to ABC and XYZ analysis that are introduced in Chap. 3. Both are standard methods in inventory management to prioritize SKUs for inventory optimization through analytical models that are introduced in the following sections.

5.3 Economic Order Quantity (EOQ)

The economic order quantity (EOQ) addresses the *transaction function* of inventories. It determines the optimal order quantity in the presence of fixed order costs and variable cost. It answers the question how many times a company should order (e.g., once per year or just in time). As the most basic inventory control model that dates back to 1913 (see [7]), it is included into many software applications (e.g., ERP systems).

5.3.1 Standard EOQ Model

The standard economic order quantity (EOQ) model, also referred to as economic purchase quantity model or Andler formula, is the standard static lot-sizing model with a lot size defined as the order quantity that is purchased within one order process. The EOQ is the cost-optimal order quantity that minimizes the sum of fixed order cost (or setup cost) and inventory holding cost. Setup costs are all costs related to ordering, transportation and storage that occur once per ordering process.

Inventory holding costs are typically provided as percentage of purchase cost and include cost for storage space (e.g., rent), inventory service cost (tax, hardware, handling, insurance), inventory risk cost (shrinkage, theft, administrative errors) and opportunity cost from capital lockup (weighted average cost of capital, WACC).

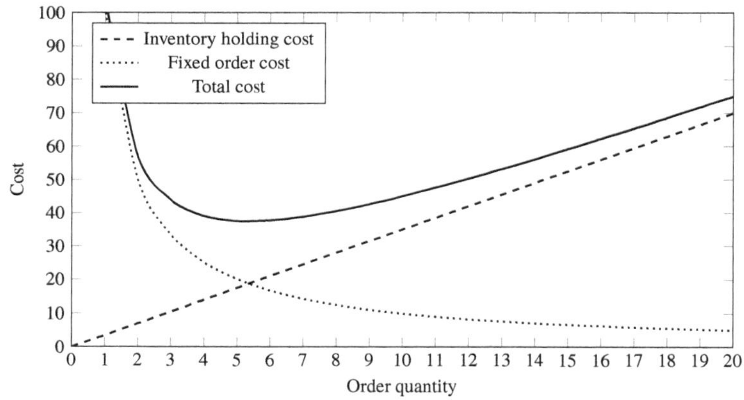

Fig. 5.2 Trade-off in the EOQ model

Numerical Example: Calculation of Inventory Holding Cost
In order to optimize purchase quantities, it is essential to correctly specify inventory holding cost. A standard approach is to sum up all (annual) inventory costs and divide it by the average inventory value. For instance, suppose that a company pays 500,000 Euro p.a. for storage, 250,000 Euro p.a. for handling, 250,000 Euro p.a. for damage and 500,000 Euro p.a. for administration. Therefore, annual inventory cost is 1,500,000 Euro. At a 15,000,000 Euro average inventory value, the percentage inventory cost is 10%. Considering additional opportunity cost of capital of 5% and insurance cost of 5%, the inventory holding cost is 20% of the inventory value driven by the purchase price.

EOQ solves in the cost trade-off that is illustrated in Fig. 5.2: If the order quantity is large, fixed order cost is low due to a reduced number of required orders, but inventory holding cost is high due to an increased inventory level. If the order quantity is small, fixed order cost is large due to a high number of required orders, but inventory holding cost is low due to a reduced inventory level.

The standard EOQ model only applies under the following assumptions, i.e., constant and predictable demand d, zero lead time ($L = 0$), unlimited storage capacity/infinite supply rate, no back orders and an infinite planning horizon. If these assumptions are met, the standard EOQ model derives the optimal order quantity Q^* based on the minimization of the cost function $C(Q)$, i.e.,

$$C(Q) = \frac{d}{Q} \cdot A + \frac{h}{2} \cdot Q + c \cdot d \tag{5.8}$$

with A as the fixed order cost (setup cost per order), h as the unit inventory holding cost and c as the unit purchase cost. The optimality condition is given by

$$\frac{\partial C}{\partial Q} = \frac{d}{Q^2} \cdot A + \frac{h}{2} \stackrel{!}{=} 0. \tag{5.9}$$

Consequently, the economic order quantity (EOQ) is calculated by

$$Q^* = \sqrt{\frac{2dA}{h}} \tag{5.10}$$

and the economic order interval (EOI) is calculated by

$$T = \sqrt{\frac{2A}{hd}}. \tag{5.11}$$

Consequently, the minimal cost is given by

$$C^*(Q^*) = \sqrt{2dhA} + cd. \tag{5.12}$$

Numerical Example: Economic Order Quantity
A firm has an annual product demand of 1000 units. Fixed order cost is 250 Euros per order process. Unit purchase cost is 10 Euro, and inventory holding cost is 2 Euro per unit per year. Given this data, the optimal order quantity is 500 units, the optimal order interval is 0.5 years (each 6 months) and the minimal cost is 11.000 Euro.

5.3.2 EOQ Model Under Quantity Discounts

In practice, quantity discounts are common if quantities are large due to economies of scale. In case of quantity discounts, the standard EOQ model that assumes that unit purchase cost c are constant needs to be extended. In this case, we need to distinguish between all-unit discounts and incremental discounts (see Fig. 5.3).

Both discount schemes are characterized by break points q_i. For all-unit discounts, the discount applies to all units, while for incremental discounts, the discount applies to the units that exceed break point q_i. The optimal purchase quantity Q^* under quantity discounts is not computable via a simple formula as it is the case for environments without discounts but require algorithms that are introduced next.

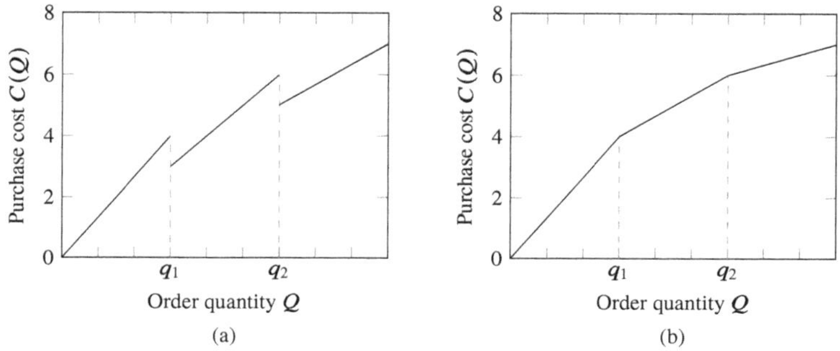

Fig. 5.3 All-unit and incremental quantity discounts. (**a**) All-unit discount scheme. (**b**) Incremental discount

All-Unit Discounts

We define an all-unit discount by (q_{n-1}, q_n, d_n) with n as the discount level where a discount d_n (e.g., in percent of purchase cost c) applies to all units if purchase quantity is within the discount interval $[q_{n-1}; q_n]$. The optimal order quantity under all-unit discounts can be derived via the following algorithm:

- **Step 1:** Calculate the EOQ according to Eq. 5.10 for the largest discount level n. If EOQ falls within the discount interval, then EOQ is the cost-optimal purchase quantity.
- **Step 2:** If EOQ is not valid because it does not fall within the discount interval, then calculate the total cost at each break point q_n according to Eq. 5.8.
- **Step 3:** Calculate the total cost at each valid EOQ for the different discounts.
- **Step 4:** The optimal order quantity is the one associated with the lowest cost from step 2 and step 3.

Numerical Example: Economic Order Quantity with All-Unit Discounts
Consider an EOQ setting with a product demand of 1,000 units per year, inventory holding cost of $h = 10$ Euros per unit per year, fixed order cost of $A = 8$ Euros per order and a purchase price of 5 Euros. The supplier provides a discount of 2% if purchase quantity is at least 30 units (discount level 1) and a discount of 4% if purchase quantity is at least 70 units (discount level 2).

In step 1, we calculate EOQ with $Q = 40$ units, which does not fall within the largest discount level (i.e., $q_2 \geq 70$ units). Therefore, in step 2, we need to calculate the total cost at each break point: At $q_1 = 30$, the total cost is $5,316.67$, and at $q_2 = 70$, the total cost is $5,264.29$. In step 3, we additionally need to calculate total cost at each valid EOQ: For discount level 2, $Q = 40$ is

(continued)

not valid. For discount level 1, $Q = 40$ is valid and yields a total cost of $5,300$. For the setup without discount, $Q = 40$ is valid and yields a total cost of $5,400$. Consequently, the cost-optimal purchase quantity under this discount scheme is 70 units with a total cost of 5,264.29. The results are graphically illustrated in Fig. 5.4. The solid line describes the area of valid decisions.

Incremental Discounts

Incremental discounts are discounts that only apply to the quantity purchased above the break point q_i. In the EOQ context, this can be considered by treating the quantity below the break point as fixed cost F_i. Consequently, the optimal order quantity Q^* under incremental discounts can be derived via the following algorithm:

- **Step 1:** Calculate fixed cost F_i (with $F_0 = 0$) for each break point q_i by

$$F_i = F_{i-1} + (c_{i-1} - c_i) \cdot q_i. \tag{5.13}$$

- **Step 2:** Calculate fixed cost-adjusted Q_i^* for each discount level by

$$Q_i^* = \sqrt{\frac{2 \cdot D \cdot (A + F_i)}{h}}. \tag{5.14}$$

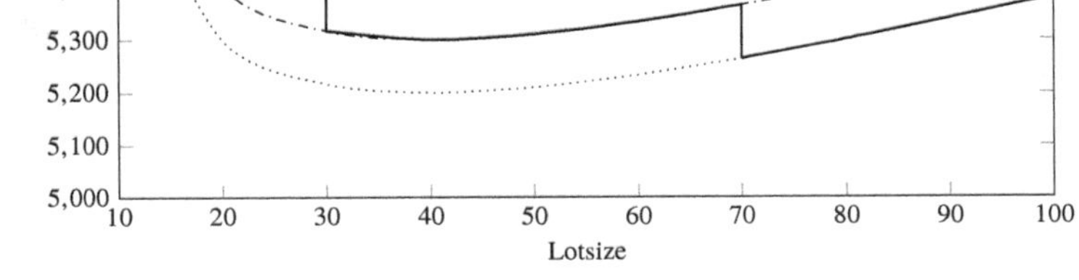

Fig. 5.4 EOQ cost functions under all-unit discounts

- **Step 3:** If Q_i^* is not within the allowable range $[q_{i-1}, q_i]$, then go to the next q_i; otherwise, calculate total cost using effective unit purchase cost c_i^e with

$$c_i^e = c_i + \frac{F_i}{Q_i}. \tag{5.15}$$

- **Step 4:** Choose Q_i with the lowest total cost.

Numerical Example: Economic Order Quantity with Incremental Discounts
Consider an EOQ setting with product demand of 1,000 units per year, unit per year inventory holding cost of 20% of the unit purchase cost, fixed order cost of $A = 250$ Euro per order and a purchase price of 10 Euro. The supplier provides a discount of 5% for the units ordered that are above or equal to 100 units (discount level 1) and a discount of 10% to all units purchased that are above or equal to 500 units (discount level 2).

In step 1, the fixed cost F_i is calculated for each discount level, i.e., $F_2 = 300$, $F_1 = 50$ and $F_0 = 0$. In step 2, the fixed cost adjusted Q_i^* is calculated for each discount level, i.e., $Q_2^* = 782$ units, $Q_1^* = 562$ units and $Q_0^* = 500$ units. $Q_2^* = 782$ is in the allowable discount range (i.e., greater or equal to 500). Therefore, the optimal order quantity is $Q^* = 782$ with total cost of $10,437.12$ Euro including purchase cost (9383.76 Euro), holding cost (733.56 Euro) and fixed order cost (319.80 Euro).

5.3.3 Dynamic Lot Sizing Model

The standard EOQ model only applies under constant demand d. If demand d deterministically fluctuates over time, the standard lot sizing model needs to be extended to the dynamic lot sizing model introduced by Wagner and Whitin in 1958. The Wagner-Whitin algorithm uses a mixed forward and backward calculation to determine possible alternatives and select the optimal strategy. We do not review dynamic lot sizing in this textbook but refer to [13] for more details. Alternatively, in practice dynamic lot sizing heuristics are applied such as the Silver-Meal heuristic (see [11]).

5.4 Safety Stock Planning

EOQ and dynamic lot sizing models assume that demand is known or perfectly predictable, which is hardly true in practice (e.g., for Z-classified items)—even not with the most advanced machine learning or deep learning models. Therefore, safety stock planning addresses the *safety function* of inventories in the presence of uncertainty. We focus on two sources of uncertainty that justify safety stocks: (i) supply uncertainty (in time, quantity or quality) and (ii) customer demand uncertainty (in time or quantity). For instance, a company might recognize that 20% of the time, delivery is on time; 50% of the time, delivery is 1 to 3 days late; 20% of the time, delivery is 4 to 6 days late; and in 10% of the time, delivery is more than 6 days late.

Safety stocks are stocks hold to prevent stockouts and therefore an effective measure to mitigate risk from variability in customer demand and lead times (Fig. 5.5). However, safety stock planning is a very complex management task due to the trade-off between too high inventory levels and too small inventory levels. On the other hand, too much inventory ties up money in working capital and decreases liquidity particularly in times of high market interest rates. Too less inventory increases the risk of stockouts, which can lead to less profit.

There are various approaches available to set safety stocks: from simple safety stock rules (see Sect. 5.4.1) to more advanced analytical safety stock models (see Sect. 5.4.2).

5.4.1 Simple Safety Stock Rules

Practitioners often use simple rules or gut feeling to plan their safety stock levels. Those rules do not include any probabilistic model and are therefore simple to apply and interpret. Two popular rules are the *period coverage rule* and the *fixed quantity rule*.

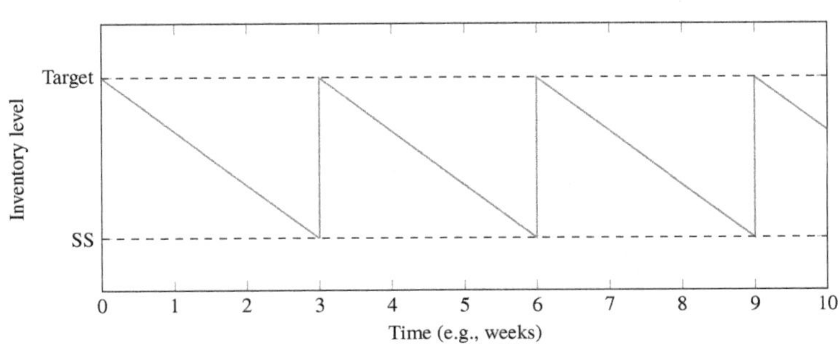

Fig. 5.5 Safety stock (SS) in inventory charts

The *period coverage rule* states to keep a specific number of weeks of supply as safety stock. For instance, a company keeps three weeks of average supply as safety stock for a specific product. The number of weeks is often derived from lead time estimates.

The *fixed quantity rule* states to keep a specific number of units as safety stock. For instance, a company keeps 30 units of safety stock for a specific product. The number of units is often derived from consumption and lead time estimates. For instance, set safety stock to 10% or 20% of the cycle stock level.

Another approach that is often used in practice is to set safety stock equal to the average daily usage multiplied by the average lead time in days. An extension is to approximate safety stock by the maximum daily usage multiplied by the maximum lead time in days minus the average daily usage times the average lead time in days.

Numerical Example: Safety Stock Placement in Practice

A company faces a daily average demand for a specific product of 900 units (up to a maximum of 1,100 units) with an average supply lead time of 10 days. Following a simple rule, the company keeps a safety stock of 9,000 units (= 900 units per day · 10 days).

During the COVID-19 pandemic, there were lead time outliers up to 30 days. Therefore, the company sets its safety stock to 24,000 units (=1,100 units per day · 30 days–900 units per day · 10 days).

Material requirements planning (MRP) in the standard ERP system of SAP (SAP S/4HANA) uses a similar approach to calculate dynamic safety stocks (see www.help.sap.com): *The system has determined an average daily requirement of 15 pieces. You have defined a minimum range of coverage of 3 days, a maximum range of coverage of 7 days and a target range of coverage of 5 days. The system calculates the following: Minimum stock level = 3 · 15 pieces = 45 pieces, maximum stock level = 7 · 15 pieces = 105 pieces, target stock level = 5 · 15 pieces = 75 pieces. The available quantity is 40 pieces and is therefore below the minimum stock level. Therefore, the system creates a procurement proposal for 35 pieces (= target stock level 75 pieces – available quantity of 40 pieces) during the planning run.*

5.4.2 Analytical Safety Stock Models

The presented simple safety stock rules are easy to execute and therefore widespread in practice but do not have any mathematical or statistical foundation and do not incorporate probabilistic information. They do not explicitly consider (i) variability and forecast inaccuracy in customer demand and supplier or manufacturing lead time and (ii) objectives regarding customer service levels. However, both factors undoubtedly affect optimal safety stock placements: The better a company can predict customer demand and lead time (e.g., through machine learning and applied artificial intelligence), the lower the safety stock levels can be. The higher the customers' service level requirements, the higher safety stock levels need to be. This considers that in some industries, stockouts might be more critical than in others. Therefore, the simple safety stock rules (see Sect. 5.4.1) often perform poor, which asks for analytical safety stock models. In the following, we introduce analytical safety stock models that optimize the balance between inventory cost and customer service level for three settings: (i) business environments with demand variability only, (ii) business environments with lead time variability only and (iii) business environments with both demand and lead time variability.

Safety Stock Planning Under Demand Variability

The following analytical safety stock (SS) formula (also known as King's method) determines the optimal safety stock level under demand variability and under the assumption that demand is an independent and identically distributed random variable drawn from a normal distribution. In this case, safety stock (SS) is given by

$$SS = z_\alpha \cdot \sigma_D \cdot \sqrt{L}. \tag{5.16}$$

z_α is a safety factor (also often called z-core), and σ_D is the demand standard deviation. L is the total lead time. Please note that the unit of lead time L (e.g., days, weeks) needs to be consistent with the time increment used for calculating the standard deviation of the demand σ_D. To address forecast errors, σ_D is often replaced by the $RMSE$ measure between actual and predicted demand, which is the standard measure in inventory management for quantifying forecast errors (see Chap. 2 for details on its calculation).

The safety factor z_α is a function of the non-stockout probability α. It can be calculated through the inverse distribution function of a standard normal distribution with cumulative probability α. z_α can easily be calculated by the `Excel` function `NORM.INV(`α`,0,1)`. This results in the exemplary values shown in Table 5.4. For instance, in order to satisfy demand with 95% confidence level, it requires a safety factor of 1.64 to prevent stockouts, which ensures to have enough inventory in 95% of the times.

Table 5.4 Safety factor z_α as a function of the non-stockout probability α

α in %	50	55	60	65	70	75	80	85	90	95	99	99.9
z_α	0.0	0.13	0.25	0.39	0.52	0.67	0.84	1.04	1.28	1.64	2.33	3.09

The numbers from Table 5.4 already show that z increases exponentially in α, which directly translates into an exponential increase in safety stocks. Please note that a 100% service level would require an infinite level of inventory.

Safety Stock Planning Under Lead Time Variability

If there is variability in supply lead time rather than customer demand, the safety stock formula requires the following adjustments:

$$SS = z_\alpha \cdot D \cdot \sigma_L \tag{5.17}$$

D is the deterministic customer demand, and σ_L is the standard deviation of the lead time. This can refer to both supplier lead time that varies due to unforeseeable events or manufacturing lead time that varies due to, for instance, machine downtime. The smaller σ_L, the more stable and predictable lead time L.

Safety Stock Planning Under Demand and Lead Time Variability

If both customer demand and lead time vary, the analytical safety stock formula needs to be adjusted accordingly. In this case, we need to distinguish between two cases: (i) demand and lead time variability are independent, and (ii) demand and lead time variability are not independent.

If demand and lead time variability are independent, then the optimal safety stock level is calculated by

$$SS = z_\alpha \cdot \sqrt{E[L] \cdot \sigma_D^2 + (E[D])^2 \cdot \sigma_L^2}. \tag{5.18}$$

$E[L]$ is the expected (average) lead time, and $E[D]$ is the expected (average) customer demand. The first term under the square root protects against demand forecast errors, while the second term protects against lead time variability. Safety stock is only zero if there is no uncertainty in demand and lead time, i.e., $\sigma_D = \sigma_L = 0$.

If demand and lead time variability are not independent, then the optimal safety stock level is calculated by

$$SS = z_\alpha \cdot \sigma_D \cdot \sqrt{E[L]} + z_\alpha \cdot E[D] \cdot \sigma_L. \tag{5.19}$$

Based on the safety stock calculations, the re-order point s can be calculated by

$$s = E[D] \cdot E[L] + SS. \tag{5.20}$$

As soon as the inventory level for a specific SKU falls to or below s, the purchasing (or production) process is started.

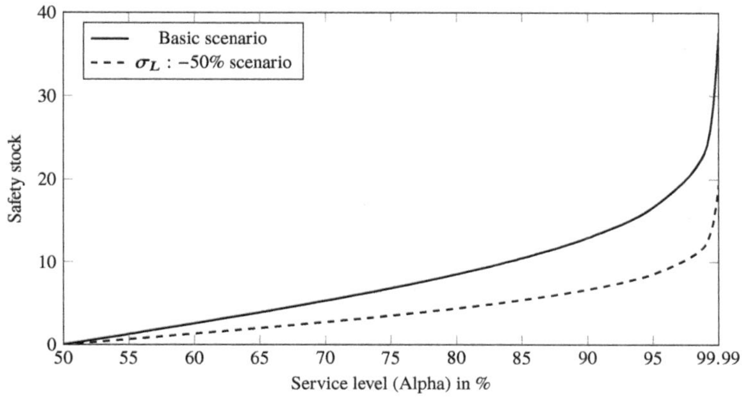

Fig. 5.6 Safety stock effects of lead time variability and desired customer service level

Numerical Example: Analytical Safety Stock Planning
A company purchases metals at a supplier with a lead time of 2 weeks that frequently deviates by 1 week. Weekly demand varies around 10 tons with a standard deviation of 1 ton. Customer demand and supplier lead time are independent. Figure 5.6 plots the optimal safety stock level for different service-level agreements. It also shows that a more stable supply (in terms of lower lead time variability) would allow to significantly reduce safety stocks.

With the emergence and improvement of internal and external data as well as data-driven forecasting methods (e.g., from the field of machine learning), inventory managers were in many places able to better understand its customer demands and consequently were able to reduce forecast errors. This has a direct effect on required safety stock levels as shown in the following example.

Numerical Example: Demand Forecast Quality and Safety Stocks
Suppose a metal trader that purchases and sells aluminum. Average weekly demand is 50 tons (point forecast). However, the current forecasting methods yields a root mean squared error of $RMSE = 5$ tons per week between actual and predicted demand. Supplier lead time is 1 week and does not vary. Figure 5.7 shows the company's safety stock implications of lower $RMSE$ through the use of, for instance, data-driven AI-based forecasting for different service levels α.

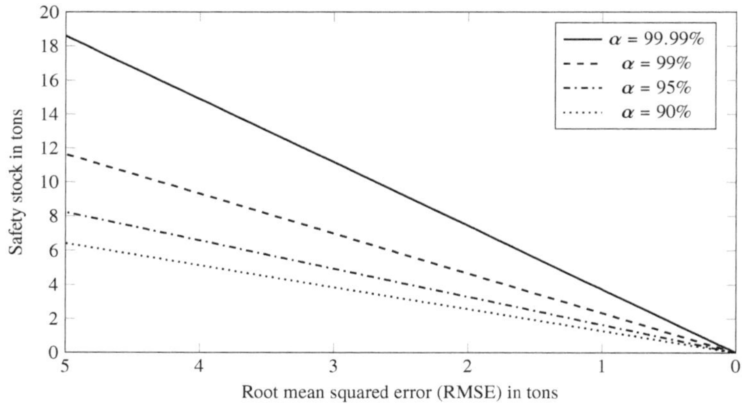

Fig. 5.7 Safety stock effects for different prediction accuracy (RMSE) and service levels α

Please note that there are various extensions of safety stock planning in multi-echelon inventory systems (e.g., guaranteed service models). For this, we refer to the standard textbooks of [2, 8, 10, 12, 14].

5.5 Newsvendor Models

For products with restricted storage life or products whose value decreases over time (e.g., perishable products such as food, newspapers, airline tickets or fast fashion), the newsvendor model describes a standard approach for determining optimal inventory levels under customer demand uncertainty in order to minimize waste (e.g., food waste or throwaway fashion). Therefore, the newsvendor model becomes particularly relevant from a sustainability perspective. In the following, we review the standard single-item newsvendor (see Sect. 5.5.1) and its data-driven extensions such as the data-driven newsvendor (see Sect. 5.5.2), the feature-based newsvendor (see Sect. 5.5.3), the machine learning-enabled newsvendor (see Sect. 5.5.3) and the deep learning-enabled newsvendor (see Sect. 5.5.4).

5.5.1 Standard Newsvendor Model

The standard newsvendor model optimizes the order quantity y under uncertain demand d that is modeled by a distribution function $f(d)$ (e.g., normal distribution). The newsvendor model originally refers to a newsvendor who needs to decide on the purchase quantity for tomorrow's newspaper without knowing how many newspapers she can sell. Therefore, the newsvendor can either purchase too little or too many newspapers. This trade-off is modeled by the following cost parameters: purchase price c, selling price p and salvage value g with the relationship $g \leq c \leq p$. If $c > p$, the product would not be profitable; if $g > c$, there would be an arbitrage opportunity. To solve the decision problem, a naïve decision-maker would set the order quantity y equal to the point forecast for the demand. An advanced purchaser however knows about the importance of uncertainty in decision-making. Consequently, the objective of the advanced purchaser is to maximize her expected profit $\pi(y)$, which is given by

$$\pi(y) = \int_{d=y}^{\infty} p \cdot y \cdot f(d)\partial d + \int_{0}^{y} (p \cdot d + g \cdot (y - d)) \cdot f(d)\partial d - c \cdot y, \qquad (5.21)$$

i.e., expected sales plus expected salvage value minus purchase cost.

The cost trade-off is solved by balancing underage cost $c_u = p - c$, i.e., the additional cost of having purchased one unit too little, and overage cost $c_o = c - g$, i.e., the additional cost of having purchased one unit too many. The optimal (i.e., profit-maximizing) purchase quantity y can be calculated by

$$y^* = F^{-1}\left(\frac{c_u}{c_u + c_o}\right) = F^{-1}\left(\frac{p - c}{p - g}\right) \qquad (5.22)$$

with F^{-1} as the inverse of the cumulative demand distribution function. If demand is modeled by a normal distribution with mean μ and standard deviation σ, then $F^{-1}(\cdot)$ can easily be computed using the `Excel` function `NORM.INV(·,μ,σ)`.

The expected profit $\pi(y)$ can also be stated as

$$\pi(y) = p \cdot ES(y) + g \cdot ELO(y) - c \cdot y. \qquad (5.23)$$

The expected lost sales (ELS) is calculated by

$$ELS(y) = \int_{y}^{\infty} (d - y) f(d)\partial d. \qquad (5.24)$$

If the demand follows a normal distribution $f(d)$ (cumulative normal distribution $F(d)$) with $f_{0,1}$ as the standard normal distribution, then $ELS(y)$ can be calculated by

$$ELS(y) = \sigma \cdot \left(f_{0,1}\left(\frac{y - \mu}{\sigma}\right) - \frac{y - \mu}{\sigma} \cdot \left(1 - F_{0,1}\left(\frac{y - \mu}{\sigma}\right)\right)\right). \qquad (5.25)$$

The expected sales (ES) is calculated by

$$ES(y) = \mu - ELS(y) \qquad (5.26)$$

with μ as the expected demand, and the expected leftover inventory (ELO) is calculated by

$$ELO(y) = y - ES(y). \tag{5.27}$$

Based on the optimized purchase quantity y, the performance indicators non-stockout probability (α service level) and fill rate (β service level) introduced in Chap. 4.7.3 can be calculated as follows:

$$\alpha = F(y) = F_{0,1}\left(\frac{y-\mu}{\sigma}\right) \tag{5.28}$$

with $F_{0,1}$ as the cumulative standard normal distribution.

$$\beta = \frac{ES(y)}{\mu} = \frac{\int_0^y d \cdot f(d)\partial d + y \cdot \int_y^\infty f(d)\partial d}{\mu} \tag{5.29}$$

Numerical Example: Standard Newsvendor Model

A newsvendor sells newspapers for 2 Euros per unit. She purchases the newspapers for 1 Euro per unit. Newspapers that cannot be sold can be returned with a refund of 0.50 Euros per unit. History shows that newspaper demand is normally distributed with a mean of 100 units per day and a standard deviation of 10 units per day.

Based on this input data, we can calculate the optimal purchase quantity $y^* = 104$ with a corresponding expected profit of $\pi^*(y) = 94.55$ Euros from expected sales $ES(y) = 98$ units, expected lost sales $ELS(y) = 2$ units and expected leftovers $ELO(y) = 7$ units. The non-stockout probability is 65.5%, and the fill rate is 98%.

Please note that the optimal purchase quantity is 4 units above the point forecast of 100 units per day. However, a naïve purchaser that ceteris paribus sets the order quantity equal to the point forecast of 100 units obtains a suboptimal profit of 94.02 Euros.

If the selling price increases by 10%, the optimal purchase quantity increases to 105 and the expected profit to 114.14 Euros. If the purchase price increases by 10%, the optimal purchase quantity decreases to 103 and the expected profit to 84.20 Euros. If the salvage value increases by 10%, the optimal purchase quantity increases to 105 and the expected profit to 94.88 Euros. If demand uncertainty increases from a standard deviation of 10 to 20, the optimal purchase quantity increases to 109, and the expected profit reduces to 89.09 Euros.

If the decision-maker is risk-averse (risk-averse newsvendor), then the optimal purchase quantity y is derived by maximizing the expected utility u rather than the expected profit π. The utility function is characterized by

$$u(x) = -e^{-\alpha \cdot x} \tag{5.30}$$

with $\alpha > 0$ as the decision-maker's coefficient of risk aversion. $\alpha = 0$ refers to the risk-neutral case. Other than the optimal risk-neutral newsvendor order quantity that can be derived analytically with a formula, the optimal risk-averse newsvendor order quantity can only be derived numerically and decreases with increasing α. Therefore, a risk-averse decision-maker would order less than a risk-neutral decision-maker, fearing more the loss through overage cost. For more details on the risk-averse newsvendor, we refer to [6].

5.5.2 Data-Driven Newsvendor Model

The standard newsvendor model as introduced in Sect. 5.5.1 works with simplistic assumptions with regard to the demand model. This works well whenever the probability distribution of demand is known and accurate. However, probability distributions are difficult to estimate and prone to errors. For instance, a normally distributed demand is often not adequate in practice. The data-driven newsvendor does not rely on any distributional assumptions but directly optimizes based on (historical) raw data $i = 1, \ldots, n$ of demand d_i. While the standard newsvendor model is a two-step approach (predictive modeling and optimization), the data-driven newsvendor is a single-step approach (integrated prediction and optimization) based on a linear programming model:

$$\text{maximize} \quad \frac{1}{n}\sum_{i=1}^{n}\Big(p \cdot s_i + g \cdot (y - s_i)\Big) - c \cdot y \tag{5.31}$$

$$\text{s.t} \quad s_i \leq d_i \qquad \forall i = 1, \ldots, n \tag{5.32}$$

$$s_i \leq y \qquad \forall i = 1, \ldots, n \tag{5.33}$$

$$y, s_i \geq 0 \qquad \forall i = 1, \ldots, n \tag{5.34}$$

The objective function maximizes the (historical) profit with sales price p, purchase price c and salvage value g and with the sales quantity s_i being restricted by demand d_i and order quantity y.

Numerical Example: Data-Driven Newsvendor Model
A company needs to decide about its purchase quantity of a specific perishable product with a selling price of $p = 12$ Euros, a purchase price of $c = 6$ Euros and a salvage value of $g = 1$ Euro. The company observed the following demand during the last 10 days, i.e., 60, 118, 114, 79, 97, 59, 76, 108, 96, 115. Based on the data-driven newsvendor model, the company should order 97 units in order to maximize its expected profit, which is 455.5 Euros.

5.5.3 *Feature-Based Newsvendor Model*

The data-driven newsvendor from Sect. 5.5.2 relies on historical demand observations $d_i, i = 1, \ldots, n$ only. However, in practice, additional information on demand drivers may be available such as weather conditions, day of the week, month of the year or location. For instance, the demand for barbecue products strongly depends on weather data such as hours of sun or rainfall. The decision-maker should chose its order quantity y under consideration of this information as optimal order quantities for barbecue products may differ between sunny and cloudy days.

To capture demand features, the data-driven newsvendor model is extended to the feature-based newsvendor model with the order quantity y as a regression-like function of features X_j, $j = 1, .., m$:

$$y = \beta_0 + \sum_{j=1}^{m} \beta_j \cdot X_j \tag{5.35}$$

The coefficients β_j are obtained by defining them as decision variables in the linear programming formulation of the data-driven newsvendor (see, e.g., [3]).

Alternatively, we can follow the approach by [4], who define the target inventory level I rather than the order quantity y as a function of features, i.e.,

$$I = \beta_0 + \sum_{j=1}^{m} \beta_j \cdot X_j, \tag{5.36}$$

and optimize the coefficients β_j with a data-driven approach using the following linear programming formulation under cost minimization objectives with holding cost c_h for excess inventories z_i and unit shortage penalty cost c_p for shortage quantity $(d_i - s_i)^+$:

$$\text{minimize} \quad \frac{1}{n} \sum_{i=1}^{n} \left(c_h \cdot z_i + c_p \cdot (d_i - s_i) \right) \tag{5.37}$$

$$\text{s.t} \qquad z_i \geq \sum_{j=0}^{m} \beta_j X_{ji} - d_i \qquad \forall i = 1, \ldots, n \tag{5.38}$$

$$s_i \leq d_i \qquad \forall i = 1, \ldots, n \tag{5.39}$$

$$s_i \leq \sum_{j=0}^{m} \beta_j X_{ji} \qquad \forall i = 1, \ldots, n \tag{5.40}$$

$$s_i, z_i \geq 0, \beta_j \in \mathbb{R} \qquad \forall i = 1, \ldots, n, j = 1, \ldots, m \tag{5.41}$$

Numerical Example: Feature-Based Newsvendor Model

Suppose a supermarket needs to decide about purchase quantities for barbecue products. This decision is heavily affected by weather conditions. Therefore, the supermarket has historical demand data available and additionally collects temperature data and data on average daily hours of sunshine (Table 5.5).

By solving the feature-based newsvendor model based on specific holding cost c_h (e.g., 1 Euro per unit per week) and shortage penalty cost c_p (e.g., 2 Euro per unit), the supermarket can derive the target inventory level I as a function of weather conditions as shown in Fig. 5.8.

Figure 5.8 shows that that there is a relationship between both temperature and hours of sun on the optimal target inventory level of the supermarket for barbecue products. Furthermore, target inventory levels are also affected by inventory holding cost c_h and penalty cost c_p.

Please note that only single-variate results are shown for two-dimensional illustration reasons. For this example, there is a positive value of using both feature time series for calculating optimal target inventory levels considering both temperature and hours of sun. The optimal target inventory levels are given by

$$\text{Target inventory} = \begin{cases} 115.5 + 4.5 \cdot \text{Temp} + 11.4 \cdot \text{Sun Hours} & \text{if } (c_h, c_p) = (1, 2) \\ 105.2 + 4.6 \cdot \text{Temp} + 11.8 \cdot \text{Sun Hours} & \text{if } (c_h, c_p) = (2, 1) \\ 105.5 + 4.6 \cdot \text{Temp} + 11.7 \cdot \text{Sun Hours} & \text{if } (c_h, c_p) = (1, 1) \end{cases}$$

This trained formula can easily be used to calculate target inventory levels by entering latest regional temperature and sum hour data that can be retrieved from any weather website or through the weather service.

Table 5.5 Input data for the feature-based newsvendor model

Week	1	2	3	4	5	6	7	8	9	10
Demand [units]	339	269	369	278	349	387	397	346	317	256
Temperature [°C]	20	24	26	22	29	33	35	31	28	25
Hours of sun	12	4	12	6	9	12	11	8	7	3

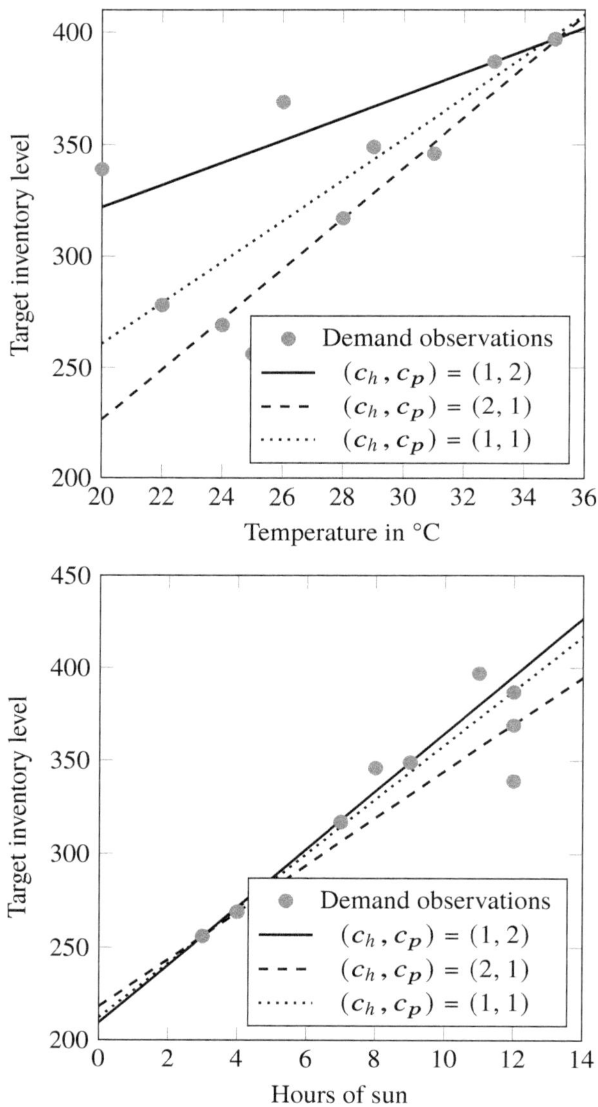

Fig. 5.8 Demand observation points (dots) and optimal target inventory levels (lines) as a function of average temperature and average daily hours of sunshine for different operational parameter settings of c_h and c_p

5.5.4 Machine Learning-Enabled Newsvendor Model

As described in Chap. 2, overfitting often deteriorates the performance of linear regression models whenever the algorithm learns the data set by heart but does not recognize the fundamental underlying pattern. This problem also occurs for the feature-based newsvendor that was described in Sect. 5.5.3.

Therefore, the feature-based newsvendor model is extended to the machine learning-enabled newsvendor model that uses regularization (see, e.g., [3]). For the machine learning-enabled newsvendor, the objective function of the linear program

$$\frac{1}{n}\sum_{i=1}^{n}\Big(c_h \cdot z_i + c_p \cdot (d_i - s_i)\Big) + \lambda \cdot R(\beta) \tag{5.42}$$

is extended by a penalty term $R(\beta)$ with λ being the regularization parameter (optimized via cross-validation) and $R(\beta)$ being the regularization function. The regularization function is typically defined by the l_1 or l_2 norm of the weights β. The literature shows that this improves the performance of the algorithm significantly and increases the realized profits (see [3]).

5.5.5 Deep Learning-Enabled Newsvendor Model

Both the feature-based and machine learning-enabled newsvendors assume a linear relationship between order quantity y (or inventory level I) and features X_j, $j = 1, \ldots, m$. This is not appropriate to capture existing nonlinear relationships. The deep learning-enabled newsvendor model (see [9]) extends the machine learning-enabled newsvendor to nonlinear relationships. Therefore, it uses a deep neural network (see Chap. 2) that connects an input layer (feature data X_j) with an output layer (order quantity y) over several hidden layers. The following loss function measures the closeness of the output of the neural network and the true values. The objective of the deep neural network is to minimize the loss function, i.e., to solve the following optimization problem:

$$\min_{y_1,\ldots,y_n} \frac{1}{n}\left(\sum_{i=1}^{n}\left(c_p(d_i - y_i)^+ + c_h(y_i - d_i)^+\right)^2\right) \tag{5.43}$$

The squared cost function penalizes order quantities y that are far from demand more than those that are close to demand. Similar to the machine learning-enabled newsvendor, regularization extensions help avoid overfitting.

The deep learning-enabled newsvendor outperforms the machine learning-enabled and feature-based newsvendor particularly when demand volatility was high or very limited training data is available. For further details on deep reinforcement learning applications in inventory control, we refer to [5].

5.6 Dynamic Stochastic Inventory Control Policies

While the newsvendor model addresses a single-period problem (with restricted storage time), the following inventory control policies address a multi-period setting where product value does not decrease during storage as it is relevant for commodities such as steel, aluminum, copper or semi-finished products. The objective is to find an inventory control policy that optimizes timing (*when?*) and quantity (*how much?*) of procurement and inventory decisions in order to minimize total cost and at the same time often guarantee a specific service level. Therefore, inventory management distinguishes between four major inventory policies (or strategies) that are characterized by the parameters reorder point s, order interval t, order-up-to-level S and order quantity Q (see Fig. 5.9). Dynamic inventory policies optimize orders based in the so-called inventory position that is defined as the net inventory plus outstanding orders (or on-order inventory) with net inventory (or inventory level) as the physical inventory (or on-hand inventory) minus back orders. Dynamic inventory control furthermore distinguishes between periodic review and continuous review. Periodic review systems track inventory levels every week or month, while continuous review systems track inventory levels permanently.

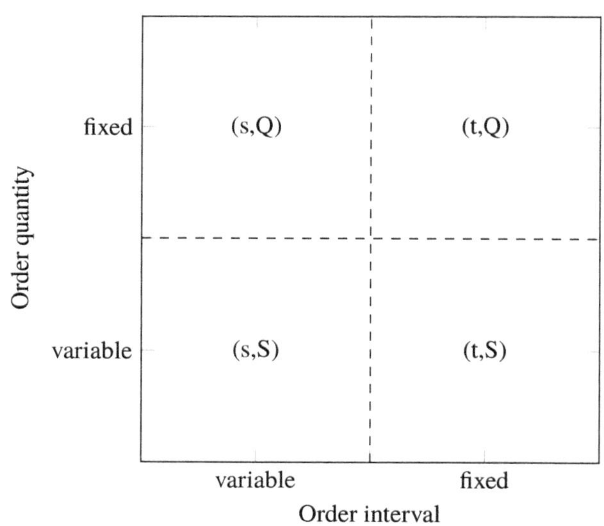

Fig. 5.9 Dynamic inventory control policies

Parameters (t, s, Q, S) of dynamic inventory control policies can be determined by dynamic programming (see Markov decision processes in Chap. 2). However, dynamic programming suffers from (i) the curse of dimensionality (see Chap. 2) and (ii) mostly relies on (wrong) distributional assumptions for modeling uncertainty. To address (i), in practice, policy parameters are often determined via approximate solutions such as the economic order quantity. To address (ii), reinforcement learning and simulation approaches are used to optimize system parameters based on data and without probabilistic assumptions.

In the following, we conceptually introduce the four major classes of dynamic inventory control policies that are applied in practice.

5.6.1 (s,Q) Inventory Policy

The (s,Q) inventory policy triggers an order quantity Q whenever the inventory position falls below or reaches a reorder point s (Fig. 5.10). Heuristically, Q can be approximated by the standard economic order quantity (EOQ), and s can be set as expected demand during supply lead time (L) plus a safety stock (see safety stock formula).

Example: (s,Q) Inventory Policy
An inventory system is characterized by the following parameters: $s = 30$, $Q = 50$, an initial inventory of 50 and a lead time of $L = 1$ week. Given the demand series from Table 5.6, this yields an alpha service level of 42.9% (=3/7) and a beta service level of 75% $(= 180/240)$.

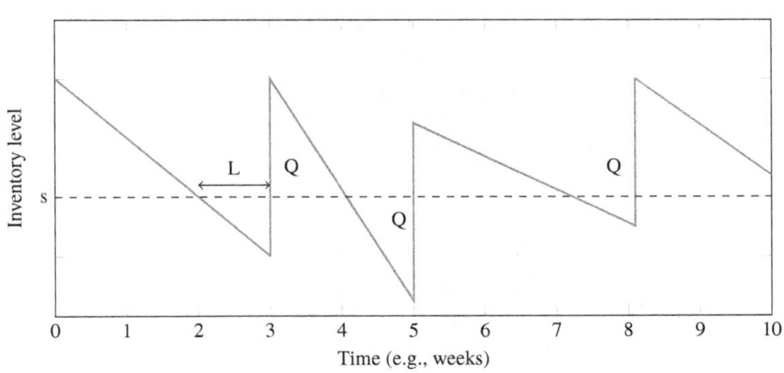

Fig. 5.10 Concept of (s,Q) inventory policies

Table 5.6 Numerical example for (s,Q) inventory policies

Week	Opening stock	Inventory position	Order quantity	Demand	Closing stock
1	50	50	0	30	20
2	20	20	50	20	0
3	0	50	0	60	−10
4	−10	−10	50	20	−30
5	−30	20	50	40	−20
6	−20	30	50	40	−10
7	−10	40	0	30	10

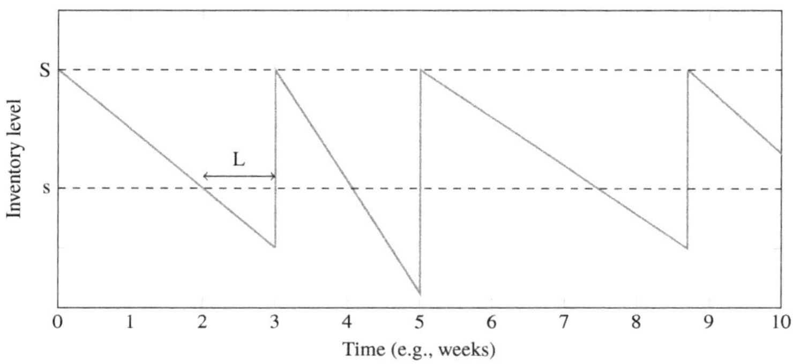

Fig. 5.11 Concept of (s,S) inventory policies

5.6.2 (s,S) Inventory Policy

The (s,S) inventory policy triggers an order-up-to level S (i.e., order quantity is S minus inventory position) whenever the inventory position falls below or reaches a reorder point s (Fig. 5.11). $S - s$ can be approximated by the standard economic order quantity (EOQ), and s can be set as expected demand during supply lead time plus safety stock. If there are no fixed order cost, the (s,S) policy reduces to a base-stock policy that is equivalent to the (s,S) policy with $s = S - 1$, meaning we place an order to replenish the inventory up to S units immediately if there is any demand consuming the inventory on a particular day.

Numerical Example: (s,S) Inventory Policy
An inventory system is characterized by the following parameters: $s = 30$, $S = 80$, an initial inventory of 50 and $L = 1$ week. Given the demand series from Table 5.7, this yields an alpha service level of 71.4% (=5/7) and a beta service level of 83.3% ($= 200/240$).

Table 5.7 Numerical example for (s,S) inventory policies

Week	Opening stock	Inventory position	Order quantity	Demand	Closing stock
1	50	50	0	30	20
2	20	20	60	20	0
3	0	60	0	60	0
4	0	0	80	20	−20
5	−20	60	0	40	20
6	20	20	60	40	−20
7	−20	40	0	30	10

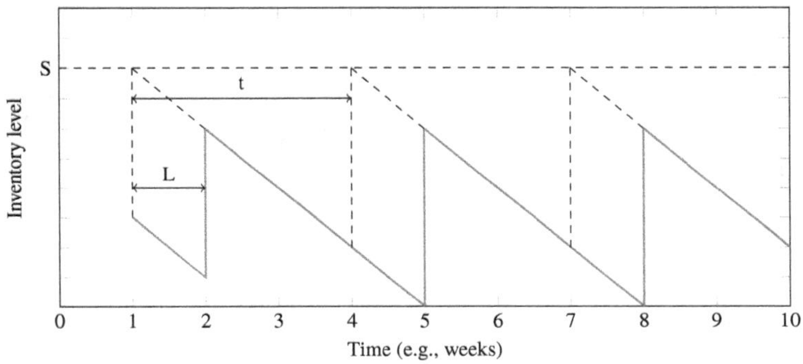

Fig. 5.12 Concept of (t,S) inventory policies

5.6.3 (t,S) Inventory Policy

The (t,S) inventory policy triggers an order up to level S each t periods (Fig. 5.12). t can be approximated by the standard economic order interval (EOI) and S as the expected demand during supply lead time plus safety stock.

Numerical Example: (t,S) Inventory Policy
An inventory system is characterized by the following parameters: $t = 1$ week, $S = 70$, an initial inventory of 70 and $L = 1$ week. Given the demand series from Table 5.8, this yields an alpha service level of 57% (=4/7) and a beta service level of 87.5% (= 210/240).

Table 5.8 Numerical example for (t,S) inventory policies

Week	Opening stock	Inventory position	Order quantity	Demand	Closing stock
1	70	70	0	30	40
2	40	40	30	20	20
3	20	50	20	60	−10
4	−10	10	60	20	−10
5	−10	50	20	40	10
6	10	30	40	40	−10
7	−10	30	40	30	0

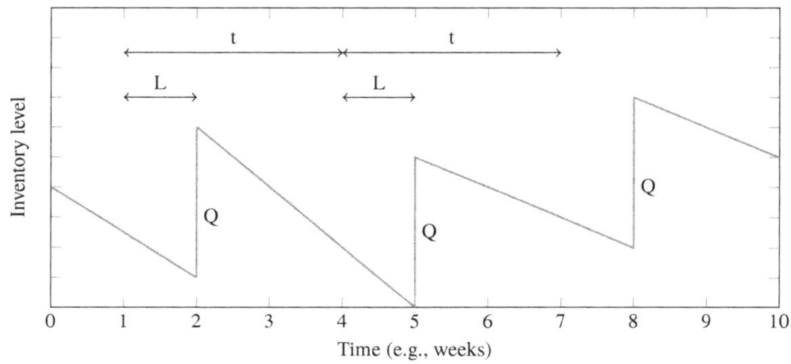

Fig. 5.13 Concept of (t,Q) inventory policies

5.6.4 (t,Q) Inventory Policy

The (t,Q) inventory policy triggers an order quantity Q each t periods (Fig. 5.13). t can be approximated by the standard economic order interval (EOI) and Q by the economic order quantity (EOQ).

Numerical Example: (t,Q) Inventory Policy
An inventory system is characterized by the following parameters: $t = 2$ weeks, $Q = 50$, an initial inventory of 70 and zero lead time. Given the demand series from Table 5.9, this yields an alpha service level of 100% (=7/7) and a beta service level of 100% (=240/240). However, the example shows that parameters t and Q may not be accurately chosen as the high service levels come along with high and therefore costly inventory levels.

For a further deep dive into analytical inventory control and management, we refer to the re-owned textbooks of [2, 8, 10, 12, 14].

Table 5.9 Numerical example for (t,Q) inventory policies

Week	Opening stock	Inventory position	Order quantity	Demand	Closing stock
1	70	70	50	30	90
2	90	90	0	20	70
3	70	70	50	60	60
4	60	60	0	20	40
5	40	40	50	40	50
6	50	50	0	40	10
7	10	10	50	30	30

References

1. Arrow KA (1958) Historical background. In: Arrow KJ, Karlin S, Scarf HE (eds) Studies in the Mathematical Theory of Inventory and Production, 1st edn. Stanford University Press, Stanford
2. Axsäter S (2015) Inventory Control, 3rd edn. Springer, Berlin
3. Ban GY, Rudin C (2020) The Big Data Newsvendor: practical insights from machine learning. Oper Res 67(1):90–108
4. Beutel AL, Minner S (2012) Safety stock planning under causal demand forecasting. Int J Prod Eco 140(2):637–645
5. Boute RN, Gijsbrechts J, van Jaarsveld W, Vanvuchelen N (2022) Deep reinforcement learning for inventory control: a roadmap. Eur J Oper Res 298(1):401–413
6. Eeckhoudt L, Gollier C, Schlesinger H (1995) The risk-averse (and prudent) newsboy. Manage. Sci. 41(5):786–794
7. Harris FW (1913) How many parts to make at once. Factory Mag Manage 10:135–136
8. Muckstadt JA, Sapra A (2011) Principles of Inventory Management. 1st edn. Springer, Berlin
9. Oroojlooyjadid A, Snyder L, Takáč M (2020) Applying deep learning to the newsvendor problem. IISE Trans 52:444–463
10. Porteus EL (2002) Foundations of Stochastic Inventory Theory, 1st edn. Stanford Business Books, Stanford
11. Silver EA, Meal HC (1973) A heuristic for selecting lot size requirements for the case of a deterministic time-varying demand rate and discrete-opportunities for replenishment. Prod Inventory Manage 14(2):64–74
12. Snyder EA, Pyke DF, Peterson R (1998) Inventory Management and Production Planning and Scheduling, 3rd edn. John Wiley & Sons, Hoboken
13. Wagner HM, Whitin TM (1958) Dynamic version of the economic lot size model. Manage Sci 5(1):89–96
14. Zipkin PH (2000) Foundations of Inventory Management, 1st edn. Irwin Professional Publishing, Burr Ridge

Chapter 6
Data-Driven Risk Management

Abstract The world is increasingly becoming volatile and uncertain. In the procurement context, this gets obvious through severe supply disruptions for semiconductors and other basic purchase materials as well as through unforeseeable upward commodity price movements in the early 2020s at metal, energy and agricultural markets. In this chapter, we provide guidance on how to measure the degree of procurement risk that a company is facing and present analytical approaches to reduce risk. Doing so, we distinguish between three major exogenous risk factors that affect procurement performance: supply disruption risk, commodity price risk and exchange rate risk.

Keywords Supply risk · Price risk · Exchange rate risk · Value at risk · Financial hedging · Operational hedging

6.1 Introduction

More than ever before, today's business decisions need to be taken in a high-risk environment. In business language, people speak about the VUCA world, which characterizes the early 2020s, i.e., volatility, uncertainty, complexity and ambiguity. In the context of procurement, there are many external potential risk factors that may affect procurement performance, for instance, supply disruption risk, commodity price risk, exchange rate risk or risks related to changes in duties, taxes and local content requirements.

In the literature, risk is generally defined as the amount of a loss L multiplied by the probability of its occurrence P, i.e.,

$$\text{Risk} = L \cdot P. \tag{6.1}$$

C. Mandl, *Procurement Analytics*, Springer Series in Supply Chain Management 22, https://doi.org/10.1007/978-3-031-43281-1_6

Table 6.1 Risk matrix

		Loss				
		Negligible	**Minor**	**Moderate**	**Major**	**Severe**
Probability	**Very likely**	Low medium	Medium	Medium high	High	High
	Likely	Low	Medium low	Medium	Medium high	High
	Possible	Low	Medium low	Medium	Medium high	Medium high
	Unlikely	Low	Medium low	Medium low	Medium	Medium high
	Very unlikely	Low	Low	Medium low	Medium	Medium

Both dimensions are often used to specify a risk in so-called risk matrices (or risk maps) that classify risk into categories such as *high, medium high, medium, medium low and low* (see Table 6.1). For being classified as high risk, it needs both a sufficient amount of loss and a sufficient probability of occurrence. *Black swans* are, for instance, events that are highly unlikely but with severe consequences.

The risk priority number known from *Failure Mode and Effects Analysis (FMEA)* goes even one step further and prioritizes risks according to the dimensions amount of loss, probability of occurrence and likelihood of detection with risk being higher if the likelihood of detection is low.

This textbook mainly focuses on decision-making in procurement. Therefore, we want to define risk also from a decision theory perspective (Fig. 6.1). Decision theory distinguishes between certainty, uncertainty, risk and ambiguity. Decisions under certainty are based on a basis of information that is complete, while decisions under uncertainty are made under incomplete information. Decisions under uncertainty furthermore split into decisions under ambiguity and decisions under risk. While for both all potential consequences of a decision (e.g., potential loss) are known, for decisions under ambiguity (also known as Knightian uncertainty), probabilities of occurrence are unknown due to, for instance, a lack of historical data. On the other hand, decisions under risk are taken under known probabilities of occurrence, i.e., a known underlying probability model that might be derived or estimated from historical data (see, e.g., scenario tree modeling or distributional modeling from Chap. 2).

There is also an important difference between uncertainty and volatility that are often used interchangeably. While uncertainty measures the difficulty to forecast, volatility measures the fluctuation, i.e., the dispersion of a parameter (e.g., price or demand) around a long-term mean.

In the business context, risk is typically classified into economic risk (e.g., market risk, price risk, supply risk, quality risk, process risk, insurance risk, currency risk, financial risk) and country risk (e.g., political risk, legal risk, regulatory risk) or into financial risk (i.e., uncertainty in payoffs) and operational risk (i.e., risk related to processes and resources). In the following, we want to focus on three risk dimensions that are particularly relevant for today's procurement organizations, i.e., supply disruption risk (see Sect. 6.2), commodity price risk (see Sect. 6.3) and exchange rate risk (see Sect. 6.4). In this chapter, we do not explicitly focus

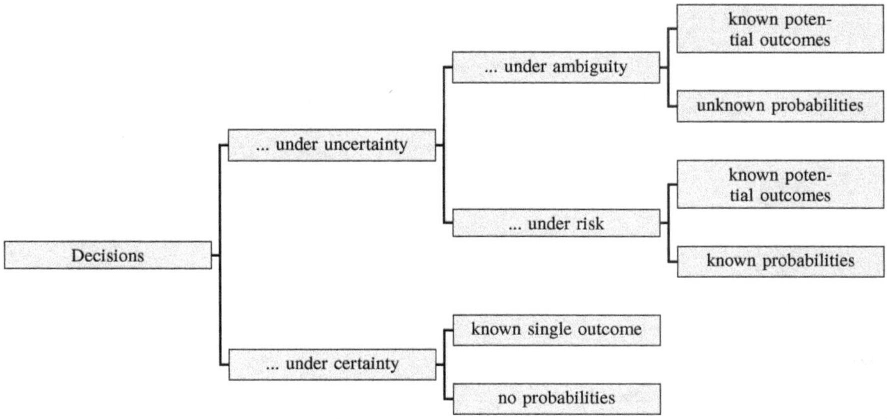

Fig. 6.1 Decision environments

on customer demand risk, which is however covered in the context of inventory management in Chap. 5 and in the context of supply network design in Chap. 4.

In order to evaluate risk, the risk management literature defines various quantitative measures such as the standard deviation of returns, variance, annualized volatility, quartiles, value at risk (VaR) and conditional value at risk (CVaR). We will introduce major measures for risk evaluation and risk mitigation and in the following.

6.2 Supply Disruption Risk

During the early 2020s, disruption risk became a prevalent external risk factor for companies. The blockade of the Suez Canal in 2021, the global chip shortage during 2020–2022 and the energy crisis as a result of the war in Ukraine in 2022/2023 are only three prominent events related to severe supply disruptions. Procurement as the company interlink to suppliers is responsible for managing and minimizing supply risk that is often divided into disruption risk (due to stochastic disruptions) and lead time risk (due to stochastic lead times).

In general, disruption or supply risk can have a variety of causes. We typically distinguish between (geo-)political risk, financial risk, fiscal risk, structural risk and operational risk. Van Mieghem [26] categorizes reasons for supply risks based on the dimensions probability of occurrence and impact (see Fig. 6.2). This includes black swans such as terror events or earthquakes at supplier locations as well as frequent risks such as stockouts, human errors or staff shortage. For instance, in 2021, shortage of truck drivers yielded significant supply disruptions in the UK.

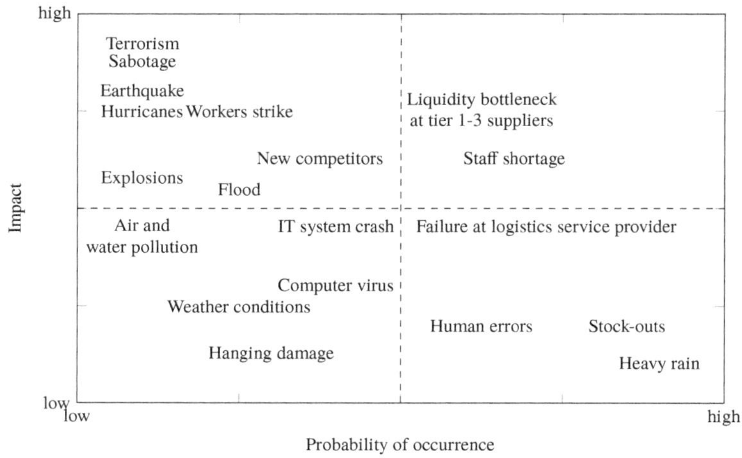

Fig. 6.2 Supply risk according to Van Mieghem [26]

6.2.1 Measuring Supply Disruption Risk

As shown above, disruption risks have various dimensions. Therefore, there cannot be a single formula to calculate a company's individual disruption risk. There should rather be a scorecard of key performance indicators to be considered. The following list gives an overview on what kind of performance indicators might be worth to be tracked over time in order to capture different causes for supply disruptions such as supplier quality risk, logistics risk, capacity risk or contract risk. For each of the metrics that are measured per supplier, thresholds can be defined that give signals when to (counter)act in order to avoid supply disruptions.

- Perfect order rate [%]
- Complaint rate [%]
- Default rate [%]
- Service levels (non-stockout probability, fill rate) [%]
- Delivery date accuracy [%]
- Delivery quantity accuracy [%]
- Average lead time [days]
- Number of suppliers per category [#]
- Single source and sole source of products and transportation services rate [%]
- Global sourcing rate [%]
- Index-based contracting rate [%]
- Contracting rate (short-term, medium-term, long-term) [%]
- Supplier liquidity score (-)

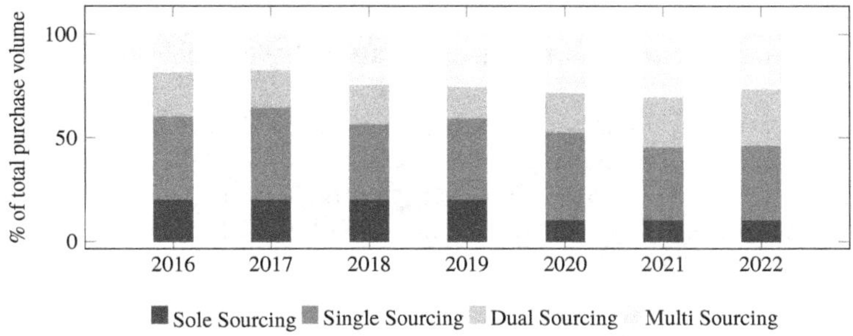

Fig. 6.3 Sole-source and single-source rates

Table 6.2 Training data for decision tree

Supplier	Geography	Liquidity	Revenue	Supplier risk
A	Local	Medium	>1 bn USD	Low
B	Local	High	<0.1 bn USD	Low
C	Global	Low	<0.1 bn USD	High
D	Global	Low	0.1–1 bn USD	High
E	Regional	Low	>1 bn USD	High
F	Regional	High	<0.1 bn USD	Low
G	Regional	Medium	0.1–1 bn USD	High
H	Regional	Medium	>1 bn USD	High
I	Global	Medium	>1 bn USD	High

Figure 6.3 gives an example for a KPI tracking over time. It shows that the company was able to decrease sole- and single-sourcing rates. The purchase portfolio in 2022 is therefore less risky compared to previous years.

In order to quantify supply risk on a supplier level, a decision tree approach can be used that is illustrated based on the following numerical example.

Numerical Example: Decision Tree for Supplier Risk Assessment
Suppose the following simplified classification problem with the target value *supplier risk* that should be classified as *high* or *low*. The following predictor values (features) should be used: supplier liquidity (low, medium, high), supplier geography (local, regional, global) and supplier revenue (>1 bn USD, 0.1 bn USD–1 bn USD, < 0.1 bn USD). The purchasing department collected the following historical training data (Table 6.2).

Based on the training data, an algorithm (e.g., CART) trains a decision tree (see Fig. 6.4) based on specific metrics such as entropy. The resulting tree can

(continued)

be used for future supplier risk assessments and subsequent risk mitigation actions.

The performance of the decision tree for supplier classification is evaluated based on accuracy metrics (see Chap. 2). Accuracy is 100% on this training set. However, for new suppliers (test set), this might decrease. A false-negative classification (i.e., a high-risk supplier is classified as low-risk supplier) is worse than a positive classification (i.e., a low-risk supplier is classified as high-risk supplier).

In addition to internal KPI monitoring and risk assessment, there are also external indices available that measure supply disruption risk per industry or country such as the *Purchasing Manager Index*, the *Supply Delivery Time Index* and the *Global Supply Chain Pressure Index*.

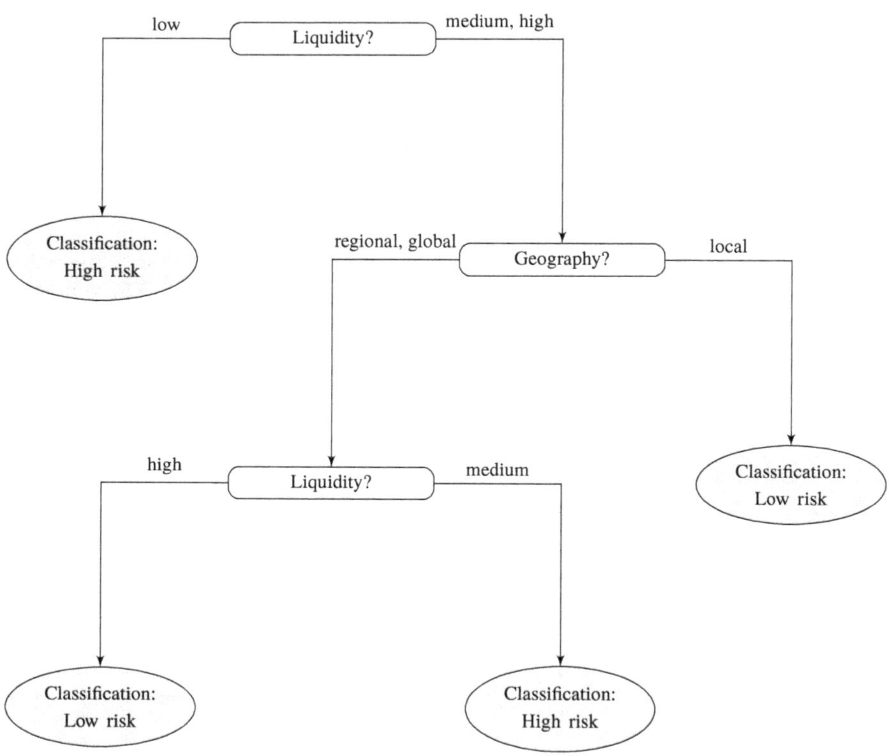

Fig. 6.4 Decision tree for supplier risk assessment

The *Purchasing Manager Index (PMI)* is a well-known monthly indicator for economic activities in the purchasing environment. It is based on a regular survey sent to purchasing managers and weights five sub-indices, i.e., order pipeline (weight 30%), production output (weight 25%), employment (weight 20%), supply delivery times (weight 15%) and inventory levels (10%).

The indices are calculated by

$$\mathrm{PMI} = 1 \cdot P_1 + 0.5 \cdot P_2 + 0 \cdot P_3 \tag{6.2}$$

with P_1 as the percentage of purchasing managers that report an improvement compared to the previous month, P_2 as the percentage of purchasing managers that report no change compared to the previous month and P_3 as the percentage of purchasing managers that report a decline compared to the previous month. Therefore, PMI is a scaled value between 0 and 100. $\mathrm{PMI} = 0$ indicates the one extreme that all purchasing managers expect or observe a decline of the situation, while $\mathrm{PMI} = 100$ indicates the other extreme that all purchasing managers tend to expect or observe an improvement of the situation. $\mathrm{PMI} > 50$ indicates an improvement, while $\mathrm{PMI} < 50$ indicates a decline. The monthly indices can be retrieved from databases such as Refinitiv Datastream.

A second index is the *Supply Delivery Time Index* that presents the change in supply delivery time compared to the previous month for different countries and sectors (see Fig. 6.5). It therefore reflects current and future supply disruption risk. Figure 6.5 shows that procurement managers across various countries and industries faced supply delays in June 2021. The greatest supply chain delays were observed in the Netherlands, Austria and Germany and particularly for technology equipment, machinery and industrial goods.

A third index that gives a monthly indication on supply disruption is the *Global Supply Chain Pressure Index (GSCPI)*. It therefore analyzes data on transportation cost (e.g., Baltic Dry Index) and manufacturing activities (e.g., inventories, backlogs and orders). Please note that GSCPI also includes some components of the *Purchasing Manager Index*.

Figure 6.6 shows the development of *GSCPI* between 2010 and 2023. It indicates a huge supply disruption risk starting in 2020 with the beginning of the COVID-19 crisis, while supply disruption risks were rather moderate prior to 2020.

6.2.2 Measures for Risk Mitigation

In practice, there are several risk mitigation strategies possible that are summarized in Table 6.3—each coming with benefits and limitations. According to Deloitte's well-regarded *2021 Global Chief Procurement Officer Survey*, number 1 risk mitigation action is supplier information sharing through the use of digital tools. For

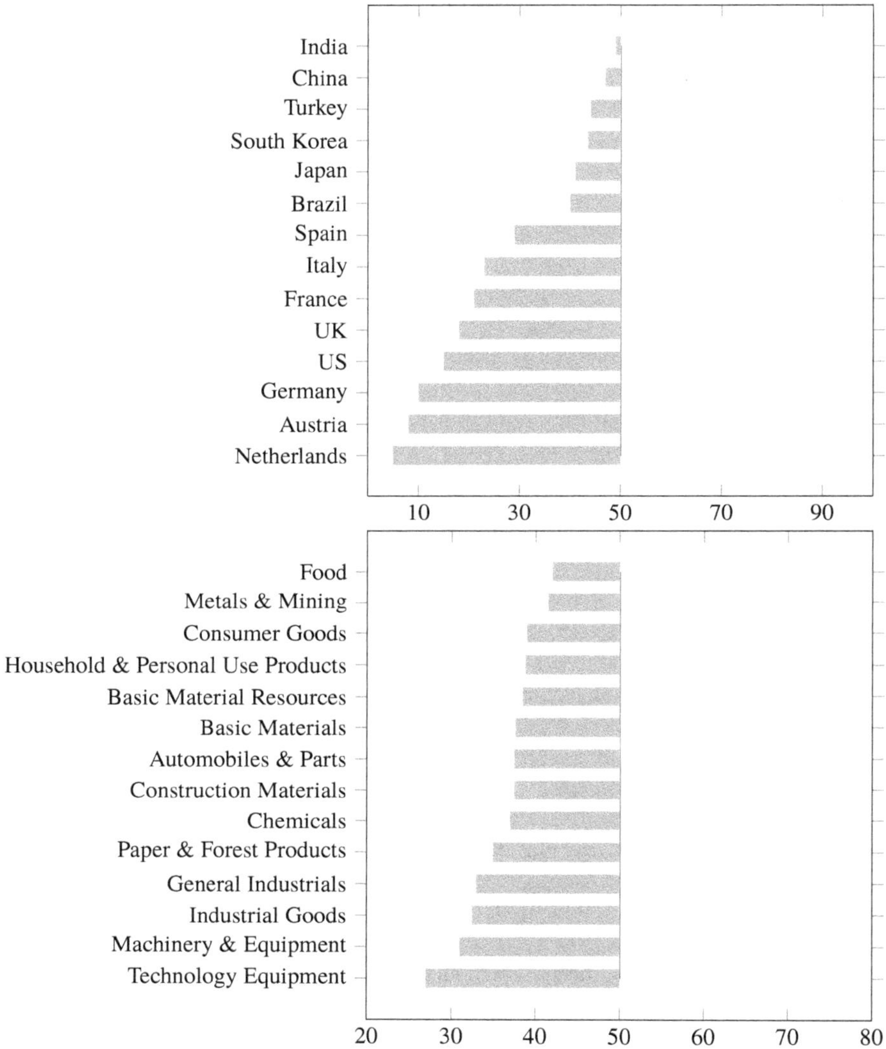

Fig. 6.5 Global supply delivery time index for manufacturing industries in June 2021 for different countries and industries (50, no change compared to previous month) (Data source: IHS Markit)

instance, the automotive industry started *Catena-X*—a collaborative data ecosystem along the entire supply chain that builds the basis for a secure data exchange in order to increase resilience. Number 2 is activating alternative supply sources (i.e., dual or multi-sourcing), while number 3 is building inventories (i.e., safety stocks).

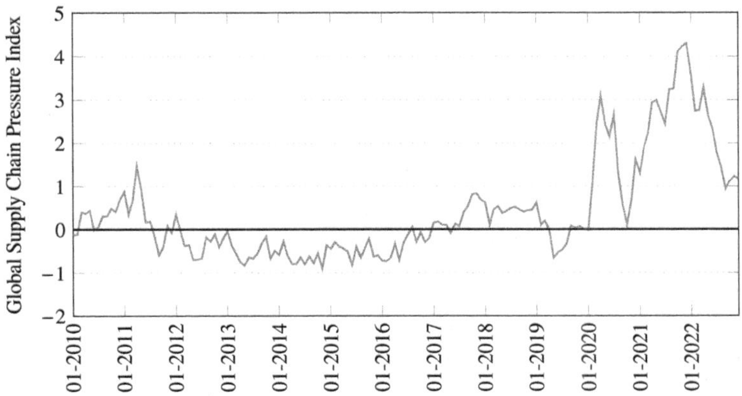

Fig. 6.6 Global supply chain pressure index (GSCPI from 2010 to 2022) (Source: IHS Markit)

Industry Example: Reactions on 2021/2022 Supply Disruptions

As a consequence of the corona pandemic and the resulting supply disruptions, many companies think about a re-design of their supply and production network. Therefore, they simulate the cost effects of re-shoring activities in order to increase resilience of supply chains. To shift production closer to suppliers and customers was even enforced by political decisions and energy cost inflation in 2023. As a consequence, European firms elaborate on shifting parts of their production to, for instance, the USA, whose government subsidies the settlement of companies from the sustainability and clean energy field through the Inflation Reduction Act and lower energy cost. Other European companies also think about alternative transportation routes from Asia to Europe. While for years, the typical shipping route was either the Suez route or the Cape route, companies increasingly evaluate the opportunity to ship goods via train using east-west rail corridors and the silk route as an (additional) alternative. Other companies used vertical control. This can either be vertical integration, i.e., the integration of suppliers, or direct sourcing, i.e., the buyer purchases the raw material requirements of its first-tier suppliers directly at the second-tier supplier.

In the following, we want to analytically investigate three measures and its effect on supply risk: safety stock optimization, multi-sourcing and supply network optimization. All three were increasingly used as a reaction on the supply chain disruptions in the early 2020s.

Table 6.3 Measures for mitigating supply disruption risk

Measure	Benefits	Limitations
Make rather than buy	Complete independence	High fixed cost
	Know-how development	Know-how requirements
	High flexibility	Capacity limitations
Safety stocks	Bypassing bottlenecks	High capital lockup
	Hedging of price risk	Storage capacity limitations
	Hedging of demand risk	Planning effort
Back-up suppliers	High flexibility	Cost of flexibility
	Argument for price negotiations	Willingness of suppliers
	Less coordination effort	No close supplier relationship
Dual/Multi-Sourcing	Independence of single source	High administrative effort
	Argument for price negotiations	Limited economies of scale
	Hedging of demand peaks	No close supplier relationship
Supplier integration	Early warnings and actions	Cost of acquisition
	Know-how acquisition	Cost of integration
	Potential competitive advantage	Potential cultural divergence
Information sharing	Early warnings	High cost and complexity
	Value of collected data	Just warning, no action
Global sourcing	Diversification of geographical risk	Administrative effort
	Argument for price re-negotiations	Cultural and linguistic barriers
		Currency risk
Local sourcing	Limitation of logistics risk	High labor cost
	Reduction of lead time	Product limitations
Multi-modal transportation	Hedging of weather risk	Coordination effort
and alternative routes	Hedging of infrastructure risk	Cost of switching
Risk-sharing agreements	Risk shift to supplier	Cost of risk premium
	Building of trust	Treating symptoms not causes
Insurance	Risk shift to insurance company	Treating symptoms not causes
		High insurance premium
Backlogging	No direct cost	Risk of customer churn
	Small administrative effort	Potential image damage

Safety Stock Optimization for Supply Risk Mitigation

While for decades of just-in-time production and lean management companies were not focusing too much on inventories and safety stock, this changed during the last years of severe supply disruptions and rapidly increased lead times. For specific companies, lead times of supply increased from 1 week to 10 weeks, and uncertainty in lead times also increases safety stocks as illustrated in the example below.

Numerical Example: Safety Stock Effects of Lead Time Uncertainty
Suppose a company wants to achieve an α service level of 95% for a demand of 150 units per week. Originally, the lead time was rather stable and varied with a standard deviation of 1 week. Therefore, according to the analytical safety stock formula introduced in Sect. 5.4.2, safety stock is

$$SS = 1.64 \cdot 150 \cdot 1 = 246. \tag{6.3}$$

During the pandemic, lead time volatility increased significantly with a standard deviation of 3 weeks. Consequently,

$$SS = 1.64 \cdot 150 \cdot 3 = 738. \tag{6.4}$$

If there is additional uncertainty in demand, then the level of the lead time increases safety stock additionally. Assume that the average customer demand of 150 units additionally varies by a standard deviation of 10 units and lead time increases from 2 weeks to 4 weeks—however without deviations. Then the original safety stock is

$$SS = 1.64 \cdot 10 \cdot \sqrt{2} = 24 \tag{6.5}$$

and the lead time-adjusted safety stock is

$$SS = 1.64 \cdot 10 \cdot \sqrt{4} = 33. \tag{6.6}$$

There is also empirical evidence that companies build inventories when supply delivery times increase. This is shown by the following *Purchasing Manager Index* data from December 2020 to May 2021.

Figure 6.7 shows that supplier lead times increased significantly in 2021 (PMI < 50), which is due to component shortages and logistical disruptions. As a consequence, companies' buying activities (quantity of purchases index) increased for building sufficient safety stock (see stocks of purchases index).

Multi-sourcing Optimization for Supply Risk Mitigation

Sourcing from more than one supplier costs money due to reduced economies of scale and administrative cost to handle several suppliers. At the same time, it decreases the probability of shortages significantly as the following simple calculations illustrate. Assume that a company has N suppliers (i.e., $N = 2$ for dual sourcing) and all have the same failure probability p. Therefore, the probability of total failure of supply can be calculated as p^N. The effects are illustrated in Fig. 6.8.

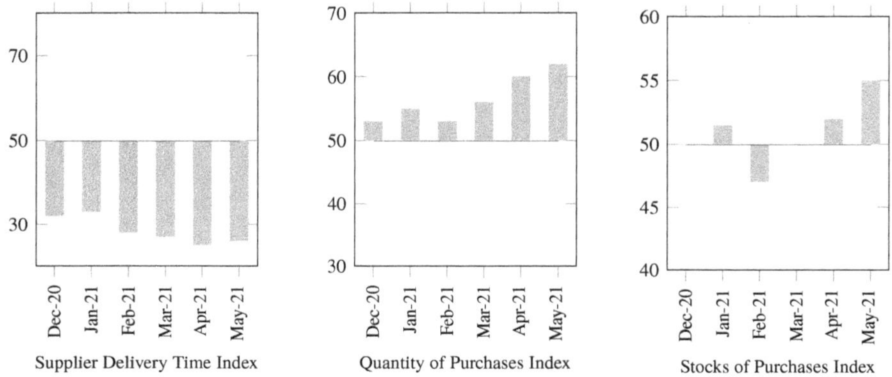

Fig. 6.7 US manufacturing purchasing manager index from December 2020 to May 2021 (50, no change compared to previous month; >50 growth or faster delivery) (Data source: IHS Markit)

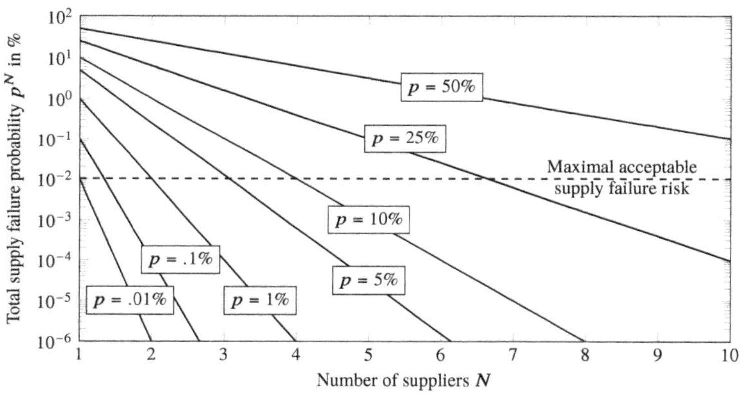

Fig. 6.8 Effect of multi-sourcing on supply failure probability (see [26])

Figure 6.8 shows that the total supply failure probability decreases with the number of suppliers. The analysis can be used to decide how many suppliers should be chosen in order to achieve a maximum acceptable supply failure risk. For instance, if the maximal acceptable supply failure risk is 0.01% (i.e., 100 ppm), then at an individual supplier failure probability of 1%, the required number of suppliers is 2 (dual sourcing).

Supply Network Optimization for Supply Risk Mitigation

Supply network optimization with explicit resilience maximization objectives (rather than pure cost minimization) is another appropriate analytics approach in order to minimize supply disruption risk. This can result in local- or dual-sourcing strategies that are paid by a total cost of resilience. For resilient supply network design, we refer to Sects. 4.6.3 and 4.6.5.

6.3 Commodity Price Risk

The Cambridge Dictionary defines a commodity as *a substance or product that can be traded, bought, or sold.*[1] We distinguish between three major classes of commodities: metals (i.e., precious metals, industrial metals and rare earth metals), agricultural products and energy. According to [4], commodities make up 27% (17%) of the total costs (purchase cost) of a firm in the sector of mechanical and plant engineering, 47% (22%) in the automotive supply industry, 56% (35%) in the packaging industry and 66% (44%) in the agri-food industry.

All commodities have in common that their prices fluctuate (see Fig. 6.9). Freight capacity and weather are also often referred to as non-storable commodities, which is due to their shared characteristic of being traded on both spot markets (or cash markets) for immediate delivery or on forward markets in the form of freight forward agreements (FFA) and weather derivatives for future delivery or risk management. Rare earth metals additionally to price risk face significant supply risk due to very limited availability. The same is expected for lithium and cobalt in the course of the electrification of mobility as both commodities are required for lithium-ion battery cell production.

Price uncertainty at commodity markets constitutes a significant exogenous risk factor for companies. Almost all (manufacturing) firms are exposed to commodity price risk that affects the direct costs of raw materials, packaging materials, energy consumed in operations or transportation costs.

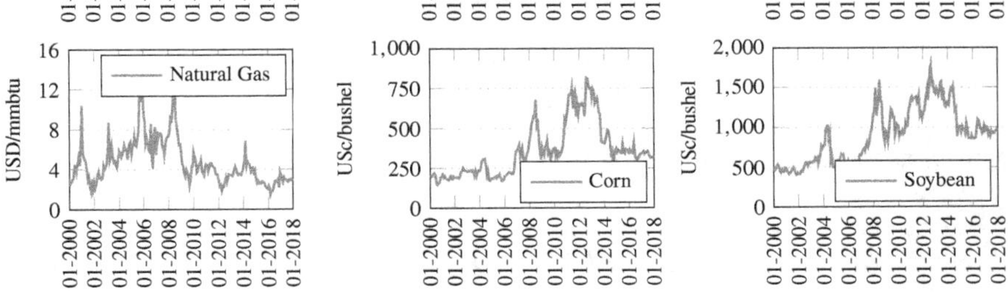

Fig. 6.9 Commodity spot prices for metals, energy and agriculturals

[1] https://dictionary.cambridge.org/dictionary/english/commodity.

Therefore, it is essential for companies to (i) measure their individual commodity price risk (see Sect. 6.3.1), model price evolution via predictive analytics (see Sect. 6.3.2) and limit their price risk through the application of various price risk mitigation strategies (see Sect. 6.3.3).

6.3.1 Measuring Commodity Price Risk

There are various risk measures available that are used to quantify commodity price risk such as variance of the profit, shortfall probability, expected shortage and the value at risk. In the following, we give an overview of volatility and value at risk measures that are predominantly used in commodity finance.

Volatility

According to [14], *volatility* is a measure of the variability of a market factor, most often the price. It needs to be distinguished between actual volatility and implied volatility. Actual volatility is calculated from historical data, while implied volatility is calculated based on the market's expectation for movement over a specified period of time.

Finance defines *volatility* σ_T over a time period $t = 1, \ldots, T$ as the square root of the *variance* σ_T^2, which is defined as

$$\sigma_T^2 = \frac{1}{T-1} \sum_{t=1}^{T} \left[(R_t - \bar{R})^2 \right] \tag{6.7}$$

with R_t as the logarithmic spot price return in period t and $\bar{R}$ as the mean return over the period $t = 1, \ldots, T$, i.e.,

$$R_t = ln\left(\frac{p_t}{p_{t-1}}\right) \approx \frac{p_t - p_{t-1}}{p_{t-1}} \tag{6.8}$$

with p_t as the spot price in period t. Therefore,

$$\bar{R} = \frac{1}{T} \cdot \sum_{t=1}^{T} R_t. \tag{6.9}$$

In practice, there are several other methods to quantify volatility that slightly differ from the volatility definition above. For instance, the German financial institute Commerzbank publishes the *Commodity Radar* (see Fig. 6.10), which is well regarded in Germany due to its biannual publication in the newspaper

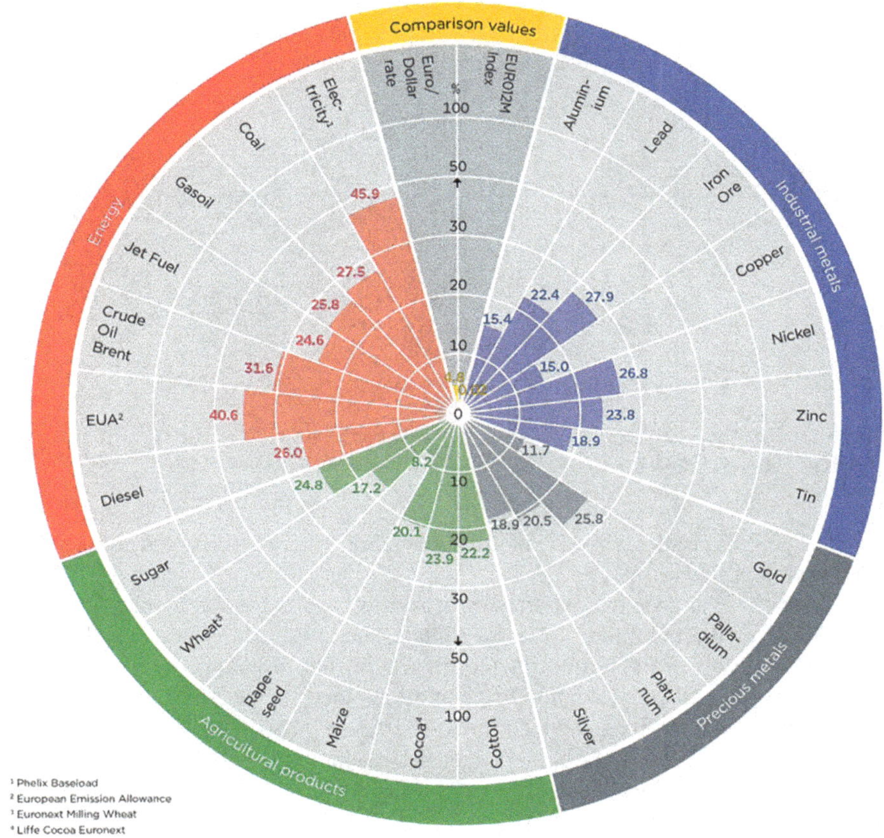

Fig. 6.10 Commerzbank's commodity radar with price volatilities (in %) from September 28, 2021 to September 27, 2022

Wirtschaftswoche. It shows the average percentage deviation of commodity prices from the average price over the last 12 months.

Annualized Volatility

A standardized volatility measure is *annualized volatility* that is based on the volatility definition σ_T but additionally incorporates the number of trading days per year, which is often set to 250. The annualized volatility σ is therefore according to [14] defined as

$$\sigma = \sigma_T \cdot \sqrt{\frac{250}{T}}. \tag{6.10}$$

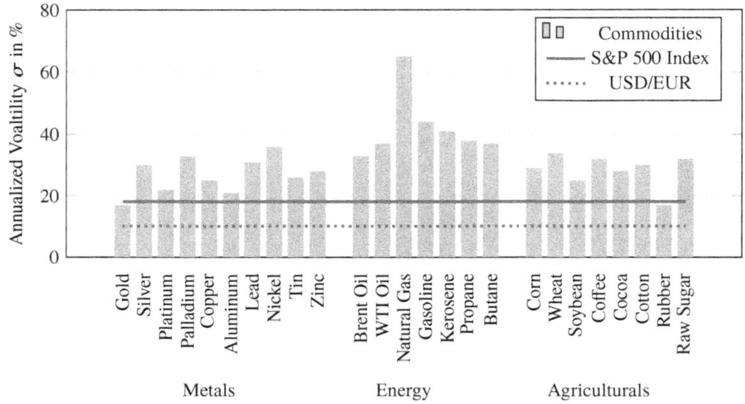

Fig. 6.11 Mean annualized price volatility σ of major commodities from 2000 to 2017 relative to corporate stocks and exchange rates (Data source: Thomson Reuters Datastream)

This definition allows for a volatility comparison across different markets and observation periods $t = 1, \ldots, T$.

Figure 6.11 shows the annualized volatility[2] at the main commodity spot markets from the commodity classes metals, energy and agriculturals. It shows that commodities are significantly more volatile than exchange rates and stocks (see [14]). Consequently, commodity operations incorporate a huge risk potential for commodity-processing and commodity-trading firms. The particularly high volatility of gas prices can be explained, besides other factors, by high storage costs, storage restrictions as well as its strong relationship to electricity, which is the most volatile commodity of all (see [14]).

Semi-variance

While risk measures such as standard deviation, variance or volatility consider both downside and upside risk, the *semi-variance* (or also called downside risk) only considers the variance σ_T^2 of returns that are below the mean $\bar{R}$ (i.e., the potential loss for a firm). The semi-variance (SV) is calculated by

$$\mathrm{SV} = \frac{1}{T-1} \sum_{t|R_t<\mu} \left[(R_t - \bar{R})^2 \right]. \tag{6.11}$$

[2] Standardized measure based on the standard deviation of daily spot price returns. For the exact mathematical definition, we refer to [14].

(Conditional) Value at Risk

Value at risk (VaR) is a standard measure in finance to evaluate risk as the tail end of an (empirical) distribution. It is defined as the loss that is not exceeded with a certain probability, i.e., confidence interval $1 - \alpha$ (e.g., 95% or 99%) within a specific time horizon (e.g., trading day or month), i.e.,

$$\text{VaR} = F^{-1}(1 - \alpha) \tag{6.12}$$

with $F^{-1}(\cdot)$ as the inverse of the cumulative empirical distribution function. Therefore, VaR uses the empirical distribution of (daily) commodity price returns R_t over a specific time period (e.g., year). It quantifies the amount that can be lost by not fixing prices but rather purchasing on the spot market under full price risk. Using spreadsheet software such as Excel and assuming a normal distribution of returns, VaR can be calculated by the formula `NORM.INV(1-α,μ,σ)` with μ as the mean return and σ as the standard deviation of returns. Shortfall probability is a related measure and defines the probability of the loss being larger than a pre-fixed value.

Conditional value at risk (CVaR) (or expected shortfall, average value at risk, expected tail loss or superquantile) on the other hand calculates the average loss if the loss x is above VaR, i.e.,

$$\text{CVaR} = E[x|x > \text{VaR}]. \tag{6.13}$$

Figure 6.12 shows the empirical distribution of daily percentage spot price returns for the commodity copper at the LME (Refinitiv source code: LCPCASH) over the time period of the year 2020.

It shows that from 262 observations, 13 observations (i.e., 5% of observations) yield a loss of more than 2.1%. Consequently, with a probability of 95%, the

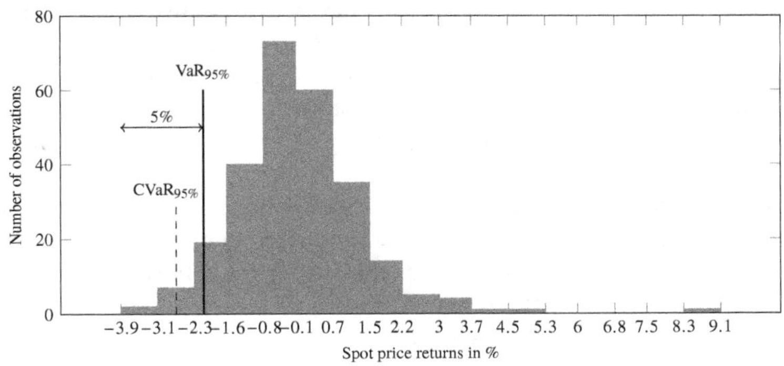

Fig. 6.12 Empirical distribution of daily percentage spot price returns for LME copper from January 2020 until December 2020

commodity price increases by not more than 2.1%. For a copper purchase volume of 100,000 USD, the VaR at 95% equals 2,100 USD (also known as spend at risk). The average loss over these 13 observations is 2.7%. This equals the CVaR. For a copper purchase volume of 100,000 USD, the CVaR consequently equals 2,700 USD. For 99% confidence level, the VaR of a purchase volume of 100,000 Euro equals 3,600 USD and the CVaR 3,700 USD.

Industry Example: Computation of Commodity Price Risk at Volkswagen

Volkswagen uses a VaR-like approach in order to quantify its individual commodity price risk for metals, coal and natural rubber. In the 2021 annual report, Volkswagen states: *If the commodity prices of the hedged nonferrous metals, coal and rubber had been 10% higher (lower) as of December 31, 2021, earnings after tax would have been 679 million Euro (previous year: 559 million Euro) higher (lower).* This equals 4.4% of its earnings.

6.3.2 *Stochastic Modeling of Commodity Prices*

In order to use simulation and optimization in commodity purchasing and risk management (see Sect. 6.3.3), it is essential to model price behavior. In the following, we give a brief overview of prevalent commodity price models from the empirical finance and economics literature.

Basic Reduced-Form Price Models

The simplest way to capture the stochastic nature of commodity prices is a probability density function (e.g., normal distribution). However, if the value of the random variable (i.e., the price) evolves over time (as in the case of commodity prices that are highly correlated across periods), a stochastic process, which typically is Markovian with the subsequent price depending on the current price, might be more appropriate.

The finance literature distinguishes between continuous-time and discrete-time stochastic processes for modeling commodity prices. For discrete-time problems, such as the multi-stage decision problems that we regard in the textbook, first-order autoregressive processes (AR(1)) are frequently used for modeling commodity price time series (see also Sect. 2.3.2). An AR(1) price process can be expressed by

$$p_t = \beta_0 + \beta_1 p_{t-1} + \epsilon_t, \tag{6.14}$$

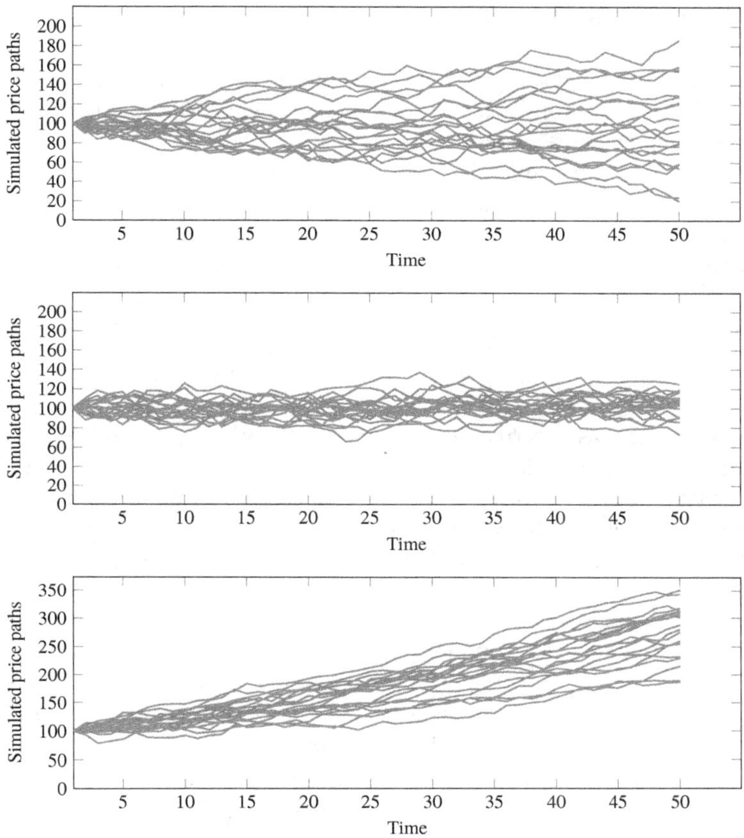

Fig. 6.13 Commodity price simulation: random walk, mean reversion and momentum

with normally distributed random error term $\epsilon_t \sim N(0, \sigma_t^2)$. If $(\beta_0, \beta_1) = (0, 1)$, the AR(1) process describes a random walk (RW) without drift. A mean-reverting (MR) price process is characterized by $(\beta_0, \beta_1) = (\kappa\mu_p, 1 - \kappa)$, with $\kappa \in [0, 1)$ as the mean reversion speed and μ_p as the mean price level. A momentum (MO) price process with $\beta_1 > 1$ models price trends (explosive behavior).

Figure 6.13 shows a simulation of random walk, mean-reverting and momentum price processes based on 20 Monte Carlo simulation runs with a starting price of 100. The RW model is based on $\sigma = 5$; the MR price model is characterized by a mean-reversion speed of $\kappa = 0.1$, a mean price level of $\mu_p = 100$ and $\sigma_t = 5$. The MO price model is simulated by $\beta_1 = 0.02$ and $\sigma_t = 5$. The simulations allow to develop scenarios for risk management. These scenarios can be used as input for stochastic programming techniques (see Chap. 2) or to simulate the implications for the profit and loss statement of the company.

Nonlinear and High-Dimensional Price Models

In reality, time series typically do not behave linearly. They are rather characterized by abrupt jumps and drops, which is due to, e.g., switches in regimes (e.g., during economic boom and bust cycles).

The state-of-the-art economic forecasting literature presents various nonlinear approaches, such as neural networks, jump diffusion models (JD), stochastic volatility models (GARCH-type models) and Markov regime switching models (MRS), that allow for time-varying parameters of the price process.

$$p_t = \begin{cases} \beta_0^{(1)} + \beta_1^{(1)} p_{t-1} + \epsilon_t^{(1)} & \text{if } s_t = 1 \\ \beta_0^{(2)} + \beta_1^{(2)} p_{t-1} + \epsilon_t^{(2)} & \text{if } s_t = 2 \end{cases} \tag{6.15}$$

In MRS models as described by Eq. (6.15), the price p_t is modeled by several stochastic processes with distinct parameters that depend on the current state s_t of a Markov chain. These states are typically not directly observable and must be learned from price observations (*Hidden Markov models*).

Furthermore, *multi-factor models* that incorporate several exogenous variables (features) typically allow for a more accurate price model than one-factor models, however with a higher computational complexity (see [14] for more details).

Another way to model commodity prices p_t is by using the term structure $\mathbf{F_t} = (f_{t,\tau} : \tau > t)$ (i.e., the futures or forward curve). The *Rational Expectations Hypothesis* implies that $f_{t,\tau} = \mathbb{E}_t^Q[p_\tau]$. That follows the *Efficient Market Hypothesis* introduced by Eugene Fama in 1970 that states that markets are efficient if all the available information (including past spot and forward prices) is incorporated into the current market price such that technical[3] and fundamental[4] analysis cannot lead to profits above average in the long run. Figure 6.14 illustrates the futures curves of natural gas showing a seasonal behavior, i.e., natural gas prices tend to be higher during winter. Those futures curves are publicly available for exchange-traded commodities.

6.3.3 *Measures for Risk Mitigation*

In practice, there are several measures in order to mitigate or at least minimize the risk of adverse commodity price movements (see Fig. 6.15). In the following, we present methods such as price scanning, price mapping, price escalation clauses (i.e., pass or share risk with suppliers or customers), the budgeting or cost averaging approach, fixed price contracting with suppliers, financial hedging at futures,

[3] Technical analysis refers to a chart analysis based on the historical price evolution.

[4] Fundamental analysis uses additional data (features) to explain price movements.

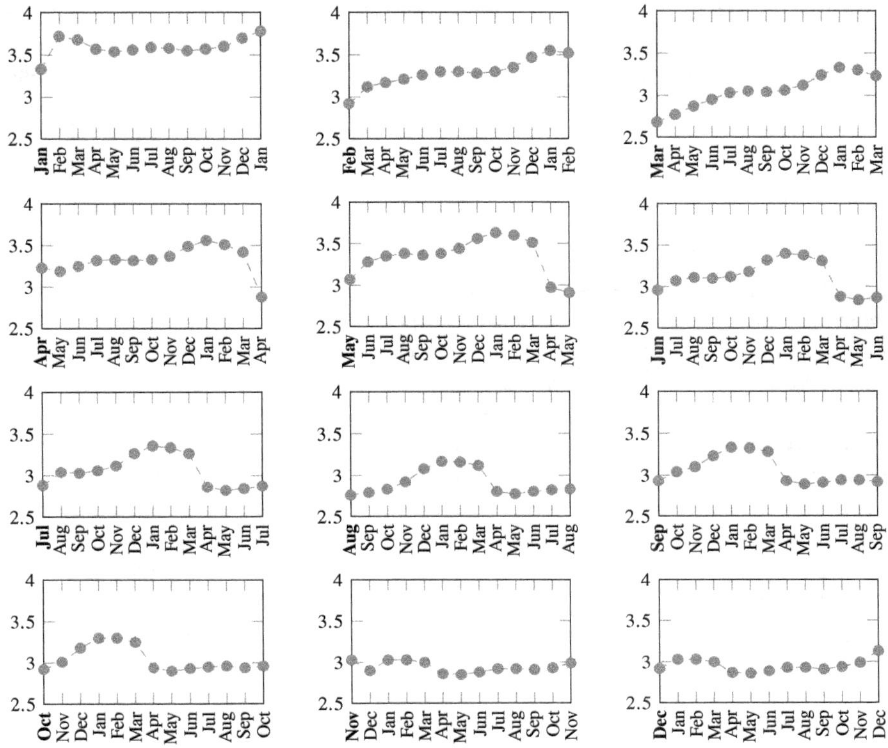

Fig. 6.14 NYMEX natural gas futures curves from January 2017 to December 2017 (Prices in USD/mmbtu refer to closing prices at the first trading day of the corresponding month)

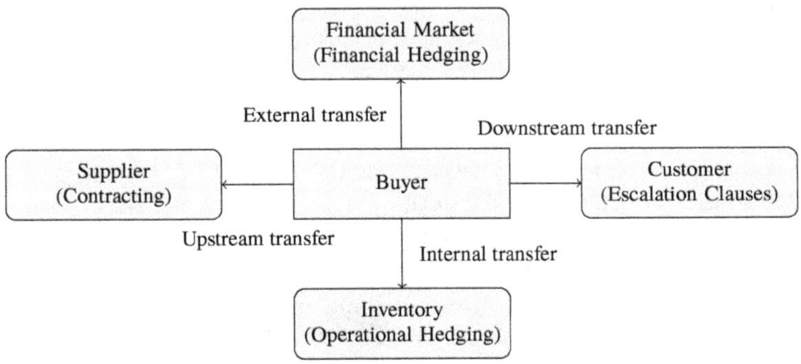

Fig. 6.15 Dimensions of commodity price risk management

forwards or options markets, cross-hedging or proxy hedging via related exchange-traded commodities and operational hedging via inventory optimization. We do not cover other mitigation strategies such as commodity substitution or demand reduction.

Price Scanning

A continuous price scanning in the sense of a technical chart analysis is crucial for risk mitigation actions. KPIs such as commodity price ratios can help identify whether a price is relatively small (which opens a purchasing opportunity) or still too high. A well-known example is the gold-silver ratio that evaluates the price valuation of gold and silver. This is based on predefined thresholds. For instance, if the ratio is above 80, then silver is rather undervalued relative to gold, while a value below 40 indicates that silver is rather overvalued relative to gold. These ratios can be developed for all relevant commodities. In contrast to technical chart analysis, fundamental analysis incorporates supply and demand (e.g., production data, global inventory data, consumption data) in order to determine price trends and consequently the best timing for purchasing. Price scanning can also be combined with price alerts, i.e., signals that indicate whenever a market price falls below a specific threshold or exceeds a specific threshold.

Price Mapping

Price mapping historically maps a company's purchase price for a specific product with the market price or price index development of a specific commodity the company's product is based on. Many suppliers work with cost-plus models for pricing their products. That means that the product price increases when the supplier's raw material cost increases. In this case, price mapping identifies whether price quotes from suppliers are fair and in accordance with the market price development.

The price mapping for aluminum profiles illustrated in Fig. 6.16 shows that the supplier's quoted price is significantly above the index-based should-cost that are connected to the raw material price development. In 2019, the buyer was not able to participate in slight downward raw material price movements, while since mid of 2020, she was charged price increases that are significantly above the market development. This mapping allows to re-negotiate prices with the supplier in a next step or connect them to the market movement via a price formula (see section on price escalation clauses).

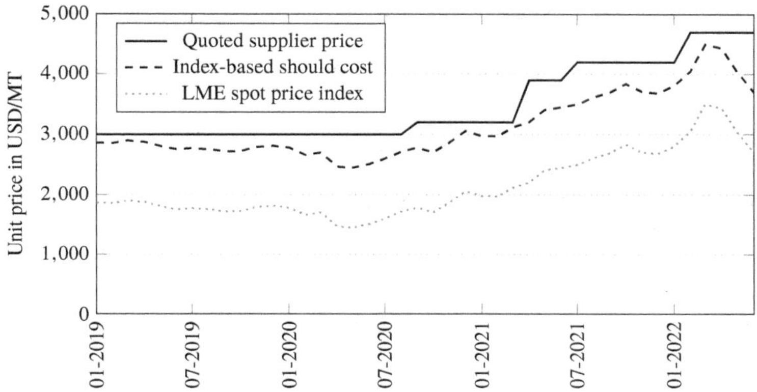

Fig. 6.16 Price mapping between purchase price for aluminum profiles and index-based should-cost

Industry Example: Cost Clawbacks During COVID-19
During the COVID-19 pandemic, many supplier justified price increases with increased raw material or energy prices. However, quoted price increases were often far above market development. In this case, price mapping can help re-negotiate prices and ask for clawbacks.

Price Escalation Clauses

Price escalation clauses (also known as price variation formulas or index-based formula pricing) are contractual agreements to pass or share commodity price risk upstream the supply chain with the suppliers (cost defense) or downstream the supply chain with the customers (cost pass-through).

Therefore, price escalation clauses adjust contract prices between the buyer and the supplier or the buyer and the customer based on the movement of the underlying commodity prices (e.g., through a public index) and are particularly applied to products with a high raw material input (e.g., metal profiles). Price escalation clauses secure suppliers from decreasing (or even negative) margins through significant price increases of their raw materials. At the same time, they allow buyers to participate in case of decreasing raw material cost of their suppliers. Furthermore, they secure companies from raw material price increases that they pass on to customers but also allow to participate in raw material price drops, which may increase customer demand.

Price escalation clauses can be index formulas of the following form:

$$P_1 = P_0 + \left(a + b \cdot \frac{M_1}{M_0} + c \cdot \frac{L_1}{L_0}\right) \tag{6.16}$$

P_1 is the price of the final product at day of delivery. P_0 is the price of the final product at day of contract closure. M_1 (L_1) is material cost of commodity 1 (2) at day of delivery, while M_0 (L_0) is material cost of commodity 1 (2) at day of contract closure. a is the percentage share of the price that stays unchanged (constant). b and c are the percentage shares of the price of commodity 1 and 2, respectively.

Another form of index-based contracting can look as follows:

$$P_t = a + b \cdot \text{Index}_t \tag{6.17}$$

with a constant price level a and an index as a third-party reference number representing the commodity spot price in a given region and providing an indication of the market trend (see [14]). A index-based price formula of this type is illustrated in Fig. 6.16 with the index being the aluminum spot price at the LME. Other important price indices are, e.g., the consumer price index, the producer price index, the Goldman Sachs Commodity Index, the Bloomberg Commodity Index, the Refinitiv/Core Commodity CRB Index, the Continuous Commodity Index and the LME Index.

For metals, the LME Index consolidates prices of the six major industrial metals with different weights, i.e., aluminum (42.8%), copper (31.2%), zinc (14.8%), lead (8.2%), nickel (2%) and tin (1%).

The Bloomberg Commodity Index considers a basket of commodities from different classes including metals, energy and agriculturals. The Bloomberg Energy and Metals Equal-Weighted Total Return Index includes an equal-weighted set of 12 energy and metal commodity futures contracts including WTI crude oil, Brent crude oil, low sulfur gas oil, natural gas, gold, silver, platinum, palladium, copper, zinc, nickel and aluminum.

Other forms of price escalation clauses that are often applied in practice are price caps, price floors and price collars that trigger a cost-sharing or revenue-sharing mechanism between the buyer and the supplier. Caps are price limits if the commodity market price p_t exceeds a specified upper bound UB, while floors are price limits if the commodity market price p_t falls below a specified lower bound LB. A price collar is a combination of caps and floors. In this case, the effective purchase price P_t at a certain point in time t is defined as follows in case of a 50–50 share:

$$P_t = \begin{cases} UB + 0.5 \cdot (p_t - UB) & \text{if } p_t > UB \\ p_t & \text{if } LB \leq p_t \leq UB \\ LB - 0.5 \cdot (LB - p_t) & \text{if } p_t < LB \end{cases} \tag{6.18}$$

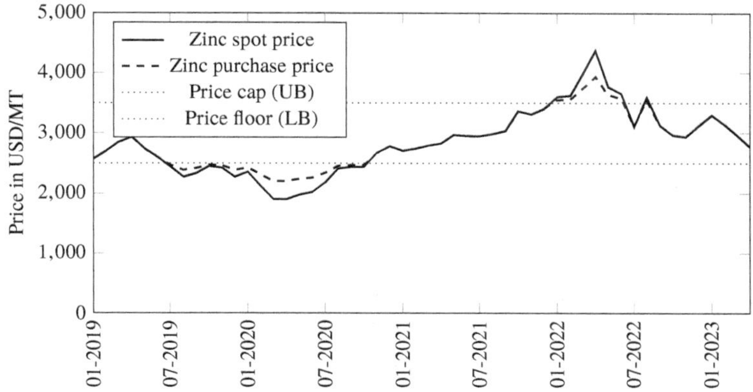

Fig. 6.17 Price collar mechanism for zinc between January 2019 and April 2023

UB and LB can, for example, be specified as 10% increase or decrease relative to the commodity spot market price observed at the date of contract closure. That means, if spot prices increase (decrease) by 10%, then the additional increase (decrease) is split equally between the buyer and the supplier.

Figure 6.17 shows a price collar mechanism for zinc with a defined upper price limit of 3,000 USD/MT and a defined lower price limit of 2,500 USD/MT. Above and below those price limits, the additional cost or gains from commodity price movements are shared equally between buyer and supplier.

Industry Example: Price Escalation Clauses at BMW
According to the *BMW Group International Terms and Conditions for the Purchase of Production Materials and Automotive Components* (see [5]), the price components for raw materials are typically determined based on raw material indices (e.g., LME stock market price) or on raw material surcharges. A few years ago, BMW used a risk-sharing mechanism that shared material cost increases equally between BMW, the 1st tier supplier and the 2nd tier supplier (see [24]).

Budgeting Approach/Cost Averaging Approach

The so-called budgeting or cost averaging approach is a commodity-purchasing approach that spends a specific amount of money in each period. Based on commodity price fluctuations, the purchaser gets more or less commodity volume (e.g., tons). This approach minimizes price risk at the cost of generating supply risk as the purchase volumes decrease with increasing prices (Table 6.4).

Table 6.4 Cost averaging approach illustrated for copper procurement from January to December 2021

Date	Price in USD/ton	Purchase volume in USD	Effective purchase volume in ton
Jan 2021	7,749	100,000	12.9
Feb 2021	7,805	100,000	12.8
Mar 2021	9,089	100,000	11.0
Apr 2021	8,794	100,000	11.4
May 2021	9,829	100,000	10.2
Jun 2021	10,234	100,000	9.8
Jul 2021	9,296	100,000	10.8
Aug 2021	9,674	100,000	10.3
Sep 2021	9,332	100,000	10.7
Oct 2021	9,135	100,000	10.9
Nov 2021	9,993	100,000	10.0
Dec 2021	9,492	100,000	10.5

Fixed Price Contracting

In practice, many commodity-processing firms secure prices (and supply) through fixed price contracts with their suppliers. While this strategy provides highest level of security (as it limits the exposure to price uncertainty) and minimizes administrative effort, it is typically not cost-optimal due to two reasons: (i) suppliers charge high fees to be able to provide fixed prices in volatile markets, and (ii) fixed price contracts do not allow to benefit from price declines. Therefore, it is essential for purchasing managers to optimize (i) price levels of fixed price contracts and (ii) contract duration. Both impact potential profits and losses compared to spot market purchasing as illustrated in Fig. 6.18.

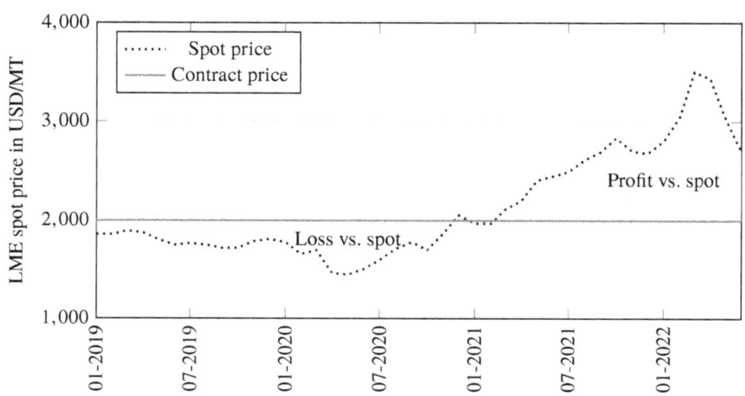

Fig. 6.18 Long-term fixed price contract for aluminum signed in January 2019 at 2000 USD/MT

Latest price information from futures markets gives a market outlook that can be leveraged for supplier negotiation and renegotiation with regard to pricing and contract duration. In practice, purchase contract duration is often balanced with sales contract duration. This allows to (re-)negotiate purchase and sales contracts at the same time under the same level of information, which can be used to eliminate price risk by transferring upstream supplier price risk downstream toward the customers. Especially during the period 2021–2023, which was characterized by huge price increases and high market volatility, many suppliers were not willing to offer fixed price contracts or only with a high risk premium and for short contract duration.

To derive data-driven decisions on whether to sign commodity-purchasing contracts, we can use stochastic programming. Suppose a commodity-purchasing company requires a known commodity volume of d_t in each future time period $t = 1, \ldots, T$ (e.g., months). Given volatile commodity prices, the company needs to decide whether to sign long-term contracts $c = 1, \ldots, C$ at known unit prices p_c or buy later at unknown future spot prices p_t. As the future spot price is unknown, it is modeled via a scenario approach with scenarios $s = 1, \ldots, S$ and scenario probabilities P_s. The stochastic programming formulation of the corresponding decision problem looks as follows:

$$\text{minimize} \quad \sum_{c=1}^{C}\sum_{t=1}^{T} p_c \cdot x_{c,t}^{\text{contract}} + \sum_{s=1}^{S} P_s \sum_{t=1}^{T} p_{t,s} \cdot x_{t,s}^{\text{spot}} \tag{6.19}$$

$$\text{s.t.} \quad \sum_{c=1}^{C} x_{c,t}^{\text{contract}} + x_{t,s}^{\text{spot}} = d_t \qquad \forall t = 1, \ldots, T, s = 1, \ldots, S \tag{6.20}$$

$$\sum_{t=1}^{T} x_{c,t}^{\text{contract}} \leq x_c^{\text{contract, max}} \qquad \forall c = 1, \ldots, C \tag{6.21}$$

$$x_{c,t}^{\text{contract}} \geq 0 \qquad \forall c = 1, \ldots, C, t = 1, \ldots, T \tag{6.22}$$

$$x_{t,s}^{\text{spot}} \geq 0 \qquad \forall t = 1, \ldots, T, s = 1, \ldots, S \tag{6.23}$$

The objective function minimizes the total cost including cost from contract purchasing and expected cost from spot purchasing. $x_{c,t}^{\text{contract}}$ is the here-and-now decision on contract quantities for contracts $c = 1, \ldots, C$ at known unit price p_c for corresponding future delivery period $t = 1, \ldots, T$, and $x_{t,s}^{\text{spot}}$ are the wait-and-see decisions on spot purchase quantities in future periods $t = 1, \ldots, T$. Future demand d_t needs either to be satisfied via contracts or via the spot market. Contract purchasing is limited by quantity limits $x_c^{\text{contract, max}}$ for each contract $c = 1, \ldots, C$.

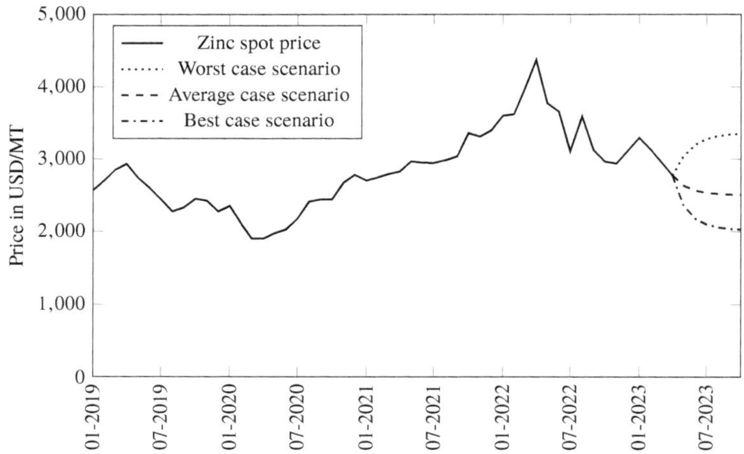

Fig. 6.19 LME zinc spot prices and future scenarios in April 2023

Numerical Example: Stochastic Programming for Fixed Price Contracting

Suppose a company faces a monthly zinc demand of 20 MT and is offered two 6 months' contracts for zinc purchasing with monthly delivery in tranches that need to be signed upfront. The first supplier offers a price of 2,770 USD per MT with a maximum contract volume of 60 MT (contract 1); the second supplier offers a price of 2,400 USD per MT with a maximum contract volume of 40 MT (contract 2). Alternatively, the company can buy zinc monthly at the corresponding spot market rate.

Based on the company's market expertise, three spot price scenarios are generated for the subsequent 6 months as illustrated in the scenario tree from Fig. 6.19: a best-case scenario, an average-case scenario and a worst-case scenario. Each scenario is expected to occur with a probability of 33.33%.

Solving the stochastic program given the presented input data, the decision-maker is recommended to secure 40 MT via contract 2 (for month 1 and 2) and buy the rest at the spot market with expected cost of 306,524 USD over 6 months. This is substantially different from the scenario recommendations: In the best-case scenario, it is recommended not to sign any zinc contract upfront; in the worst-case scenario, both contracts are signed up to capacity limit. However, we also notice for this specific decision problem that an expected value approach (based on the expected value scenario) would yield the same decision recommendation as the stochastic approach, which is not per se true (see, e.g., the numerical example from Sect. 4.6 on stochastic supply network design).

Please note that this stochastic programming formulation can also be extended with regard to risk minimization aspects via, for instance, value-at-risk constraints.

Financial Hedging

Financial hedging describes hedging of price risk with financial contracts. This can be forward contracts, futures contracts, swaps or options.

Forward contracts are agreements made in period t to buy (or sell) a commodity at a pre-specified price (i.e., the forward price) at a fixed future date $\tau > t$ (often called maturity or expiration date).

Futures contracts are financial derivatives that have very similar characteristics. However, while forward contracts are over-the-counter (OTC) agreements directly between two parties, *futures contracts* are traded on commodity exchanges and highly standardized.

The main commodity exchanges are the New York Mercantile Exchange (NYMEX), the Chicago Mercantile Exchange (CME), the London Metal Exchange (LME), the European Energy Exchange (EEX), the Intercontinental Exchange (ICE), the Commodity Exchange (COMEX) as part of NYMEX for metals, the Chicago Board of Trade (CBOT) as part of CME for mainly agricultural commodities, Dalian Commodity Exchange (DCE) in China, Dubai Mercantile Exchange (DME) and Multi Commodity Exchange (MCX) in India (Table 6.5).

At those exchanges, futures contracts are available for different (typically monthly) maturities, from one month (front-month contract) up to several years in the future (whereas typically only close maturities are liquidly traded).

The relationship between the forward price $f_{t,\tau}$ for any future maturity $\tau \geq t$ and the spot price p_t is given by the cost-of-carry model, i.e.,

$$f_{t,\tau} = p_t e^{(r+c_h-\tilde{Y})(\tau-t)} = p_t e^{(r-Y)(\tau-t)}, \tag{6.24}$$

with $f_{\tau,\tau} \equiv p_\tau$. r is the risk-free interest rate and c_h are the storage costs per unit and per unit of time typically expressed as a percentage of p_t. $\tilde{Y}$ is the marginal convenience yield on the commodity. The marginal convenience yield is the benefit of physically holding an additional unit of inventory, rather than a forward contract.

Equation (6.24) is often referred to as the no-arbitrage condition as it avoids cash-and-carry arbitrage through buying at the spot market and simultaneously selling

Table 6.5 Important commodity exchanges

Commodity type	Exchange
Metals	COMEX, NYMEX, LME, MCX, TOCOM
Energy	NYMEX, ICE, EEX, DCE, Powernext, Nordpool, DME, MCX
Agriculturals	CBOT, NYMEX, DCE, MCX, ICE, MGEX
Freight capacity	Baltic exchange

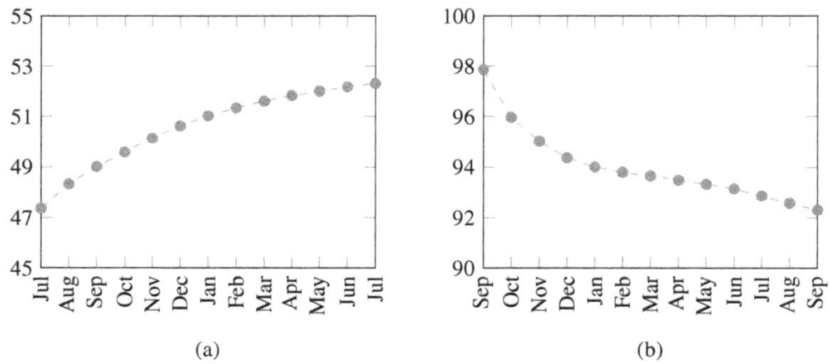

Fig. 6.20 (**a**) Contango and (**b**) backwardation at the WTI crude oil market (USD/barrel) in July 2016 and September 2014

at the forward market. Equation (6.24) furthermore characterizes the forward curve $\mathbf{F_t} = (f_{t,\tau} : \tau > t)$ (sometimes referred to as the term structure): if $(r - Y) > 0$, then the forward curve is an increasing function of the maturity τ, and the market is said to be in contango (normal market). In case of contango, speculators experience so-called negative roll yield by rolling positions across the forward curve. Purchasers have incentives to purchase commodities and put them into storage if storage is possible at a price less than the curve differential. If $(r - Y) < 0$, then the forward curve is a decreasing function of the maturity τ, and the market is said to be in backwardation (inverted market) (Fig. 6.20).

The difference between spot and forward price is called the basis $B_{t,\tau}$ with

$$B_{t,\tau} = p_t - f_{t,\tau}. \tag{6.25}$$

It can be explained by the *Theory of Storage* and equals the forgone interest by a purchase in period t plus the marginal cost of storage from period t until period τ minus the marginal convenience yield. An important implication of the *Theory of Storage* is that the price and the price volatility of commodities are both negatively correlated with the level of global inventories.

Under the *Rational Expectations Hypothesis*, the forward price $f_{t,\tau}$ determines the best estimator of the future spot price p_τ under the risk-neutral probability measure Q (sometimes also referred to as the equivalent martingale measure), i.e.,

$$f_{t,\tau} = \mathbb{E}_t^Q[p_\tau]. \tag{6.26}$$

However, statistical tests on empirical data reject the hypothesis in most cases (see [14]). If Eq. (6.26) is violated, then $f_{t,\tau}$ is a biased estimator of p_τ, which is typically explained by a *risk premium*, i.e., $f_{t,\tau}$ reflects both the forecast of the future spot price and the risk premium the decision-maker is willing to pay to secure a fixed price in t for delivery in τ.

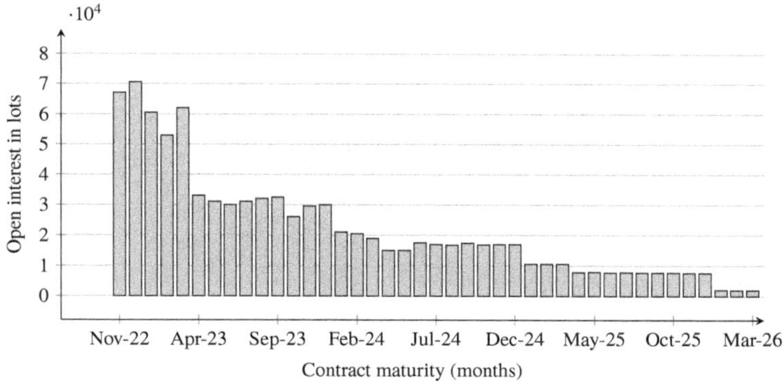

Fig. 6.21 Liquidity of futures contracts measured by open interest: Example of Dutch TTF gas futures as of October 10, 2022 (Source: ICE data)

The difference between forward price $f_{t,\tau}$ and future spot price at maturity p_τ determines the forecast ability of futures prices to predict spot prices. However, it turns out that the forecast ability of futures prices is rather poor (see [6]) and might be outperformed by no-change (naïve) forecasts (see [2]) or analyst forecasts of major financial institutions (see [7]).

Measures for market or contract liquidity are, for instance, the number of traded contracts, volume, open interest (see Fig. 6.21) or the bid/ask spread, where bid is the price level at which buyers are willing to buy and ask is the price level at which sellers are willing to sell. The thinner the spread, the higher liquidity.

Swaps are generalizations of forward contracts with the agreement made over a specified period of time.

In contrast, *options contracts* give the commodity purchaser the right but not the obligation to take off a pre-specified quantity at a pre-specified price (exercise or strike price) at a future date τ (European option) or until a future date τ (American option) by paying a certain reservation price or premium. Therefore, in contrast to futures/forward contracts, the loss due to adverse price movements (price decreases) is limited to the premium as shown in the payoff diagram of Fig. 6.22.

Figure 6.22 shows a forward or futures contract at a price of 5. If the underlying commodity spot price increases, the delta between spot price and futures price defines the profit. If the underlying commodity spot price decreases, the delta between futures price and spot price defines the loss. If the future spot price equals the futures price, then there is breakeven. For an options contract, if the commodity spot price is above the strike price, then the option is exercised with unlimited upside potential. However, the strike price is not the breakeven point as there is a premium to be paid in any case (sunk cost). If the commodity spot price falls below the strike price at expiration, the option expires without execution. In this case, the downside risk is limited to the premium.

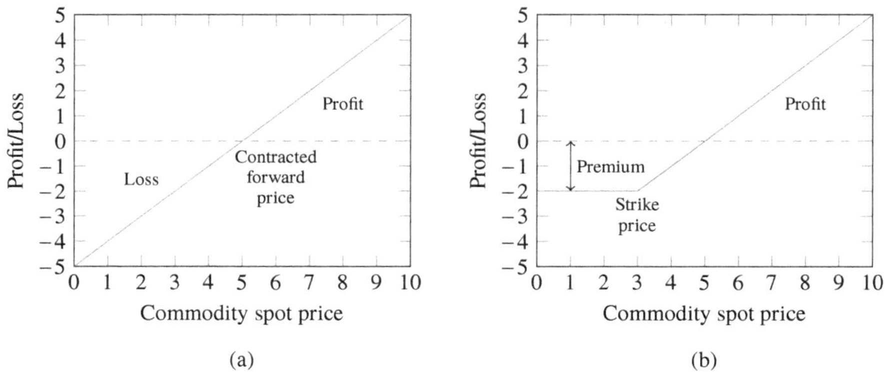

Fig. 6.22 Payoff diagram of commodity forward/futures contracts and commodity options contracts. (**a**) Forward/Futures contract. (**b**) Options contract

Forward Contracting Strategies

Financial hedging through optimal forward contracting, i.e., the optimization of the firm's procurement position in the forward contract market, exhibits a growing liquidity during the past decades. A large-scale empirical study by Bartram et al. [3] shows that 50.4% of the oil-processing companies and 30.5% of the steel-processing companies have implemented some kind of commodity price risk hedging using financial contracts. Financial contracting might especially be relevant for firms that act in just-in-time environments (e.g., the automotive industry with copper or aluminum as important raw materials) or firms that purchase commodities that can hardly be stored (e.g., energy or freight capacity).

Industry Example: Hedging Gains and Hedging Losses

A prominent example for a firm that has benefited greatly from commodity hedging is the food manufacturer General Mills, which realized hedging gains of $151 million in volatile agricultural and energy markets during the first quarter of 2008 (see [27]). On the other hand, by contractually hedging future demand, firms become inflexible to react to price declines. In 2015, the world's second-largest airline, United, lost $960 million, while the world's third-largest airline, Delta, even $2.3 billion by hedging 100% of their fuel costs via long-term contracts prior to the big drop in crude oil prices (see [29]).

In practice, different contracting strategies can be applied that support the purchase quantity decision y_t^τ at a specific forward price p_t^τ for commodity delivery in period $t + \tau$ in order to minimize total purchase cost or risk (see [21] for an overview). Please note that there is no one-size-fits-all approach, but the performance of

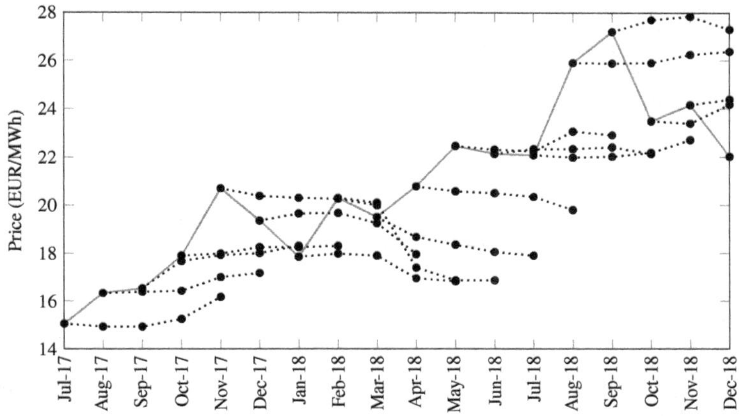

Fig. 6.23 TTF natural gas futures curves of M1–M4 (dotted curves) and realized spot price (solid curve) from July 2017 to December 2018

the different strategies needs to be evaluated based on backtests for each specific commodity and different market situations (e.g., upward market trends, downward market trends). For instance, given the market situation of natural gas at the European trading hub TTF (see Fig. 6.23), it would have been beneficial to lock in futures prices in July 2017 for August 2017 (M1 contract), September 2017 (M2 contract), October 2017 (M3 contract) and November 2017 (M4 contract).

In the following, we give a brief overview of existing forward contracting strategies—from simple static strategies to advanced dynamic strategies that are supported by machine learning techniques.

The *pure spot purchase strategy (P-S)* (or just-in-time strategy) is a simple static strategy where the whole commodity demand d_t of a period t is purchased at the spot market (i.e., $\tau = 0$) at full risk, i.e., $y_t^0 = d_t$. This strategy is particularly beneficial on downward-trending markets, while it often is unfavorable whenever prices increase.

The *pure forward purchase strategy (P-Mx)* eliminates price risk by purchasing the entire commodity demand at commodity forward or futures markets. This can be futures or forward contracts of different maturities (e.g., M1 as the front-month contract, M2 as the two-months ahead contract, etc.). For instance, a pure front-month purchase strategy yields $y_t^1 = d_{t+1}$. However, this comes at a price, i.e., lower flexibility with regard to price decreases.

The *1/N purchase strategy (1/N)* diversifies risk through the procurement of demand tranches at different points in time. While P-S and P-Mx do either use spot or forward purchases, 1/N equally splits future commodity demand across futures contracts (of different maturities) and spot purchases. An often used rule (see [21]) is a split between spot (20%), M1 (20%), M2 (20%), M3 (20%) and M4 (20%).

The *reoptimization purchase strategy (REO)* (or naïve purchase strategy) assumes that spot and futures prices do not vary over time and purchases at the lowest currently quoted price. As soon as new price information gets available, it reoptimizes its purchasing strategy accordingly. Given 4 forward months contracts (M1, M2, M3, M4) with forward prices p_t^1, p_t^2, p_t^3, p_t^4 and commodity demand d_t, the corresponding decision rule looks as follows:

- If $p_t^4 \leq \min\{p_t^0, p_t^1, p_t^2, p_t^3\}$, then buy d_{t+4} via M4
- If $p_t^3 \leq \min\{p_t^0, p_t^1, p_t^2\}$ and d_{t+3} not hedged yet, then buy d_{t+3} via M3
- If $p_t^2 \leq \min\{p_t^0, p_t^1\}$ and d_{t+2} not hedged yet, then buy d_{t+2} via M2
- If $p_t^1 \leq \min\{p_t^0\}$ and d_{t+1} not hedged yet, then buy d_{t+1} via M1

The *forecast-based purchase strategy (FC)* optimizes purchase quantities at spot and forward markets based on price forecasts. Price forecasts can be calculated with simple forecasting methods such as moving average models, auto-regressive models or regression models or by more advanced machine learning techniques (see Sect. 2.3). The decision rule looks as follows: If the forward price p_t^τ is lower than forecast for $t+\tau$, then buy contract at forward price p_t^τ if not sourced yet; otherwise, wait.

The *integrated data-driven purchase strategy* (or data-driven approach, DDA) presented by Mandl and Minner [21] derives purchase-or-wait signals for forward contracts of different maturities. The data-driven purchase signals have the following regression-like form that compares quoted futures prices p_t^τ with optimized threshold prices, i.e.,

$$p_t^\tau \leq \beta_0 + \sum_{i=1}^{N} \beta_i^\tau X_{it} \tag{6.27}$$

with β_0 as an estimated intercept of a threshold price and X_{it} as feature values of features $i = 1, \ldots, N$ (e.g., temperature, macroeconomic data) of the threshold price function. If the quoted commodity forward price p_t^τ is smaller or equal to the feature-based threshold price, then the commodity purchaser gets a purchase signal for forward contract with maturity τ, otherwise not. The coefficients of the threshold functions β_0 and β_i are trained based on historical price and feature data via a mixed-integer linear programming model under cost minimization objectives.

Performance Evaluation

The performance assessment of different financial hedging strategies is based on different KPIs. Procurement organizations that are risk-averse may use value-at-risk (VaR) and conditional value-at-risk (CVaR) assessment, while risk-neutral procurement organizations may evaluate the resulting purchase cost that should be minimized.

An important reference value is the perfect foresight cost, i.e., the cost resulting from the perfect foresight strategy (or also called clairvoyant strategy) under the assumption that future price developments are known to the decision-maker. The delta of a specific commodity procurement strategy to the perfect foresight cost quantifies the missed potential. The perfect foresight strategy and cost can be

Table 6.6 Zinc spot and futures prices at London Metal Exchange (LME) from November 2021 to June 2022 in USD/MT

	Nov-21	Dec-21	Jan-22	Feb-22	Mar-22	Apr-22	May-22	Jun-22
Spot	3410	3269	3590	3622	3767	4408	4151	3885
M1 (front-month)	3410	3217	3580	3624	3764	4388	4141	3878
M2 (2-months-ahead)	3387	3211	3563	3623	3762	4376	4125	3871
M3 (3-months-ahead)	3365	3205	3548	3608	3755	4361	4113	3868
M4 (4-months-ahead)	3354	3200	3527	3595	3741	4336	4101	3864

calculated in hindsight (backtests) based on the following linear programming formulation:

$$\text{minimize} \quad \frac{1}{T}\sum_{t=1}^{T} p_t^\tau \cdot y_t^\tau \tag{6.28}$$

$$\text{s.t.} \quad \sum_{\tau} y_{t-\tau} = d_t \qquad \forall t = 1, \dots, T \tag{6.29}$$

$$y_t^\tau \geq 0 \qquad \forall t = 1, \dots, T, \tau = 0, \dots, n \tag{6.30}$$

The objective function minimizes the average period purchase cost over a back-testing horizon of T months with p_t^τ being the commodity prices at period t for maturity τ, i.e., p_t^0 is the spot price, p_t^1 is the front-month price and p_t^4 is the 4-months ahead price. y_t^τ is the purchase quantity at period t for commodity delivery period $t+\tau$ that needs to satisfy the commodity demand d_t. The clairvoyant strategy therefore purchases commodity demand at the cheapest source of spot and forward markets. Under maximization objective, the LP formulation yields the worst case procurement strategy. Both objectives therefore define a bandwidth for the resulting purchase cost.

Numerical Example: Procurement Strategies at Forward Markets
Suppose spot and futures prices for zinc from November 2021 until June 2022 quoted at the first trading day of the month as illustrated in Table 6.6.

The perfect foresight strategy is to cover Mar-22 demand by M3 in Dec-21 at a contract price of 3205 USD/MT, to cover Apr-22 demand by M4 in Dec-21 at a contract price of 3200 USD/MT, May-22 demand by M4 in Jan-22 at a contract price of 3527 USD/MT and Jun-22 demand by M4 in Feb-22 at a price of 3595 USD/MT. This yields an ex-post optimal (perfect foresight) average purchase price of 3382 USD/MT between March and June 2022.

(continued)

A pure spot purchase strategy achieves an average purchase price of 3382 USD/MT in this time frame, which is 19.8% above the perfect foresight strategy (see Fig. 6.24). That means with a perfect forward purchase strategy a firm could have saved more than 15% compared to spot procurement. Pure forward contracting achieves average purchases prices of 3979 USD/MT (M1), 3831 USD/MT (M2), 3529 USD/MT (M3) and 3419 USD/MT (M4), respectively. This means that 4-months ahead purchasing can achieve purchase costs that are only 1.1% above perfect foresight cost. The REO approach recognizes the benefits of M4 at upward markets and achieves an average purchase price of 3419 USD/MT by always buying at M4. The 1/N purchase strategy on the other hand diversifies risk and leads to an average purchase cost of 3762 USD/MT, which is far better than spot purchasing but clearly outperformed by dynamic forward contracting in the example above.

Application: Freight Forward Agreements

Similar to commodities from the classes *metals*, *energy* and *agriculturals*, ocean and sea freight rates vary significantly as shown by the *Baltic Dry Index* from Fig. 6.25. A prominent example in the media was the price jump in early 2021, where prices increased by 500% in a short period of time. The Baltic Dry Index is the most important price index for ocean transportation of bulk freight such as coal, iron ore, grain, copper, synthetic granules, gravel and cement at the 26 most important routes (e.g., Richards Bay/South Africa to Rotterdam/Netherlands or Gladstone/Australia to Rotterdam/Netherlands). It is published by the Baltic Exchange and consists of the following indices depending on four main vessel classes, i.e., Baltic Capesize Index (BCI), Baltic Panamax Index (BPI), Baltic Supramax Index (BSI) and Baltic Handysize Index (BHSI). Other freight indices exist for oil products (e.g., Baltic Dirty Tanker Index, Baltic Clean Tanker Index) and container (e.g., HARPEX, Howe Robinson Container Index).

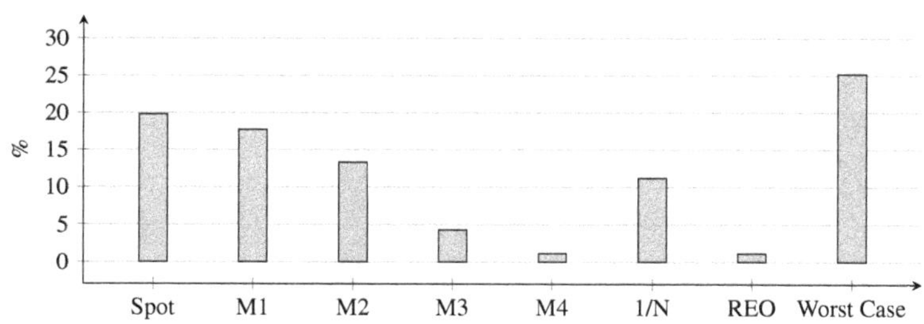

Fig. 6.24 Performance evaluation: Percentage above perfect foresight purchase cost

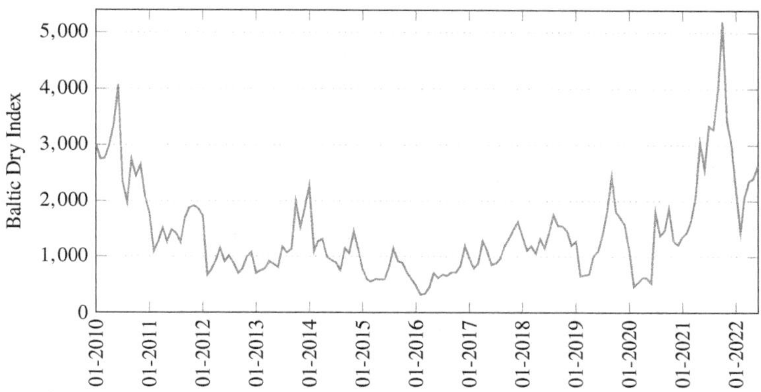

Fig. 6.25 Baltic dry index from January 2010 until June 2022

For risk management purposes, freight forward agreements (FTAs) exist for various tanker shipping routes and vessel classes (see, e.g., [15]). They are over-the-counter (OTC) agreements between, e.g., the shipowner and the charterer to fix a freight rate for a specific good, route and future date in advance. FFAs allow ship owners and charterers to hedge against price volatility. The forward contracting strategies therefore do also apply to freight capacity purchasing. According to [14], 40% of goods transported in ships are hired on the spot market, while 60% are purchased via forward markets. Besides, FFAs, freight futures are traded at, for instance, International Martime Exchange (IMAREX) and New York Mercantile Exchange (NYMEX) as more standardized contracts.

Cross-Hedging or Proxy Hedging

Some commodities are not or not liquidly traded at futures markets. Examples are, for instance, standard plastics such as high-density polyethylen (HDPE), low-density polyethylen (LDPE), linear low-density polyethylene (LLDPE) or polypropylen (PP). Another example is jet fuel. Therefore, it is not possible to directly secure these commodities via financial hedging. However, a cross-hedge allows to indirectly hedge these commodities through futures contracts of related commodities that are characterized by a similar price movement as the actual commodity. For instance, airlines often use liquid crude oil futures for hedging jet fuel. Another example is HDPE, LLDPE and PP, which are based on ethylene and propylene, respectively (see Fig. 6.26). Both ethylene and propylene are again based on ethane/propane and naphtha, respectively. While ethane and propane are derived from natural gas, naphtha is derived from crude oil in an oil refining process. Therefore, the price of HDPE, LLDPE and PP is affected by the price of natural gas and crude oil and might move similarly. This correlation can be used for financial

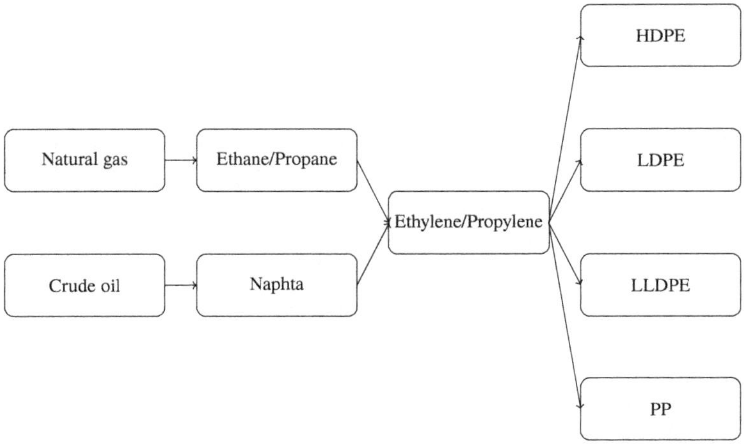

Fig. 6.26 Plastics supply chain

Table 6.7 Correlation matrix: Correlation coefficients of monthly commodity spot prices from January 2011 until December 2017

	Natural gas	Crude oil	Ethylene	Propylene	Naphta	PP	LDPE	LLDPE
Natural gas	1.0	0.63	0.54	0.67	0.58	0.67	0.72	0.71
Crude oil	0.63	1.0	0.92	0.90	0.96	0.87	0.90	0.85
Ethylene	0.54	0.92	1.0	0.81	0.87	0.85	0.86	0.82
Propylene	0.67	0.90	0.81	1.0	0.91	0.85	0.87	0.84
Naphta	0.58	0.96	0.87	0.91	1.0	0.84	0.83	0.77
PP	0.67	0.87	0.85	0.85	0.84	1.0	0.88	0.84
LDPE	0.72	0.90	0.86	0.87	0.83	0.88	1.0	0.99
LDPE	0.71	0.85	0.82	0.84	0.77	0.84	0.99	1.0

hedging as both crude oil and natural gas are liquidly traded at commodity futures markets.

In order to identify the cross-hedging potential, correlation and regression analysis is applied in order to identify the relationship in price movements. R^2 is used to evaluate hedge effectiveness as it shows the percentage of variance in a specific commodity price that can be explained by a liquidly traded commodity price. Table 6.7 presents the results of a correlation analysis between different plastics commodities and related upstream products (e.g., WTI crude oil or Henry Hub natural gas). According to the International Accounting Standard IAS 39 (now IFRS 9) that regulate hedge accounting, there was originally a correlation requirement. Today, there is no formal requirement, but 80% of correlation is a recommendation for hedge effectiveness that is wide-spread in practice and literature.

Operational Hedging

If price risk cannot be passed toward the supplier or customer (via escalator clauses), financial hedging is not possible due to liquidity issues and cross-hedging is not an option due to the absence of correlation, operational hedging via inventory optimization may be an appropriate measure for price risk (but also supply risk) mitigation of storable commodities.

A specific example for operational decision-making under price uncertainty is optimal inventory management under random demand and price, i.e., how to effectively control inventory in order to avoid stock-outs and simultaneously exploit low purchase prices. If a commodity's price is anticipated to increase, an inventory manager may purchase more than required, and if the price is expected to decrease, one may wait with purchasing. Stockpiling inventory is particularly prevalent for firms that want to exploit inter-temporal price differentials (e.g., commodity-trading firms) and for firms that have warehouse space available. According to the Metals Service Centers Institute, the stock of steel-processing companies increased from 2.4 to 2.7 months of inventory in November 2010 due to raising prices and the firms' anticipation of further price increases (see [28]). Companies that actively use inventory management for price risk mitigation are, for instance, Unilever and Caterpillar (see [1, 28]).

Compared to forward contracts, spot markets provide a higher flexibility in procurement. Due to the fact that there is no equilibrium in inventory holding costs (i.e., some firms may store cheaper than the market), a firm might also operationally hedge price risk via forward buying at the spot market and carrying inventory.

In the following, we give a brief introduction to operational hedging via inventories. For an early but fundamental discussion on inventory control under stochastic raw material prices, we refer to [18]. For a more general view of commodity storage from an economist's perspective, we refer to [30].

According to [1], there are three motives for holding inventories: safety motives, speculation motives and transaction motives. Stochastic inventory control theory traditionally focuses on uncertain demand in order to address safety motives, i.e., keeping a safety stock to guarantee defined customer service levels. However, in volatile commodity markets, also speculation motives play a potentially important role in terms of procurement in advance and stockpiling of commodities for which one expects a price increase $p_{t+1} - p_t$ that is larger than the inventory holding costs c_h (see [13]).

Deterministic Analysis

In order to quantify (maximum) savings potential from stockpiling under fluctuating prices compared to just-in-time purchasing under full price risk, it is recommended to start with a deterministic backtest. This can be executed based on the following

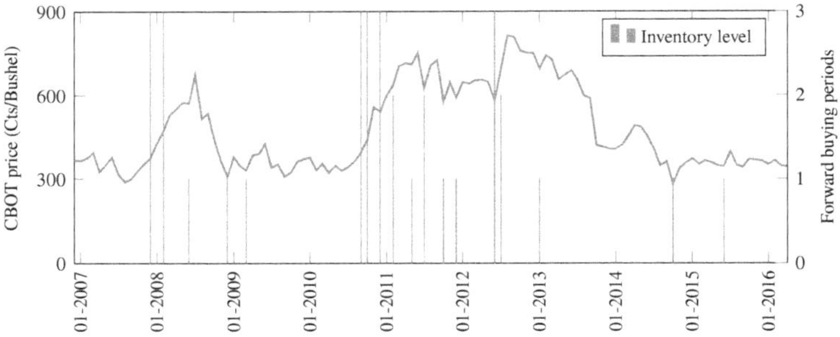

Fig. 6.27 Price evolution and optimal inventory levels

linear programming formulation:

$$\text{minimize} \quad \sum_{t=1}^{T} p_t \cdot y_t + c_h \cdot I_t + c_c \cdot p_t \cdot I_t \tag{6.31}$$

$$\text{s.t.} \quad I_{t+1} = I_t + y_t - d_t \qquad \forall t = 1, \ldots, T-1 \tag{6.32}$$

$$y_t \leq C - I_t + d_t \qquad \forall t = 1, \ldots, T \tag{6.33}$$

$$y_t \geq 0 \qquad \forall t = 1, \ldots, T \tag{6.34}$$

The objective function minimizes the total cost over a planning horizon $t = 1, \ldots, T$ by optimizing purchase quantities y_t. Total cost consists of purchase cost $p_t \cdot y_t$ with fluctuating purchase price p_t, inventory holding cost $c_h \cdot I_t$ with per unit per period holding cost c_h and inventory level I_t and cost of capital $c_c \cdot p_t \cdot I_t$ with c_c as the interest rate. The first constraint ensures inventory balance with period demand d_t, and the second constraint considers capacity restrictions by warehouse capacity C.

Using this perfect foresight model, companies can benchmark their current strategy based on their individual data input (i.e., inventory holding cost, cost of capital, demand and warehouse capacity). This results in price-dependent inventory profiles as illustrated in Fig. 6.27.

In addition, the linear programming model allows to quantify maximum savings potential through anticipative inventory control compared to just-in-time spot market procurement under full price risk. Figure 6.28 illustrates the savings potential for the commodities aluminum and polypropylen. Please note that this is the maximum savings potential under perfect forecast assumptions. Figure 6.28 shows that the savings potential of optimized inventory control versus just-in-time purchasing decreases with increasing holding cost and decreasing warehouse capacity, which is intuitive.

In practice, depending on the forecast accuracy, the savings typically can be significantly smaller. However, the deterministic perfect foresight analysis allows to

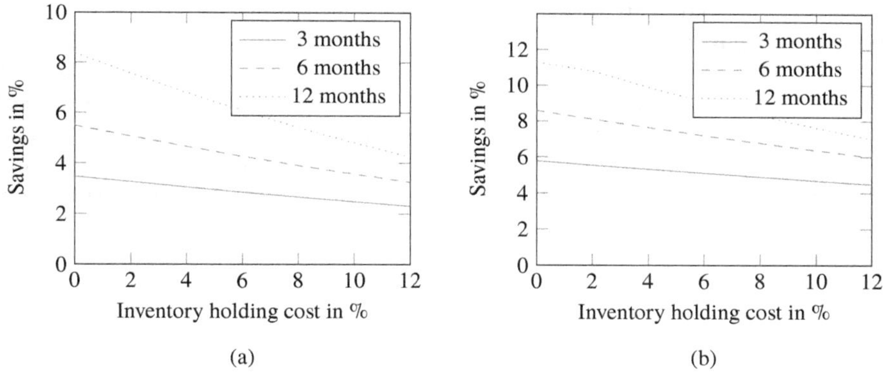

Fig. 6.28 Cost savings potential through inventory optimization versus just-in-time spot market procurement from January 2010 until January 2020 for different inventory holding cost (in % p.a.) and warehouse capacity (in months). (**a**) Aluminum. (**b**) Polypropylen

understand whether in general there is sufficient potential to invest time and money in sophisticated forecasting tools (e.g., based on artificial intelligence or machine learning) to support inventory decisions for price risk management.

Stochastic Analysis

In case the deterministic backtests show a significant savings potential, one needs to switch to a stochastic analysis. Suppose a multi-period setting with a planning horizon of n periods and deterministic period demand $d_t \;\; \forall t = 1, \ldots, n$ that takes place uniformly over the period and needs to be satisfied. One chooses the order quantity y_t that minimizes the expected cost C_t over the planning horizon by solving the dynamic programming equation

$$C_t(I_t, p_t) = \min_{\substack{y_t + I_t \geq d_t \\ y_t \geq 0}} \left\{ p_t y_t + c_h(y_t + I_t - \frac{1}{2} d_t) + \mathbb{E}_t[C_{t+1}(I_{t+1}, p_{t+1})] \right\}$$

$$\forall t = 1, \ldots, n, \tag{6.35}$$

with the system state $z_t = (I_t, p_t)$ characterized by the inventory level I_t that evolves according to $I_{t+1} = I_t + y_t - d_t$ (endogenous state information) and the spot price p_t (exogenous state information). According to the seminal work by Kingsman [17], the optimal procurement policy is of the form

$$y_t^*(z_t) = \begin{cases} (d_t - I_t)^+ & \text{if } p_t > P_2, \\ (D_k - I_t)^+ & \text{if } P_{k+1} < p_t \leq P_k \quad \forall k = 2, \ldots, n-1, \\ (D_n - I_t)^+ & \text{if } p_t \leq P_n. \end{cases} \tag{6.36}$$

D_k denotes the cumulative demand up to period k including the current period. The optimal policy is characterized by price thresholds P_k that are interpreted as the price at which the purchaser is indifferent between covering the cumulative demands for the next k or $k-1$ periods ahead including the present period. This is the lowest price that the purchaser expects to pay over the next $k-1$ periods for each unit of consumption in the kth period ahead in time, unless it is bought now at the price offer p_t. Under the assumption of serially independent prices modeled by distribution function ϕ, P_k can be determined analytically by

$$P_k = \int_{0}^{P_{k-1}} p_{t+1}\ \phi_{t+1}(p)\partial p_{t+1} + \int_{P_{k-1}}^{\infty} P_{k-1}\ \phi_{t+1}(p)\partial p_{t+1} - c_h\ \ \forall k = 3, 4, \ldots, n, \tag{6.37}$$

$$P_2 = \int_{0}^{\infty} p_{t+1}\ \phi_{t+1}(p)\partial p_{t+1} - c_h. \tag{6.38}$$

This results in stepwise price thresholds (i.e., price breaks) that indicate how much to buy in advance. Given above's formulas, the price breaks can be obtained using any programming language or calculation software (e.g., MATLAB).

Numerical Example: Price Break Policy for Aluminum Purchasing
Assume the situation of aluminum purchasing with a current price level of around 2,500 USD/MT at the London Metal Exchange (as of February 2023). Assume that price volatility of aluminum is measured by a standard deviation of $\sigma = 250$ USD/MT. Therefore, the inventory manager could argue to purchase in advance and build inventories whenever a supplier offers a competitive price. However, building inventories comes at a price, i.e., inventory holding costs in addition to the aluminum demand (i.e., 10 tons per month) and the maximum warehouse capacity (i.e., 90 tons). The following price break policy derived from the formulas mentioned above gives decision-support on the optimal inventory levels as a function of the supplier's price offer. The stepwise function shows that the lower the price offer and the lower the inventory holding cost, the higher the target stock level. For instance, a supplier's price offer of 1,750 USD per ton results in an optimal target stock level of 50 tons (i.e., buying 4 months in advance given a monthly demand of 10 tons) (Fig. 6.29).

However, under stochastic demand structures and more advanced and realistic price models, the inventory control problem becomes much more complicated.

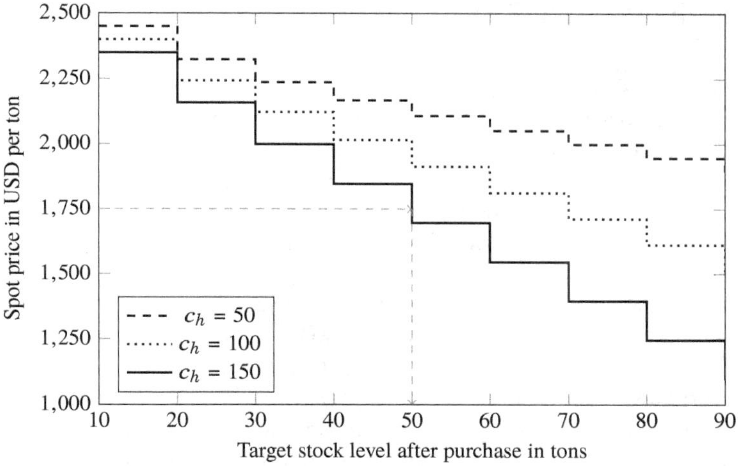

Fig. 6.29 Decision chart with price breaks for aluminum forward purchasing at different holding cost c_h (in USD/ton)

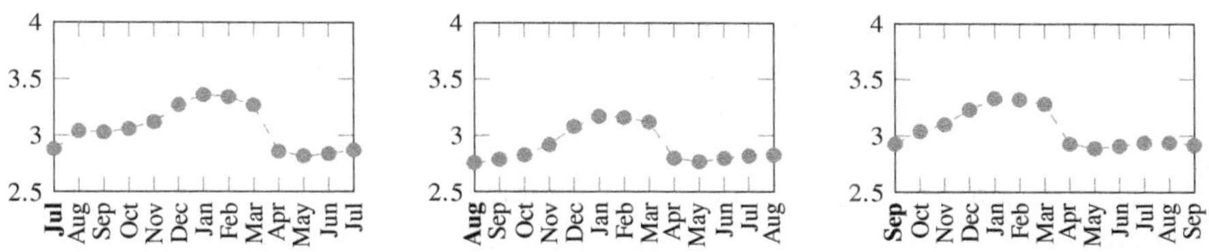

Fig. 6.30 Concept of rolling forecast updates illustrated based on futures curves of NYMEX natural gas from July 2017 to September 2017 (Prices in USD/mmbtu)

Therefore, for practical applications, a *rolling intrinsic approach* (or also called *reoptimization heuristic*) is widely applied when it comes to inventory trading of commodities with purchase, storage and selling decisions (see, e.g., [22]). This approach uses quoted futures prices as best estimates for future spot price developments (see Fig. 6.30). These point forecasts can easily be included into the deterministic linear programming formulation from above.

After solving the linear program over a specific planning horizon (e.g., 12 months), the first-period purchase decision is implemented (e.g., purchase decision from July in Fig. 6.30). As soon as new futures price information arrives in the next period (i.e., August), the decision-maker updates price forecasts and runs the model again based on current inventory information in order to derive another purchase decision (i.e., for August). This repeats over and over again.

Please note that the performance of the reoptimization heuristic for operational hedging strongly depends on the accuracy of futures prices to forecast the spot market direction.

6.4 Exchange Rate Risk

Exchange rate risk is the risk that results from trading in different currencies. For instance, if a European company operates with a US supplier, both need to agree on a currency for transactions. If the supplier asks for US dollar, then the European buyer is affected by the risk of exchange rate fluctuations. There are various dimensions of exchange rate risk such as transaction risk through currency exchange from imports and exports or strategic risk whenever competitors can source and offer products at a cheaper price due to exchange rate benefits (Fig. 6.31).

Whenever the exchange rate increases, we speak of an **appreciation** of the foreign currency (e.g., Euro) against the USD, which refers to a strong foreign currency and a weak USD. In this case, you get more USD for one unit of the foreign currency. This is negative for exporters to the USA because exports get more expensive because one gets less of a foreign currency for one USD. On the other hand, it is positive for importers that import goods from the USA because imports get cheaper because one gets more USD per unit of the foreign currency.

Whenever the exchange rate decreases, we speak of a **depreciation** of the foreign currency (e.g., Euro) against the USD, which refers to a strong USD and a weak foreign currency. In this case, you get less USD for one unit of the foreign currency. This is positive for exporters to the USA because exports get cheaper because one gets more foreign currency for one USD. On the other hand, it is negative for importers that import goods from the USA because imports get more expensive because one gets less USD for one unit of the foreign currency.

Figure 6.32 shows the exchange rates of four major currencies against the USD measured in USD.

6.4.1 *Measuring Exchange Rate Risk*

The computation of exchange rate risk is strongly related to commodity price risk. Both exchange rate and commodity price risk affect the effective price that a company needs to pay for its products or services.

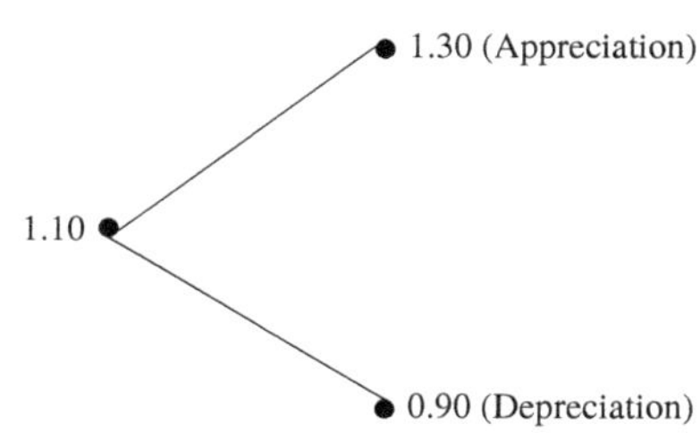

Fig. 6.31 Appreciation and depreciation of the USD based on the USD/EUR exchange rate of 1.10 (1.10 USD = 1 EUR)

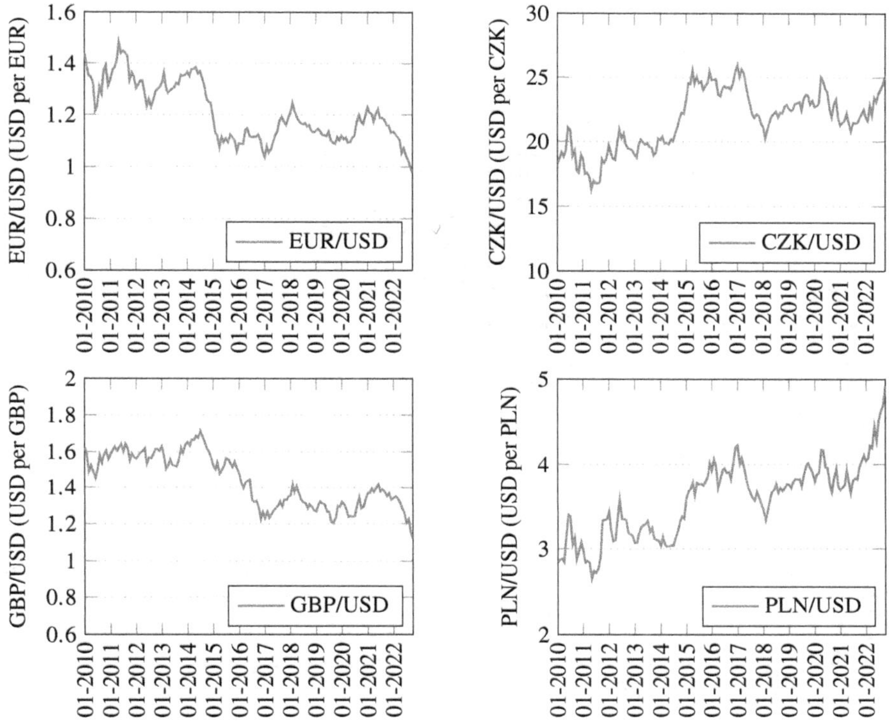

Fig. 6.32 Exchange rates of major currencies versus USD from 2010 to 2022

Standard Metrics

KPIs that are used for commodity price risk valuation can also be used for exchange rate risk valuation. Therefore, annualized volatility and value-at-risk measures are widely applied in practice (see Sect. 6.3.1).

Exchange Rate Exposure

To quantify their individual exchange rate risk, procurement departments can also use backtests to simulate their risk based on historical exchange rate and historical purchase volume data. Exchange rate exposure measures the impact that exchange rate fluctuations have on the overall spend. This needs to be considered in quantifying the savings performance of procurement organizations because a specific percentage of savings can come from favorable exchange rate developments.

For 2020, we observe from Table 6.8 that there is not too much of a gain or lose by linking the contract sum (100.000 USD per month) with the supplier to EUR or USD. Agreeing on EUR (January rate of 89,285.70 Euro) for the 2020 contract

Table 6.8 Backtesting of currency exchange rate risks (1/2)

Date	USD/EUR rate	Payment in USD	Effective purchase cost in EUR	Savings against EUR contract
Jan 2020	1.12	100,000	89,285.70	0
Feb 2020	1.11	100,000	90,090.09	−804.39
Mar 2020	1.11	100,000	90,090.09	−804.39
Apr 2020	1.09	100,000	91,743.12	−2,457.42
May 2020	1.09	100,000	91,743.12	−2,457.42
Jun 2020	1.11	100,000	90,090.09	−804.39
Jul 2020	1.12	100,000	89,285.70	0
Aug 2020	1.17	100,000	85,470.10	3,815.60
Sep 2020	1.20	100,000	83,333.33	5,952.37
Oct 2020	1.18	100,000	84,745.76	4,539.94
Nov 2020	1.17	100,000	85,470.10	3,815.60
Dec 2020	1.20	100,000	83,333.33	5,952.37
Total				16,747.87 (1.6%)

rather than USD would yield an exchange profit of 1.6%, which is typically eaten up by a risk premium the US supplier would charge for Euro invoicing.

However, for other years, this might look the other way around. For instance, for the year 2021 (see Fig. 6.9), we observe that agreeing on EUR would yield an exchange loss of 3.6% (Table 6.9).

Table 6.9 Backtesting of currency exchange rate risks (2/2)

Date	USD/EUR rate	Payment in USD	Effective purchase cost in EUR	Savings against EUR contract
Jan 2021	1.23	100,000	81,300.81	0
Feb 2021	1.21	100,000	82,644.63	−1,343.82
Mar 2021	1.21	100,000	82,644.63	−1,343.82
Apr 2021	1.17	100,000	85,470.09	−4,159.28
May 2021	1.20	100,000	83,333.33	−2,032.52
Jun 2021	1.22	100,000	81,967.21	−666.40
Jul 2021	1.19	100,000	84,033.61	−2,732.80
Aug 2021	1.19	100,000	84,033.61	−2,732.80
Sep 2021	1.18	100,000	84,745.76	−3,444.95
Oct 2021	1.16	100,000	86,206.90	−4,906.09
Nov 2021	1.16	100,000	86,206.90	−4,906.09
Dec 2021	1.13	100,000	88,495.58	−7,194.77
Total				−35,463.34 (3.6%)

Simulation

Simulation based on fitted price models introduced in Sect. 6.3.2 (e.g., random walk, mean-reversion or momentum) can also be used to simulate exchange rate risk.

> **Industry Example: Currency Risk Valuation at Volkswagen**
> According to the 2021 annual report, Volkswagen uses value-at-risk based on historical simulation and sensitivity analysis in order to assess currency risk. Sensitivity analysis is based on calculating the profit and loss effects of a 10% appreciation and a 10% depreciation of specific foreign currencies. VaR calculations are based on a 99% probability that a specific loss is not exceeded within 40 days. 1,000 historical trading days are used for evaluation.

6.4.2 Measures for Risk Mitigation

There are several measures to minimize risk of exchange rates, i.e.,

- financial FX rate hedging,
- natural FX rate hedging,
- invoicing in domestic currency (e.g., all payments in Euro),
- currency risk-sharing agreements between supplier and buyer
- insurance against currency risk.

For the latter three, risk minimization is typically not for free of charge but needs to be paid through a risk premium to the insurance company or the supplier. The size of the premium depends on the market power of the buyer and is often part of the negotiation process between the buyer and the supplier.

In the following, we deep-dive into the first two instruments, i.e., financial and natural FX rate hedging.

Financial FX Rate Hedging

Forward exchange contracts allow currency exchange (e.g., Euro to USD) at a fixed future point in time at a today's agreed rate. The exchange typically happens between a company and a financial institution. This is similar to forward contracting at commodity markets, and same methods can be applied (see Chap. 6).

Figure 6.33 shows a contango market for EUR/USD exchange rate in December 2022, i.e., the market expects that the EUR/USD rate will increase over the next year. On the other hand, the EUR/JPY exchange rate is characterized by a backwardation market, i.e., the market expects the EUR/JPY rate to decrease over the next months.

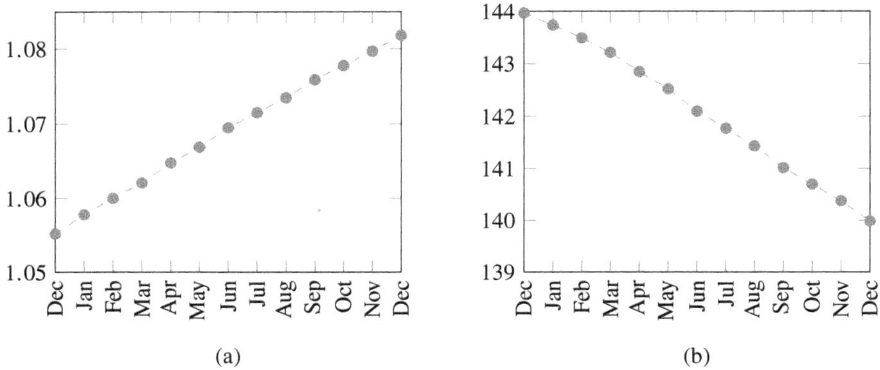

Fig. 6.33 (**a**) EUR/USD and (**b**) EUR/JPY futures contracts on December 8, 2022 (Source: EUREX)

Besides currency forward, there are also currency options and currency swaps available. Similar to commodity options, currency options are typically more expensive due to the higher flexibility. But they do not lead to a negative market value of a hedge.

Industry Example: Financial FX Rate Hedging at Volkswagen
According to the 2021 annual report, Volkswagen actively hedges currency risk for the following currencies, i.e., the Australian Dollar, Brazilian Real, British Pound, Chinese Renminbi, Hongkong Dollar, Indian Rupee, Japanese Yen, Canadian Dollar, Mexican Peso, Norwegian Crown, Polish Zloty, Russian Rubel, Swedish Crown, Swiss Franc, Singapore Dollar, South African Rand, South Korean Won, Taiwanese Dollar, Czech Crown, Hungarian Forint and US Dollar. Therefore, Volkswagen uses FX futures, FX options and FX swaps.

Natural FX Rate Hedging

Through natural hedging, a company can match its currency flows (e.g., USD inflow and USD outflow) that means an offset of revenues and cost in the same currency. An effective natural FX rate hedging requires optimized supply and production footprints. Therefore, standard supply network design models are extended to exchange rate risk (see Sect. 4.6).

Industry Example: Natural Hedging at BMW
Besides financial hedges, BMW uses natural hedging at its US plant in Spartanburg where cash inflows from selling cars to US customers are used to finance production and to pay US suppliers in USD (see [10]). This local-for-local strategy reduces currency exchange and therefore currency exchange rate risk significantly.

Closely related to natural FX rate hedging however without the requirement for exchange rate-optimized footprint decisions is *exposure netting*, i.e., a company's cash inflows and outflows are charged out. This reduces the number of payments (and therefore transaction cost) and the volume (and therefore currency risk).

Industry Example: Exposure Netting at Bosch
Bosch established a netting center in Germany that focuses on cross-border settlement transactions among the different Bosch subsidiaries. For instance, Deutsche Bank helped Bosch to consolidate 2,000 payments in Chinese Renminbi into one single transaction.

References

1. 2016 Annual Report and Accounts. https://www.unilever.com/investor-relations/annual-report-and-accounts/archive-of-unilever-annual-report-and-accounts.html. Accessed 17 Jul 2022
2. Alquist R, Kilian L (2010) What do we learn from the price of crude oil futures? J Appl Econom 25(1):539–573
3. Bartram SM, Brown GW, Fehle FR (2009) International evidence on financial derivatives usage. Finan Manag 38(1):185–206
4. Beschaffungsmanagement (2009) Rohstoffkosten-management: Einkaufsexperten fordern jetzt aktives Management von Rohstoffkosten für schlechtere Zeiten. Beschaffungsmanagement 04/2009:12–13
5. BMW Group (2008) BMW Group International Terms and Conditions for the Purchase of Production Materials and Automotive Components. https://b2b.bmw.com/. Accessed 01 Jun 2023
6. Borovkova S, Geman H (2008) Forward curve modeling in commodity markets. In: Geman H (ed) Risk Management in Commodity Markets - From Shipping to Agriculturals and Energy. 1st edn. Wiley Finance, Hoboken
7. Cortazar G, Millard C, Ortega H, Schwartz E (2018) Commodity price forecasts, futures prices and pricing models. Manag Sci 65(9):3949–4450
8. DeMarzo PM, Duffie D (1991) Corporate financial hedging with proprietary information. J Econ Theory 53(1):261–286

9. FIA (2015) 2015 Annual Survey: Global Derivatives Volume. Market Voice - The Magazine of the Global Futures, Options and Cleared Swaps Markets
10. Financial Times (2012) The Case Study: How BMW Dealt with Exchange Rate Risk. Financial Times, October 29
11. Froot KA, Scharfstein DS, Stein JC (1993) Risk management: coordinating corporate investment and financing policies. J Finance 47(5):1629–1658
12. Gaur V, Seshadri S (2005) Hedging inventory risk through market instruments. Manufact Serv Oper Manag 7(2):103–120
13. Gavirneni S, Morton TE (1999) Inventory control under speculation: myopic heuristics and exact procedures. Europ J Oper Res 117(2):211–221
14. Geman H (2005) Commodities and Commodity Derivatives: Modeling and Pricing for Agriculturals, Metals and Energy, 1st edn. Wiley Finance, Hoboken
15. Geman H (2009). Risk Management in Commodity Markets - From Shipping to Agriculturals and Energy, 1st edn. Wiley, Hoboken
16. Hull JC (2018) Options, Futures, and Other Derivatives, 9th edn. Pearson Prentice Hall, Hoboken
17. Kingsman BG (1969) Commodity purchasing. Oper Res Quart 20(1):59–79
18. Kingsman BG (1985) Raw Materials Purchasing: An Operational Research Approach, 1st edn. Pergamon, Oxford
19. Malkiel BG (2003) The Efficient market hypothesis and its critics. J Econ Perspect 17(1):59–82
20. Mandl C (2019) Optimal Procurement and Inventory Control in Volatile Commodity Markets - Advances in Stochastic and Data-Driven Optimization. Dissertation. Technical University Munich
21. Mandl C, Minner S (2023) Data-driven optimization for commodity procurement under price uncertainty. Manufact Serv Oper Manag 25(2):371–390
22. Mandl C, Nadarajah S, Minner S, Gavirneni S (2022) Data-driven storage operations: cross-commodity backtest and structured policies. Prod Oper Manag 31(6):2438–2456
23. Modigliani F, Miller MH (1958) The cost of capital, corporation finance and the theory of investment. Amer Econ Rev 48(3):261–297
24. Schuh C, Raudabaugh JL, Kromoser R, Strohmer MF, Triplat A, Pearce J (2017) The Purchasing Chessboard - 64 Methods to Reduce Costs and Increase Value with Suppliers, 3rd edn. Springer, Berlin
25. Smith CW, Stulz RM (1985) The determinants of Firms' hedging policies. J Finan Quant Analy 20(4):391–405
26. Van Mieghem J (2010) Risk management and operational hedging: an overview. In: Kouvelis P, Dong L, Boyabatli O, Li R (eds) Handbook of Integrated Risk Management in Global Supply Chains, 1st end. Wiley, Hoboken
27. Wall Street Journal (2008) Against the Grain: Food Firms Hedge Costs. http://www.wsj.com/articles/SB120632251149658521. Accessed 21 Feb 2022
28. Wall Street Journal (2011) Steel Price Increases Creep into Supply Chain. https://www.wsj.com/articles/SB10001424052748704775604576120382801078352. Accessed 21 Feb 2022
29. Wall Street Journal (2016) Airlines Pull Back on Hedging Fuel Costs. http://www.wsj.com/articles/airlines-pull-back-on-hedging-fuel-costs-1458514901. Accessed 21 Feb 2022
30. Williams JC, Wright BD (1991) Storage and Commodity Markets, 1st edn. Cambridge University Press, Cambridge

Chapter 7
Conclusion

Abstract This short concluding chapter summarizes the content of the textbook and provides a brief outlook on potential developments in procurement analytics during the next decade based on advancements in, e.g., generative artificial intelligence, cognitive analytics, quantum computing, cloud computing and 3D printing.

Keywords Generative AI · Cognitive analytics · Quantum computing · Cloud computing · 3D printing

In the course of digitization, advanced analytics, artificial intelligence, machine learning and operations research are buzzwords that gain increasing attention across industries. Additionally, companies increasingly have access to immense amounts of internal and external data. This is in particular the case in procurement as the company's intersection to thousands of incumbent and potential suppliers as well as to worldwide commodity markets. However, similar to other business functions, procurement is still only leveraging a small fraction of the available data for better decision-making. We only can guess that this is due to a lack of know-how or the unawareness of successful use cases.

Therefore, this textbook gives a state-of-the-art overview of advanced analytics and data-driven methodologies for solving important decision problems in procurement practice by focusing on the dimensions, *data-driven spend management*, *data-driven supplier management*, *data-driven inventory management* and *data-driven risk management*. Therefore, we presented methods to leverage procurement data most effectively, from machine learning-based forecasting and classification to linear programming to game theory. We presented use cases and comprehensive data examples that help readers quickly understand, implement and test data-driven approaches in the procurement field. Therefore, we hope the textbook is useful for both (future) practitioners in procurement departments and professionals in the ProcureTech and procurement consulting area.

This book also addressed some timely and fundamental challenges that occurred in procurement and supply management during the last few years, and for which, we strongly believe that data is key to tackling them, whether it is a resilient supply

C. Mandl, *Procurement Analytics*, Springer Series in Supply Chain Management 22, https://doi.org/10.1007/978-3-031-43281-1_7

network design, efficient multi-sourcing strategies and appropriate safety stocks in the face of supply disruptions or effective hedging strategies against commodity price and exchange rate risk. Data and analytics are disrupting procurement, which opens plenty of new opportunities for both procurement professionals and data scientists. We hope that this textbook could help both groups – the former in getting an understanding about basic analytics methods and how data can be leveraged to optimize their procurement decisions and the latter in getting insights into the procurement world, what data is available and what decision problems need to be solved there.

During the next years of ongoing technological advancement in artificial intelligence (e.g., generative AI and cognitive analytics), computer power (e.g., cloud computing and quantum computing) and data quantity and quality (e.g., web crawling and large-scale RFI/RFQ), we expect many new applications in the procurement analytics area. Those can be chatbots that lead supplier negotiations (see, e.g., Walmart), satellite-driven forecasting of supply disruptions and price developments, blockchain technology as the single source of truth for smart contracting without any intermediary and with fully transparent and consistent pricing, predictive policing in supply chains, nearshoring and local ESG-optimized supply networks that are profitable with the use of 3D printing, quantum computing for algorithmic supply network optimization across many stages with hundreds of suppliers under consideration or how to effectively leverage the immense amount of data produced during RFI/RFQ processes.

Procurement analytics stays exciting.